Counseling & Psychotherapy:

Classics On Theories & Issues

Other books by the editor:

HANDBOOK OF MARRIAGE COUNSELING (Co-edited)
TREATING PSYCHOSEXUAL DYSFUNCTION

Counseling
&
Psychotherapy:

Classics On
Theories & Issues

Compiled and Edited by
Ben N. Ard, Jr., Ph. D.

Revised Edition

1975

Science and Behavior Books, Inc.
Palo Alto, California

Science and Behavior Books, Inc.
Palo Alto, California 1975

Library of Congress Card Number 66-23291
ISBN 0-8314-0048-X

*Dedicated affectionately to: Myrtle May
. . . who always encouraged hewing away
at the truth, and letting the chips fall
where they may.*

CONTRIBUTORS

Nathan Adler, Ph.D., Psychologist, San Francisco, California.

Ben N. Ard, Jr., Ph.D., Professor of Counseling, San Francisco State University, San Francisco, California.

Breffni Barrett, Ph.D., Satori Project Director, YMCA, San Diego, California.

Nathaniel Branden, Ph.D., Founder and Director of the Biocentric Institute, Los Angeles, California.

Robert L. Browning, Ph.D., Associate Professor of Christian Education, Ohio Methodist Theological School, Delaware, Ohio.

Jack Dusay, M.D., Psychiatrist, San Francisco, California.

Albert Ellis, Ph.D., Executive Director, Institute for Rational Living, New York, New York.

William Glasser, M.D., Psychiatrist, founder, Institute of Reality Therapy, Los Angeles, California.

Harold Greenwald, Ph.D., Professor of Clinical Psychology, United States International University, San Diego, California.

Don D. Jackson, M.D., Deceased, formerly psychiatrist, Mental Research Institute, Palo Alto, California.

John D. Krumboltz, Ph.D., Professor of Education and Psychology, Stanford University, Stanford, California.

Abraham H. Maslow, Ph.D., Deceased, formerly Professor of Psychology, Brandeis University, Waltham, Massachusetts.

O. Hobart Mowrer, Ph.D., Research Professor, University of Illinois, Urbana, Illinois.

Fritz Perls, M.D., Ph.D., Deceased, founder of the Gestalt approach.

Herman J. Peters, Ph.D., Associate Professor of Education, Ohio State University, Columbus, Ohio.

Carl R. Rogers, Ph.D., Psychologist, Center for Studies of the Person, La Jolla, California.

Joseph Samler, Ph.D., Chairman, Vocational Rehabilitation Board, Veterans Administration, Washington, D.C.

Frederick C. Thorne, M.D., Ph.D., Editor, JOURNAL OF CLINICAL PSYCHOLOGY, Branden, Vermont.

Leona E. Tyler, Ph.D., Dean, Graduate School, University of Oregon, Eugene, Oregon.

E. G. Williamson, Ph.D., formerly Dean of Students, University of Minnesota, Minneapolis, Minnesota.

C. Gilbert Wrenn, Ph.D., Professor of Educational Psychology, Arizona State University, Tempe, Arizona.

TABLE OF CONTENTS

Table of Contents

Canst thou not minister to a mind diseased,
Pluck from the memory a rooted sorrow,
Raze out the written troubles of the brain,
And with some sweet oblivious antidote
Cleanse the stuff'd bosom of that perilous matter
Which weighs upon the heart?

Shakespeare
Macbeth

PREFACE

Since the reader of any book is entitled to know somewhat the story of how or why the book one is reading came into existence, I would like to say that, as a university professor teaching graduate students about counseling and psychotherapy, I was unhappy with the books then available to give to my graduate students. As Jules Henry (1973, p. 105) has said,

"The books we are compelled to give our students—largely because there are no better ones—are often boring and irritating, not because their authors lack brains but because they lack courage."

So I tried to pick out some courageous, thought-provoking, controversial writing that would stretch my students' minds and stimulate my students into some deep, critical thinking. I wanted to stir their minds up about the important theories and issues in counseling and psychotherapy. This revised, second edition continues within this early framework, only more so.

There are many books available these days on counseling and psychotherapy and there were some available when the first edition of the present book was first published in 1966. However, many of the books available then (and still today) are discussions of what other theorists have said and thus are what might be termed "second hand" interpretations, rather than first hand accounts, of theories and issues relevant in counseling and psychotherapy. This book is still rather unique in that it presents the various theories as put forth by the theorists themselves. It also shows them in clearer, sharper contrast by presenting the various theories and issues in juxtaposition and thus reveals more clearly their differences and agreements. There are even debates between various theorists.

Preface

Many colleagues in various colleges and universities have adopted the first edition of this book as a textbook and I am indebted to several of them for comments and suggestions regarding this revised second edition. I am also indebted to my graduate students over the years at San Francisco State University for many suggestions, not all of which I could follow (!), as regards to what I could do with the book. Many of them have argued, debated and discussed (and learned to disagree agreeably) about the various issues and theories involved in the first edition. They have suggested new ideas and theories for inclusion in this revised edition.

Several new theories have been included in this revised edition, including behavioral counseling, Gestalt therapy, transactional analysis, decision therapy, existential approaches, radical approaches, biocentric therapy and conjoint family therapy.

Many practitioners in the field of counseling operate from within the framework of one theoretical outlook or model, frequently because, during their training, they themselves studied under a teacher who espoused one theory as the only way to view problems and issues in the field. This book is offered as an aid to graduate students in training and also to practitioners already in the field in the hope that it will provide a broader background by considering a variety of theories and several different positions on some significant issues in the field, as expressed first-hand by the authors of the ideas themselves. Some of the presentations have appeared previously elsewhere (in journals and books) and some have been written especially for this revised edition and thus appear here for the first time.

The papers selected or commissioned for this revised edition deal basically with any *psychological* technique used in the treatment of what might be roughly termed the normal range of problems faced by children, adults, and young adults. This excludes from consideration here many of the psychiatric therapies intended primarily for psychotics, the therapies involving drugs or other medical treatment, electric or insulin shock treatments, lobotomies, and those conditioning or aversive treatments of some of the so-called "behavior" therapies which involve giving medication or electric shocks to clients, as well as the orthodox Freudian and neo-Freudian theories (which latter have been presented elsewhere in abundance). Group counseling, encounter groups, and group therapy are usually included in separate courses in most universities and therefore will not be discussed here.

Most of the aforementioned approaches (outside the group sessions) require a medical degree and other specialized training (e.g., at a psychoanalytical training institute). The theories in this revised second edition deal primarily with *verbal interaction* (and some non-verbal) between clients and the counselor or psychotherapist and do not, therefore, require the medical training presupposed in the theories mentioned above. Therefore these theories and issues discussed herein should be of interest to practitioners who function (or plan to function) as counselors in schools, agencies, prisons, probation or parole departments, juvenile halls, rehabilitation centers, as well as psychologists, social workers, marriage counselors and other members of the helping professions.

This revised edition, then, presents the student or practitioner in the field with a variety of points of view or frames of reference. The papers were purposefully chosen and compiled as provocative, opposing, controversial points of view. In order to make it more feasible for the student or practitioner to consider these contrasting views (and to stretch the reader's mind), the papers have been grouped in such a fashion as to bring out their opposing positions and present them in sharp contrast.

The reader is urged to consider each theory or issue in relation to each of the others, to contrast them, to weigh them critically and thoughtfully, and not to agree with any author unless the reader feels forced to by the weight of the author's evidence and arguments. For, as W. K. Clifford (1947, p. 96) has said,

"It is wrong in all cases to believe on insufficient evidence, and where it is presumption to doubt and investigate, there it is worse than presumption to believe."

Ben N. Ard, Jr.
San Francisco, 1975

INTRODUCTION

Ben N. Ard, Jr., Ph.D.

Before getting right into specific theories and issues about counseling and psychotherapy, perhaps a few words about the basic terms of our discourse would not be out of order. What is meant by the terms "counseling," "psychotherapy," "theories," and "issues"?

Some authorities have gone to considerable lengths to try and maintain distinctions between "counseling" and "psychotherapy." A variety of concepts have been brought to bear in these attempts, such as depth, goals, techniques, length of time or duration, etc. However, despite all this effort and the many pages of writing spent on this topic, a fine-line distinction between counseling and psychotherapy is admittedly difficult if not impossible to draw. Many of the papers that follow will deal in some instances with psychotherapy and in other instances, counseling. It is hoped that this usage will not confuse or bother the reader unnecessarily. Perhaps a useful thought to keep in mind is that the two terms overlap and therefore, rather than trying to maintain distinctions which will not hold up under logical analysis, let the reader allow the two terms to be used interchangeably.

What is a "theory" in this context? What is the function or purpose of theories in counseling and psychotherapy? In a very basic or fundamental sense, a theory in counseling and psychotherapy tells you *what to look for*, since you cannot realistically look for everything. If a client comes to the counselor or therapist with a personal problem, the helping person cannot possibly cover every event in the client's life as a possible cause. More specifically, a theory (i.e., a good theory, a productive theory, one that has heuristic value) tells you *what causes certain behavior* in clients. Next, a good theory tells you *what changes certain behavior* (presumably the problematic behavior) and, in so far as the theory is really helpful, *how*. That is, a good theory tells you how certain troublesome behavior can be changed. Then, the ultimate function or purpose of a good theory is to tell the counselor or therapist *what he (or she) had better do and not do,* and *why*. That is, the theory tells the therapist what to do if he or she wants to change certain behaviors in the client, or help the client to change certain behaviors. Not only should a good theory tell the counselor what to do but the theory should be explicit (that is, if we want the theory to be used wisely and well) about why.

Each of the following theories may be evaluated as to how they help counselors or therapists in the above mentioned ways. How do the theories help counselors and therapists help clients? That is the question we must ask of each theory, if we want to assess it properly. Some theories will be more explicit in some of the above matters and less so in other matters. Sometimes the above concepts are implicit in what the theorists say but the reader needs to make the implicit assumptions as explicit in his own mind as possible.

Another factor that is important in the assessment of any theory is for the reader to understand clearly the often *implicit assumptions* about the "nature of man" (or "human nature"). Are human beings essentially good or evil? Is aggressiveness (hostility) an essential part of every human being? How changeable is human nature? Do human beings have instincts? If so, what kind? If not, what follows from that fact? Are the problems which people bring to the helping professions largely inherited, constitutional, organic, or are the problems largely learned? What are the determining factors in the problematic behavior which clients present? Cultural factors, the influence of society, groups, peers, gangs, parents and significant others are considered more important by some theorists than some others. How much of the presenting problems are intra-psychic (within the individual person) and how much are caused by factors outside the client? Is there such a thing as reality, outside the client? Are there distorted perceptions of that reality? How much can human beings control their actions? Can they control their emotions, their feelings, their desires, their thoughts? How much are human beings aware of the causes of their behavior? How can they become more aware? Is there only one way to do so or are there several ways? Should the counselor or therapist be more passive and merely listen, or should he or she be more active and direct? How responsible are clients for their problematic behavior? Is there such a thing as free will? Do clients make choices or decisions (conscious, unconscious, or preconscious; explicit or implicit) which cause or affect their problematic behavior? Is sin a pertinent concept in counseling and psychotherapy? These are some of the basic questions which the reader may pursue while reading the following pages.

A professional counselor or psychotherapist needs to know not only *what* to do in various situations with a wide variety of clients in this pluralistic society of ours, but also *why*. The *what* may be considered to be the *techniques* of counseling and psychotherapy. But these techniques depend, or at least had better depend, upon logically prior conceptions of *why* a given technique is called for at a particular time in a specific situation. Thus techniques, ideally, depend upon *prior theories*.

The growth of any science depends, at least in an important part, upon tracing the consequences of *false hypotheses*. In the various helping professions (including medicine and others here), there have been many false hypotheses such as, for example, the wandering uterus as the cause of hysteria; "ducking" in water (sometimes to the point of drowning) to determine if certain women then called "witches" were possessed of "demons"; also various other, sometimes deadly, attempts to "exorcize" these supposed "devils"; bleeding, a specific form of removing or releasing blood in early English medicine to supposedly "cure" many illnesses (but which actually hurried death, in many instances); "black boxes" which supposedly cured cancer, etc. I leave it to the perceptive reader to ferret out some of the more recent examples in theories influential and current today. The reason for mentioning some of these examples of false hypotheses from history is to make the important point that a theory can kill you. What theories the therapist chooses to employ are going to have a very fundamental effect on his clients. He, the therapist, is *responsible* for what theory he chooses. Flipping a coin and taking your choice may be all right in a gambling situation but it is not a professional stance in counseling and psychotherapy where people's lives are at stake.

Growth in enlightenment can result from the drawing out and

elaboration of the consequences of any theory—provided that a proper climate of opinion encourages the development of theory, and provided that its espousal remains in the universe of discourse and debate. This book is intended to make a contribution to the field by aiding just such discourse and debate.

In common usage "theory" is usually contrasted with "practice." However, as Norman R. Campbell (1953, p. 289), in a discussion of the structure of theories, has pointed out,

"The desire of many half-educated persons to rely on 'practical conclusions' rather than on the reasoning of the 'theorist' is founded merely on ignorance and on an inability to differentiate between the kinds of thought likely to lead to truth and those which may be associated with error."

Nevertheless, as Campbell (1953, p. 289) has also noted,

"The views of 'practical men' are usually derived from assumptions and arguments no less complex than those on which theory is based; they are more and not less liable to error because they are less openly expressed. The idea that there are no propositions 'true in theory but false in practice' has its foundation only in the incompetence of the uninitiated to understand theory, and in their habit of applying propositions to circumstances entirely foreign to the theory. To those who have not the power to think, theory will always be dangerous."

Some people are critical of theorizing because they say theories cannot be proven true, or at least not completely so. Following this line of reasoning, these people are loath to "waste time" with theories. But, as Campbell (1953, p. 300) has pointed out,

"Theories are often accepted and valued greatly, by part of the scientific world at least, even if it is known that they are not quite true and are not strictly equivalent to any experimental laws, simply because the ideas which they bring to mind are intrinsically valuable."

The reader is urged to keep this thought in mind as he or she considers the various theories in this book.

Since we are considering here some of the antitheoretical views in the field, Ford and Urban (1963, pp. 24-25) have noted that:

"Some theorists, such as phenomenologists, are concerned about imposing an inappropriate conceptual scheme on an individual's behavior. This is a legitimate concern, but the solution is not the alternative of simply adopting the individual's own conceptual scheme which may be loaded with many inadequacies, as in disordered individuals, although some extremists in the phenomenological movement propose its adoption."

Too often some practitioners operate in the field simply on the basis of what "feels" to them at the moment like the proper thing to do. Some authorities have even urged this attitude be adopted toward counseling and psychotherapy in general. Hopefully, a thoughtful consideration of a variety of theoretical approaches may provide a more justifiable basis for practice.

There are too many practitioners, also, who do what they do in counseling and psychotherapy merely because (by chance factors usually) that is what they were taught to do in their professional training. That is, practitioners in their training have too often been taught only one theoretical approach. After they enter the field, they work in only one fashion—that of their major professor. Rather than creating such a specific image so early in training, it would seem wiser to clarify more fully the range of possibilities. Thus we must attempt to build into training programs the many possible theories and procedures within that range of possibilities.

This book is intended to provide just such a broad introduction to a variety of theoretical approaches to counseling and psychotherapy. It is intended to provide what might be called a multi-track approach rather than a single-track approach.

Some authorities in the field have recommended that the student in training adopt a particular theoretical position without reservation—that he become a "true believer." It has been suggested that the student be enthusiastically imbued with the theory *before* he commences to examine it critically. However, not everyone would agree with this blind acceptance of one theory to the exclusion of all other possibilities. Carl Rogers (1959, p.191) has commented in this regard,

". . . I am distressed at the manner in which small caliber minds immediately accept a theory—almost any theory—as a dogma of truth."

The present book tries an entirely different approach. The assumption here is that it is better for the student to become aware of the variety of different theories available in the field. It is hoped that the student will read each of the theories critically and not merely absorb one theory, revel in it, and identify with it as practically a religious badge of honor.

The reader may wisely keep in mind several critical concepts in his or her reading of the various theorists. William of Occam left us a critical concept that has come to be known as Occam's razor (in that it cuts away a lot of unnecessary verbiage) and that concept is that whatever explanation involves the fewest assumptions is to be preferred. This concept has been put another way: entities (or concepts) should not be multiplied unnecessarily (or beyond necessity). Some theorists seem to like to build and multiply concepts on top of concepts, many of which are not really necessary.

Two other concepts which may be helpful to the critical reader are those of meaninglessness and inapplicability. Perhaps one of the most serious difficulties for the reader in critically analyzing various theories arises in trying to distinguish the concepts which are highly abstract from those which are pretentious but empty. As Michael Scriven (in Calvin, 1961, p. 9) has pointed out:

"The vast vocabularies of physiognomy (the "science" of telling people's character from their face) or phrenology (same trick but using the shape of their head) or astrology (determining character and fortune on the basis of date of birth) stand as tombstones to the memory of the thousands of highly educated people who thought them scientific. In fact, it requires great care to avoid the trap of supposing that any set of verbal formulae that *sounds* sensible gives some meaning to the terms in it."

In explaining the concept of meaninglessness, Michael Scriven has pointed out that a term can have meaning even if it only occurs in an unlikely hypothesis, as long as we can see how the hypothesis could be supported by certain discoveries and disproved by others (Scriven, in Calvin, 1961, p. 9). But when we cannot even tell what evidence would support or disprove a hypothesis, we call it *meaningless*; and any terms whose meaning depends on it will themselves be meaningless.

So the reader may wisely ask of each of the theories in this book, what would count for or against the claim of the theorist (i.e., is it meaningful?) and secondly, is it applicable (if so, in what circumstances?), and finally, what evidence is there so that one could say that the theory is well or poorly supported?

SECTION I

THEORIES

*A clash of doctrines is not a disaster —
it is an opportunity.*

Alfred North Whitehead

1

THE GESTALT APPROACH

Fritz Perls, M.D., Ph.D.

The approach here presented rests on a set of premises that are neither abstruse nor unreasonable. The approach outlined is in many ways new. This does not mean that this approach has no relationship to any other theory of human behavior or to any other applications of theory to the problems of daily life or psychotherapeutic practice. Nor does it mean that this approach is composed exclusively of new and revolutionary elements. Most of the elements in it are to be found in many other approaches to the subject. What is new here is not necessarily the individual bits and pieces that go to make up the theory, *rather it is the way they are used and organized which gives this approach its uniqueness and its claim on your attention.* The first basic premise is implicit in that last sentence. The premise is that it is the organization of facts, preceptions, behavior or phenomena, and not the individual items of which they are composed, that defines them and gives them their specific and particular meaning.

Originally, this concept was developed by a group of German psychologists working in the field of perception, who showed that man does not perceive things as unrelated isolates, but organizes them in the perceptual process into meaningful wholes. The school of psychology which developed out of these observations is called the Gestalt School. Gestalt is a German word for which there is no exact English equivalent. A gestalt is a pattern, a configuration, the particular form of organization of the individual parts that go into its make up. The basic premise of Gestalt psy-

---

This material was excerpted from *The Gestalt Approach* (Palo Alto: Science and Behavior Books, 1973), with the permission of the publishers.

chology is that human nature is organized into patterns or wholes, that it is experienced by the individual in these terms, and that it can only be understood as a function of the patterns or wholes of which it is made.

The healthy organism seems to operate within what we might call a hierarchy of values. Since it is unable to do more than one thing properly at a time, it attends to the dominant survival need before it attends to any of the others; it operates on the principle of first things first.

Formulating this principle in terms of Gestalt psychology, we can say that the dominant need of the organism, at any time, becomes the foreground figure, and the other needs recede, at least temporarily, into the background. The foreground is that need which presses most sharply for satisfaction, whether the need is the need to preserve life itself, or whether it is related to less physically vital areas—whether it is physiological or psychological.

For the individual to satisfy his needs, to close the gestalt, to move on to other business, he must be able to sense what he needs and he must know how to manipulate himself and his environment, for even the purely physiological needs can only be satisfied through the interaction of the organism and the environment.

Given, then, that the human being has a built-in ability to use symbols and to abstract (and even the most rigid behaviorist has to admit this; if the ability did not exist he could not conduct an argument about its existence) what is the human being doing when he uses it? He is, I maintain, acting in effigy. He is doing *symbolically* what he could do *physically*.

In all of these mental activities, the relationship between what we do and what we think is very clear. When we are aware of something, or focus attention on it, or attempt to exert our will on it, there are at least some overt signs by which the spectator can see that these processes are at work.

But let me return to the area of thinking. It is here that most of the confusion arises. We understand thinking to include a number of activities—dreaming, imagining, theorizing, anticipating—making maximum use of our capacity to manipulate symbols. For the sake of brevity, let us call all of this *fantasy* activity rather than thinking. We tend to attach the notion of reason to thinking and of unreason to dreaming, and yet the two activities are very much alike. Let me make it very clear, however, that I do not mean, by using the word fantasy, to imply that there is anything unreal, eerie, strange, or false about these activities. Fantasy activity, in the broad sense in which I am using the term, is that activity of the human being which through the use of symbols tends to reproduce reality on a diminished scale. As activity involving the use of symbols, it derives from reality, since symbols themselves are initially derived from reality. Symbols begin as labels for objects and processes; they proliferate and grow into labels for labels and labels for labels for labels. The symbols may not even be approximated in reality, but they start in reality.

Thus, mental activity seems to act as a time, energy, and work saver for the individual. We think about problems in fantasy in order to be able to solve them in reality.

Now we are ready to formulate a definition of the functions of the mind and a definition of mental activity as a part of the whole organism we call the human being. Mental activity seems to be activity of the whole person carried on at a lower energy level than those activities we call physical. Here I must stop to point out that by using the word "lower" I am implying no value judgment at all. I simply mean that the activities that we call mental require less expenditure of the body substance than do those we call physical.

Our capacity to act on a level of diminished intensity—to engage in mental behavior—is of tremendous advantage not only for the individual human being in solving his own particular problems, but for the entire species. The energy man saves by thinking out instead of acting them out in every situation can now be invested in enriching his life. Once we recognize that thoughts and actions are made of the same stuff, we can translate and tranpose from one level to another.

In psychotherapy, this concept gives us a tool for dealing with the whole man. Now we can see how his mental and physical actions are meshed together. Neither patient nor therapist is limited by what the patient says and thinks, both can now take into consideration what he *does*. What he does provides clues as to what he thinks, as what he thinks provides clues as to what he does, and what he would like to do. Between the levels of thinking and doing there is an intermediate stage, the stage of playing at, and in therapy, if we observe keenly, we will notice that the patient plays at a lot of things. He himself will know what his actions, his fantasies and his play-actions mean, if we but call them to his attention. He himself will provide his own interpretations.

Through his experience of himself on the three levels of fantisizing, play-acting, and doing, he will come to an understanding of himself. Psychotherapy then becomes not an excavation of the past, in terms of repressions, Oedipal conflicts, and primal scenes, but an experience in living in the present. In this living situation, the patient learns for himself how to integrate his thoughts, feelings, and actions not only while he is in the consulting room, but during the course of his everyday life.

With this new outlook, the environment and the organism stand in a relationship of mutuality to one another. Neither is the victim of the other. To satisfy its needs, the organism has to find its required supplements in the environment. The system or orientation discovers what is wanted; all living creatures are observably able to sense what the outside objects are that will satisfy their needs.

Once the system or orientation has done its job, the organism has to manipulate the object it needs in such a way that the organismic balance will be restored, the gestalt will be closed.

These concepts, too, have meaning in psychotherapy. First of all, the conception that effective action is action directed towards the satisfaction of a dominant need gives us a clue as to the meaning of specific forms of behavior. Secondly, it gives us a further tool for an understanding of neurosis. If, through some disturbance in the homeostatic process, the individual is unable to sense his dominant needs or to manipulate his environment in order to attain them, he will behave in a disorganized and ineffective way. He will try to do too many things at once.

The neurotic has lost the ability (or perhaps he never developed it) to organize his behavior in accordance with a necessary hierarchy of needs. He literally cannot concentrate. In therapy, he has to learn how to distinguish the myriad of needs from one another, and how to attend to them, one at a time. He must learn to discover and identify himself with his needs, he must learn how, at every moment, to become totally involved in what he is doing; how to stick with a situation long enough to close the gestalt and move on to other business.

Not only does he have needs and a system of orientation and manipulation with which to achieve their satisfaction, he has attitudes towards those things in the environment that can help or hinder his search for satisfaction.

Magic annihilation is well known in psychotherapy under the name of *scotoma*, that is, blind spot. There are people who literally do not see what they don't want to see, don't hear what they don't want to hear, don't feel what they don't want to feel—all this in order to shut out what they consider to be dangerous—the objects or situations that have a negative cathexis for them. Magic annihilation is a partial withdrawal, a substitute for actual withdrawal.

Withdrawal per se is neither good nor bad, it is simply a means of coping with danger. The question of whether or not it is pathological can only be answered by our answers to these questions: withdrawal from what, withdrawal to what, and withdrawal for how long?

The same applies to contact. Contact itself is neither good nor bad, although in our age of concern for "social adjustment" we tend to value the capacity to make contact almost above all others. Yet some forms of contact are anything but healthy. Hence, not every contact is healthy and not every withdrawal unhealthy. One of the characteristics of the neurotic is that he can neither make good contact nor can he organize his withdrawal.

This brings us to the question of force which basically energizes all our action. That force seems to be emotion. For although modern psychiatry treats emotions as if they were a bothersome surplus that had to be discharged, emotions are the very life of us. We can theorize and interpret the motions any way we will. But this is a waste of time. For emotions are the very language of the organism; they modify the basic excitement according to the situation which has to be met. Excitement is transformed into specific emotions, and the emotions are transformed into sensoric and motor actions. The emotions energize the cathexes and mobilize the ways and means of satisfying needs.

We now see something else about the neurotic. His contact-withdrawal rhythm is out of kilter. He cannot decide for himself when to participate and when to withdraw because all the unfinished business of his life, all the interruptions to the ongoing process, have disturbed his sense of orientation, and he is no longer able to distinguish between those objects or persons in the environment which have a positive cathexis and those which have a negative cathexis; he no longer knows when or from what to withdraw. He has lost his freedom of choice, he cannot select appropriate means to his end goals, because he does not have the capacity to see the choices that are open to him.

2

TRANSACTIONAL ANALYSIS IN COUNSELING

Jack M. Dusay, M.D.

Transactional analysis (popularly known as T.A.) is a complete theory of human behavior and a method of psychotherapy. Its innovator and chief theoretician, was the late Dr. Eric Berne, who was initially trained in classical psychoanalysis. He amiably parted ways with psychoanalysis, in lieu of his newly-developed theories, and he opted for an active participation role on the part of the therapist. T.A. was originally formulated to be applied as an adjunct therapy in groups. It also lends itself easily to problems of family systems and couples. It is effective on a one-to-one counseling basis as well as in a group. As therapies go, T.A. is relatively new, having its origin in the mid 1950s. Since that time, it has developed a rich literature, both in the scientific field as well as in popular publication. Dr. Eric Berne's best seller, *Games People Play* (1964), familiarized the general public with T.A.; Dr. Thomas Harris' book, *I'm O.K.–You're O.K.* (1970), also reached a large audience. Berne's early work, *Transactional Analysis in Psychotherapy* (1961) and his *Principles of Group Treatment* (1966) were designed for a scientific group. Dusay and Steiner's formal chapter, entitled "Transactional Analysis in Groups," appeared in *The Comprehensive Textbook of Group Psychotherapy* (1971). It outlines the theory and application of T.A. for both professionals and students.

The following synopsis is a restatement of the principles and tenets of T.A., focusing upon both the theory and the clinical applications.

The International Transactional Analysis Association, 1772 Vallejo Street, San Francisco, California, sponsors ongoing seminars, training programs, worldwide conferences; and it certifies competent clinicians.

THE TRANSACTIONAL ANALYSIS THEORY OF PERSONALITY AND SOCIAL BEHAVIOR

Basic Motivation

The basic motivating factor for all human social behavior is the need for *strokes*. Dr. Rene Spitz (1945), a child psychoanalyst, studied two groups of infants in two types of foundling homes (orphanages). He discovered that infants who were physically touched, cuddled and poked, had a far higher survival rate than infants who were not. The limited-contact home prided itself on being medically sterile and impeccable. The children were surrounded by boiled, white sheets in separate cribs, and the masked nurses seldom touched the infants. This home did everything imaginable to protect the children from dreaded bacteria, in conformity to the popular germ theories of the day. A shockingly high percentage of these children died from a condition known as marasmus, or spinal cord shrinkage. Many of those who lived were "disturbed." In the "unhealthy" touching home, the staff were volunteer "mommies," who rocked and tickled the kids; kept them in large playpens; and let the kids dirty each other. In this home the remarkably small mortality rate occurred from the normal childhood diseases that infants contract. Spitz concluded that infants and children need a great deal of physical contact for survival. This contact is what transactional analysts term strokes, and they are the backbone and the motivating need for all human transactions. The lack of strokes has both physical and mental deleterious effects.

Various experiments support this notion. At Princeton (1961), several student volunteers were placed in sensory isolation chambers, for up to seventy-two hours. It was found that sensory deprivation had an undesirable influence upon the volunteers, which manifested itself in the loss of body weight (although food was provided); inability to walk a straight line; visual problems in color differentiation; pen and pencil test errors; hallucinations; auditory problems; and tactile difficulties. The researchers, fortunately, put a "panic button" in the isolation chamber, so that the subjects could get out if necessary. Out of the sixty subjects, only forty-one completed their stays (even though money-making was the featured enticement for the graduate students). It is not difficult to understand that a favored form of punishment and torture for criminals and war prisoners has been solitary confinement and isolation.

The primate studies of Dr. Harry Harlow demonstrated that monkeys who were reared outside of the presence of other monkeys, exhibited bizarre behavior. It was not possible for them to recover to normalcy for the rest of their lives.

The vital contact and touching (*strokes*) is an inherent biological drive in higher animals and humans. At first, the human baby needs actual physical touching from mother or others. Later, the growing child discovers that it is possible to get strokes in more symbolic ways by the use of words and voice tones. Mother's voice, in a nurturing, or even critical tone, will sometimes gratify the infant. In later life, spoken words become the major source of strokes; although, throughout the entire realm of life, it is doubtful that words can completely take the place of actual physical touching.

Strokes are received in several ways. Some people, who got and became used to negative, "put-down" strokes in early childhood, may feel comfortable in the role of criminal, being constantly berated and sent to their rooms (or to jail) over and over. There is a high recidivism rate among institutionalized criminals. Their histories frequently include a "rap sheet," going back to their early days. This makes it apparent that the need for strokes is vital; and that getting negative strokes is better than no strokes at all. People would prefer to thrive on punishment, apprehension, scolding, and abuse rather than not be recognized as a human being at all. The worst form of torture is the receiving of no strokes—positive *or* negative.

Occasionally, people may wait for a long time to receive their strokes. A concert pianist may practice at length, in relative seclusion, before performing publicly to receive a resounding applause at the end of his recital. A lab researcher may toil in privacy for many months, before his professor congratulates him for a well-done job. A gourmet chef may work for weeks to prepare a banquet, and will not receive strokes until the patrons smile and pat their full bellies. From a negative standpoint, a burglar sometimes has to pull several jobs before he gets caught. A schlemiel-type[1] waitress may have to spill many soups and cups of coffee before she gets her strokes yelled at her by an indignant patron.

So, infants literally need to be touched. And, as mentioned, as they grow older, they find that strokes come in increasingly sym-

---

[1]Schlemiel is the colloquial name for the person who gets recognition for making a mess out of things.

bolic ways, through words or non-verbal gestures. There is a vast array of ingenious methods which people use to get strokes; and they learn their predominate methods when they are young. When people incorporate rich and varied ways of getting strokes, they may experience autonomous, non-stereotyped lives. If their methods incorporate highly repetitive patterns, this could lead to destructive game behavior. Either decision is generally made at a young age, and the child may continue this behavior by thinking, "It worked for me once, so it will always work."

Ego States

Ego states are of a fundamental interest to transactional analysts. They are defined as a coherent system of thoughts and feelings, with the corresponding pattern of behavior. An ego state is observable, real, and usually obvious. Each person has incorporated in himself, specific parts from his actual parents (the Parent Ego State); an adult part, which developed along the lines of logical thinking (the Adult Ego State); and finally, his own unique Child ego state.[2]

Because the Parent ego state in an individual, is introjected directly from his actual parents, the individual may find himself expressing *exactly* the same words, thoughts, and gestures that his parents do or did. Occasionally, these opinions, morals, and ethics will spill out; and the person will look puzzled and say, "Where did that come from?" A Parent ego state may include a "see-no-evil" position, or concern itself with values, principles, and opinions. The judicial words "good" and "bad" are expressions from a Parent ego state. The Adult ego state is basically a computer, and it conforms to the rules of logic. The Adult ego state is free of emotion; it does not laugh, cry, pout, berate, or show concern. (The Adult ego state is not to be confused with "adult." This needs to be clear, because some people have been told that being and behaving like an adult is a perfect and a desirable quest.) The Adult is not concerned with being perfect or imperfect. Its sole function is to think in a rational way. The Child ego state is the part of the person, which is ideally uninhibited, free, spontaneous, and prone to

---

[2]For clarity, the ego states are capitalized as Parent, Adult, and Child for easy identification. This distinguishes them from biological parents, chronological adults, and under-twelve children.

imagination and fantasy. In it is lodged intuition and creativity. The Child can be the most delightful and beautiful part of any person. However, there is another type of Child inside each person who may not be so attractive. Indeed, it may manifest itself in being resentful, shy, rebellious, inhibited, sulky; or perhaps by compliant thoughts, and conforming behavior.[3]

Ego states have little to do with an individual's chronological age, except that during early childhood, the Adult and Parent are not fully developed. A four-year-old girl who is changing the diaper on her Betsy-Wetsy doll, is "coming-on" with her fledgling Parent state and behaving exactly the way her mother or father did when changing her diapers. Her mannerisms, speech, and inflections come out just the same. Another youngster, standing at the street curb, portrays Adult behavior when she stops and looks in both directions, and decides to stand back on the curb, because an automobile is bearing down upon her path. Her logic tells her that her small frame could not withstand the impact from the truck. This is rapid, logical, computer-like thinking. The sixty-five-year-old chairman of the board, who is gleefully in the lively pursuit of his pretty secretary, is exhibiting his Child ego state.

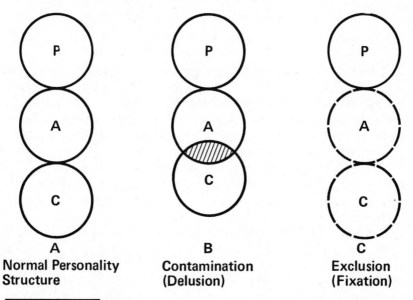

A	B	C
Normal Personality Structure	**Contamination (Delusion)**	**Exclusion (Fixation)**

---

[3]These subdivided ego states have been divided into five functional parts: the Critical Parent (CP); the Nurturing Parent (NP); the Adult (A); the Free Child (FC); and the Adapted Child (AC).

Figure 1-A represents a diagram of the normal structure of the personality. It shows the primary Parent, Adult, and Child ego states as being separate and distinct entities. Figure 1-B illustrates delusional thinking, which could be a spontaneous or chemical psychosis, and it is diagrammed as the Child and Adult being contaminated and inseparable from one another. A woman in a mental hospital told the doctor that all the television commercials pertained especially to her, and that they emitted secret messages to her. Her Child ego state (like the Child of most people) felt that she was special. Her Adult ego state knew where to watch and how to turn on the television set. When the Child and the Adult functions got mixed together in this situation, the patient had delusions of grandeur. Another type of pathology is known as a fixation of one ego state which excludes the others (Figure 1-C). In this example, the Parent is operating as the effective ego state. The Adult and Child have been excluded from this person's functioning. A fundamentalist country preacher, who is obsessed and intent upon finding "sin under every bush," would be operating from a fixated Parent ego state. Another example of a fixated Parent, shows up as abject prejudice, e.g., "all people with long hair are Communists."

Transactions

A transaction is defined as a stimulus (or statement) directed to one person, followed by a corresponding reply from the other. A transaction is a unit of communication. It disects and clarifies, in a simple manner, the complex ways of how people interact with each other. There are three general types of transactions: the complementary; the crossed; and the ulterior.

Figure 2-A illustrates a simple, complementary transaction. In this situation, the stimulus (the top arrow) and the response (the corresponding arrow) are parallel with each other. The boss says to his secretary, "What time is it?" and the secretary responds, "3:00." In this case, two Adult ego states are talking with one another. The arrows are parallel and straight data is being transacted. Of course, complementary transactions could occur between Parent to Child and back; Parent to Parent and back, Child to Child and back, and so forth. This illustrates the first rule of communication: *Whenever the arrows are parallel, communication on that subject may proceed indefinitely.*

A second type of transaction is shown in Figure 2-B. In this one,

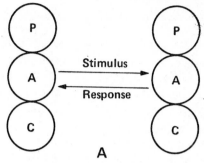

A
Complementary

Boss: What time is it?   Secretary: 3:00
(Stimulus)   (Response)

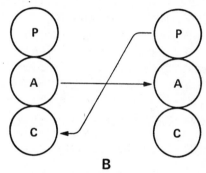

B
Crossed

Boss: What time is it?   Secretary: Look at your own
(Stimulus)   (Response) watch, (stupid).

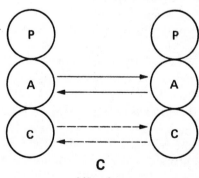

C
Ulterior

Boss: What time is it?   Secretary: Wouldn't you like
(Stimulus)   (Response) to know. . .(hee, hee).

the two arrows are *crossed*, and not parallel. The boss gives the same stimulus, "What time is it?" and the secretary responds from her Parent to the boss's Child by saying, "Look at your own watch, (stupid)." The arrows are crossed, and this leads to the second rule of communication: *Whenever the arrows become crossed, communication on the original subject, ceases abruptly.* At this point, it will be impossible for the boss and secretary to continue with the initial discussion about time. The predictable topics will be, "Why do you always criticize me?" or "You're fired!" A logical corollary, to the second rule of communication is: *Whenever the arrows become parallel again, communication on a topic can proceed as before.*

Figure 2-C represents two levels of transactions occurring at the same time. The solid line (social level) transactions are readily observable and contain the overt message. The broken line (psychological level) is hidden and contains the ulterior message. The boss and the secretary again are discussing time on the social level, but on the psychological level, they are discussing fun and hankypanky. "What time is it?" "Wouldn't you like to know . . . (Hee Hee)." The third rule of communication is: *One cannot predict behavior by focusing on the social level of transactions alone; the psychological level must also be considered.* The ulterior transaction has been found to be the basis and core of games, in the psychological sense.

Games

Games are ways of behaving; and are played by two or more people. There is always an ulterior transaction, a gimmick, and a switch, which culminates in the respective psychological pay-off. An illustration of a game is demonstrated by Fanny. Fanny, an expert secretary, came to the psychiatrist's office because she wanted, but was unable to hold a job. She had a horrible work record, in that she had been fired twenty times in ten years. She said that she wanted a good working relationship with an employer. The therapist agreed that this was a valid goal (contract) for treatment and committed himself to work with her to achieve this result. After five minutes had elapsed in the initial interview, Fanny suddenly turned to the therapist, pointed at his necktie and said haughtily, "Where did you get *that*?" The therapist, being professional (which means being able to keep a straight face in times of sudden stress) maintained his decorum, and continued with the interview.[4]

After about fifteen minutes, Fanny proceeded to rearrange the chairs in the office to make herself more comfortable. In doing so, she knocked over the therapist's favorite lamp.[5] Finally, the therapist's anger became more evident as he chomped on his pipe. Fanny profusely apologized, leaned over to replace the lamp, and as she bent over, she positioned her "fanny" about two feet from the therapist's foot. With this distinctive target in front of him, the therapist burst out laughing. With a knowing look, Fanny began to laugh also, and they both intuitively recognized the "Kick Me" game. Recognition is helpful, but not a cure in itself. And so Fanny joined an ongoing psychotherapy group. She performed similar antics with a different cast of players. One evening she brought her own thermos of coffee, and "unwittingly" spilled it onto the lap of the man sitting next to her. Sarge was a hostile man who was in treatment to control his rage toward women.[6] The outcome of Fanny's escapade was obvious; several group members worked frantically at restraining Sarge. The group worked diligently at breaking her Kick Me game by taking an antithetical position. This meant that they would seek out her positive attributes, and carefully restrain themselves from getting angry at her. Frustrated by this, Fanny tried harder and harder to get "put down," but the perseverance of the group, which was operating from a predominantly nurturing, creative, and logical position (NP, FC, and A) eventually paid off. Fanny finally fulfilled her treatment contract; she has been working peacefully at the same job for over four years.

Fanny picked up her game early in life. She remembered that she had been kicked out of almost everything, her sorority at college; a social club in high school; high school itself; as well as most of the lower grades; Brownies and summer camp. Her earliest

---

[4]This is a professional stance that many therapists adopt: how to maintain a straight face when things like this are happening. This is one reason that male therapists frequently smoke pipes.

[5]This doesn't usually happen in a therapist's office, or in anyone's office, and was rather unsettling.

[6]Two things are to be noted here: 1) She did something unusual, as other members did not bring their own coffee, and 2) somehow she intuitively positioned herself next to the person who was most likely to lash out at her.

recollection was knocking an ashtray off of her mother's coffee table, and receiving a violent slap on the hand as well as a stinging swat on her bottom.[7]

She learned that the way to get the necessary survival strokes from her mother was to do something naughty, and get slapped and berated. She stated as well as anyone could, "Negative strokes are better than no strokes at all."

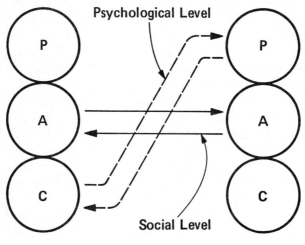

A Game Diagram

The above diagram illustrates Fanny's game. On the social level, she said to the therapist, "I have a difficult problem." The therapist responded, "I agree. Let's work on it." On the surface, this looked like parallel Adult to Adult transactions, and Fanny responded, "O.K." On the ulterior level, however, she was saying, "Please kick me," a Child-to-Parent transaction. Before the therapist caught on to her game, he responded with angry looks, and a broken pipe stem, which came from his Parent.

---

[7]This was her earlist intact memory—she had frequent dreams and vague memories of being punished by Mother. Her mother's recognition of her was mainly through swats on her bottom and saying "no-no." Fanny was impoverished in eliciting positive praise. She later came to depend upon spankings and cross words.

All varieties and types of game behavior conform to this general formula (1972):

$$C + G \quad R \quad S \quad X \quad P.O.$$

"C" stands for the "con," which shows that a transaction is ulterior (hidden). On the surface, it looks as though it's a straight request for help, but underneath, there is a hidden request for something else. For a game to develop and succeed, it must "hook" into a weakness of the respondent. The respondent's desire to help or rescue is represented by the letter "G" which means "gimmick." The gimmick is the device which hooks the respondent. This brings forth the predictable "response," or "R," in which the rescue is forthcoming. Next, comes the dramatic "switch," or "S." Fanny, rather than being a grateful recipient of the therapist's wisdom and advice, switched from her "poor victim" role into someone who was intent upon criticizing the therapist, his necktie, rearranging his furniture, and spilling coffee on another group member. The therapist switched to being angry. Anger became a temporary "cross-up" in their relationship, signified by "X," and the entire episode ended with a definite "pay-off" for both of them. The therapist was entitled to be angry at the ungrateful patient, and the patient got her cherished rejection and possible banishment. The pay-off can be viewed as the cashing in of a collection of "trading stamps" in exchange for the big pay-off.[8] With Fanny, the big pay-off was a free "get fired," or "get kicked out of the group" type of prize. (If Fanny collected enough of these "black and blue," existential trading stamps, she might be able to cash in on a full-blown beating or even a potential suicide.)

The switch and cross-up positions have been illustrated in Dr. S. Karpman's Drama Triangle (1968). He recognized certain similarities between psychological games and theatre drama. In game relationships, there is a dramatic switch between the two people involved. (See Figure 4.)

Fanny came into the therapist's office as a "victim" of her miserable childhood; the therapist jumped into the "rescuer" role to help the "damsel in distress." The first switch occurred when Fanny changed from "victim" to "persecutor," by criticizing the

---

[8]Because of the diagnosis of the game and its interruption by correct antithesis, the big pay-off was avoided in this case.

therapist and breaking his lamp. The therapist's corresponding switch was from "rescuer" to "victim." The completion of the game rotated the positions again, with the therapist switching back to "persecutor" and becoming angry with Fanny. She promptly went back to the "victim" role.[9]

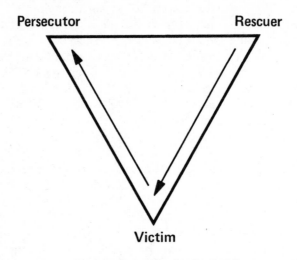

Persecutor   Rescuer

Victim

Drama Triangle (A Switch)

The transactional diagram of games, the game formula, and the drama triangle, are important aids in understanding games. Note that authentic behavior may appear similar, but it is not gamey. For example, Diane enters the therapist's office and says, "Help! I need some reassurance." The therapist gives her reassurance, and she says, "Thank you." No dramatic switch has occurred, and this remains a simple set of transactions.

Scripts

People have unique game repertoires. A common question that arises is, "why does one individual choose a particular game, and a

---

[9]Had the therapist not been a transactional analyst, it might have ended with her being called an unsuitable candidate for treatment, and she could have been fired from the therapist's office, just as she had been repetitively fired from her jobs.

different individual, another?" For the answer, attention to life scripts is essential. Dr. C. Steiner (1974) composed a script matrix, which completes the theory of social relations and personality function.

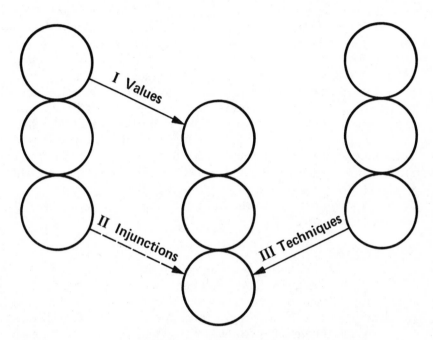

I   Values; i.e.; Go to college, make money
II   Injunction; i.e.; "Get lost"
III   Technique; i.e.; Be a pest

A Script Matrix

Fanny was given a young American's "S.S.S." (Standard Success Story) by her parents: i.e., "Go to college, make money, get married, and have children." Those were Fanny's values, which were drummed securely into her head, until they became part of her own Parent ego state. This "SSS" is represented by No. I, which is the "value part" of the script, and is initially accepted by the individual. Constructed with a solid line, it represents those transactions between the father and daughter (the Parent ego state of the father, and the developing Parent ego state of the daughter), which the parent is willing to openly discuss.[10]

No. II is the hidden-level injunction (or the curse) and is represented by dotted lines. It is not freely discussed or admitted. With Fanny, her father insinuated, "Get lost." This is a "don't be" transaction. Therefore, Fanny had two contradictory messages from her father: "Be a success" and "Get lost." Fanny turned to her mother for a solution to this dilemma. In essence, she felt, "How can I live with these two types of incompatible messages?" By observing Mother, who pestered Father, she saw that she irritated him; and was the recipient of his wrath and an occasional black eye. Mother would then retire to her separate room after being physically and mentally assaulted. This is the "Here's How" message, depicted by No. III. This technique informed Fanny's Child to "Be a pest and get rejected." Values (I); Injunctions (II); and Techniques (III); combine and make up the script. A script explains game choices, and gives the clues as to how a person will structure his or her time throughout life. Severe problems may develop by *conforming* to the hidden messages and curse-like elements of the script.

Reinforcement

Because of "scripting," people choose playmates, friends, enemies, spouses, and occupations which blend with their early life programming. These choices reinforce the early, basic, decisions that they have made about themselves. When Fanny's father gave her the "get lost" message, she ultimately *decided* that the thing to do was to look like she was succeeding, but in essence, get lost and be rejected. Once this decision was made, she led her life accordingly. Fanny intentionally sat next to the group member with the biggest temper and provoked him. Her entire life was filled with these purposeful activities, until they were diagnosed and interrupted in treatment. After Fanny had mastered and perfected a positive way of eliciting strokes, her new personality (as reflected in her "after" egogram) as well as her new behavior, was in itself, reinforcing.

---

[10]Most fathers would not be at all reticent to tell their neighbors, a doctor, or anyone else that they gave their daughter a common success inspiration.

CLINICAL APPLICATION

Fortunately, all people are born *O.K.*, with the potential and drive to grow in happy and creative ways. When this growth potential gets thwarted, the developing person may decide that he is not O.K. and may proceed to live an unproductive or tragic life. The therapist's challenge is to interrupt the losing patterns. This may be accomplished at any one of three different levels, which will be discussed.[11]

Script Change

Fanny's earliest recollection was being spanked by her mother at the coffee table. This is a prototype memory. This early intact social memory, as distinguished from fleeting or incomplete recollections, is indicative of the reinforcements a person will seek. A developing child formulates questions of "How am I?" "Am I an O.K. person?" and "How do I stack up, compared to others?" Fanny was given the message, "You're bothering me, Clumsy! You're not O.K.!" Fanny, overwhelmed by continual negative injunctions, finally *decided* that she was not O.K. and would live her life from this standpoint.

Through script re-decision, the transactional analyst works with the client, so that the initial moment of decision is rediscovered. This has two immediate advantages: 1) a person recognizes when and under what circumstances his life-style deviated from growth and positive potential, and 2) the individual client is empowered.[12] This is the implied notion that an individual is captain of his own destiny, and that he himself made the decision on how to live his life. He can then avoid blaming the parents, for their role and actions, and recognize his accountability in arranging his life pattern. This may be upsetting to the person, but finally, in an enlightened position, he is able to develop both the understanding and attitude that he himself can change.

A "double chair"[13] technique is an effective procedure, where-

---

[11]The transactional analyst may effect a cure on any of the three levels. They are not totally distinct entities; when one level is affected, the others are also.

[12]Empowered is the self-realization of the person, that he has the necessary ingredients to make his own choices and be personally responsible.

[13]Fritz Perl's confronting technique.

by the individual may sort out the various components of his ego states, by "placing" them in different chairs and re-experiencing their impact. He readily views his Adapted Child, which is highly conformed and compliant with the predominant negative influences. The person becomes aware of the life decisions he made during the first six years of his life. At a peak moment, he experiences a re-decision, which is based upon his informed, rational elements. In essence, his Adult talks to his hurt, deviant Child and this affects a re-decision. This process has been well demonstrated in the work of R. Goulding (1972), particularly with those who are self-destructive and suicidal.

Another type of script intervention has been to regress the client to an early childlike position. At this point, the individual is re-raised by positive parenting, in a totally new re-learning environment, with positive nurturing messages and values. This concept is known as re-parenting. It was innovated and successfully used by J. Schiff. She and her associates have found it to be effective with the "uncurable" disease known as schizophrenia.

As employed by Dr. Berne, the original technique of script change relied chiefly upon an intense, trusting relationship between the client and the therapist. When the client moved into a position of extreme susceptability to the therapist, a counter-injunction to the script would be given. A person who had been told "drop dead" or "kill yourself," early in life, would receive the potent counter-injunction, "Do not kill yourself." Several patients reported later, "No one ever said that to me before."

Game Interruption

When someone has made a personal decision about being not "O.K.," a continual reinforcement of their basic position is necessary. If this is not forthcoming, the original decision or the life plan is weakened. Games are a vehicle of reinforcing a person's basic life decision. If the predominant game is interrupted or broken up, the pathological behavior will desist. This explains the clinical phenomena of why people become miserable after a phone call, letter, or visit from their parents. This stirs up the dormant coals of the old life plan, which had its inception from parental influences. Even though the individual has grown up, shifted his thought patterns, and is separated by distance, his earlier misery and discomfort is renewed from the parental stimulus. Frequently, persons who are unwilling to break their script, marry others who are a direct reflection of their parents.[14]

Fanny had no trouble in finding players for her "Kick Me" game. There are an abundance of "Kick Me" players, waiting for their chance. Her therapy group took an antithetical position by refusing to kick her, in spite of the tempting stimuli she offered. They interrupted the pattern by giving her a massive infusion of positive strokes. She tried harder to elicit "kicks," but the therapist and group resisted—frustrating her attempts at re-establishing her destructive course. (They were able to maintain a "growth" position because of a logical analysis of the situation and because it simply feels better to give positive strokes.) Frustration and despair occur when the old familiar patterns aren't working any more. This anxiety ultimately leads to a unique exploration of new methods to get strokes. Although most psychotherapy sessions may last for only a couple hours a week, their impact has a long-reaching effect. If Fanny were to continue being kicked outside of the group, and elicit the opposite responses in the group, she would most likely notice what she was doing. When a game pattern is habitual, the person is performing it in a state of limited awareness. During frequent rigorous confrontations, it becomes difficult to continue playing the game naively. This heightened sense of awareness within the group setting also is experienced outside the group.

Ego State Change

Shifting energies from an ineffective ego state to an effective one is an exhilirating and self-reinforcing experience.[15] Fanny usually "came on" as a naughty little pest, intent upon provoking angry responses from others. A relationship diagram, which illustrates the intensity of the various ego states, is called an egogram (1972). These egograms are diagnosed intuitively and represent the five aspects of the personality: the Critical Parent (CP), the Nurturing Parent (NP), the Adult (A), the Free Child (FC) and the Adapted Child (AC). They are lined up in this order on a bar graph and reveal the functional and intensity aspects of a personality.

---

[14]This is similar to a stubborn child, who would rather stick to a decision and be miserable instead of changing.

[15]For an authentic change, an accurate personality assessment is necessary.

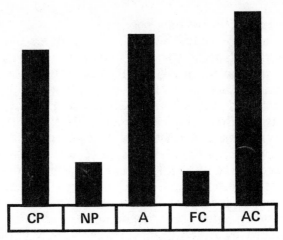

Fanny's Egogram

CP	NP	A	FC	AC

Her Adapted Child, that part of her Child ego state which had decided that she was not O.K. and kickable was her predominant ego state. It is represented by the highest column in the egogram. Her Free Child was very low in relation to this, and she had little fun, sexual enjoyment, or satisfaction. Her Adult was solid; she was bright and a good thinker. She seldom had spare energy to console or help other people, and this is reflected in her low NP. Because her biological parent was judgmental and angry with her, during her youth she learned well how to criticize and "pick apart" others, and this is represented by the height of her Critical Parent. Fanny's initial egogram, drawn by her as well as the group, was supported by her personal history and customary actions.

To facilitate an egogram change, it has been found that it is easier to raise a deficient ego state than it is to lower a high one. In Fanny's before egogram, her Free Child and Nurturing Parent were the lowest, and this was related to her problem. Innumerable techniques have been devised, which, when practiced, will raise any of the low ego states.[16]

In the protective, permissive setting of the transactional analysis group, Fanny learned how to exercise her Free Child. Psychodrama, role-playing, and shared-fantasy were among the techniques she used. She was authentically stroked and complimented when

---

[16]Each ego state has a positive as well as a negative side. Persons with too little CP will get pushed around and intimidated; those with low AC are unable to compromise and get along with others, and so forth.

she was creative.[17] Her Nurturing Parent was strengthened by physically hugging and being concerned about other people. It feels good at both poles: the giving, which is the NP, as well as the receiving, which is the FC. Raising a low or dormant ego state is generally met with powerful resistances. The personality will wage a terrific battle to protect its status quo. Fanny and the group persevered and persisted and she ultimately underwent an egogram (personality) change. A good portion of the energy, previously spent in her Adapted Child, shifted to her Free Child, while some of the energy formerly spent in her Critical Parent transmigrated to her Nurturing Parent. This was evidenced spontaneously one evening, when she shared her home-baked cookies with the group.[18] Her post-cure egogram symbolized that she was less prone to kick and get kicked by others. Fanny's case succinctly illustrates the three different levels at which transactional analysis operates and works: the script change, the interruption of game patterns, and the actual ego state change.

A prime consideration in transactional analysis is that both the therapist and the client form a distinct mutual treatment *contract*.[19] This contract is unique to T.A. and, simply stated, it answers the question, "How will you and I both know when you get what you are coming for?" Sometimes an answer may be easily attained; at other times it is fought for rigorously. Without the contract, the therapist could be viewed in a rescuing Parent position, while the client is viewed as a victimized patient. The ensuing therapy would have no clear-cut, pre-determined course. A contract serves to emphasize the attitude of the T.A. therapist, in that both he and the client agree that change can occur, and both commit themselves to action. Ultimately, the therapist provides the patient with permission, protection, and potency.

T.A. lends itself nicely to the incorporation of various theories, including psychodrama, gestalt, psychoanalysis, and so forth. Its

---

[17]Phony or sociable strokes are not allowed.

[18]A group member humorously remarked, "That's how you can tell when somebody's cured."

[19]A T.A. *contract* consists of mutual assent; a legal, agreeable goal; consideration (payment of a fee); and competency; it illustrates the same elements of a legal contract.

vocabulary is as easily learned by a third grader, as a college professor. After acquiring a solid foundation of T.A. theory and techniques, the therapist freely uses his own creative and insightful abilities in the treatment setting.

REFERENCES

Berne, E. *Games People Play*. New York: Grove Press, 1964.

Berne, E. *Transactional Analysis in Psychotherapy*. New York: Grove Press, 1961.

Berne, E. *Principles of Group Treatment*. New York: Oxford University Press, 1966.

Berne, E. *What Do You Say after You Say Hello?* New York: Grove Press, 1972.

Dusay, J. Egograms and the Constancy Hypothesis. *Trans. Anal. J., 2:*3, 1972.

Dusay and Steiner, T.A. in Groups, in *Comprehensive Textbook of Group Psychotherapy*. Ed. H. Kaplan & B. Sadock, Williams & Wilkins, Baltimore, 1971.

Goulding, R. New Directions in Transactional Analysis. Creating an Environment for Redecision and Change, in *Progress and Family Therapy*. New York: Brunner/Mazel, 1972.

Harris, T. *I'm OK – You're OK*. New York: Harper & Row, 1970.

Karpman, S. Script Drama Analysis, *Trans. Anal. Bull., 7:*26, 1968.

Spitz, R. Hospitalism, genesis of psychiatric conditions in early childhood. *Psychoanal. Study Child., 1:*53, 1945.

Steiner, C. *Scripts People Live*. New York: Grove Press, 1974.

Vernon, J., et al. The Effect of Human Isolation upon some Perceptual and Motor Skills, in *Sensory Deprivation*. Ed. Solomon, et al., Harvard University Press, Cambridge, 1961.

3

A THEORY OF THERAPY
AS DEVELOPED IN THE
CLIENT-CENTERED FRAMEWORK

Carl R. Rogers, Ph.D.

No theory can be adequately understood without some knowledge of the cultural and personal soil from which it springs. This
means that I must take the reader through some autobiographical
material since, although the client-centered orientation has become very much of a group enterprise in every respect, I, as an
individual, carry a considerable responsibility for its initiation and
for the beginning formulation of its theories. I shall, therefore,
mention briefly some cultural influences and personal experiences
which may or may not have relevance to the theory itself. I shall
not attempt to evaluate these influences, since I am probably a
poor judge of the part they have played.

I lived my childhood as a middle child in a large, close-knit
family, where hard work and a highly conservative (almost fundamentalist) Protestant Christianity were about equally revered.
When the family moved to a farm at the time I was twelve, I
became deeply interested and involved in scientific agriculture.
The heavy research volumes I read on my own initiative in the
next few years regarding feeds and feeding, soils, animal hus-
bandry, and the like, instilled in me a deep and abiding respect for
the scientific method as a means of solving problems and creating
new advances in knowledge. This respect was reinforced by my
first years in college, where I was fond of the physical and

Reprinted and abridged, by permission of the author and the publisher, from
Sigmund Koch (Ed.), *Psychology: A Study of a Science,* Vol. 3. New York:
McGraw-Hill, 1959. Pp. 184-256.

biological sciences. In my work in history I also realized something of the satisfactions of scholarly work.

Having rejected the family views of religion, I became interested in a more modern religious viewpoint and spent two profitable years in Union Theological Seminary, which at that time was deeply committed to a freedom of philosophical thought which respected any honest attempt to resolve significant problems, whether this led into or away from the church. My own thinking led me in the latter direction, and I moved "across the street" to Teachers College, Columbia University. Here I was exposed to the views of John Dewey, not directly, but through William H. Kilpatrick. I also had my first introduction to clinical psychology in the warmly human and common-sense approach of Leta Hollingworth. There followed a year of internship at the Institute for Child Guidance, then in its chaotic but dynamic first year of existence. Here I gained much from the highly Freudian orientation of most of its psychiatric staff, which included David Levy and Lawson Lowrey. My first attempts at therapy were carried on at the Institute. Because I was still completing my doctorate at Teachers College, the sharp incompatibility of the highly speculative Freudian thinking of the Institute with the highly statistical and Thorndikean views at Teachers College was keenly felt.

There followed twelve years in what was essentially a community child guidance clinic in Rochester, New York. This was a period of comparative isolation from the thinking of others. The psychology department of the University of Rochester was uninterested in what we were doing because our work was not, in its opinion, in the field of psychology. Our colleagues in the social agencies, schools, and courts knew little and cared less about psychological ideologies. The only element which carried weight with them was the ability to get results in working with maladjusted individuals. The staff was eclectic, of diverse background, and our frequent and continuing discussion of treatment methods was based on our practical everyday working experience with the children, adolescents, and adults who were our clients. It was the beginning of an effort, which has had meaning for me ever since, to discover the order which exists in our experience of working with people. The volume on the *Clinical Treatment of the Problem Child* (Rogers, 1939) was one outcome of this effort.

During the second half of this period there were several individuals who brought into our group the controversial therapeutic views of Otto Rank and the Philadelphia group of social workers and psychiatrists whom he had influenced. Personal contact with Rank was limited to a three-day institute we arranged; nevertheless his thinking had a very decided impact on our staff and helped me to crystallize some of the therapeutic methods we were groping toward. For by this time I was becoming more competent as a therapist, and beginning to sense a discoverable orderliness in this experience, an orderliness which was inherent *in* the experience, and (unlike some of the Freudian theories which had grown so far from their original soil) did not have to be imposed *on* the experience.

Though I had carried on some part-time university teaching throughout the Rochester years, the shift to a faculty position at Ohio State University was a sharp one. I found that the emerging principles of therapy, which I had experienced largely on an implicit basis, were by no means clear to well-trained, critically minded graduate students. I began to sense that what I was doing and thinking in the clinical field was perhaps more of a new pathway than I had recognized. The paper I presented to the Minnesota chapter of Psi Chi in December, 1940, which later became Chapter 2 of *Counseling and Psychotherapy* (1942), was the first conscious attempt to develop a relatively new line of thought. Up to that time I had felt that my writings were essentially attempts to distill out more clearly the principles which "all clinicians" were using.

The new influence at Ohio State, which continued to be felt in my years at Chicago, was the impact of young men and women — intellectually curious, often theoretically oriented, eager to learn from experience and to contribute through research and theory to the development of a field of knowledge. Through their mistakes as well as their successes in therapy, through their research studies, their critical contributions, and through our shared thinking, have come many of the recent developments in their orientation.

In the decade at the University of Chicago the new elements which stand out most sharply are the opportunity for and the encouragement of research, the inclusion of graduate students from education, theology, human development, sociology, industrial relations, as well as psychology, in the ramified activities of the Counseling Center, and the creative thinking of my faculty colleagues, especially those connected with the Center.

The persistent influence which might not be fully recognized, because it is largely implicit in the preceding paragraphs, is the continuing clinical experience with individuals who perceive themselves, or are perceived by others to be, in need of personal help. Since 1928, for a period now approaching thirty-five years, I have spent probably an average of 15 to 20 hours per week, except during vacation periods, in endeavoring to understand and be of therapeutic help to these individuals. To me, they seem to be the major stimulus to my psychological thinking. From these hours, and from my relationships with these people, I have drawn most of whatever insight I possess into the meaning of therapy, the dynamics of interpersonal relationships, and the structure and functioning of personality.

SOME BASIC ATTITUDES

Out of this cultural and personal soil have grown certain basic convictions and attitudes which have undoubtedly influenced the theoretical formulation which will be presented. I will endeavor to list some of these views which seem to me relevant:

1. I have come to see both research and theory as being aimed toward the inward ordering of significant experience. This research is not something esoteric, nor an activity in which one engages to gain professional kudos. It is the persistent, disciplined effort to make sense and order out of the phenomena of subjective experience. Such effort is justified because it is satisfying to perceive the world as having order and because rewarding results often ensue when one understands the orderly relationships which appear to exist in nature. One of these rewarding results is that the ordering of one segment of experience in a theory immediately opens up new vistas of inquiry, research, and thought, thus leading one continually forward.

Thus the primary reason for research and systematic theory in the field of therapy is that it is personally dissatisfying to permit the cumulating experiences of therapeutic hours to remain as a conglomeration of more or less isolated events. It feels as though there is an order in these events. What could it be? And of any hunch regarding the inherent order, it is necessary to ask the question, is this really true, or am I deceiving myself? Thus slowly there is assembled a body of facts, and systematic constructs to explain those facts, which have as their basic function the satisfaction of a need for order which exists in me.

(I have, at times, carried on research for purposes other than the above to satisfy others, to convince opponents and skeptics, to gain prestige, and for other unsavory reasons. These errors in judgment and activity have only deepened the above positive conviction.)

2. It is my opinion that the type of understanding which we call science can begin anywhere, at any level of sophistication. To observe acutely, to think carefully and creatively—these activities, not the accumulation of laboratory instruments, are the beginnings of science. To observe that a given crop grows better on the rocky hill than in the lush bottom land, and to think about this observation, is the start of science. To notice that most sailors get scurvy but not those who have stopped at islands to pick up fresh fruit is a similar start. To recognize that, when a person's views of himself change, his behavior changes accordingly, and to puzzle over this, is again the beginning of both theory and science. I voice this conviction in protest against the attitude, which seems too common in American psychology, that science starts in the laboratory or at the calculating machine.

3. A closely related belief is that there is a natural history of science—that science, in any given field, goes through a patterned course of growth and development. For example, it seems to me right and natural that in any new field of scientific endeavor the observations are gross, the hypotheses speculative and full of errors, the measurements crude. More important, I hold the opinion that this is just as truly science as the use of the most refined hypotheses and measurements in a more fully developed field of study. The crucial question in either case is not the degree of refinement but the direction of movement. If in either instance the movement is toward more exact measurement, toward more clear-cut and rigorous theory and hypotheses, toward findings which have greater validity and generality, then this is a healthy and growing science. If not, then it is a sterile pseudo-science, no matter how exact its methods. Science is a *developing* mode of inquiry, or it is of no particular importance.

4. I have been asked to cast our theoretical thinking in the terminology of the independent-intervening-dependent variable, in so far as this is feasible. I regret that I find this terminology somehow uncongenial. I cannot justify my negative reaction very adequately, and perhaps it is an irrational one, for the logic behind these terms seems unassailable. But to me the terms seem static— they seem to deny the restless, dynamic, searching, changing aspects of scientific movement. There is a tendency to suppose that a variable thus labeled, remains so, which is certainly not true.

The terms also seem to me to smack too much of the laboratory, where one undertakes an experiment *de novo* with everything under control, rather than of a science which is endeavoring to wrest from the phenomena of experience the inherent order which they contain. Such terms seem to be more applicable to the advanced stages of scientific endeavor than to the beginning stages.

Please do not misunderstand. I quite realize that *after the fact* any research investigation, or any theory constructed to relate the discovered facts, should be translatable into the language of independent and dependent variables or there is something wrong with the research or theory. But the terms seem to me better adapted to such autopsies than to the living physiology of scientific work in a new field.

5. It should be quite clear from the foregoing that the model of science which I find most helpful is not taken from the advanced stages of theoretical physics. In a field such as psychotherapy or personality the model which seems more congenial to me would be taken from the much earlier stages of the physical sciences. I like to think of the discovery of radioactivity by the Curies. They had left some pitchblende ore, which they were using for some purpose or other, in a room where they stored photographic plates. They discovered that the plates had been spoiled. In other words, first there was the observation of a dynamic event. This event might have been due to a multitude of causes. It might have been a flaw in the manufacture of the plates. It might have been the humidity, the temperature, or any of a dozen other things. But acute observation and creative thinking fastened on a hunch regarding the pitchblende, and this became a tentative hypothesis. Crude experiments began to confirm the hypothesis. Only slowly was it discovered that it was *not* the pitchblende, but a strange element *in* the pitchblende which was related to the observed effect. Meanwhile a theory had to be constructed to bring this strange phenomenon into orderly relationship with other knowledge. And although the theory in its most modest form had to do with the effect of radium on photographic plates, in its wider and more speculative reaches it was concerned with the nature of matter and the composition of the universe. By present-day standards in the physical sciences, this is an example of a primitive stage of investigation and theory construction. But in the field in which I am most deeply interested I can only hope that we are approaching such a stage. I feel sure that we are not beyond it.

6. Another deep-seated opinion has to do with theory. I believe

that there is only one statement which can accurately apply to all theories—from the phlogiston theory to the theory of relativity, from the theory I will present to the one which I hope will replace it in a decade—and that is that at the time of its formulation every theory contains an unknown (and perhaps at that point an unknowable) amount of error and mistaken inference. The degree of error may be very great, as in the phlogiston theory, or small, as I imagine it may be in the theory of relativity, but unless we regard the discovery of truth as a closed and finished book, then there will be new discoveries which will contradict the best theories which we can now construct.

To me this attitude is very important, for I am distressed at the manner in which small-calibre minds immediately accept a theory —almost any theory—as a dogma of truth. If theory could be seen for what it is—a fallible, changing attempt to construct a network of gossamer threads which will contain the solid facts—then a theory would serve as it should, as a stimulus to further creative thinking.

I am sure that the stress I place on this grows in part out of my regret at the history of Freudian theory. For Freud, it seems quite clear that his highly creative theories were never more than that. He kept changing, altering, revising, giving new meaning to old terms—always with more respect for the facts he observed than for the theories he had built. But at the hands of insecure disciples (so it seems to me), the gossamer threads became iron chains of dogma from which dynamic psychology is only recently beginning to free itself. I feel that every formulation of a theory contains this same risk and that, at the time a theory is constructed, some precautions should be taken to prevent it from becoming dogma.

7. I share with many others the belief that truth is unitary, even though we will never be able to know this unity. Hence any theory, derived from almost any segment of experience, if it were complete and completely accurate, could be extended indefinitely to provide meaning for other very remote areas of experience. Tennyson expressed this in sentimental fashion in his *Flower in the Crannied Wall.* I too believe that a complete theory of the individual plant would show us "what God and man is."

The corollary, however, is of equal importance and is not so often stated. A slight error in a theory may make little difference in providing an explanation of the observed facts out of which the theory grew. But when the theory is projected to explain more remote phenomena, the error may be magnified, and the inferences from the theory may be completely false. A very slight error in the understanding of Tennyson's flower may give a grossly false understanding of man. Thus every theory deserves the greatest respect in the area in which it was drawn from the facts and a decreasing degree of respect as it makes predictions in areas more and more remote from its origin. This is true of the theories developed in our group.

8. There is one other attitude which I hold, which I believe has relevance for the proper evaluation of any theory I might present. It is my belief in the fundamental predominance of the subjective. Man lives essentially in his own personal and subjective world, and even his most objective functioning, in science, mathematics, and the like, is the result of subjective purpose and subjective choice. In relation to research and theory, for example, it is my subjective perception that the machinery of science as we know it—operational definitions, experimental method, mathematical proof—is the best way of avoiding self-deception. But I cannot escape the fact that this is the way it appears to me, and that had I lived two centuries ago, or if I were to live two centuries in the future, some other pathway to truth might seem equally or more valid. To put it more briefly, it appears to me that though there may be such a thing as objective truth, I can never know it; all I can know is that some statements appear to me subjectively to have the qualifications of objective truth. Thus there is no such thing as Scientific Knowledge; there are only individual perceptions of what appears to each person to be such knowledge.

Since this is a large and philosophical issue, not too closely related to what follows, I shall not endeavor to state it more fully here but refer any who are interested to an article in which I have tried to expound this view somewhat more fully (Rogers & Dymond, 1954, chapter 13). I mention it here only because it is part of the context in which my theoretical thinking has developed.

THE GENERAL STRUCTURE OF OUR SYSTEMATIC THINKING

Before proceeding to the detailed statement of some of our theoretical views, I believe it may be helpful to describe some of the interrelationships between various portions of our theoretical formulations.

The earliest portion, most closely related to observed fact, most heavily supported by evidence, is the theory of psychotherapy and personality change which was constructed to give order to the phenomena of therapy as we experienced it. In this theory there were certain hypotheses regarding the nature of personality and the dynamics of behavior. Some of these were explicit, some implicit. These have been developed more fully into a theory of personality. The purpose has been to provide ourselves with a tentative understanding of the human organism and its developing dynamics—an attempt to make sense of this person who comes to us in therapy.

Implicit in the theories of therapy and of personality are certain hypotheses regarding the outcomes of therapy—hence, hypotheses regarding a more socially constructive or creative individual. In the last few years we have endeavored to spell out the picture of the theoretical end point of therapy, the maximally creative, self-actualizing, or fully functioning person.

In another direction, our understanding of the therapeutic relationship has led us to formulate theoretical statements regarding all interpersonal relationships, seeing the therapeutic relationship simply as one special case. This is a very new and tentative development, which we believe has promise.

Finally, it has seemed that if your views of therapy have any validity they have application in all those fields of human experience and endeavor which involve (a) interpersonal relationships and (b) the aim or potentiality of development or change in personality and behavior. Consequently, a cluster of partially developed theories exists in relation to such fields as family life, education, group leadership, and situations of group tension and conflict.

Before proceeding to set forth something of the theories themselves, I should like gratefully to stress the extent to which this is basically a group enterprise. I have drawn upon specific written contributions to theory made by Victor Raimy, Richard Hogan, Stanley Standal, John Butler, and Thomas Gordon. Many others have contributed to my thinking in ways known and unknown, but I would particularly like to mention the valuable influence of Oliver Bown, Desmond Cartwright, Arthur Combs, Eugene Gendlin, A. H. Maslow, Julius Seeman, John Shlien, and Donald Snygg on the theories which I am about to present. Yet these individuals are by no means to be held responsible for what follows, for their own attempts to order experience have often led them into somewhat different channels of thinking.

DEFINITIONS OF CONSTRUCTS

In the development of our theories various systematic constructs have emerged, gradually acquiring sharper and more specific meaning. Also terms in common usage have gradually acquired somewhat specialized meanings in our theoretical statements. In this section I have endeavored to define, as rigorously as I am able, these constructs and terms. These definitions supply the means by which the theory may be more accurately understood.

In this section one will find all of the constructs defined, grouped in related clusters. There are eleven of these clusters, each with a focal concept. If these focal concepts are understood, the understanding of each of the related terms should not be difficult, since each of the constructs within a group has a close and meaningful relationship to the others.

It is quite possible that such a section, devoted entirely to definitions, will prove dull reading. The reader may prefer to go at once to the theory of therapy in the following section, where he will find each defined term in italic type. He may then refer back to this section for the exact meaning of each such term.

1. *Actualizing tendency.* This is the inherent tendency of the organism to develop all its capacities in ways which serve to maintain or enhance the organism. It involves not only the tendency to meet what Maslow (1954) terms "deficiency needs" for air, food, water, and the like, but also more generalized activities. It involves development toward the differentiation of organs and of functions, expansion in terms of growth, expansion of effectiveness through the use of tools, expansion and enhancement through reproduction. It is development toward autonomy and away from heteronomy, or control by external forces. Angyal's (1941) statement could be used as a synonym for this term: "Life is an autonomous event which takes place between the organism and the environment. Life processes do not merely tend to preserve life but transcend the momentary status quo of the organism, expanding itself continually and imposing its autonomous determination upon an ever increasing realm of events."

It should be noted that this basic actualizing tendency is the only motive which is postulated in this theoretical system. It should also be noted that it is the organism as a whole, and only the organism as a whole, which exhibits this tendency. There are no homunculi, no other sources of energy or action in the system. The self, for example, is an important construct in our theory, but the self does not "do" anything. It is only one expression of the general tendency of the organism to behave in those ways which maintain and enhance itself.

It might also be mentioned that such concepts of motivation as are termed need-reduction, tension-reduction, drive-reduction, are included in this concept. It also includes, however, the growth motivations which appear to go beyond these terms: the seeking of pleasurable tensions, the tendency to be creative, the tendency to learn painfully to walk when crawling would meet the same needs more comfortably.

2. *Tendency toward self-actualization.* Following the development of the self-structure, this general tendency toward actualization expresses itself also in the actualization of that portion of the experience of the organism which is symbolized in the self. If the self and the total experience of the organism are relatively congruent, then the actualizing tendency remains relatively unified. If self and experience are incongruent, then the general tendency to actualize the organism may work at cross purposes with the subsystem of that motive, the tendency to actualize the self.

This definition will be better understood when various of its terms—self, incongruence, etc.—are defined. It is given here because it is a subaspect of motivation. It should perhaps be reread after the other terms are more accurately understood.

3. *Experience* (noun). This term is used to include all that is going on within the envelope of the organism at any given moment which is potentially available to awareness. It includes events of which the individual is unaware, as well as all the phenomena which are in consciousness. Thus it includes the psychological aspects of hunger, even though the individual may be so fascinated by his work or play that he is completely unaware of the hunger; it includes the impact of sights and sounds and smells on the organism, even though these are not in the focus of attention. It includes the influence of memory and past experience, as these are active in the moment, in restricting or broadening the meaning given to various stimuli. It also includes all that is present in immediate awareness or consciousness. It does not include such events as neuron discharges or changes in blood sugar, because these are not directly available to awareness. It is thus a psychological, not a physiological, definition.

Synonyms are "experiential field," or the term "phenomenal field" as used by Snygg and Combs, which also covers more than the phenomena of consciousness. I have in the past used such phrases as "sensory and visceral experiences" and "organic experiences" in the attempt to convey something of the total quality of this concept.

It is to be noted that experience refers to the given moment, not to some accumulation of past experience. It is believed that this makes the operational definition of experience, or of *an* experience, which is a given segment of the field, more possible.

4. *Experience* (verb). To experience means simply to receive in the organism the impact of the sensory or physiological events which are happening at the moment.

Often this process term is used in the phrase "to experience in awareness" which means to symbolize in some accurate form at the conscious level the above sensory or visceral events. Since there are varying degrees of completeness in symbolization, the phrase is often "to experience more fully in awareness," thus indicating that it is the extension of this process toward more complete and accurate symbolization to which reference is being made.

5. *Feeling, Experiencing a feeling.* This is a term which has been heavily used in writings on client-centered therapy and theory. It denotes an emotionally tinged experience, together with its personal meaning. Thus it includes the emotion but also the cognitive content of the meaning of that emotion in its experiential context. It thus refers to the unity of emotion and cognition as they are experienced inseparably in the moment. It is perhaps best thought of as a brief theme of experience, carrying with it the emotional coloring and the perceived meaning to the individual. Examples would include "I feel angry at myself," "I feel ashamed of my desires when I am with her," "For the first time, right now, I feel that you like me." This last is an example of another phenomenon which is relevant to our theory, and which has been called *experiencing a feeling fully,* in the immediate present. The individual is then congruent in his experience (of the feeling), his awareness (of it), and his expression (of it).

6. *Awareness, Symbolization, Consciousness.* These three terms are defined as synonymous. To use Angyal's expression, consciousness (or awareness) is the symbolization of some of our experience. Awareness is thus seen as the symbolic representation (not necessarily in verbal symbols) of some portion of our experience. This representation may have varying degrees of sharpness or vividness, from a dim awareness of something existing as ground,

to a sharp awareness of something which is in focus as figure.

7. *Availability to awareness.* When an experience can be symbolized freely, without defensive denial and distortion, then it is available to awareness.

8. *Accurate symbolization.* The symbols which constitute our awareness do not necessarily match, or correspond to, the "real" experience, or to "reality." Thus the psychotic is aware of (symbolizes) electrical impulses in his body which do not seem in actuality to exist. I glance up quickly and perceive a plane in the distance, but it turns out to be a gnat close to my eye. It seems important to distinguish between those awarenesses which, in common-sense terms, are real or accurate and those which are not. But how can this be conceptualized if we are trying to think rigorously?

The most adequate way of handling this predicament seems to me to be to take the position of those who recognize that all perception (and I would add, all awareness) is transactional in nature, that it is a construction from our past experience and a hypothesis or prognosis for the future. Thus the examples given are both hypotheses which can be checked. If I brush at the gnat and it disappears, it increases the probability that what I was aware of *was* a gnat and not a plane. If the psychotic were able to permit himself to check the electric currents in his body, and to see whether they have the same characteristics as other electric currents, he would be checking the hypothesis implicit in his awareness. Hence when we speak of accurate symbolization in awareness, we mean that the hypotheses implicit in the awareness will be borne out if tested by acting on them.

We are, however, well over the border line of simple awareness and into the realm which is usually classified as perception, so let us proceed to a consideration of that concept.

9. *Perceive, Perception.* So much has the meaning of this term changed that one definition has been given as follows: "Perception is that which comes into consciousness when stimuli, principally light or sound, impinge on the organism from the outside" (Kelly, 1955, p. 250). Although this seems a bit too general, it does take account of the work of Hebb, Riesen, and others, which indicates that the impingement of the stimuli and the meaning given to the stimuli are inseparable parts of a single experience.

For our own definition we might say that a perception is a hypothesis or prognosis for action which comes into being in awareness when stimuli impinge on the organism. When we perceive "this is a triangle," "that is a tree," "this person is my mother," it means that we are making a prediction that the objects from which the stimuli are received would, if checked in other ways, exhibit properties we have come to regard from our past experience as being characteristic of triangles, trees, mother.

Thus we might say that perception and awareness are synonymous, perception being the narrower term, usually used when we wish to emphasize the importance of the stimulus in the process, and awareness the broader term, covering symbolizations and meanings which arise from such purely internal stimuli as memory traces, visceral changes, and the like, as well as from external stimuli.

To define perception in this purely psychological fashion is not meant to deny that it can be defined in physiological fashion by referring to the impact of a pattern of light rays upon certain nerve cells, for example. For our purpose, however, the psychological definition seems more fruitful, and it is in this sense that the term will be used in our formulations.

10. *Subceive, Subception.* McCleary and Lazarus (1949) formulated this construct to signify discrimination without awareness. They state that "even when a subject is unable to report a visual discrimination he is still able to make a stimulus discrimination at some level below that required for conscious recognition." Thus it appears that the organism can discriminate a stimulus and its meaning for the organism without utilizing the higher nerve centers involved in awareness. It is this capacity which, in our theory, permits the individual to discriminate an experience as threatening, without symbolization in awareness of this threat.

11. *Self-experience.* This is a term coined by Standal (1954), and defined as being any event or entity in the phenomenal field discriminated by the individual which is also discriminated as "self," "me," "I," or related thereto. In general, self-experiences are the raw material of which the organized self-concept is formed.

12. *Self, Concept of self, Self-structure.* These terms refer to the organized, consistent conceptual gestalt composed of perceptions of the characteristics of the "I" or "me" and the perceptions of the relationships of the "I" or "me" to others and to various aspects of life, together with the values attached to these perceptions. It is a gestalt which is available to awareness though not necessarily in awareness. It is a fluid and changing gestalt, a process, but at any given moment it is a specific entity which is at

least partially definable in operational terms by means of a Q sort or other instrument of measure. The term self or self-concept is more likely to be used when we are talking of the person's view of himself, self-structure when we are looking at this gestalt from an external frame of reference.

13. *Ideal self.* Ideal self (or self-ideal) is the term used to denote the self-concept which the individual would most like to possess, upon which he places the highest value for himself. In all other respects it is defined in the same way as the self-concept.

14. *Incongruence between self and experience.* In a manner which will be described in the theory of personality a discrepancy frequently develops between the self as perceived, and the actual experience of the organism. Thus the individual may perceive himself as having characteristics *a, b,* and *c,* and experiencing feelings *x, y,* and *z.* An accurate symbolization of his experience would, however, indicate characteristics *c, d,* and *e,* and feelings *v, w,* and *x.* When such a discrepancy exists, the state is one of incongruence between self and experience. This state is one of tension and internal confusion, since in some respects the individual's behavior will be regulated by the actualizing tendency, and in other respects by the self-actualizing tendency, thus producing discordant or incomprehensible behaviors. What is commonly called neurotic behavior is one example, the neurotic behavior being the product of the actualizing tendency, whereas in other respects the individual is actualizing the self. Thus the neurotic behavior is incomprehensible to the individual himself, since it is at variance with what he consciously "wants" to do, which is to actualize a self no longer congruent with experience.

15. *Vulnerability.* Vulnerability is the term used to refer to the state of incongruence between self and experience, when it is desired to emphasize the potentialities of this state for creating psychological disorganization. When incongruence exists, and the individual is unaware of it, then he is potentially vulnerable to anxiety, threat, and disorganization. If a significant new experience demonstrates the discrepancy so clearly that it must be consciously perceived, then the individual will be threatened, and his concept of self disorganized by this contradictory and unassimilable experience.

16. *Anxiety.* Anxiety is phenomenologically a state of uneasiness or tension whose cause is unknown. From an external frame of reference, anxiety is a state in which the incongruence between the concept of self and the total experience of the individual is

approaching symbolization in awareness. When experience is *obviously* discrepant from the self-concept, a defensive response to threat becomes increasingly difficult. Anxiety is the response of the organism to the "subception" that such discrepancy may enter awareness, thus forcing a change in the self-concept.

17. *Threat.* Threat is the state which exists when an experience is perceived or anticipated (subceived) as incongruent with the structure of the self. It may be regarded as an external view of the same phenomenon which, from the internal frame of reference, is anxiety.

18. *Psychological maladjustment.* Psychological maladjustment exists when the organism denies to awareness, or distorts in awareness, significant experiences, which consequently are not accurately symbolized and organized into the gestalt of the self-structure, thus creating an incongruence between self and experience.

It may help to clarify this basic concept of incongruence if we recognize that several of the terms we are defining are simply different vantage points for viewing this phenomenon. If an individual is in a state of incongruence between self and experience and we are looking at him from an external point of view we see him as vulnerable (if he is unaware of the discrepancy), or threatened (if he has some awareness of it). If we are viewing him from a social point of view, then this incongruence is psychological maladjustment. If the individual is viewing himself, he may even see himself as adjusted (if he has no awareness of the discrepancy) or anxious (if he dimly subceives it) or threatened or disorganized (if the discrepancy has forced itself upon his awareness).

19. *Defense, Defensiveness.* Defense is the behavioral response of the organism to threat, the goal of which is the maintenance of the current structure of the self. This goal is achieved by the perceptual distortion of the experience in awareness, in such a way as to reduce the incongruity between the experience and the structure of the self, or by the denial to awareness of an experience, thus denying any threat to the self. Defensiveness is the term denoting a state in which the behaviors are of the sort described.

20. *Distortion in awareness, Denial to awareness.* It is an observed phenomenon that material which is significantly inconsistent with the concept of self cannot be directly and freely admitted to awareness. To explain this the construct of denial or distortion has been developed. When an experience is dimly perceived (or "subceived" is perhaps the better term) as being incon-

gruent with the self-structure, the organism appears to react with a distortion of the meaning of the experience (making it consistent with the self) or with a denial of the existence of the experience, in order to preserve the self-structure from threat. It is perhaps most vividly illustrated in those occasional moments in therapy when the therapist's response, correctly heard and understood, would mean that the client would necessarily perceive openly a serious inconsistency between his self-concept and a given experience. In such a case, the client may respond, "I can hear the words you say, and I know I should understand them, but I just can't make them convey any meaning to me." Here the relationship is too good for the meaning to be distorted by rationalization, the meaning too threatening to be received. Hence the organism denies that there is meaning in the communication. Such outright denial of experience is much less common than the phenomenon of distortion. Thus if the concept of self includes the characteristic "I am a poor student" the experience of receiving a high grade can be easily distorted to make it congruent with the self by perceiving in it such meanings as, "That professor is a fool"; "It was just luck"; etc.

21. *Intensionality.* This term is taken from general semantics. If the person is reacting or perceiving in an intensional fashion he tends to see experience in absolute and unconditional terms, to overgeneralize, to be dominated by concept or belief, to fail to anchor his reactions in space and time, to confuse fact and evaluation, to rely upon abstractions rather than upon reality-testing. This term covers the frequently used concept of rigidity but includes perhaps a wider variety of behaviors than is generally thought of as constituting rigidity.

It will perhaps be evident that this cluster of definitions all have to do with the organism's response to threat. Defense is the most general term: distortion and denial are the mechanisms of defense; intensionality is a term which covers the characteristics of the behavior of the individual who is in a defensive state.

22. *Congruence, Congruence of self and experience.* This is a basic concept which has grown out of therapeutic experience, in which the individual appears to be revising his concept of self to bring it into congruence with his experience, accurately symbolized. Thus he discovers that one aspect of his experience if accurately symbolized, would be hatred for his father; another would be strong homosexual desires. He reorganizes the concept he holds of himself to include these characteristics, which would

previously have been inconsistent with self.

Thus when self-experiences are accurately symbolized and are included in the self-concept in this accurately symbolized form, then the state is one of congruence of self and experience. If this were completely true of all self-experiences, the individual would be a fully functioning person, as will be made more clear in the section devoted to this aspect of our theory. If it is true of some specific aspect of experience, such as the individual's experience in a given relationship or in a given moment of time, then we can say that the individual is to this degree in a state of congruence. Other terms which are in a general way synonymous are these: integrated, whole, genuine.

23. *Openness to experience.* When the individual is in no way threatened, then he is open to his experience. To be open to experience is the polar opposite of defensiveness. The term may be used in regard to some area of experience or in regard to the total experience of the organism. It signifies that every stimulus, whether originating within the organism or in the environment, is freely relayed through the nervous system without being distorted or channeled off by any defensive mechanism. There is no need of the mechanism of "subception" whereby the organism is forewarned of experiences threatening to the self. On the contrary, whether the stimulus is the impact of a configuration of form, color, or sound in the environment on the sensory nerves, or a memory trace from the past, or a visceral sensation of fear, pleasure, or disgust, it is completely available to the individual's awareness. In the hypothetical person who is completely open to his experience, his concept of self would be a symbolization in awareness which would be completely congruent with his experience. There would, therefore, be no possibility of threat.

24. *Psychological adjustment.* Optimal psychological adjustment exists when the concept of the self is such that all experiences are or may be assimilated on a symbolic level into the gestalt of the self-structure. Optimal psychological adjustment is thus synonymous with complete congruence of self and experience, or complete openness to experience. On the practical level, improvement in psychological adjustment is equivalent to progress toward this end point.

25. *Extensionality.* This term is taken from general semantics. If the person is reacting or perceiving in an extensional manner he tends to see experience in limited, differentiated terms, to be aware of the space-time anchorage of facts, to be dominated by

facts, not by concepts, to evaluate in multiple ways, to be aware of different levels of abstraction, to test his inferences and abstractions against reality.

26. *Mature, Maturity.* The individual exhibits mature behavior when he perceives realistically and in an extensional manner, is not defensive, accepts the responsibility for his own behavior, evaluates experience in terms of the evidence coming from his own senses, changes his evaluation of experience only on the basis of new evidence, accepts others as unique individuals different from himself, prizes himself, prizes others. (If his behavior has these characteristics, then there will automatically follow all the types of behavior which are more popularly thought of as constituting psychological maturity.)

These last five definitions form a cluster which grows out of the concept of congruence. Congruence is the term which defines the state. Openness to experience is the way an internally congruent individual meets new experience. Psychological adjustment is congruence as viewed from a social point of view. Extensional is the term which describes the specific types of behavior of a congruent individual. Maturity is a broader term describing the personality characteristics and behavior of a person who is, in general, congruent.

The concepts in the group of definitions which follow have all been developed and formulated by Standal (1954), and have taken the place of a number of less satisfactory and less rigorously defined constructs. Essentially this group has to do with the concept of positive regard, but since all transactions relative to this construct take place in relationships, a definition of psychological contact, or minimal relationship, is set down first.

27. *Contact.* Two persons are in psychological contact, or have the minimum essential of a relationship, when each makes a perceived or subceived difference in the experiential field of the other.

This construct was first given the label of "relationship," but it was found that this led to much misunderstanding, for it was often understood to represent the depth and quality of a good relationship, or a therapeutic relationship. The present term has been chosen to signify more clearly that this is the *least* or minimum experience which could be called a relationship. If more than this simple contact between two persons is intended, then the additional characteristics of that contact are specified in the theory.

28. *Positive regard.* If the perception by me of some self-

experience in another makes a positive difference in my experiential field, then I am experiencing positive regard for that individual. In general, positive regard is defined as including such attitudes as warmth, liking, respect, sympathy, acceptance. To perceive oneself as receiving positive regard is to experience oneself as making a positive difference in the experiential field of another.

29. *Need for positive regard.* It is postulated by Standal that a basic need for positive regard, as defined above, is a secondary or learned need, commonly developed in early infancy. Some writers have looked upon the infant's need for love and affection as an inherent or instinctive need. Standal is probably on safer ground in regarding it as a learned need. By terming it the need for positive regard, he has, it is believed, selected out the significant psychological variable from the broader terms usually used.

30. *Unconditional positive regard.* Here is one of the key constructs of the theory, which may be defined in these terms: If the self-experience of another is perceived by me in such a way that no self-experience can be discriminated as more or less worthy of positive regard than any other, then I am experiencing unconditional positive regard for this individual. To perceive oneself as receiving unconditional positive regard is to perceive that of one's self-experiences none can be discriminated by the other individual as more or less worthy of positive regard.

Putting this in simpler terms, to feel unconditional positive regard toward another is to "prize" him (to use Dewey's term, recently used in this sense by Butler). This means to value the person, irrespective of the differential values which one might place on his specific behaviors. A parent "prizes" his child, though he may not value equally all of his behaviors. Acceptance is another term which has been frequently used to convey this meaning, but it perhaps carries more misleading connotations than the phrase which Standal has coined. In general, however, acceptance and prizing are synonymous with unconditional positive regard.

This construct has been developed out of the experiences of therapy, where it appears that one of the potent elements in the relationship is that the therapist "prizes" the whole person of the client. It is the fact that he feels and shows an unconditional positive regard toward the experiences of which the client is frightened or ashamed, as well as toward the experiences with which the client is pleased or satisfied, that seems effective in bringing about change. Gradually the client can feel more acceptance of all of his own experiences, and this makes him again more of a whole or congruent person, able to function effectively. This clinical explanation will, it is hoped, help to illuminate the meaning contained in the rigorous definition.

31. *Regard complex.* The regard complex is a construct defined by Standal as all those self-experiences, together with their interrelationships, which the individual discriminates as being related to the positive regard of a particular social other.

This construct is intended to emphasize the gestalt nature of transactions involving positive or negative regard, and their potency. Thus, for example, if a parent shows positive regard to a child in relationship to a specific behavior, this tends to strengthen the whole pattern of positive regard which has previously been experienced as coming from that parent. Likewise specific negative regard from this parent tends to weaken the whole configuration of positive regard.

32. *Positive self-regard.* This term is used to denote a positive regard satisfaction which has become associated with a particular self-experience or a group of self-experiences, in which this satisfaction is independent of positive regard transactions with social others. Though it appears that positive regard must first be experienced from others, this results in a positive attitude toward self which is no longer directly dependent on the attitudes of others. The individual, in effect, becomes his own significant social other.

33. *Need for self-regard.* It is postulated that a need for positive self-regard is a secondary or learned need, related to the satisfaction of the need for positive regard by others.

34. *Unconditional self-regard.* When the individual perceives himself in such a way that no self-experience can be discriminated as more or less worthy of positive regard than any other, then he is experiencing unconditional positive self-regard.

35. *Conditions of worth.* The self-structure is characterized by a condition of worth when a self-experience or set of related self-experiences is either avoided or sought solely because the individual discriminates it as being less or more worthy of self-regard.

This important construct has been developed by Standal to take the place of "introjected value," which was a less exact concept used in earlier formulations. A condition of worth arises when the positive regard of a significant other is conditional, when the individual feels that in some respects he is prized and in others not. Gradually this same attitude is assimilated into his own self-regard complex, and he values an experience positively or negatively solely because of these conditions of worth which he has taken over from others, not because the experience enhances or fails to enhance his organism.

It is this last phrase which deserves special note. When the individual has experienced unconditional positive regard, then a new experience is valued or not, depending on its effectiveness in maintaining or enhancing the organism. But if a value is "introjected" from a significant other, then this condition of worth is applied to an experience quite without reference to the extent to which it maintains or enhances the organism. It is an important specific instance of inaccurate symbolization, the individual valuing an experience positively or negatively, *as if* in relation to the criterion of the actualizing tendency, but not actually in relation to it. An experience may be perceived as organismically satisfying, when in fact this is not true. Thus a condition of worth, because it disturbs the valuing process, prevents the individual from functioning freely and with maximum effectiveness.

36. *Locus of evaluation.* This term is used to indicate the source of evidence as to values. Thus an internal locus of evaluation, within the individual himself, means that he is the center of the valuing process, the evidence being supplied by his own senses. When the locus of evaluation resides in others, their judgment as to the value of an object or experience becomes the criterion of value for the individual.

37. *Organismic valuing process.* This concept describes an ongoing process in which values are never fixed or rigid, but experiences are being accurately symbolized and continually and freshly valued in terms of the satisfactions organismically experienced; the organism experiences satisfaction in those stimuli or behaviors which maintain and enhance the organism and the self, both in the immediate present and in the long range. The actualizing tendency is thus the criterion. The simplest example is the infant who at one moment values food, and when satiated, is disgusted with it; at one moment values stimulation, and soon after, values only rest; who finds satisfying that diet which in the long run most enhances his development.

38. *Internal frame of reference.* This is all of the realm of experience which is available to the awareness of the individual at a given moment. It includes the full range of sensations, perceptions, meanings, and memories which are available to consciousness.

The internal frame of reference is the subjective world of the individual. Only he knows it fully. It can never be known to another except through empathic inference and then can never be perfectly known.

39. *Empathy.* The state of empathy, or being empathic, is to perceive the internal frame of reference of another with accuracy, and with the emotional components and meanings which pertain thereto, as if one were the other person, but without ever losing the "as if" condition. Thus it means to sense the hurt or the pleasure of another as he senses it, and to perceive the causes thereof as he perceives them, but without ever losing the recognition that it is *as if* I were hurt or pleased, etc. If this "as if" quality is lost, then the state is one of identification.

40. *External frame of reference.* To perceive solely from one's own subjective internal frame of reference without empathizing with the observed person or object, is to perceive from an external frame of reference. The "empty organism" school of thought in psychology is an example of this. Thus the observer says that an animal has been stimulated when the animal has been exposed to a condition which, in the observer's subjective frame of reference, is a stimulus. There is no attempt to understand, empathically, whether this is a stimulus in the animal's experiential field. Likewise the observer reports that the animal emits a response when a phenomenon occurs which, in the observer's subjective field, is a response.

We generally regard all "objects" (stones, trees, or abstractions) from this external frame of reference since we assume that they have no "experience" with which we can empathize. The other side of this coin is that anything perceived from an external frame of reference (whether an inanimate thing, an animal, or a person) becomes for us an "object" because no empathic inferences are made.

This cluster of three ways of knowing deserves some further comment. In so far as we are considering knowledge of human beings we might say that these ways of knowing exist on a continuum. They range from one's own complete subjectivity in one's own internal frame of reference to one's own complete subjectivity about another (the external frame of reference). In between lies the range of empathic inference regarding the subjective field of another.

Each of these ways of knowing is essentially a formulation of hypotheses. The differences lie in the way the hypotheses are checked. In my own internal frame of reference if I experience love or hate, enjoyment or dislike, interest or boredom, belief or disbelief, the only way I can check these hypotheses of experience is by further focusing on my experience. Do I really love him? Am I really enjoying this? Do I really believe this?—all are questions which can only be answered by checking with my own organism. (If I try to find out whether I really love him by checking with others, then I am observing myself as an object, am viewing myself from an external frame of reference.)

Although in the last analysis each individual lives in and by his own subjective knowledge, this is not regarded socially as "knowledge" and certainly not as scientific knowledge.

Knowledge which has "certainty," in the social sense, involves the use of empathic inference as a means of checking, but the direction of that empathy differs. When the experience of empathic understanding is used as a source of knowledge, one checks one's empathic inferences with the subject, thus verifying or disproving the inferences and hypotheses implicit in such empathy. It is this way of knowing which we have found so fruitful in therapy. Utilizing empathic inference to the fullest, the knowledge thus gained of the client's subjective world has led to understanding the basis of his behavior and the process of personality change.

In knowing a person or an object from the external frame of reference, our implicit hypotheses are checked with other people but *not* with the subject of our concern. Thus a rigorous behaviorist believes that S is a stimulus for his experimental animal and R is a response, because his colleagues and even the man in the street agree with him and regard S and R in the same way. His empathic inferences are made in regard to the internal frame of reference of his colleagues, rather than in regard to the internal frame of reference of the animal.

Science involves taking an external frame of reference, in which we check our hypotheses basically through empathic inferences as to the internal frame of reference of our colleagues. They perform the same operations we have (either actually or through symbolic representation), and if they perceive the same events and meanings, then we regard our hypotheses as confirmed.

The reason for thus elaborating the different ways of knowing is that it seems to us that all ways of knowing have their usefulness, and that confusion arises only when one is not clear as to the type of knowledge which is being specified. Thus in the theory of therapy which follows one will find certain conditions of therapy specified as subjective experiencing states, another as empathic knowledge of the client, and yet the scientific checking of the hypotheses of the theory can only be done from an external frame of reference.

A THEORY OF THERAPY AND PERSONALITY CHANGE

This theory is of the if-then variety. If certain conditions exist (independent variables), then a process (dependent variables) will occur which includes certain characteristic elements. If this process (now the independent variable) occurs, then certain personality and behavioral changes (dependent variables) will occur. This will be made specific.

In this and the following sections the formal statement of the theory is given briefly. The italic terms or phrases in these formal statements have been defined in the previous section and are to be understood as defined. The remaining paragraphs are explanatory and do not follow the rigorous pattern of the formal statements.

A. *Conditions of the Therapeutic Process*

For therapy to occur it is necessary that these conditions exist:

1. That two persons are in *contact*.

2. That the first person, whom we shall term the client, is in a state of *incongruence*, being *vulnerable* or *anxious.*

3. That the second person, whom we shall term the therapist, is *congruent* in the *relationship.*

4. That the therapist is *experiencing unconditional positive regard* toward the client.

5. That the therapist is *experiencing* an *empathic* understanding of the client's *internal frame of reference.*

6. That the client *perceives,* at least to a minimal degree, conditions 4 and 5, the *unconditional positive regard* of the therapist for him, and the *empathic* understanding of the therapist.

Comment. These seem to be the necessary conditions of therapy, though other elements are often or usually present. The process is more likely to get underway if the client is anxious, rather than merely vulnerable. Often it is necessary for the contact or relationship to be of some duration before the therapeutic process begins. Usually the empathic understanding is to some degree expressed verbally, as well as experienced. But the process often commences with only these minimal conditions, and it is hypothesized that it never commences *without* these conditions being met.

The point which is most likely to be misunderstood is the omission of any statement that the therapist *communicates* his empathic understanding and his unconditional positive regard to the client. Such a statement has been omitted only after much consideration, for these reasons. It is not enough for the therapist to communicate, since the communication must be received, as pointed out in condition 6, to be effective. It is not essential that the therapist *intend* such communication, since often it is by some casual remark, or involuntary facial expression, that the communication is actually achieved. However, if one wishes to stress the communicative aspect which is certainly a vital part of the living experience, then condition 6 might be worded in this fashion:

6. That communication to the client of the therapist's empathic understanding and unconditional positive regard is, at least to a minimal degree, achieved.

The element which will be most surprising to conventional therapists is that the same conditions are regarded as sufficient for therapy, regardless of the particular characteristics of the client. It has been our experience to date that although the therapeutic relationship is used differently by different clients, it is not necessary nor helpful to manipulate the relationship in specific ways for specific kinds of clients. To do this damages, it seems to us, the most helpful and significant aspect of the experience, that it is a genuine relationship between two persons, each of whom is endeavoring, to the best of his ability, to be himself in the interaction.

The "growing edge" of this portion of the theory has to do with point 3, the congruence or genuineness of the therapist in the relationship. This means that the therapist's symbolization of his own experience in the relationship must be accurate, if therapy is to be most effective. Thus if he is experiencing threat and discomfort in the relationship and is aware only of acceptance and understanding, then he is not congruent in the relationship and therapy will suffer. It seems important that he should accurately "be himself" in the relationship, whatever the self of that moment may be.

Should he also express or communicate to the client the accurate symbolization of his own experience? The answer to this question is still in an uncertain state. At present we would say that such feelings should be expressed, if the therapist finds himself persistently focused on his own feelings rather than on those of the client, thus greatly reducing or eliminating any experience of empathic understanding, or if he finds himself persistently experiencing some feeling other than unconditional positive regard. To know whether this answer is correct demands further testing of the hypothesis it contains, and this is not simple since the courage to do this is often lacking, even in experienced therapists. When the therapist's real feelings are of this order: "I find myself fearful that you are slipping into a psychosis," or "I find myself frightened because you are touching on feelings I have never been able to resolve," then it is difficult to test the hypothesis, for it is very difficult for the therapist to express such feelings.

Another question which arises is this: is it the congruence, the wholeness, the integration of the therapist in the relationship which is important, or are the specific attitudes of empathic understanding and unconditional positive regard vital? Again the final answer is unknown, but a conservative answer, the one we have embodied in the theory, is that for therapy to occur the wholeness of the therapist in the relationship is primary, but a part of the congruence of the therapist must be the experience of unconditional positive regard and the experience of empathic understanding.

Another point worth noting is that the stress is upon the experience *in the relationship.* It is not to be expected that the therapist is a completely congruent person at all times. Indeed if this were a necessary condition there would be no therapy. But it is enough if in this particular moment of this immediate relationship with this specific person he is completely and fully himself, with his experience of the moment being accurately symbolized and integrated into the picture he holds of himself. Thus it is that imperfect human beings can be of therapeutic assistance to other imperfect human beings.

The greatest flaw in the statement of these conditions is that they are stated as if they were all-or-none elements, whereas conditions 2 to 6 all exist on continua. At some later date we may be able to say that the therapist must be genuine or congruent to such and such a degree in the relationship, and similarly for the other items. At the present we can only point out that the more marked the presence of conditions 2 to 6, the more certain it is that the process of therapy will get under way, and the greater the degree of reorganization which will take place. This function can only be stated qualitatively at the present time.

B. *The Process of Therapy*

When the preceding conditions exist and continue, a process is set in motion which has these characteristic directions:

1. The client is increasingly free in expressing his *feelings,* through verbal and/or motor channels.

2. His expressed feelings increasingly have reference to the *self,* rather than nonself.

3. He increasingly differentiates and discriminates the objects of his *feelings* and *perceptions,* including his environment, other persons, his *self,* his *experiences,* and the interrelationships of these. He becomes less *intensional* and more *extensional* in his *perceptions,* or to put it in other terms, his experiences are more *accurately symbolized.*

4. His expressed *feelings* increasingly have reference to the *incongruity* between certain of his *experiences* and his *concept of self.*

5. He comes to experience in awareness the threat of such *incongruence.*

    a. This *experience of threat* is possible only because of the continued *unconditional positive regard* of the therapist, which is extended to *incongruence* as much as to *congruence,* to *anxiety* as much as to absence of *anxiety.*

6. He *experiences* fully, in *awareness,* feelings which have in the past been *denied to awareness* or *distorted in awareness.*

7. His *concept of self* becomes reorganized to assimilate and include these *experiences* which have previously been *distorted in,* or *denied to, awareness.*

8. As this reorganization of the *self-structure* continues, his *concept of self* becomes increasingly *congruent* with his *experience,* the *self* now including *experiences* which previously would have been too *threatening* to be in *awareness.*

    a. A corollary tendency is toward fewer perceptual *distortions in awareness* or *denials to awareness* since there are fewer *experiences* which can be *threatening.* In other words, *defensiveness* is decreased.

9. He becomes increasingly able to *experience*, without a feeling of *threat*, the therapist's *unconditional positive regard.*

10. He increasingly feels an *unconditional positive self-regard.*

11. He increasingly experiences himself as the *locus of evaluation.*

12. He reacts to experience less in terms of his *conditions of worth* and more in terms of an organismic valuing process.

Comment. It cannot be stated with certainty that all of these are *necessary* elements of the process, though they are all characteristic. Both from the point of view of experience and from the logic of the theory, items 3, 6, 7, 8, 10, and 12 are necessary elements in the process. Item 5a is not a logical step in the theory but is put in as an explanatory note.

The element which will doubtless be most puzzling to the reader is the absence of explanatory mechanisms. It may be well to restate scientific purpose in terms of an example. *If* one strokes a piece of steel with a magnet, and *if* one places the piece of steel so that it can rotate freely, *then* it will point to the north. This statement of the if-then variety has been proved thousands of times. Why does it happen? There have been various theoretical answers, and one would hesitate to say, even now, that we know with certitude why this occurs.

In the same way I have been saying in regard to therapy, "If these conditions exist, then these subsequent events will occur." Of course we have speculations as to why this relationship appears to exist, but the most basic element of our theory is that if the described conditions exist, then the process of therapy occurs, and the events which are called outcomes will be observed. We may be quite wrong as to *why* this sequence occurs. I believe there is an increasing body of evidence to show that it *does* occur.

C. *Outcomes in Personality and Behavior*

There is no clear distinction between process and outcome. Items of process are simply differentiated aspects of outcome. Hence the statements which follow could have been included under process. For reasons of convenience in understanding, there have been grouped here those changes which are customarily associated with the terms "outcomes" or "results," or are observed outside of the therapeutic relationship. These are the changes which are hypothesized as being relatively permanent:

1. The client is more *congruent,* more *open to his experience,* less *defensive.*

2. He is consequently more realistic, objective, *extensional* in his *perceptions.*

3. He is consequently more effective in problem-solving.

4. His *psychological adjustment* is improved, being closer to the optimum.

    a.   This is owing to, and a continuation of, the changes in *self-structure* described in B7 and B8.

5. As a result of the increased *congruence* of *self* and *experience* (C4 above) his *vulnerability* to *threat* is reduced.

6. As a consequence of C2 above, his perception of his *ideal self* is more realistic, more achievable.

7. As a consequence of the changes in C4 and C5 his *self* is more *congruent* with his *ideal self.*

8. As a consequence of the increased *congruence* of *self* and *ideal self* (C6) and the greater *congruence of self* and *experience,* tension of all types is reduced—physiological tension, psychological tension, and the specific type of psychological tension defined as *anxiety.*

9. He has an increased degree of *positive self-regard.*

10. He *perceives* the *locus of evaluation* and the locus of choice as residing within himself.

    a.   As a consequence of C9 and C10 he feels more confident and more self-directing.

    b.   As a consequence of C1 and C10, his values are determined by an *organismic valuing process.*

11. As a consequence of C1 and C2, he *perceives* others more realistically and accurately.

12. He *experiences* more *acceptance* of others, as a consequence of less need for distortion of his perceptions of them.

13. His behavior changes in various ways.

    a.   Since the proportion of *experience* assimilated into the *self-structure* is increased, the proportion of behaviors which can be "owned" as belonging to the *self* is increased.

    b.   Conversely, the proportion of behaviors which are disowned as *self-experiences,* felt to be "not myself," is decreased.

    c.   Hence his behavior is *perceived* as being more within his control.

14. His behavior is perceived by others as more socialized, more *mature.*

15. As a consequence of C1, 2, 3, his behavior is more creative, more uniquely adaptive to each new situation, and each new problem, more fully expressive of his own purposes and values.

Comment. The statement in part C which is essential is statement C1. Items 2 through 15 are actually a more explicit spelling out of the theoretical implications of statement 1. The only reason for including them is that though such implications follow readily enough from the logic of theory, they are often not perceived unless they are pointed out.

Comments on the theory of therapy. It is to be noted that this theory of therapy involves, basically, no intervening variables. The conditions of therapy, given in A, are all operationally definable, and some have already been given rather crude operational definitions in research already conducted. The theory states that if A exists, then B and C will follow. B and C are measurable events, predicted by A.

It should also be pointed out that the logic of the theory is such that: if A, then B; if A, then B and C; if A, then C (omitting consideration of B); if B, then C (omitting consideration of A).

Specification of functional relationships. At this point, the functional relationships can only be stated in general and qualitative form. The greater the degree of the conditions specified in A, the more marked or more extensive will be the process changes in B, and the greater or more extensive the outcome changes specified in C. Putting this in more general terms, the greater the degree of anxiety in the client, congruence in the therapist in the relationship, acceptance and empathy experienced by the therapist, and recognition by the client of these elements, the deeper will be the process of therapy, and the greater the extent of personality and behavioral change. To revert now to the theoretical logic, all we can say at present is that

$$B = (f)A \qquad C = (f)A \qquad B + C = (f)A \qquad C = (f)B$$

Obviously there are many functional interrelationships not yet specified by the theory. For example, if anxiety is high, is congruence on the part of the therapist less necessary? There is much work to be done in investigating the functional relationships more fully.

D. *Some Conclusions Regarding the Nature of the Individual*

From the theory as stated above, certain conclusions are implicit regarding the nature of man. To make them explicit involves little more than looking at the same hypotheses from a somewhat different vantage point. It is well to state them explicitly, however, since they constitute an important explanatory link of a kind which gives this theory whatever uniqueness it may possess. They also constitute the impelling reason for developing a theory of personality. If the individual is what he is revealed to be in therapy, then what theory would account for such an individual? We present these conclusions about the characteristics of the human organism:

1. The individual possesses the capacity to *experience in awareness* the factors in his *psychological adjustment,* namely, the *incongruences* between his *self-concept* and the totality of his *experience.*
2. The individual possesses the capacity and has the tendency to reorganize his *self-concept* in such a way as to make it more *congruent* with the totality of his *experience,* thus moving himself away from a state of *psychological maladjustment,* and toward a state of *psychological adjustment.*
3. These capacities and this tendency, when latent rather than evident, will be released in any interpersonal *relationship* in which the other person is *congruent* in the *relationship,* experiences *unconditional positive regard* toward, and *empathic* understanding of the individual, and achieves some communication of these attitudes to the individual. (These are, of course, the characteristics already given under IA3, 4, 5, 6.)

It is this tendency which is elaborated into the tendency toward actualization.

I believe it is obvious that the basic capacity which is hypothesized is of very decided importance in its psychological and philosophical implications. It means that psychotherapy is the releasing of an already existing capacity in a potentially competent individual, not the expert manipulation of a more or less passive personality. Philosophically it means that the individual has the capacity to guide, regulate, and control himself, providing only that certain definable conditions exist. Only in the absence of these conditions, and not in any basic sense, is it necessary to provide external control and regulation of the individual.

REFERENCES

Angyal, A. *Foundations for a science of personality.* New York: Commonwealth Fund, 1941.

Kelley, E. C. Education in communication. *ETC,* Summer, 1955, 12: 248-256.

Maslow, A. H. *Motivation and personality.* New York: Harper, 1954.

McCleary, R. A., & Lazarus, R. S. Autonomic discrimination without awareness. *J. Pers.,* 1949, 18: 171-179.

Rogers, C. R. *Clinical treatment of the problem child.* Boston: Houghton Mifflin, 1939.

Rogers, C. R. *Counseling and psychotherapy.* Boston: Houghton Mifflin, 1942.

Rogers, C. R., & Dymond, R. F. (Eds.) *Psychotherapy and personality change.* Chicago: Univer. Chicago Press, 1954.

Standal, S. The need for positive regard: a contribution to client-centered theory. Unpublished doctoral dissertation, Univer. of Chicago, 1954.

SUGGESTED READINGS

Rogers, C. R. *Client-centered therapy.* Boston: Houghton Mifflin, 1951.

Rogers, C. R. *On becoming a person.* Boston: Houghton Mifflin, 1961.

4

PRINCIPLES OF DIRECTIVE COUNSELING
AND PSYCHOTHERAPY

Frederick C. Thorne, M.D., Ph.D.

Clinical psychology has emerged from the prescientific into the scientific era of development. There is urgent need for a comprehensive integration of all scientific data into a "system" of practice which would be genuinely eclectic and provide a basis for the standardization of practice throughout the world. Such a system would be based upon the most modern scientific principles and methods, and would attempt to relate the most recent discoveries with the great mass of information accumulated during the history of the profession. An example of this phase of development in the medical field was the work of Sir William Osler who wrote the first systematic text on the practice of medicine and laid the foundations of the great medical center at Johns Hopkins University. Characteristic of the newer theory of professional education has been the insistence that the orientation must be genuinely eclectic with every student being required to familiarize himself with the latest developments in every clinical specialty.

Prior to World War II, uniform training was non-existent in clinical psychology and every student operated more or less on his own with whatever tools and qualifications he had been able to acquire informally. This situation is being rapidly remedied during the post-war period through the efforts of the APA committees on graduate training in cooperation with the universities, but in spite

Condensed from a paper presented at a symposium under the auspices of the Division of Consulting Psychology at the Detroit meeting of the American Psychological Association, September 10, 1947. Reprinted by permission of the author and *American Psychologist*, 1948, *3:* 160-165.

of this desirable trend clinical psychology in America is still characterized by a primitive state of organization in which the leaders in the field operate more or less independently. Until the recent popularity of nondirective methods, there was no general agreement on any theoretical viewpoint with the result that there were almost as many brands of clinical psychology as there were clinical psychologists. Lacking any formally systemized viewpoint, the theoretical biases of clinical psychologists literally represented all the permutations and combinations of behaviorism, experimentalism, Gestalt psychology, Freudianism, Alderian individual psychology, Jungian analytic psychology, purposivism and many other minor schools. Most of the leaders in clinical psychology were represented by groups of adherents who were well-trained only in the methods of their teachers. So divergent were the different ideologies and terminologies that proponents of the various schools were frequently unable to communicate with each other. In view of these theoretical differences, it is easy to understand why clinical psychologists have been viewed with suspicion by their experimental colleagues to say nothing of psychiatrists and psychoanalysts who have theoretical biases all their own.

ORIGINS OF DIRECTIVE PSYCHOTHERAPY

The purpose of this paper is to review the basic principles of the comprehensive system of directive psychotherapy described in the series of papers appearing in the *Journal of Clinical Psychology* beginning in 1945, and to make a definitive statement concerning the eclectic orientation which is the basis for the proposed system of practice. The primary motivation was to formulate a comprehensive system of counseling and psychotherapy which would integrate and relate the positive values of newer viewpoints with traditional methods. This system would be more than a compilation of isolated facts, and would be based primarily on the objective foundations of experimental psychology. Its basic orientation would be determined by a detailed system of psychopathology derived from a more comprehensive method of personality analysis than had ever been attempted before. Modifying the classical psychiatric methods involving (a) Kraepelinian descriptive classifications, (b) psychobiological longitudinal studies, and (c) psychoanalytic depth analysis, the new method would seek to systematically evaluate and, if indicated, to modify all known important personality traits by the eclectic utilization of all available methods according to their indications and contraindications.

Although recognizing the undesirability of designating a system of psychotherapy by the term "directive," the choice was partially determined by our apprehension that the sudden popularity of Rogerian nondirective methods to the exclusion of traditional methods was a dangerous development both for the profession and for the student. This critical attitude was directed not so much toward nondirective methods which are admitted to have great value in their place, but toward the attitude of uncritical enthusiasm and cultism associated with the new development. It appeared that there was definite need for a comprehensive system which would relate directive and nondirective methods in their proper perspective and emphasize the values of eclecticism in clinical science.

TERMINOLOGICAL CONSIDERATIONS

The term *directive* seemed particularly appropriate to designate a system of therapy which is based upon a formal plan for the identification and modification of etiologic factors in maladjustment. Based upon the historical study of the evolution of clinical methods in science which have been outlined elsewhere (Thorne, 1947), it was our opinion that any valid therapeutic system must be oriented about a comprehensive knowledge of psychopathology and the uses and limitations of *all* known clinical methods. It is presupposed that persons representing themselves as clinical psychologists should have training and experience to enable them to adequately utilize all known methods according to the standards of time and place. Possession of such training and experience beyond that which might be expected of the most intelligent and best-informed layman implies that the basic responsibility for the *direction* of all stages of case handling lies with the therapist even though he may choose to delegate some portion of this responsibility to other persons including the client himself. In our opinion the possibility of a completely nondirective method is nonexistent since by the very nature of the therapist-client relationship (a) the client comes to a therapist considered to be of superior experience and training which thereby establishes a relationship of dominance through prestige, (b) the therapist determines the method to be used, and (c) what happens in the therapeutic relationship must be evaluated not only in terms of what the therapist thinks he is doing but also in terms of what the therapy means to the patient. Rather than involving a dichotomy of either-or directive or nondirective, we are dealing with a continuum involving various degrees of directiveness of which nondirective methods may be regarded as being at one extreme along with other "passive" techniques. We are in disagreement with Rogers' contention that any lapse from complete nondirectiveness is a grave therapeutic error, since our experience indicates that all degrees of directiveness may be used with a single case according to the indications of each individual situation.

The concepts of *directive* and *direction* also imply straightforwardness, i.e., straight, leading by the shortest way to a point or end. *Directed* movements of an organism are those which are observed to be related to a specific stimulus or goal. *Direction* is an attribute of behavior indicative of specific function and variously expressed in terms of needs, drives, goals, purposes and other concepts descriptive of integrated behavior. One of the principle characteristics of the maladjusted or disordered person is the inability to resolve problems unaided. Although self-direction is the highest democratic goal and evidence of integration, the maladjusted person either asks for help spontaneously or is induced to do so for his own good. Until such time as the person demonstrates his ability to regulate his behavior within the limits of what is socially acceptable, he is subjected to varying degrees of direction or regulation from the environment. The general rule may be stated that the need for direction is inversely correlated with the person's potentialities for effective self-regulation, i.e., the healthier the personality, the less the need for direction; the sicker the personality, the more the need for direction. It is to be assumed that the well-trained psychological scientist is the person best equipped to provide whatever degree of direction may be necessary to catalyze therapeutic processes by the shortest route. Judiciously utilized, psychological knowledge may have specific action in facilitating curative processes in much shorter time than might be accomplished by the client working by trial and error even assuming that homeostatic resources would be sufficient. While recognizing the dangers of over-regulation and over-interpretation in cases of mild personality disorder, it is our opinion that failure to institute the indicated degrees of direction in more serious cases may constitute malpractice since the therapist has the obligation to protect the interests of the client when the client is unable to do so himself.

The significance of these facts is that the therapist is supposed to *direct* the overall details of case handling according to tested scientific procedures whether he is utilizing nondirective methods or authoritarian methods in an institution. It is assumed that training and experience will provide the therapist with the knowledge concerning when to be directive or relatively nondirective. The validity of the results will be determined by the skill with which any method is used with reference to etiological diagnosis and the indications of each individual case. The critical factor is not what method is used but rather the skill with which it is used. We are not in agreement with the ideological bias of many nondirective therapists to the effect that all which is directive is bad, while all that is nondirective is good. In his basic text, Rogers (1942) attacks directive methods by setting up the straw man of criticizing the most crude and unacceptable forms of directive methods and implying that all directive techniques are subject to the same handicaps. Directive methods can only be fairly judged when they are employed with maximum skill; it is unrepresentative to base criticisms on atypical examples which would be condemned by all experienced directive therapists. Long before the development of nondirective methods, psychoanalysis had demonstrated the errors of over-interpretation, too much leading, crude interference and other pitfalls of the beginning counselor. The nondirective viewpoint appears to have gone to the extreme of rejecting direction in any form simply because it has frequently been misused. Hahn and Kendall (1947) and others have recently pointed out the logical inconsistencies involved in many of the theoretical criticisms made by Rogers and his pupils against directive methods. Perhaps most important is to emphasize that all valid therapy is client-centered and that nondirective therapy has no monopoly on methods which are to the best interests of the client. As pointed out by Blain (1947), effective therapy frequently involves a compromise between what a patient sincerely believes he wants and what he needs according to the most objective judgment of the experienced therapist. Although it is theoretically desirable to place major dependence upon the growth principle and homeostatic processes as emphasized by Rogers and many others before him, there are many cases in which the client's resources and growth potentialities are so deficient or damaged that adjustment without outside help and direction is impossible.

A further application of the concept of *directness* is illustrated

in our attempt toward a systematic application of the Law of Par- ·
simony (Lloyd Morgan's canon). In contrast with the current popularity of psychoanalytically oriented approaches which seek to
discover latent meanings, symbolism, unconscious complexes and
other depth processes in personality, our viewpoint is that primary
weight should be assigned to direct interpretations of manifest
behavior according to the principles of scientific psychology and
particularly the laws of learning. Much is lost by failing to make
the simplest possible interpretations and also by proceeding in the
most direct manner consistent with the needs of the client. In our
own practice, we systematically avoid complex psychoanalytic
interpretations, preferring to communicate whatever minimum
amount seems indicated in the simplest of terms. It is an axiom of
directive therapy, as well as nondirective, that the less said by the
therapist the better.

Finally, we would specifically refute the implication made by
Snyder (1947) and apparently accepted by others, that the term
"directive psychotherapy" was coined by us simply to refer to
traditional methods of therapy and involving little which is new.
While it is true that many of the methods included under directive
therapy have long been utilized, there has not been any systematic
attempt known to us in the English literature to reevaluate them
in terms of modern psychopathology with the objectives of determining their nature, indications and contraindications. Traditionally, these methods have been described and utilized as isolated
units with no attempt being made to construct an integrated system about a central theory of personality.

THE BASIC METHOD

The theoretical foundations for directive psychotherapy are derived from a survey of the historical development of clinical
science carrying over the principles and methods which appear to
be valid for clinical psychology. As pointed out elsewhere (Thorne,
1947), clinical psychology has a medico-psychological heritage dat-
ing back to ancient Egypt and one must be familiar with the evolution of medical psychology in order to evaluate any development
in proper perspective. Utilizing standard techniques of description,
classification, statistical evaluation and integrative interpretation,
directive psychotherapy attempts to discover the causal conditions
resulting in maladaptation and then to utilize treatments specific

for each pathological condition. Unless comprehensive etiologic studies are carried out with every case, it is difficult to understand how any objective evaluation in case handling may be made. However, this unending search for the causation of morbidity must never be allowed to conceal the basic objective of satisfying the needs of the client.

The basic pattern of directive therapy in which the therapist, though client-centered, assumes responsibility for the conduct of all details of case handling according to the highest ethical and professional standards of time and place is given in another paper (Thorne, 1947).

Gregg (1947) states a cardinal axiom that the human organism involves such a complex relationship of constituent parts that one cannot be modified without affecting all others; that, therefore, a given result comes usually not from one cause but from a combination of causes, sometimes a sequence, sometimes a constellation or pattern; and similarly, that a given cause has not one but many results, sometimes in sequence, sometimes in pattern. With such a complex situation, it is inevitable that a wide armamentarium of therapeutic tools will be needed, each used as skillfully as possible based on a valid knowledge of what each tool can be expected to accomplish.

PSYCHOPATHOLOGICAL RATIONALE

One of the most important contributions of Adolf Meyer's psychobiological approach to personality was his recognition that pathological processes of different types may involve personality functions as a whole or in parts. By careful appraisal of all the known functions of personality, it becomes possible to identify areas of dysfunction, to postulate etiologic factors, and to outline specific plans of treatment. The psychobiologic approach is genuinely eclectic in the sense that it seeks to assess all known functions with proper weight being assigned to dysfunctions of each in the longitudinal study of personality. In this respect, the psychobiological viewpoint may be contrasted with that of psychoanalysis in its various forms. In our opinion, psychoanalytic theory is one-sided in that it overemphasizes latent, unconscious, affective-impulsive components of personality while almost disregarding the direct, manifest, rational intellectual components characteristic of the higher mental functions and which are best understood by the psychology of learning and thinking. When the psychoanalytic viewpoint is carried to its logical conclusions as in nondirective therapy, the main emphasis is placed on affective-impulsive components which are regarded as involving the principal etiologic factors in maladjustment. Snyder (1947) even defines the objective of psychotherapeutic counseling as to "modify emotional attitudes that are socially maladjusted" and omits any reference to intellectual factors which may also be productive of maladjustment.

The system of directive psychotherapy which has been outlined in our published series of papers is theoretically oriented upon psychobiological approaches to the whole organism with perhaps more emphasis on rational intellectual components than on affective-impulsive since we believe that the highest potentialities for adaptation are related to the maturation and effective utilization of the higher cortical functions. The developmental phenomena associated with the maturation of the cerebral cortex are now well known and may be summarized in the statement that although the biologically more primitive affective-impulsive components of personality are constantly operative throughout life, the maturation of the cortex with the development of the higher mental functions results in the achievement of rational intellectual control through cerebral inhibition of lower functions and the acquisition of tremendously enhanced powers of learning. The dominance of the cerebrum over mid and hind-brain functions is achieved very slowly and only incompletely in the average person so that learning self-regulation, making the most of one's resources, and achieving insight into the meanings of behavior and life in general is a very gradual process.

In outlining the theoretical foundations of directive psychotherapy, we have attempted to integrate the principal contributions of the main schools of psychology. From behaviorism comes a major emphasis on the role of learning and of environmental stimulation in the development of acquired patterns of behavior. Experimental psychology of the traditional type contributes important information concerning sensation, memory, association, physiological reactions, and other relatively elemental phenomena. Gestalt psychology is important because of its emphasis on wholes, and its detailed studies of the perceptual process. Psychoanalysis gives most important emphasis to depth psychology, with its developmental studies of the affective-impulsive life. Finally, hormic psychology contributes the stimulating viewpoint that organic phenomena are largely determined by purposive factors as yet not clearly understood. Following the psychobiological approach which assumes that the psychologist will have detailed and extensive training and experience in the basic sciences of anatomy, biochemistry, physiology, pathology, as well as in normal psychology, directive psychotherapy depends for its validity upon the psychological sophistication and broadness of the person who attempts to utilize it. The better oriented is the clinician to the psychological sciences and to life in general, the more able is he to avoid the pitfalls which are recognized as inherent in any active (directive) method. Any method is no better than the skill of the person who makes it. We have come to regard psychotherapy as involving the hardest kind of work for both therapist and client, since deviant personality patterns become chronic over the years and can hardly be expected to be unlearned and relearned with startling rapidity.

Directive psychotherapy accepts the concept of *distributive analysis and treatment* developed by Meyer and described by Diethelm (1936). The distributive principle assumes that it is most effective to budget time and energy during the treatment process giving major emphasis to trends which appear to be most etiologically important. Instead of spending hundreds of hours more or less passively exploring the channels taken by the client, considerable saving may be accomplished without violence to the client-centered principle by directing the course of treatment along what may seem to be the most profitable lines. In addition to etiologic studies exploring the developmental history of the person, it seems important also to assess learning ability and accomplishment in all areas of activity. Directive psychotherapy is particularly concerned with maximizing the self-regulatory functions of personality with particular emphasis on self-control and conative life. It seems important to deal with certain phenomena usually denied or ignored in traditional psychology including the study of the nature of consciousness, nonconscious mental functions, volition, suggestion, hypnosis, deviant personalities of all types, and other phenomena which have important significance for psychopathology.

The directive principle that intellectual resources constitute the highest potentialities for adaptation in the organism and that therapy must be realistically distributed to deal with both affective-impulsive and rational-intellectual factors as they are encountered in the individual case, is based on the important distinction concerning primary and secondary etiologic factors in maladaptation. Etiologic factors may be identified as precipitating, predisposing or perpetuating. To explain our conception of the relative psychopathological importance of affective vs. intellectual factors in personality would require much more time than is here available. In summary, it seems important to reevaluate the entire etiologic role of affective factors in maladjustment with particular reference to the distinction between (a) reactive affective disorders, and (b) deeper habitual affective reactions based on constitutional or acquired personality complexes. In our opinion, affective disorders of reactive type have a much higher incidence and have most hopeful prognosis with or without treatment (although perhaps more quickly with treatment) when the stimulating factors are modified. In these cases, affective disorders are recognized to be symptomatic and therapy is primarily directed toward the intellectual failure to react adaptively. It may be necessary to treat affective-impulsive disorders first in order to prepare the stage for rational problem-solving activity but it should clearly be recognized that treatment of such reactive affective disorders results in only transient alleviation of symptoms which are prone to recur unless effective intellectual solutions are achieved. A basic diagnostic question therefore becomes: "Is the client maladjusted because he is emotionally disturbed, or is he emotionally disturbed because he is maladjusted?" The solution to this hen-egg problem is not always easily achieved, since reactive affective states may be of long duration. The degree of directiveness indicated in the individual case will be determined by the client's demonstrated ability to solve the problem alone.

Recognition of the need for maximally potentiating intellectual resources of personality in problem-solving behavior has important implications in both theoretical orientation and practical application. If human behavior is determined by unconscious, instinctual, affective-impulsive components in personality, it follows that maladjustment is caused by mechanistic, physiological factors over which a person can exert little conscious, voluntary control unless his growth resources or homeostatic tendencies are sufficiently strong to fortunately effect a cure. On the other hand, if it is accepted that rational-intellectual factors may supersede and control impulsive behavior, then the normal person may be expected to achieve some success in solving problems by conscious use of intellectual resources. This viewpoint does not necessarily involve the postulation of such mental functions as will or volition. On the contrary, the acquisition of self-regulatory abilities is regarded as a function of past training, usually by directive methods since few individuals are gifted enough to work out optimal methods by themselves, nor would such a trial and error process be economically desirable even if possible. Important areas of maladjustment are regarded as being caused by failure to learn to solve such problems using intellectual resources. This learning would normally take place in early life, thus normally preventing maladaptation. Since the basic factor in most psychotherapy is commonly recognized to be reeducation, it follows that the treatment process is essentially a training situation. It is occasionally necessary to resolve emotional attitudes before training can be begun, but this is not inevitable, since training may proceed even in unfavorable conditions. If latent, subconscious, unverbalized affective-impulsive reactions are important determiners of behavior, so are acquired intellectual traits and attitudes operating on manifest conscious levels. The goal of therapy is to replace emotional-compulsive behavior with deliberate rational-adaptive behavior based on the highest utilization of intellectual resources. To accomplish this may require the use of many directive techniques over and above the simple nondirective handling of emotional reactions which may be understood as simply the first step in therapy.

STATUS OF DIRECTIVE METHODS

Unfortunately, the traditional discussions of directive methods have dealt primarily with theoretical considerations with very little detail concerning the actual mechanics of case handling. Since each clinician has largely been forced to develop techniques by himself, it is understandable that the actual execution of these techniques ranged from literal perfection in the hands of the masters to the crudest bungling in the hands of amateurs. The situation is further complicated by the fact that the practical details have been taught by the apprenticeship method and only rarely described objectively. One of the purposes of the medical internship is to teach many small details of case handling which have never appeared in print, and which can only be learned by actually doing. No matter how rigidly and experimentally the treatment process may be controlled, the actual success is largely a function of the skill and intuitiveness of the individual practitioner in making the patient comfortable while attempting to treat the basic condition.

Before any extensive research program could be planned or undertaken, it has been necessary to achieve a theoretical formulation of the principles and methods of directive therapy and this has been attempted in the series of papers appearing in the *Journal of Clinical Psychology*. The failure to produce more quantitative evidence in support of the validity of directive psychotherapy is a function of its youth. Experimental work with any of the traditional methods has been almost completely lacking. Directive methods are only now being formally described and related to a system of therapy, and it will take many years to accumulate objective validation as evidenced by the fact that the basic outlines of psychoanalysis have still not been confirmed after almost fifty years of research. Although slightly more objective research has been accomplished with nondirective methods, it is insufficient either to establish the rather optimistic claims of its proponents or, conversely, to offer objective evidence that directive methods are invalid.

The status of all methods of psychotherapy is in such an elementary stage of evolution that clinical psychologists find themselves in the position of the chemists who having discovered some of the rarer elements did not know what to do with them. Some of the neglected methods such as suggestion, hypnosis, reconditioning or reassurance may well turn out to have such startling possibilities when properly used as did uranium in relation to the atom bomb. When psychologists devote as much time and energy to training themselves in the use of any of these methods as do professional athletes or craftsmen, much of the crudeness which is now so much in evidence will inevitably disappear. In our experience, nondirective methods constitute just a beginning with respect to what the clinical psychologist .may be expected to do. Some cases will show some improvement with the use of any superficial method, but others become progressively more maladjusted and constitute a challenge which will require the most effective use of all resources if the problem is to be solved. Directive psychotherapy requires that the therapist will be trained and able to make use of every known method in his field as indication may arise.

REFERENCES

Alexander, F. & French, T. M., et al. *Psychoanalytic Therapy*. New York: Ronald, 1946.

Blain, D. The psychiatrist and the psychologist. *J. Clin. Psychol.*, 1947, *3:* 4-9.

Diethelm, O. *Treatment In Psychiatry*. New York: Macmillian, 1936.

Gregg, A. Transition in medical education. *J. Assoc. Med. Coll.*, 1947, *22:* 226-232.

Hahn, M. E., and Kendall, W. E. Some comments in defense of "non-directive" counseling. *J. Consult. Psychol.*, 1947, *11:* 74-81.

Rogers, C. R. *Counseling and Psychotherapy*. Boston: Houghton Mifflin, 1942.

Rogers, C. R. Significant aspects of client-centered therapy. *Amer. Psychologist*, 1946, *1:* 415-422.

Snyder, W. U. The present status of psychotherapeutic counseling. *Psychol. Bull.*, 1947, *44:* 297-386.

Thorne, F. C. The clinical method in science. *Amer. Psychologist*, 1947, *2:* 159-166.

Thorne, F. C. Theoretical foundations of directive psychotherapy. *Annals N. Y. Acad. Sci.*, 1948, *49:* 869-877.

5

PROMOTING ADAPTIVE BEHAVIOR:
BEHAVIORAL APPROACH

John D. Krumboltz, Ph.D.

Counselors and psychologists are in the business of helping people learn how to solve certain kinds of problems more adequately. Some of these problems concern important educational and career decisions, such as : "What college should I attend?"; "What job should I enter?" Some of the problems concern personal, social and emotional difficulties, for example, "How can I save my marriage?"; "How can I overcome these horrible feelings of anxiety, loneliness and depression?"; "How can I learn to stand up for my own rights?"; "How can I get along better with others?"

As a result of consulting a counselor or psychologist a person with problems like these ought to be better able to find solutions. In addition he ought to be able to solve future problems more independently and effectively. In short, the counselor is interested in helping to promote a more adaptive problem-solving kind of behavior.

But how? There are four questions that counselors have traditionally asked themselves as they wrestled with the complex problems of their clients: 1) How should the counselor conceptualize client problems? 2) How should the counselor define client goals? 3) What techniques and procedures will best accomplish the goals? 4) How should the counselor evaluate the success of his work?

Reprinted with permission of the author and Stanford Univ. Publishers, from *Revolution in Counseling,* ed. by John D. Krumboltz. Boston: Houghton Mifflin, 1966, pp. 3-26. ©1966.

These questions are old and familiar. But the answers many of us would give to them differ so much from the answers we would have given just a few years ago that the theme of this conference, "Revolution in Counseling," seems well justified. The degree to which you judge these answers to be revolutionary, of course, will depend to some extent upon your familiarity with previous thought and practice in the field of counseling. I hope that you will consider them with the open-minded thoughtfulness that has characterized our profession. While most of us have a tendency to defend our present practices, we at the same time want to find new and better ways of being of service.

I would like to present my answers to each of these four familiar questions and allow you to judge for yourself, not just whether they are revolutionary, but whether they suggest some possible ways in which counselors and psychologists can be of greater service to their clients.

HOW SHOULD COUNSELORS CONCEPTUALIZE CLIENT PROBLEMS?

The way we think about problems determines to a large degree what we will do about them. Therefore, I think it is crucial that we conceptualize human problems in ways that suggest possible steps we can take to help solve them. The traditional ways of conceptualizing problems have made useful contributions, but they are weak in that they do not suggest a sufficient number of effective counselor activities.

Client Problems as Problems in Learning

My answer to the question is that counselors should conceive of client problems as problems in learning. The counselor should think of his job as one in which he helps his client learn more effective ways of solving his own problems. The counselor should think of himself as an aid in the learning process. He should see his job as arranging conditions so that his client will learn more adaptive ways of coping with difficulties.

At first glance, conceptualizing counseling as part of the learning process does not seem particularly revolutionary. Counselors and psychotherapists have talked about the process of counseling as learning for many years. Counselors of many theoretical persuasions would maintain that their techniques are employed as a means of helping the client learn. Several excellent books and articles have been written showing how psychotherapeutic or counseling techniques could be explained in terms of certain learning theories (e.g., Pepinsky and Pepinsky, 1954; Dollard and Miller, 1950; Shoben, 1949). However, these authors have tended to explain in learning theory terms counseling and psychotherapeutic techniques that had already been established. They did not attempt to construct *new* counseling procedures from a knowledge of the learning process. The revolutionary development, in my opinion, is that now new counseling procedures are being developed from our knowledge of the learning process.

Many people consider human behavior problems as learning problems for only certain limited types of behavior, particularly intellectual and physical skills. Let us consider some examples.

Suppose that you observe that Mike appears confused and uncertain and is unable to reply when someone says to him, "Como esta usted, señor?" How are we to conceptualize Mike's inability to reply to a question in Spanish? Would you say that Mike is mentally ill? Would you say that Mike has the capacity to understand the question in Spanish but simply has not yet had a sufficient amount of empathic understanding and unconditional positive regard? Or would you say that Mike has not yet learned to use the Spanish language? If Mike wished to master the Spanish language, we would probably all agree that he should be given certain kinds of educational experiences which would help him learn to respond appropriately in Spanish. Very few of us would claim that he was mentally ill. Very few of us would assert that merely listening to him express his feelings about his inability to speak Spanish and our communicating to him our understanding of his feelings would aid him in speaking it any better. Mike's inability to respond appropriately is clearly due to his lack of appropriate educational experiences, and the solution to the problem, therefore, is in providing appropriate conditions so that the necessary skills can be learned.

I have my difficulties playing golf. My drives all too often slice off and get lost in the woods. How shall we conceptualize this problem? Is it because my state of mental health is not sufficiently strong? Is it because no one provided me with the sufficient amount of empathic understanding when I complained about my inability to hit a drive straight? Or would you say that my difficulty is due to the fact that I simply have not learned how to hit a drive correctly? I presume that most of us would recommend that, if I wish to correct my inappropriate behavior, I allow myself to undergo some appropriate relearning experiences.

Application of the Learning Paradigm to Client Problems. My basic point here is that the same conceptualizations which are useful in explaining the acquisition of intellectual behaviors and the acquisition of physical skill behaviors are equally useful in explaining the acquisition of decision-making behaviors as well as emotional and social behaviors. Suppose Susan is unable to decide which college to attend. Shall we blame her indecision on some disease which is afflicting her mind? Shall we say that she has not been sufficiently understood? Or shall we say that she has not yet learned enough about the alternatives that are facing her and has not yet learned how to make decisions in a wise and rational way? I shall try to make clear why I think it will be far more helpful if we think about her problem as a problem in learning.

And then consider a social problem. Jim is painfully shy and withdrawn. How shall we think about his problem? Would you prefer to say that he has the beginnings of a mental illness? Would you say that no one has ever understood exactly how Jim feels about his problem? Or would you say that Jim has not yet learned the social skills involved in communicating with other people. I shall argue that we will be in a much better position to help Jim if we think of his problem as a problem in learning.

The Disease Paradigm. I shall not go into the difficulties and inconsistencies engendered by thinking about all behavior problems as diseases, though, of course, some problems do have clear organic bases. These difficulties are already well documented by Szasz (1961), Smith (1961), Glasser (1965), and Ullmann and Krasner (1965). The way we think about a problem determines to a large degree what we do about it. If we say, "That boy acts like a bully because he is sick," we refer him to a physician, expect a diagnosis, feed him pills and perhaps send him to a "mental hospital." If we say, "That boy acts like a bully because he has learned to act that way," we look for ways to help him learn more adaptive and effective ways of behaving. We are more likely to refer him to someone who can educate him. An appropriate type of instruction may be the most effective therapy by far.

Understanding–Necessary but not Sufficient. An alternative notion for conceptualizing a client's problem is to conceive of behavior as already present in the client, waiting to be released by a suitably warm, permissive, nonjudgmental counselor. It is as if good behavior has already been bottled up and needs merely to be uncorked. Under this conception of human behavior each person already knows how to behave, and once he comes in contact with a warm empathic counselor who understands his feelings and reflects them back so the client also recognizes his own feelings, then the desirable behavior will be released. Most of us who have taken courses in counseling are very familiar with this point of view.

I must make my position perfectly clear. I do not disagree with the importance of a counselor's understanding. On the contrary, it is essential that the counselor understand the client's problems. Of course he must be empathic and warm. Of course he must hold the client in high regard. Of course he must make it clear that he understands how the client feels. I agree that these conditions are necessary. How else can the counselor find out what is really bothering his client? How else can the client gain that sense of confidence and trust so necessary for an effective working relationship? But I disagree that these conditions are sufficient. More is needed. After the client's problem is clarified and the feelings about it are understood by both client and counselor, the client must still learn how to resolve his difficulty. Understanding alone is not enough. It provides only the beginning step upon which appropriate learning experiences can be arranged.

Advantages of the Learning Paradigm

I think that a number of advantages will immediately accrue to counselors and psychologists as they begin to conceptualize client problems as learning problems.

We already have a great deal of accumulated evidence and thinking about the problems of learning from psychology and educational psychology (Bijou, 1965). There is a theoretical and research base from which we can generate new ideas.

We are immediately integrated with the educational enterprise. No longer are we working at cross purposes with teachers and administrators. All of us are concerned with helping young people to learn. Different ones of us may take responsibility for different aspects of the job, but if we conceive of counseling as a learning process and communicate this to teachers and administrators, the fundamentals for co-operative action are greatly strengthened.

We shall be better able to define our goals so that they can be reached. More about this shortly.

We can concentrate our attention on what should be done to develop more adaptive behavior. We shall be less concerned with mere talk about problems and more concerned about effective action. On the basis of what we know about learning it seems certain that if we merely encourage our clients to talk about their feelings, we shall increase the extent to which they can talk about their feelings; and if we merely encourage our clients to analyze and label past events with psychoanalytic terminology, we shall increase the extent to which they analyze and label past events with psychoanalytic terminology. On the other hand, if we encourage our clients to engage in constructive problem-solving activities, we shall find that they will be more able to deal effectively with their problems.

We shall expect clients to feel an increased sense of responsibility for their own actions. By making clients aware of the consequences of their own actions and the fact that they can learn effective ways of dealing with their problems, we shall produce a heightened sense of responsibility. This is in contrast to the lack of responsibility implied by the notion that one's behavior is inappropriate because one has an unavoidable illness.

Now, whether or not I have convinced you that it may be helpful to think about counseling problems in terms of learning, let us turn to the second question traditionally asked by counselors.

HOW SHALL COUNSELORS DEFINE CLIENT GOALS?

In the past the general approach to stating counseling goals had two characteristics: 1) the goals were stated as broad generalities; and 2) it was assumed that all the goals were appropriate for every client.

We are all familiar with some of these all-encompassing goals of counseling. Here are some examples: "to fulfill one's full potentialities," "to achieve self-actualization," "to achieve a better understanding of self," and, in all fairness, I should add "to promote adaptive behavior." All of these ways of stating goals suffer from being so global and general that they provide no guidelines for what is to be accomplished.

Let me hasten to make perfectly clear, however, that I am not opposed to these goals. Quite the contrary. I am very much in favor of self-actualization, self-understanding, fulfillment of potential and adaptive behavior just as every politician is in favor of peace, justice and goodwill. However, in order to make such generalities useful they must be translated into specific kinds of behavior appropriate to each client's problems so that everyone concerned with the counseling relationship knows exactly what is to be accomplished.

Goals Stated as Mutually Accepted Changes in Behavior

Thus, my answer to the question is that the goals of counseling must be stated in terms of specific behavior changes desired by each individual client and agreed to by his counselor (Krumboltz, 1966). Three categories of goals can be constructed, each calling for a somewhat different approach by the counselor.

Altering Maladaptive Behavior. Suppose that Mary comes to the counselor and complains that she gets very nervous and uncomfortable whenever she is in a group of three or more persons so that she cannot talk with them at all. With just one other person, she is able to carry on a comfortable conversation, but add the third person and she cannot speak. How can the counselor define the goal in this case? The goal depends upon what the client wishes, first of all, and secondly upon whether the counselor agrees that such an end is desirable. The goal, however, must be stated in terms of a change in behavior by the client. In this case the client wishes to be able to communicate with other human beings when there are more than two people in the group. *The goal, then, is an increase in the frequency with which the client is able to talk when there are three or more people present.* The related goal would be a decrease in the amount of negative affect reported by the client when in groups of three or more. This may not be the client's only problem. It seldom is. But it is one problem, and it has been suggested (Bijou, 1965) that we take one problem at a time. The problem can be stated as a behavior change and can be described specifically. The goal can be explicitly agreed to by both the client and the counselor. Both will be working toward the same goal. Both will know when progress toward this goal is being achieved. The goal is clear, unambiguous, open and above board.

Note an additional feature of stating the goals in this way. The goal is individually tailored to the particular problem of each client. The goal of counseling *in general for all clients* is *not* to increase the frequency of talking in groups of three or more. As a matter of fact with some clients, the goal may be to decrease the amount of talking in groups of three or more! When we can state individual goals for individual clients, we are achieving, in the best sense of the term, dignity of the individual.

Consider another case, the case of George, a young man who has a terrible feeling of loneliness. For him weekends and vacations are the worst times of all. He reports dreadful sensations of being alone. It took every last ounce of courage on his part to approach the counselor and tell him the problem. How might the goal be defined in this case? Again it depends on what the client wishes, but let us assume that in this case George wishes that he were better at making friends so that he could have some companionship. The counselor's understanding of his problem will help to establish the counselor as one of his friends. But this is not sufficient. In the long run, the counselor cannot be his only friend. *The goals, then, are that George initiate contacts with other people, that he learn to communicate with them, and that he decrease his anxiety in the company of other people.* Goals such as these are established at the request of the client, can be agreed to by the counselor, are individually tailored to this one client's problems, and enable progress to be assessed.

Learning the Decision-Making Process. Consider Herb, a young man who has no idea what kind of occupation he would like to enter. Herb definitely wants to prepare himself for some type of occupation but is completely at a loss concerning what it might be and how he might go about deciding. How might the counselor define the objectives in this case? Once again it depends upon the client's request. But here it is obvious that the client does not know how to go about making a wise occupational choice.

The counselor may propose that the client learn how to make decisions of this type by going through the various stages in connection with his own problem. If the client wished to do this, the counselor might then help to define some specific steps which Herb should learn how to do: 1) how to gather feasible alternatives to consider, 2) how to gather relevant information about each alternative, 3) how to estimate his own chances of success in each alternative, 4) how to consider his own values and purposes in relation to various occupations under consideration, 5) how to deliberate and weigh the various values, possible outcomes and facts in relation to each alternative, and 6) how to formulate a tentative plan of action subject to new developments and new opportunities. The goal, then, is learning to use this sequence of problem-solving steps in the solution of personal, educational and vocational decisions.

Preventing Problems. There is a third kind of goal which has some intriguing possibilities—the prevention of problems. What could counselors do to prevent misery, suffering, waste and discouragement? How many problems in school are caused by harsh and punitive grading policies? How many marriages are on the rocks because the partners were ill-suited to each other and ignorant of their responsibilities? How many students fail to complete their education because their curriculum was inappropriate and teaching methods were ineffective? How many men and women go through life feeling rejected and unwanted because they never learned to approach other people in a friendly manner? How many children are permanently damaged by the neglect and harmful child-rearing practices used by their parents? Here are human problems which society at large implicitly, if not explicitly, wants to have solved. Does the counselor have any responsibility for the prevention of problems such as this? If we do have a responsibility (and I think we do), counselors and psychologists will need to have some policy-making role in the establishment of grading systems, in family life education, and in curricular and extracurricular programs. Most of all counselors and psychologists, as well as educators, will need a soundly based knowledge of the consequences of alternative educational practices.

Now that we have decided that the counselor ought to think of his problems in learning terms, and now that he is going to state his goals in terms of specific changes in the client's behavior that both he and the client desire, we turn to the third major question.

WHAT METHODS AND PROCEDURES WILL BEST ACCOMPLISH THE GOALS?

Four general approaches to the development of new counseling techniques are being derived from our current knowledge of the learning process.

Promoting Adaptive Behavior: Behavioral Approach

Operant Learning

The first approach is derived from our knowledge of operant learning. The application to counseling is that the timing of reinforcement can be useful in producing the kind of behavior desired by the client. We are all familiar with the psychological studies in which rats learn to turn either to the left or to the right as a result of finding pellets of food at one spot or the other. For the rat these pellets of food are reinforcers. If they receive these reinforcers after turning right, it is more likely that they will turn right in the future. We human beings are also affected by the reinforcers we receive, and we learn to do those things which produce certain kinds of desirable conditions for us. For example, we engage in certain kinds of occupational activity because we receive money as well as other benefits for so doing. Money is a reinforcer. Students write certain kinds of papers in school because teachers give *A* grades to people who write these kinds of papers. *A* grades are another kind of reinforcer. Most of us find that the attention and approval of our friends, neighbors and associates have reinforcing consequences. And so it seems quite likely that the attention and approval of a counselor might have reinforcing effects for a client, especially if the client feels that the counselor understands his problem and can do something to help.

Nature of Client's Talk Affected by Counselor Reinforcement. The evidence from several studies confirms that the counselor's attention and approval following certain kinds of responses makes a big difference in the kinds of responses the client makes in the future (Krumboltz and Schroeder, 1965; Krumboltz and Thoresen, 1964; Ryan and Krumboltz, 1964). Consider an illustration. Suppose the client says, "I feel all confused by this business of trying to decide about my future plans. I don't know where to begin." Notice that there are two elements in the client's statement: (a) his feelings of confusion, and (b) his not knowing where to begin. Suppose the counselor responds by saying, "You feel all confused by this business." The counselor is then giving his attention, and thus reinforcing, the client's talk about his feelings of confusion. We would expect from our knowledge of learning theory that the client would continue to talk more about his feelings of confusion. Suppose the counselor replied, instead, "You feel you want to know where to begin." He would then be reinforcing talk about where to begin and we might therefore expect more of this talk from the client in the future.

The kind of response made by the counselor will determine to some extent the direction that the client will take in the future. Counselors reinforce by their attention, interest and approval certain kinds of client responses. By their inattention, lack of interest and failure to respond, they extinguish or diminish the tendency of the client to talk about certain other things. The counselor is reinforcing some kind of response or failing to reinforce some other kind of response whether he knows it or not.

The problem for counselors is to decide on the timing of their reinforcements. The reinforcements should be arranged to promote the objectives desired by the client. If the client wants to learn how to make wise vocational decisions, then it might be more important for him to start talking about where to begin than to continue to wallow around in his own feelings of confusion.

Importance of Reinforcements Outside the Interview. But the reinforcements that occur during a brief counseling interview are of only minor importance compared to the reinforcements which occur constantly outside. Thus the school counselor must have the cooperation of teachers, administrators, parents and others if he is to help some of his clients.

Take the problem of underachievement, one of the most common school difficulties. This problem is produced in a youngster when his efforts to master school tasks are not reinforced. Since by definition only half the class can be above average, some youngsters are constantly receiving low grades. This is the result of grading systems which compare each child's present achievement with the group's achievement rather than with the child's own past achievement. If each child could be reinforced for showing improvement over his own past performance, we could predict a marked increase in achieving behavior. To bring this about teachers, parents and administrators must be prepared to reinforce any improvement in a child's school work no matter how much it may still deviate from what they consider ideal. Counselors and psychologists who understand the importance of well-timed reinforcement can help to arrange more encouraging consequences when underachievers start to show some effort in the right direction.

One of the revolutionary developments in counseling is the awareness that the counselor can reinforce or fail to reinforce either at appropriate or inappropriate times. He cannot avoid the responsibility which this brings to him. Thus, the question is not whether the counselor should or should not use reinforcement— the question is how the counselor can time his use of reinforcement in the best interests of his client.

Imitative Learning

A second approach in generating new procedures comes from our knowledge of imitative learning. The application to counseling is that the counselor can arrange for the client to observe *models* of the more adaptive behavior. Sometimes the client has so little idea of what might be more appropriate modes of behavior that he does not engage in any kind of talk or other behavior which constitutes even the beginning of a behavior to be reinforced. The work of Albert Bandura and his colleagues has contributed substantially to our knowledge of the conditions under which the observation of models is effective in changing behavior (e.g., Bandura and McDonald, 1963; Bandura, Ross and Ross, 1963; Bandura and Walters, 1963). A good deal of evidence has also been accumulated to show that the counselor's use of models may influence the behavior of a client. How can this be done?

One way is to present tape recordings of people who are successfully engaged in appropriate problem-solving activities. One effective model consisted of a 15-minute tape recording of a high school boy who was engaged in seeking information relevant to his education and vocational plans (Krumboltz and Schroeder, 1965; Krumboltz and Thoresen, 1964). Another model tape contributed substantially to helping high school students to make better use of their unscheduled time (Smith, 1965). Other media are also appropriate. The use of programmed instruction and other forms of written material has been shown to be effective (Bruner, 1965). Video taped television presentations and movies may well be effective if appropriately designed (Krumboltz, Varenhorst, and Thoresen, in press). Well chosen books may have a marked influence as models. Autobiographies, biographies and appropriate fiction may be selected or developed in an effort to provide appropriate models for the kind of behavior a particular client may desire (Young, 1963).

Cognitive Learning

A third general approach to new procedures, though not distinct from the others, is related to developments in cognitive learning. Sometimes people ask, "If the client is clear on what he wants to do, why mess around with reinforcement and models? Why not just *tell* him to do it?" There are times when appropriate verbal instructions may be most helpful. Although simply telling a client some needed information has very little appeal to theoreticians and others who write about counseling, its usefulness should not be overlooked.

Making Behavior Contracts. One particularly intriguing way of incorporating verbal instructions into the counseling of psychotherapeutic process consists of making contracts between the counselor and client (Sultzer, 1962). Keirsey (1965) has described the use of the "behavior contract" in the case of aggressive, destructive or disruptive acts by children in school. A contract is prepared and signed by each party who agrees to play a certain role for a certain period of time. The child agrees that any disruptive act on his part will immediately result in his being asked to leave school. The teacher agrees to signal the child to leave the classroom whenever the child makes a disruptive act. The principal agrees to enforce the agreement even if it entails carrying the child out of the class. The parent agrees to avoid conversation with the child about school and to avoid punishing or scolding the child for being sent home. The psychologist negotiates the contract and agrees to be available for counsel. The beauty of this system from my point of view is that the behavior desired by the child is explicitly stated; the contingencies of reinforcement are known in advance to all parties; and when the child does act properly, he gets full credit for his improved behavior.

Keirsey described other variations of the contract approach. For example, for reluctant learners, it is agreed that when the child is in seat number one, he is part of the class and is given instruction just as the other students are; but when he is in seat number two, he is not part of the class and is given no instruction whatsoever. As long as the child upholds his end of the agreement, he may elect to sit in either seat. If he violates the agreement by refusing to work when he is in seat number one, he is banished to seat number two for the rest of the day. The agreement must be written down and countersigned by the teacher, the principal, the student and the student's parents. Many variations are possible. Keirsey stated that the essential contract is, "in return for getting off the kid's back, the adults are assured in writing by the student that he will take over the responsibility for educating himself and that whatever events ensue must be credited to him and not to them . . ." (p. 12).

Role-Playing. Clients may be instructed to play new roles for certain periods of time. Role-playing is another way of presenting models and of allowing the client to practice and be reinforced for good approximations to the desired behavior. In my own counseling I find that role-playing is a very effective way of getting a client to practice a task under low-stress conditions. For example, a young man who was so timid that he was afraid to return an unsatisfactory article to a store and complain about it, though this was exactly what he wanted to do, was encouraged to practice the act while I played the role of the store manager. A couple of role-playing sessions were sufficient to enable him to return the article to the store and get his money refunded. The fact that he was successful in this venture was reinforcing to him, and he generalized the experience to strengthen his assertive responses in other encounters of a like nature.

Role-playing need not be confined to the interview situation. Indeed, the only purpose of any of these techniques is to set in motion the process of getting the client to learn a more appropriate role outside the interview. Keirsey has described a technique called the "role-shift," which involves persuading the client to try out a new pattern of behavior just so that some information about it can be gained. Keirsey described the case of the child who had maneuvered his mother into the position of having to nag at him continuously in the morning to get him out of bed, dressed, fed and off to school. Clearly, the roles that the two people were playing were unsatisfactory. Keirsey believed that it would be important for the mother to try out almost any other kind of role in order to break the pattern. The first he tried was to have her play the role of the helpless bystander. Her task was simply to do practically nothing. This included saying practically nothing to the child who was dawdling, not eating his breakfast or not dressing himself. Occasionally the mother might say, "Is there anything that I can do to help you?" and then simply walk away. Her task in short was to *not* be very helpful to the child. For several days the child ". . . bumbles around and is late to school or doesn't even get to school, in which case the mother is to just helplessly stand by without trying to do much of anything. Eventually, the child takes over and gets himself to school without further ploys" (p. 7).

Sometimes it is difficult to persuade a client to take on a new role. Keirsey suggested that the counselor or psychologist can obtain more cooperation by asking clients to try out these roles in order to permit the counselor or psychologist to gain more diagnostic information. Of course this is exactly the purpose—to gain some information regarding how well an alternative role might work in solving the client's problem. If the new role does work, the client is immediately reinforced by the more positive reaction of people around him. If it does not work, a different role can be tried.

Timing Cues. Still another application from cognitive learning concerns the timing of cues. A study demonstrating the importance of cueing in improving study habits has been reported by Ryan (1965).

Telling a person what to do may sometimes be effective, but the timing of the remark is often crucial and the importance of this timing is often overlooked. One parent I know consulted a psychologist about how her children were driving her crazy because they constantly forgot to do the things she asked of them. One of the most annoying habits the children had was to run in or out of the house without closing the door. The difficulty was that the mother reminded the children to close the door after they had already passed it. The psychologist pointed out that the most effective cues are those that occur just prior to the behavior, not those that occur afterwards. The mother was told to observe her children and as they approached the door to give the reminder: "Close the door." Just a few days of extra-attentiveness on the part of the mother enabled her to give the reminders to each child just prior to touching the door so that soon thereafter the child needed no further reminders. (One of my graduate students said it would have been easier to put a spring on the door!)

Emotional Learning

The fourth general approach is derived from the classical conditioning paradigm. The application to counseling is that unpleasant emotional reactions can be systematically reduced by pairing the eliciting stimuli with more pleasant stimuli. The work of Wolpe (1958) and Lazarus (1961) illustrates this approach. Clients with severe feelings of anxiety are relaxed and then the stimuli which cause their anxieties are presented in a gradually increasing fashion while the client remains relaxed. It is a form of "innoculating against stress" by presenting small portions of the stressful situation while the client remains in a state of relaxation.

Obviously, some of the most effective treatment procedures would not rely on any one of these four general approaches that I have described. Some techniques incorporate combinations of reinforcement, the use of models, cognitive learning and the systematic reduction of fears or anxieties.

Now that we have adopted a learning model, specified some behavior changes in concrete language and described four general kinds of useful techniques derived from our knowledge of learning, let us turn to the fourth and final question.

HOW SHOULD THE COUNSELOR EVALUATE THE SUCCESS OF HIS WORK?

Thomas Huxley once said, ". . . new truths . . . begin as heresies and . . . end as superstitions." The new truths about effective counseling procedures may begin as heresies, but a rigorous evaluation will prevent their ending as superstitions.

Inadequate Evidence for Traditional Practices

Most of the counseling and psychotherapeutic procedures currently in use have virtually no research base for their existence. The research that does exist generally shows the techniques to have no measurable effect. The few effects that are shown are usually trivial. Of course there are many difficulties with performing adequate experimental studies with complex human behavior, but it is quite clear that we do not already know the most effective ways of helping people.

For example, Gonyea's study (1964), which won a research award from the American Personnel and Guidance Association in 1965, showed that there was a negative relationship between the extent to which counselors developed the "ideal therapeutic relationship" and the degree to which their clients reported themselves to be improved. The correlation was a −.14, not significantly different from zero, but in the direction that those counselors who were most "ideal" produced the least improvement in clients. Certainly evidence such as this should cause us to hesitate before preaching that we already know what the ideal therapeutic relationship is.

One of the primary difficulties in our profession at the present time is that dogmatic statements about the nature and conditions of ideal counseling relationships are made without adequate evidence. We are faced with the fact that outstanding leaders in the field give lists of a few conditions they believe necessary for personality change to occur and then assert "no other conditions are necessary." Consider what statements like this mean. They mean that the search for new and more effective procedures is over. They imply that all the necessary and sufficient conditions of counseling have already been discovered and validated, and there is nothing for the rest of us to do but follow them. I hope you will agree that all the ideas for improving counseling have *not* already been devised and that there are still a few new ideas that ought at least to be tried before we consign them to the scrap heap.

Experimental Evaluation of Specific Procedures for Specific Goals

My answer, then, to the question on how we should evaluate our work is this: counselors must conduct careful experimental studies to determine which kind of procedures work best to accomplish which objectives with which kinds of clients. This suggestion is revolutionary only in that precise experimental studies are rare in counseling. The few well designed experimental studies that have been conducted attempted to evaluate counseling or guidance services as a whole (e.g., Volsky, Magoon, Norman and Hoyt, 1965). They have asked in essence: "Is counseling any good?" "Are guidance services valuable?"

I suggest to you that counseling in its totality cannot be evaluated. It is as foolish to say that counseling is or is not effective as it is to say that medicine is or is not effective. It is useless to evaluate counseling as compared with no counseling unless we specify the kind of problem, the direction of change desired by the client, the precise counseling procedure used and the circumstances under which counseling occurred. What we need to know is which procedures and techniques, when used to accomplish which kinds of behavior change, are most effective with what kinds of clients when applied by what kinds of counselors.

A useful approach is to compare alternative methods of helping people to solve the same kind of problems. The previously cited study by Krumboltz and Thoresen (1964) provides an example.

High school students with problems of career indecision were randomly assigned to counselors who used various procedures designed to encourage them to explore possible alternatives and relevant information. For some of the students the counselors used verbal reinforcement, encouraging them to explore further possibilities. Some of the students received, in addition, tape-recorded interviews so that they could hear how other students had explored similar problems. Still other students were assigned to various kinds of control groups so that there would be a basis for comparing the effects of the experimental procedures. Not only were all of these procedures tried in individual counseling interviews, but they were also tried in small groups. The experiment revealed that the use of models and the reinforcement counseling produced significantly more exploratory information-seeking activity on the part of the students than did the control group procedures. We found that the model was particularly useful for the male students (probably because the model used was a male student discussing typical male concerns). And although we found no significant differences on the average between group and individual counseling, we did find significant interactions indicating that some counselors were better at group counseling, whereas other counselors were more effective working with individuals.

Studies such as this raise more questions than they answer, but if we continue to test our new ideas, we shall gradually accumulate some reliable knowledge about which kinds of procedures will work best for which purposes under what kinds of circumstances.

A variety of experimental counseling procedures are currently being developed. Some of them have already been subjected to rigorous experimental tests. Others are undergoing experimental testing, and still others are hunches that may or may not work. The procedures do not constitute final answers or proven techniques. Most of them are in the very beginning stages of development, but they do represent some new possibilities. Perhaps they will not work out satisfactorily in their present state. Perhaps other persons will have ideas of ways in which the procedures can be improved and made more effective.

CONCLUSION

I am sure that each one of us as a counselor, psychologist,

teacher or administrator wants to find more effective ways of helping the young people who come in contact with us. Additional readings which expand some of the notions expressed here include Krasner and Ullmann (1965), Krumboltz (1964, 1965, 1966), Michael and Meyerson (1962), and Ullmann and Krasner (1965).

I have tried to show that a useful way of thinking about the problem would be to see ourselves as helpers in the learning process. Though we might be guided by some general goals, we would work to specify the precise kinds of behavior change desired by our clients as well as ourselves. I have tried to show that developments in our knowledge about the learning process might be fruitful in suggesting techniques and procedures useful in helping clients learn to accomplish more adaptive kinds of behavior. And finally I have emphasized that whatever techniques and procedures we derive must be experimentally tested to determine their possible usefulness.

In closing, the words of Franklin Delano Roosevelt, uttered at another time in the face of other problems, seem pertinent now to counselors and psychologists: "The country needs . . . bold, persistent experimentation. It is common sense to take a method and try it. If it fails, admit it frankly and try another. But above all, try something."

REFERENCES

Bandura, A., and McDonald, F. J. Influence of social reinforcement and the behavior of models in shaping children's moral judgments. *J. Abnormal Social Psychology*, 1963, 67:274-281.

Bandura, A., Ross, Dorothea, and Ross, Sheila A. A comparative test of the status of envy, social power, and secondary reinforcement theories of identificatory learning. *J. Abnormal Social Psychology*, 1963, 67:527-534.

Bandura, A., and Walters, R. H. *Social Learning and Personality Development*. New York: Holt, Rinehart & Winston, Inc., 1963.

Bijou, Sidney W. Implications of behavioral science for counseling and guidance, in Krumboltz, John D. (Ed.) *Revolution in Counseling*. Boston: Houghton Mifflin, 1966, pp. 27-48.

Bruner, Fern. "The effect of programmed instruction on information-seeking behavior in tenth-grade students." Unpublished doctoral dissertation, Stanford University, 1965.

Dollard, J., and Miller, N. E. *Personality and Psychotherapy.* New York: McGraw-Hill Book Co., Inc., 1950.

Glasser, W. *Reality Therapy.* New York: Harper & Row, Publishers, 1965.

Gonyea, G. The ideal therapeutic relationship and counseling outcome. *J. Clinical Psychology,* 1964, *19*:481-487.

Keirsey, D. W. Transactional casework: a technology for inducing behavior change. Paper presented at the Annual Convention of the California Association of School Psychologists and Psychometrists, San Francisco, 1965 (mimeo., 24 pp.).

Krasner, L., and Ullmann, L. P. *Research in Behavior Modification.* New York: Holt, Rinehart & Winston, Inc., 1965.

Krumboltz, J. D. Parable of the good counselor. *Personnel Guid. Journal,* 1965, *44*:383-387.

Krumboltz, J. D. Behavioral counseling: rationale and research. *Personnel Guid. Journal,* 1965, *44*:383-387.

Krumboltz, J. D. Behavioral goals for counseling. *J. Counsel. Psychology,* 1966, *13*:153-159.

Krumboltz, J. D., and Schroeder, W. W. Promoting career exploration through reinforcement. *Personnel Guid. Journal,* 1965, *44*:19-26.

Krumboltz, J. D., and Thoresen, C. E. The effect of behavioral counseling in group and individual settings on information-seeking behavior. *J. Counsel. Psychology,* 1964, *11*:324-333.

Krumboltz, J. D., Varenhorst, Barbara B., and Thoresen, C. E. Nonverbal factors in the effectiveness of models in counseling. *J. Counsel. Psychology,* in press.

Lazarus, A. A. Group therapy of phobic disorders by systematic desensitization. *J. Abnorm. Social Psychol.,* 1961, *63*:504-510.

Michael, J., and Meyerson, L. A behavioral approach to counseling and guidance. *Harvard Educ. Rev.,* 1962, *32*:382-402.

Pepinsky, H. B., and Pepinsky, Pauline N. *Counseling Theory and Practice.* New York: The Ronald Press Company, 1954.

Ryan, T. Antoinette. Influence of different cueing procedures on counseling effectiveness. *Proceedings of the 73rd Annual Convention of the American Psychological Association.* Washington, D.C.: American Psychological Association, 1965, pp. 351-352.

Shoben, E. J. Psychotherapy as a problem in learning theory. *Psychol. Bull.,* 1949, *46*:366-392.

Smith, J. E. "Encouraging students to utilize their unscheduled time more effectively through reinforcement and model counseling." Unpublished doctoral dissertation, Stanford University, 1965.

Smith, M. B. "Mental health" reconsidered: a special case of the problems of values in psychology. *American Psychologist,* 1961, *16*:299-306.

Sultzer, E. Reinforcement and the therapeutic contract. *J. Counseling Psychology,* 1962, *9*:271-276.

Szasz, T. S. *The Myth of Mental Illness.* New York: Paul B. Hoeber, Inc., 1961.

Ullmann, L. P., and Krasner, L. Introduction, in L. P. Ullmann and L. Krasner (Eds.), *Case Studies in Behavior Modification.* New York: Holt, Rinehart & Winston, Inc., 1965.

Volsky, T., Jr., Magoon, T. M., Norman, W. T., and Hoyt, D. P. *The Outcomes of Counseling and Psychotherapy.* Minneapolis: University of Minnesota Press, 1965.

Wolpe, J. *Psychotherapy by Reciprocal Inhibition.* Stanford, Calif.: Stanford University Press, 1958.

Young, Olive S. "Literary materials as aids in group guidance." Unpublished Master of Arts thesis, Chico State College, Chico, Calif., 1963.

6

SOME BASIC PROPOSITIONS OF A GROWTH AND SELF-ACTUALIZATION PSYCHOLOGY

Abraham H. Maslow, Ph.D.

When the philosophy of man (his nature, his goals, his potentialities, his fulfillment) changes, then everything changes, not only the philosophy of politics, of economics, of ethics and values, of interpersonal relations and of history itself, but also the philosophy of education, the theory of how to help men become what they can and deeply need to become.

We are now in the middle of such a change in the conception of man's capacities, potentialities and goals. A new vision is emerging of the possibilities of man and of his destiny, and its implications are many, not only for our conceptions of education, but also for science, politics, literature, economics, religion, and even our conceptions of the non-human world.

I think it is now possible to begin to delineate this view of human nature as a total, single, comprehensive system of psychology even though much of it has arisen as a reaction *against* the limitations (as philosophies of human nature) of the two most comprehensive psychologies now available—behaviorism (or associationism) and classical, Freudian psychoanalysis. Finding a single label for it is still a difficult task, perhaps a premature one. In the past I have called it the "holistic-dynamic" psychology to express my conviction about its major roots. Some have called it "organismic" following Goldstein. Sutich and others are calling it the Self-psychology or Humanistic psychology. We shall see. My own guess is that, in a few decades, if it remains suitably eclectic and

---

Reprinted by permission of the author and publisher from Abraham H. Maslow, *Toward a Psychology of Being.* Princeton, N.J.: Van Nostrand, 1962.

comprehensive, it will be called simply "psychology."

I think I can be of most service by speaking primarily for my-self and out of my own work rather than as an "official" delegate of this large group of thinkers, even though I am sure that the areas of agreement among them are very large. A selection of works of this "third force" is listed in the bibliography. Because of the limited space I have, I will present here only some of the major propositions of this point of view, especially those of importance to the educator. I should warn you that at many points I am way out ahead of the data. Some of these propositions are more based on private conviction than on publicly demonstrated facts. However, they are all in principle confirmable or disconfirmable.

1. We have, each one of us, an essential inner nature which is instinctoid, intrinsic, given, "natural," i.e., with an appreciable hereditary determinant, and which tends strongly to persist (Maslow, 1954, Chapter 7).

It makes sense to speak here of the hereditary, constitutional and very early acquired roots of the *individual* self, even though this biological determination of self is only partial, and far too complex to describe simply. In any case, this is "raw material" rather than finished product, to be reacted to by the person, by his significant others, by his environment, etc.

I include in this essential inner nature instinctoid basic needs, capacities, talents, anatomical equipment, physiological or temperamental balances, prenatal and natal injuries, and traumata to the neonate. This inner core shows itself as natural inclinations, propensities or inner bent. Whether defense and coping mechanisms, "style of life," and other characterological traits, all shaped in the first few years of life, should be included is still a matter for discussion. This raw material very quickly starts growing into a self as it meets the world outside and begins to have transaction with it.

2. These are potentialities, not final actualizations. Therefore they have a life history and must be seen developmentally. They are actualized, shaped or stifled mostly (but not altogether) by extra-psychic determinants (culture, family, environment, learning, etc.). Very early in life these goalless urges and tendencies become attached to objects ("sentiments") by canalization (Murphy, 1947) but also by arbitrarily learned associations.

3. This inner core, even though it is biologically based and "instinctoid," is weak in certain senses rather than strong. It is easily overcome, suppressed or repressed. It may even be killed

off permanently. Humans no longer have instincts in the animal sense, powerful, unmistakable inner voices which tell them unequivocally what to do, when, where, how and with whom. All that we have left are instinct-remnants. And furthermore, these are weak, subtle and delicate, very easily drowned out by learning, by cultural expectations, by fear, by disapproval, etc. They are hard to know, rather than easy. Authentic selfhood can be defined in part as being able to hear these impulse-voices within oneself, i.e., to know what one really wants or doesn't want, what one is fit for and what one is *not* fit for, etc. It appears that there are wide individual differences in the strength of these impulse-voices.

4. Each person's inner nature has some characteristics which all other selves have (species-wide) and some which are unique to the person (idiosyncratic). The need for love characterizes every human being that is born (although it can disappear later under certain circumstances). Musical genius however is given to very few, and these differ markedly from each other in style, e.g., Mozart and Debussy.

5. It is possible to study this inner nature scientifically and objectively (that is, with the right kind of "science") and to discover what it is like (discover—not invent or construct). It is also possible to do this subjectively, by inner search and by psychotherapy, and the two enterprises supplement and support each other.

6. Many aspects of this inner, deeper nature are either (a) actively repressed, as Freud has described, because they are feared or disapproved of or are ego-alien, or (b) "forgotten" (neglected, unused, overlooked, unverbalized or suppressed), as Schachtel has described. Much of the inner, deeper nature is therefore unconscious. This can be true not only for impulses (drives, instincts, needs) as Freud has stressed, but also for capacities, emotions, judgments, attitudes, definitions, perceptions, etc. Active repression takes effort and uses up energy. There are many specific techniques of maintaining active unconsciousness, such as denial, projection, reaction-formation, etc. However, repression does not kill what is repressed. The repressed remains as one active determinant of thought and behavior.

Both active and passive repressions seem to begin early in life, mostly as a response to parental and cultural disapprovals.

However, there is some clinical evidence that repression may arise also from intra-psychic, extra-cultural sources in the young child, or at puberty, i.e., out of fear of being overwhelmed by its own impulses, of becoming disintegrated, of "falling apart," exploding, etc. It is theoretically possible that the child may spontaneously form attitudes of fear and disapproval toward its own impulses and may then defend himself against them in various ways. Society need not be the only repressing force, if this is true. There may also be intra-psychic repressing and controlling forces. These we may call "intrinsic counter-cathexes."

It is best to distinguish unconscious drives and needs from unconscious ways of cognizing because the latter are often easier to bring to consciousness and therefore to modify. Primary process cognition (Freud) or archaic thinking (Jung) is more recoverable by, e.g., creative art education, dance education, and other nonverbal educational techniques.

7. Even though "weak," this inner nature rarely disappears or dies, in the usual person, in the U.S. (such disappearance or dying is possible early in the life history, however). It persists underground, unconsciously, even though denied and repressed. Like the voice of the intellect (which is part of it), it speaks softly but it will be heard, even if in a distorted form. That is, it has a dynamic force of its own, pressing always for open, uninhibited expression. Effort must be used in its suppression or repression from which fatigue can result. This force is one main aspect of the "will to health," the urge to grow, the pressure to self-actualization, the quest for one's identity. It is this that makes psychotherapy, education and self-improvement possible in principle.

8. However, this inner core, or self, grows into adulthood only partly by (objective or subjective) discovery, uncovering and acceptance of what is "there" beforehand. Partly it is also a creation of the person himself. Life is a continual series of choices for the individual in which a main determinant of choice is the person as he already is (including his goals for himself, his courage or fear, his feeling of responsibility, his ego-strength or "will power," etc.). We can no longer think of the person as "fully determined" where this phrase implies "determined only by forces external to the person." The person, insofar as he is a real person, is his own main determinant. Every person is, in part, "his own project" and makes himself.

9. If this essential core (inner nature) of the person is frustrated, denied or suppressed, sickness results, sometimes in obvious forms, sometimes in subtle and devious forms, sometimes immediately, sometimes later. These psychological illnesses include many more than those listed by the American Psychiatric Association. For

instance, the character disorders and disturbances are now seen as far more important for the fate of the world than the classical neuroses or even the psychoses. From this new point of view, new kinds of illness are most dangerous, e.g., "the diminished or stunted person," i.e., the loss of any of the defining characteristics of humanness, or personhood, the failure to grow to one's potential, valuelessness, etc.

That is, general-illness of the personality is seen as any falling short of growth, or of self-actualization, or of full-humanness. And the main source of illness (although not the only one) is seen as frustrations (of the basic needs, of the B-values,[1] of idiosyncratic potentials, of expression of the self, and of the tendency of the person to grow in his own style and at his own pace) especially in the early years of life. That is, frustration of the basic needs is not the only source of illness or of human diminution.

10. This inner nature, as much as we know of it so far, is definitely not "evil," but is either what we adults in our culture call "good," or else it is neutral. The most accurate way to express this is to say that it is "prior to good and evil." There is little question about this if we speak of the inner nature of the infant and child. The statement is much more complex if we speak of the "infant" as he still exists in the adult. And it gets still more complex if the individual is seen from the point of view of B-psychology rather than D-psychology.

The conclusion is supported by all the truth-revealing and uncovering techniques that have anything to do with human nature: psychotherapy, objective science, subjective science, education and art. For instance, in the long run, uncovering therapy lessens hostility, fear, greed, etc., and increases love, courage, creativeness, kindness, altruism, etc., leading us to the conclusion that the latter are "deeper," more natural, and more basic than the former, i.e., that what we call "bad" behavior is lessened or removed by uncovering, while what we call "good" behavior is strengthened and fostered by uncovering.

11. We must differentiate the Freudian type of superego from intrinsic conscience and intrinsic guilt. The former is in principle a taking into the self of the disapprovals and approvals of persons

---

[1]Editor's note: "B-values" = *Being* values, as contrasted with "D-values" = *Deficiency* values. The contrasts between Being and Deficiency are discussed more fully later in this article.

other than the person himself, fathers, mothers, teachers, etc. Guilt then is recognition of disapproval by others.

Intrinsic guilt is the consequence of betrayal of one's own inner nature or self, a turning off the path to self-actualization, and is essentially justified self-disapproval. It is therefore not as culturally relative as is Freudian guilt. It is "true" or "deserved" or "right and just" or "correct" because it is a discrepancy from something profoundly real within the person rather than from accidental, arbitrary or purely relative localisms. Seen in this way it is good, even necessary, for a person's development to have intrinsic guilt when he deserves to. It is not just a symptom to be avoided at any cost but is rather an inner guide for growth toward actualization of the real self, and of its potentialities.

12. "Evil" behavior has mostly referred to unwarranted hostility, cruelty, destructiveness, "mean" aggressiveness. This we do not know enough about. To the degree that this quality of hostility is instinctoid, mankind has one kind of future. To the degree that it is reactive (a response to bad treatment), mankind has a very different kind of future. My opinion is that the weight of the evidence so far indicates that indiscriminately destructive hostility is reactive, because uncovering therapy reduces it, and changes its quality into "healthy" self-affirmation, forcefulness, selective hostility, self-defense, righteous indignation, etc. In any case, the ability to be aggressive and angry is found in all self-actualizing people, who are able to let it flow forth freely when the external situation "calls for" it.

The situation in children is far more complex. At the very least, we know that the healthy child is also able to be justifiably angry, self-protecting and self-affirming, i.e., reactive aggression. Presumably, then, a child should learn not only how to control his anger, but also how and when to express it.

Behavior that our culture calls evil can also come from ignorance and from childish misinterpretations and beliefs (whether in the child or in the repressed or "forgotten" child-in-the-adult). For instance, sibling rivalry is traceable to the child's wish for the exclusive love of his parents. Only as he matures is he in principle capable of learning that his mother's love for a sibling is compatible with her continued love for him. Thus out of a childish version of love, not in itself reprehensible, can come unloving behavior.

The commonly seen hatred or resentment of or jealousy of goodness, truth, beauty, health or intelligence ("counter-values") is largely (though not altogether) determined by threat of loss of self-esteem, as the liar is threatened by the honest man, the homely girl by the beautiful girl, or the coward by the hero. Every superior person confronts us with our own shortcomings.

Still deeper than this, however, is the ultimate existential question of the fairness and justice of fate. The person with a disease may be jealous of the healthy man who is no more deserving than he.

Evil behaviors seem to most psychologists to be reactive as in these examples, rather than instinctive. This implies that though "bad" behavior is very deeply rooted in human nature and can never be abolished altogether, it may yet be expected to lessen as the personality matures and as the society improves.

13. Many people still think of "the unconscious," of regression, and of primary process cognition as necessarily unhealthy, or dangerous or bad. Psychotherapeutic experience is slowly teaching us otherwise. Our depths can also be good, or beautiful or desirable. This is also becoming clear from the general findings from investigations of the sources of love, creativeness, play, humor, art, etc. Their roots are deep in the inner, deeper self, i.e., in the unconscious. To recover them and to be able to enjoy and use them we must be able to "regress."

14. No psychological health is possible unless this essential core of the person is fundamentally accepted, loved and respected by others and by himself (the converse is not necessarily true, i.e., that if the core is respected, etc., then psychological health must result, since other prerequisite conditions must also be satisfied).

The psychological health of the chronologically immature is called healthy growth. The psychological health of the adult is called variously, self-fulfillment, emotional maturity, individuation, productiveness, self-actualization, authenticity, full-humanness, etc.

Healthy growth is conceptually subordinate, for it is usually defined now as "growth toward self-actualization," etc. Some psychologists speak simply in terms of one overarching goal or end, or tendency of human development, considering all immature growth phenomena to be only steps along the path to self-actualization (Goldstein, Rogers).

Self-actualization is defined in various ways but a solid core of agreement is perceptible. All definitions accept or imply, a) acceptance and expression of the inner core of self, i.e., actualization of these latent capacities and potentialities, "full functioning," availability of the human and personal essence. b) They all imply minimal presence of ill health, neurosis, psychosis, of loss or diminution of the basic human and personal capacities.

15. For all these reasons, it is at this time best to bring out and encourage, or at the very least, to recognize this inner nature, rather than to suppress or repress it. Pure spontaneity consists of free, uninhibited, uncontrolled, trusting, unpremeditated expression of the self, i.e., of the psychic forces, with minimal interference by consciousness. Control, will, caution, self-criticism, measure, deliberateness are the brakes upon this expression made intrinsically necessary by the laws of the social and natural worlds outside the psychic world, and secondarily, made necessary by fear of the psyche itself (intrinsic counter-cathexis). Speaking in a very broad way, controls upon the psyche which come from fear of the psyche are largely neurotic or psychotic, or not intrinsically or theoretically necessary. (The healthy psyche is not terrible or horrible and therefore doesn't have to be feared, as it has been for thousands of years. Of course, the unhealthy psyche is another story.) This kind of control is usually lessened by psychological health, by deep psychotherapy, or by any deeper self-knowledge and self-acceptance. There are also, however, controls upon the psyche which do not come out of fear, but out of the necessities for keeping it integrated, organized and unified (intrinsic counter-cathexes). And there are also "controls," probably in another sense, which are necessary as capacities are actualized, and as higher forms of expression are sought for, e.g., acquisition of skills through hard work by the artist, the intellectual, the athlete. But these controls are eventually transcended and become aspects of spontaneity, as they become self.

The balance between spontaneity and control varies, then, as the health of the psyche and the health of the world vary. Pure spontaneity is not long possible because we live in a world which runs by its own, non-psychic laws. It *is* possible in dreams, fantasies, love, imagination, sex, the first stages of creativity, artistic work, intellectual play, free association, etc. Pure control is not permanently possible, for then the psyche dies. Education must be directed then both toward cultivation of controls and cultivation of spontaneity and expression. In our culture and at this point in history, it is necessary to redress the balance in favor of spontaneity, the ability to be expressive, passive, unwilled, trusting in processes other than will and control, unpremeditated, creative, etc. But it must be recognized that there have been and will be other cultures and other areas in which the balance was or will be in the other direction.

16. In the normal development of the normal child, it is now known that, most of the time, if he is given a really free choice, he will choose what is good for his growth. This he does because it tastes good, feels good, gives pleasure or delight. This implies that *he* "knows" better than anyone else what is good for him. A permissive regime means not that adults gratify his needs directly but make it possible for *him* to gratify his needs, and make his own choices, i.e., let him *be*. It is necessary in order for children to grow well that adults have enough trust in them and in the natural processes of growth, i.e., not interfere too much, not make them grow, or force them into predetermined designs, but rather let them grow and *help* them grow in a Taoistic rather than an authoritarian way.

17. Coordinate with this "acceptance" of the self, of fate, of one's call, is the conclusion that the main path to health and self-fulfillment for the masses is via basic need gratification rather than via frustration. This contrasts with the suppressive regime, the mistrust, the control, the policing that is necessarily implied by the belief in basic, instinctive evil in the human depths. Intrauterine life is completely gratifying and non-frustrating and it is now generally accepted that the first year or so of life had better also be primarily gratifying and non-frustrating. Asceticism, self-denial, deliberate rejection of the demands of the organism, at least in the West, tend to produce a diminished, stunted or crippled organism, and even in the East, bring self-actualization to only a very few, exceptionally strong individuals.

18. But we know also that the complete absence of frustration is dangerous. To be strong, a person must acquire frustration-tolerance, the ability to perceive physical reality as essentially indifferent to human wishes, the ability to love others and to enjoy their need-gratification as well as one's own (not to use other people only as means). The child with a good basis of safety, love and respect-need-gratification, is able to profit from nicely graded frustrations and become stronger thereby. If they are more than he can bear, if they overwhelm him, we call them traumatic, and consider them dangerous rather than profitable.

It is via the frustrating unyieldingness of physical reality and of animals and of other people that we learn their nature, and thereby learn to differentiate wishes from facts (which things wishing makes come true, and which things proceed in complete disregard of our wishes), and are thereby enabled to live in the world and adapt to it as necessary.

We learn also about our own strengths and limits and extend them by overcoming difficulties, by straining ourselves to the utmost, by meeting challenge and hardship, even by failing. There can be great enjoyment in a great struggle and this can displace fear.

Overprotection implies that the child's needs are gratified for him by his parents, without effort of his own. This tends to infantilize him, to prevent development of his own strength, will and self-assertion. In one of its forms it may teach him to use other people rather than to respect them. In another form it implies a lack of trust and respect for the child's own powers and choices, i.e., it is essentially condescending and insulting, and can help to make a child feel worthless.

19. To make growth and self-actualization possible, it is necessary to understand that capacities, organs and organ systems press to function and express themselves and to be used and exercised, and that such use is satisfying, and disuse irritating. The muscular person likes to use his muscles, indeed, *has* to use them in order to "feel good" and to achieve the subjective feeling of harmonious, successful, uninhibited functioning (spontaneity) which is so important an aspect of good growth and psychological health. So also for intelligence, for the uterus, the eyes, the capacity to love. Capacities clamor to be used, and cease their clamor only when they *are* well used. That is, capacities are also needs. Not only is it fun to use our capacities, but it is also necessary for growth. The unused skill or capacity or organ can become a disease center or else atrophy or disappear, thus diminishing the person.

20. The psychologist proceeds on the assumption that for his purposes there are two kinds of worlds, two kinds of reality, the natural world and the psychic world, the world of unyielding facts and the world of wishes, hopes, fears, emotions, and the world which runs by non-psychic rules and the world which runs by psychic laws. This differentiation is not very clear except at its extremes, where there is no doubt that delusions, dreams and free associations are lawful and yet utterly different from the lawfulness of logic and from the lawfulness of the world which would remain if the human species died out. This assumption does not deny that these worlds are related and may even fuse.

21. Immaturity can be contrasted with maturity from the motivational point of view, as the process of gratifying the deficiency-needs in their proper order. Maturity, or self-actualization, from this point of view, means to transcend the deficiency-needs. This

state can be described then as metamotivated, or unmotivated (if deficiencies are seen as the only motivations). It can also be described as self-actualizing, Being, expressing, rather than coping. This state of Being, rather than of striving, is suspected to be synonymous with selfhood, with being "authentic," with being a person, with being fully human. The process of growth is the process of becoming a person. Being a person is different.

22. Immaturity can also be differentiated from maturity in terms of the cognitive capacities (and also in terms of the emotional capacities). Immature and mature cognition have been best described by Werner and Piaget. We can now add another differentiation, that between D-cognition and B-cognition (D = Deficiency, B = Being). D-cognition can be defined as the cognitions which are organized from the point of view of basic needs or deficiency-needs and their gratification and frustration. That is, D-cognition could be called selfish cognition, in which the world is organized into gratifiers and frustrators of our own needs, with other characteristics being ignored or slurred. The cognition of the object, in its own right and its own Being, without reference to its need-gratifying or need-frustrating qualities, that is, without primary reference to its value for the observer or its effects upon him, can be called B-cognition (or self-transcending, or unselfish, or objective cognition). The parallel with maturity is by no means perfect (children can also cognize in a selfless way), but in general, it is mostly true that with increasing selfhood or firmness of personal identity (or acceptance of one's own inner nature) B-cognition becomes easier and more frequent. (This is true even though D-cognition remains for *all* human beings, including the mature ones, the main tool for living-in-the-world.)

To the extent that perception is desire-less and fearless, to that extent it is more veridical, in the sense of perceiving the true, or essential or intrinsic whole nature of the object (without splitting it up by abstraction). Thus the goal of objective and true description of any reality is fostered by psychological health. Neurosis, psychosis, stunting of growth—all are, from this point of view, cognitive diseases as well, contaminating perception, learning, remembering, attending and thinking.

23. A by-product of this aspect of cognition is a better understanding of the higher and lower levels of love. D-love can be differentiated from B-love on approximately the same basis as D-cognition and B-cognition, or D-motivation and B-motivation. No ideally good relation to another human being, especially a child, is

possible without B-love. Especially is it necessary for teaching, along with the Taoistic, trusting attitude that it implies. This is also true for our relations with the natural world, i.e., we can treat it in its own right, or we can treat it as if it were there only for our purposes.

24. Though, in principle, self-actualization is easy, in practice it rarely happens (by my criteria, certainly in less than 1% of the adult population). For this, there are many, many reasons at various levels of discourse, including all the determinants of psychopathology that we now know. We have already mentioned one main cultural reason, i.e., the conviction that man's intrinsic nature is evil or dangerous,. and one biological determinant for the difficulty of achieving a mature self, namely that humans no longer have strong instincts which tell them unequivocally what to do, when, where and how.

There is a subtle but extremely important difference between regarding psychopathology as blocking or evasion or fear of growth toward self-actualization, and thinking of it in a medical fashion, as akin to invasion from without by tumors, poisons or bacteria, which have no relationship to the personality being invaded. Human diminution (the loss of human potentialities and capacities) is a more useful concept than "illness" for our theoretical purposes.

25. Growth has not only rewards and pleasures but also many intrinsic pains and always will have. Each step forward is a step into the unfamiliar and is possibly dangerous. It also means giving up something familiar and good and satisfying. It frequently means a parting and a separation, even a kind of death prior to rebirth, with consequent nostalgia, fear, loneliness and mourning. It also often means giving up a simpler and easier and less effortful life, in exchange for a more demanding, more responsible, more difficult life. Growth forward is in spite of these losses and therefore requires courage, will, choice, and strength in the individual, as well as protection, permission and encouragement from the environment, especially for the child.

26. It is therefore useful to think of growth or lack of it as the resultant of a dialectic between growth-fostering forces and growth-discouraging forces (regression, fear, pains of growth, ignorance, etc.). Growth has both advantages and disadvantages. Non-growing has not only disadvantages, but also advantages. The future pulls, but so also does the past. There is not only courage but also fear. The total ideal way of growing healthily is, in principle, to enhance. all the advantages of forward growth and all the disadvantages of

not-growing, and to diminish all the disadvantages of growth forward and all the advantages of not-growing.

Homeostatic tendencies, "need-reduction" tendencies, and Freudian defense mechanisms are not growth-tendencies but are often defensive, pain-reducing postures of the organism. But they are quite necessary and not always pathological. They are generally prepotent over growth-tendencies.

27. All this implies a naturalistic system of values, a byproduct of the empirical description of the deepest tendencies of the human species and of specific individuals. The study of the human being by science or by self-search can discover where he is heading, what is his purpose in life, what is good for him and what is bad for him, what will make him feel virtuous and what will make him feel guilty, why choosing the good is often difficult for him, what the attractions of evil are. (Observe that the word "ought" need not be used. Also such knowledge of man is relative to man only and does not purport to be "absolute.")

28. A neurosis is not part of the inner core but rather a defense against or evasion of it, as well as a distorted expression of it (under the aegis of fear). It is ordinarily a compromise between the effort to seek basic need gratifications in a covert or disguised or self-defeating way, and the fear of these needs, gratifications and motivated behaviors. To express neurotic needs, emotions, attitudes, definitions, actions, etc., means not to express the inner core or real self fully. If the sadist or exploiter or pervert says, "Why shouldn't *I* express myself?" (e.g., by killing), or, "Why shouldn't *I* actualize myself?" the answer to them is that such expression is a denial of, and not an expression of, instinctoid tendencies (or inner core).

Each neuroticized need, or emotion or action is a *loss of capacity* to the person, something that he cannot do or *dare* not do except in a sneaky and unsatisfying way. In addition, he has usually lost his subjective well-being, his will, and his feeling of self-control, his capacity for pleasure, his self-esteem, etc. He is diminished as a human being.

29. The state of being without a system of values is psychopathogenic, we are learning. The human being needs a framework of values, a philosophy of life, a religion or religion-surrogate to live by and understand by, in about the same sense that he needs sunlight, calcium or love. This I have called the "cognitive need to understand." The value-illnesses which result from valuelessness are called variously anhedonia, anomie, apathy, amorality, hope-

lessness, cynicism, etc., and can become somatic illness as well. Historically, we are in a value interregnum in which all externally given value systems have proven to be failures (political, economic, religious, etc.), e.g., nothing is worth dying for. What man needs but doesn't have, he seeks for unceasingly, and he becomes dangerously ready to jump at any hope, good or bad. The cure for this disease is obvious. We need a validated, usable system of human values that we can believe in and devote ourselves to (be willing to die for), because they are true rather than because we are exhorted to "believe and have faith." Such an empirically based *Weltanschauung* seems now to be a real possibility, at least in theoretical outline.

Much disturbance in children and adolescents can be understood as a consequence of the uncertainty of adults about their values. As a consequence, many youngsters in the United States live not by adult values but by adolescent values, which of course are immature, ignorant and heavily determined by confused adolescent needs. An excellent projection of these adolescent values is the cowboy, "Western" movie, or the delinquent gang.

30. At the level of self-actualizing, many dichotomies become resolved, opposites are seen to be unities and the whole dichotomous way of thinking is recognized to be immature. For self-actualizing people, there is a strong tendency for selfishness and unselfishness to fuse into a higher, superordinate unity. Work tends to be the same as play; vocation and avocation become the same thing. When duty is pleasant and pleasure is fulfillment of duty, then they lose their separateness and oppositeness. The highest maturity is discovered to include a childlike quality, and we discover healthy children to have some of the qualities of mature self-actualization. The inner-outer split, between self and all else, gets fuzzy and much less sharp, and they are seen to be permeable to each other at the highest levels of personality development. Dichotomizing seems now to be characteristic of a lower level of personality development and of psychological functioning; it is both a cause and an effect of psychopathology.

31. One especially important finding in self-actualizing people is that they tend to integrate the Freudian dichotomies and trichotomies, i.e., the conscious, preconscious and the unconscious (as well as id, ego, superego). The Freudian "instincts" and the defenses are less sharply set off against each other. The impulses are more expressed and less controlled; the controls are less rigid, inflexible, anxiety-determined. The superego is less harsh and punishing and

less set off against the ego. The primary and secondary cognitive processes are more equally available and more equally valued (instead of the primary processes being stigmatized as pathological). Indeed, in the "peak-experience" the walls between them tend to fall together.

This is in sharp contrast with the early Freudian position in which these various forces were sharply dichotomized as (a) mutually exclusive, (b) with antagonistic interests, i.e., as antagonistic forces rather than as complementary or collaborating ones, and (c) one "better" than the other.

Again we imply here (sometimes) a healthy unconscious, and desirable regression. Furthermore, we imply also an integration of rationality and irrationality with the consequence that irrationality may, in its place, also be considered healthy, desirable or even necessary.

32. Healthy people are more integrated in another way. In them the conative, the cognitive, the affective and the motor are less separated from each other, and are more synergic, i.e., working collaboratively without conflict to the same ends. The conclusions of rational, careful thinking are apt to come to the same conclusions as those of the blind appetites. What such a person wants and enjoys is apt to be just what is good for him. His spontaneous reactions are as capable, efficient and right as if they had been thought out in advance. His sensory and motor reactions are more closely correlated. His sensory modalities are more connected with each other (physiognomical perception). Furthermore, we have learned the difficulties and dangers of those age-old rationalistic systems in which the capacities were thought to be arranged dichotomously-hierarchically, with rationality at the top, rather than in an integration.

33. This development toward the concept of a healthy unconscious, and of a healthy irrationality, sharpens our awareness of the limitations of purely abstract thinking, of verbal thinking and of analytic thinking. If our hope is to describe the world fully, a place is necessary for preverbal, ineffable, metaphorical, primary process, concrete-experience, intuitive and esthetic types of cognition, for there are certain aspects of reality which can be cognized in no other way. Even in science this is true, now that we know 1) that creativity has its roots in the nonrational, 2) that language is and must always be inadequate to describe total reality, 3) that any abstract concept leaves out much of reality, and 4) that what we call "knowledge" (which is usually highly abstract and verbal and

sharply defined) often serves to blind us to those portions of reality not covered by the abstraction. That is, it makes us more able to see some things, but *less* able to see other things. Abstract knowledge has its dangers as well as its uses.

Science and education, being too exclusively abstract, verbal and bookish, don't have enough place for raw, concrete, esthetic experience, especially of the subjective happenings inside oneself. For instance, organismic psychologists would certainly agree on the desirability of more creative education in perceiving and creating art, in dancing, in (Greek style) athletics and in phenomenological observation.

The ultimate of abstract, analytical thinking, is the greatest simplification possible, i.e., the formula, the diagram, the map, the blueprint, the schema, the cartoon, and certain types of abstract paintings. Our mastery of the world is enhanced thereby, but its richness may be lost as a forfeit, *unless* we learn to value B-cognitions, perception-with-love-and-care, free-floating attention, all of which enrich the experience instead of impoverishing it. There is no reason why "science" should not be expanded to include both kinds of knowing.

34. This ability of healthier people to dip into the unconscious and preconscious, to use and value their primary processes instead of fearing them, to accept their impulses instead of always controlling them, to be able to regress voluntarily without fear, turns out to be one of the main conditions of creativity. We can then understand why psychological health is so closely tied up with certain universal forms of creativeness (aside from special-talent), as to lead some writers to make them almost synonymous.

This same tie between health and integration of rational and irrational forces (conscious and unconscious, primary and secondary processes) also permits us to understand why psychologically healthy people are more able to enjoy, to love, to laugh, to have fun, to be humorous, to be silly, to be whimsical and fantastic, to be pleasantly "crazy," and in general to permit and value and enjoy emotional experiences in general and peak experiences in particular and to have them more often. And it leads us to the strong suspicion that learning *ad hoc* to be able to do all these things may help the child move toward health.

35. Esthetic perceiving and creating and esthetic peak-experiences are seen to be a central aspect of human life and of psychology and education rather than a peripheral one. This is true for several reasons. 1) All the peak-experiences are (among other character-

istics) integrative of the splits within the person, between persons, within the world, and between the person and the world. Since one aspect of health is integration, the peak-experiences are moves toward health and are themselves, momentary healths. 2) These experiences are life-validating, i.e., they make life worth while. These are certainly an important part of the answer to the question, "Why don't we all commit suicide?" 3) They are worth while in themselves, etc.

36. Self-actualization does not mean a transcendence of all human problems. Conflict, anxiety, frustration, sadness, hurt and guilt can all be found in healthy human beings. In general, the movement, with increasing maturity, is from neurotic pseudo-problems to the real, unavoidable, existential problems, inherent in the nature of man (even at his best) living in a particular kind of world. Even though he is not neurotic he may be troubled by real, desirable and necessary guilt rather than neurotic guilt (which isn't desirable or necessary), by an intrinsic conscience (rather than the Freudian superego). Even though he has transcended the problems of Becoming, there remain the problems of Being. To be untroubled when one *should* be troubled can be a sign of sickness. Sometimes, smug people have to be scared *"into* their wits."

37. Self-actualization is not altogether general. It takes place via femaleness or maleness, which are prepotent to general-humanness. That is, one must first be a healthy, femaleness-fulfilled woman or maleness-fulfilled man before general-human self-actualization becomes possible.

There is also a little evidence that different constitutional types actualize themselves in somewhat different ways (because they have different inner selves to actualize).

38. Another crucial aspect of healthy growth of selfhood and full-humanness is dropping away the techniques used by the child, in his weakness and smallness for adapting himself to the strong, large, all-powerful, omniscient, godlike adults. He must replace these with techniques of being strong and independent and of being a parent himself. This involves especially giving up the child's desperate wish for the exclusive, total love of his parents while learning to love others. He must learn to gratify his own needs and wishes, rather than the needs of his parents, and he must learn to gratify them himself, rather than depending upon the parents to do this for him. He must give up being good out of fear and in order to keep their love, and must be good because *he* wishes to be. He must discover his own conscience and give up his internalized

parents as a sole ethical guide. All these techniques by which weakness adapts itself to strength are necessary for the child but immature and stunting in the adult (Maslow, Rand and Newman, 1960). He must replace fear with courage.

39. From this point of view, a society or a culture can be either growth-fostering or growth-inhibiting. The sources of growth and of humanness are essentially within the human person and are not created or invented by society, which can only help or hinder the development of humanness, just as a gardener can help or hinder the growth of a rosebush, but cannot determine that it shall be an oak tree. This is true even though we know that a culture is a *sine qua non* for the actualization of humanness itself, e.g., language, abstract thought, ability to love; but these exist as potentialities in human germ plasm prior to culture.

This makes theoretically possible a comparative sociology, transcending and including cultural relativity. The "better" culture gratifies all basic human needs and premits self-actualization. The "poorer" cultures do not. The same is true for education. To the extent that it fosters growth toward self-actualization, it is "good" education.

As soon as we speak of "good" or "bad" cultures, and take them as means rather than as ends, the concept of "adjustment" comes into question. We must ask, "What kind of culture or subculture is the 'well adjusted' person well adjusted *to*?" Adjustment is, very definitely, *not* necessarily synonymous with psychological health.

40. The achievement of self-actualization (in the sense of autonomy) paradoxically makes more possible the transcendence of self, and of self-consciousness and selfishness. It makes it easier for the person to be homonomous, i.e., to merge himself as a part in a larger whole than himself (Angyal, 1941). The condition of the fullest homonomy is full autonomy, and to some extent, vice versa, one can attain to autonomy only via successful homonomous experiences (child dependence, B-love, care for others, etc.). It is necessary to speak of levels of homonomy (more and more mature), and to differentiate a "low homonomy" (of fear, weakness, and regression) from a "high homonomy" (of courage and full, self-confident autonomy), a "low Nirvana" from a "high Nirvana," union downward from union upward (Weisskopf, 1958).

41. An important existential problem is posed by the fact that self-actualizing persons (and *all* people in their peak-experiences) occasionally live out-of-time and out-of-the-world (atemporal and

aspatial) even though mostly they must live in the outer world. Living in the inner psychic world (which is ruled by psychic laws and not by the laws of outer-reality), i.e., the world of experience, of emotion, of wishes and fears and hopes, of love, of poetry, art, and fantasy, is different from living in and adapting to the non-psychic reality which runs by laws he never made and which are not essential to his nature even though he has to live by them. (He could, after all, live in other kinds of worlds, as any science fiction fan knows.) The person who is not afraid of this inner, psychic world, can enjoy it to such an extent that it may be called Heaven by contrast with the more effortful, fatiguing, externally responsible world of "reality," of striving and coping, of right and wrong, of truth and falsehood. This is true even though the healthier person can also adapt more easily and enjoyably to the "real" world, and has better "reality testing," i.e., doesn't confuse it with his inner psychic world.

It seems clear now that confusing these inner and outer realities, or having either closed off from experience, is highly pathological. The healthy person is able to integrate them both into his life and therefore has to give up neither, being able to go back and forth voluntarily. The difference is the same as the one between the person who can visit the slums and the one who is forced to live there always. (Either world is a slum if one can't leave it.) Then, paradoxically, that which was sick and pathological and the "lowest" becomes part of the healthiest and "highest" aspect of human nature. Slipping into "craziness" is frightening only for those who are not fully confident of their sanity. Education must help the person to live in both worlds.

42. The foregoing propositions generate a different understanding of the role of action in psychology. Goal-directed, motivated, coping, striving, purposeful action is an aspect or by-product of the necessary transactions between a psyche and a non-psychic world.

a) The D-need gratifications come from the world outside the person, not from within. Therefore adaptation to this world is made necessary, e.g., reality-testing, knowing the nature of this world, learning to differentiate this world from the inner world, learning the nature of people and of society, learning to delay gratification, learning to conceal what would be dangerous, learning which portions of the world are gratifying and which dangerous, or useless for need-gratification, learning the approved and permitted cultural paths to gratification and techniques of gratification.

b) The world is in itself interesting, beautiful and fascinating. Exploring it, manipulating it, playing with it, contemplating it, enjoying it are all motivated kinds of action (cognitive, motor, and esthetic needs).

But there is also action which has little or nothing to do with the world, at any rate at first. Sheer expression of the nature or state or powers (*Funktionslust*) of the organism is an expression of Being rather than of striving (Buhler, 1924). And the contemplation and enjoyment of the inner life not only is a kind of "action" in itself but is also antithetical to action in the world, i.e., it produces stillness and cessation of muscular activity. The ability to wait is a special case of being able to suspend action.

43. From Freud we learned that the past exists *now* in the person. Now we must learn, from growth theory and self-actualization theory that the future also *now* exists in the person in the form of ideals, hopes, duties, tasks, plans, goals, unrealized potentials, mission, fate, destiny, etc. One for whom no future exists is reduced to the concrete, to hopelessness, to emptiness. For him, time must be endlessly "filled." Striving, the usual organizer of most activity, when lost, leaves the person unorganized and unintegrated.

Of course, being in a state of Being needs no future, because it is already *there.* Then Becoming ceases for the moment and its promissory notes are cashed in the form of the ultimate rewards, i.e., the peak-experiences, in which time disappears and hopes are fulfilled.

REFERENCES

Angyal, A. *Foundations for a Science of Personality.* New York: Commonwealth Fund, 1941.

Buhler, K. *Die geistige Entwickling des Kindes.* 4th ed. Jena: Fischer, 1924.

Maslow, A. H. *Motivation and Personality.* New York: Harper, 1954.

Maslow, A. H., Rand, H., & Newman, S. Some parallels between the dominance and sexual behavior of monkeys and the fantasies of psychoanalytic patients. *J. nerv. ment. Dis.,* 1960, 131:202-212.

Murphy, G. *Personality.* New York: Harper, 1947.

Weisskopf, W. Existence and values. In A. H. Maslow (Ed.) *New Knowledge of Human Values.* New York: Harper, 1959.

7

REALITY THERAPY:
A REALISTIC APPROACH TO THE YOUNG OFFENDER

William Glasser, M.D.

The first important step in correcting a young offender's behavior is to find out what it is you are trying to correct. Most of
the theories contained in the literature on juvenile delinquency
are psychoanalytic in nature (emphasizing unconscious intraper-
sonal conflict), sociological (stressing environmental difficulties), or
some combination of both. To illustrate, let me present the case of
a sixteen-year-old girl who has run away from home, indulged in
heterosexual and homosexual activity, prostituted, experimented
with narcotics, tatooed herself, and, in final custody, attempted
suicide by slashing her wrists. If I stopped now and asked you the
cause of her behavior I'm sure no one would venture an opinion.
Rather, you would ask me to give more information than this brief
description. From your training and experience, you would feel
uncomfortable about committing yourself without some history,
psychological tests, and background investigation of the girl. Very
likely you would call on someone to make a psychiatric evaluation.
Even with this information, many of you would still disagree,
according to the way you have been taught, your experience, and
the amount of introspection you have done.

One value of the theory [of reality therapy], and the therapy
based upon it, is that it circumvents any disagreement over what
caused the girl's behavior and it sharply reduces the need for the
usual diagnostic procedures. Further, this theory, if clearly under-

Adapted from a speech presented to the British Columbia Correctional Association, Vancouver, Canada, Nov. 3, 1962. Reprinted by permission of the
author and *Crime and Delinquency*, 1964, April: 135-144.

stood, can be used not only by trained psychotherapists but by everyone who comes in contact with the young offender, from the arresting officer to the parole officer. Only a consistent method of treatment, an approach that can be used to some extent by everyone in correction, will help young people in trouble.

THE THEORY

Personal Responsibility. The theory of "reality therapy" has been developed in the past seven years in consultation with a colleague, Dr. G. L. Harrington, who uses it exclusively with mental patients at the Los Angeles Veterans' Administration Center Neuropsychiatric Hospital and in his private practice. It is based on our belief that regardless of what he has done, how he feels, where he comes from, his size, shape, mental ability, physical condition, or heredity, the young offender suffers from a universal malady: he is unwilling to take responsibility for his behavior. We further believe that correctional problems are only a more dramatic expression of the lack of responsibility which is really a basic problem in all psychiatric work. The children and adults we deal with in correction express this irresponsibility directly by the act of breaking the law. Patients in mental hospitals express it by partially or completely withdrawing into a world of their own creation. The homosexual, for example, cannot take a responsible sex role although he may be perfectly responsible in other areas. The depressed patient is unable responsibly to express the intense anger he feels, so he turns it inward and becomes depressed. The obsessive-compulsive neurotic tries desperately to compensate for his basic lack of responsibility by becoming superresponsible—so much so that he can accomplish little because of his compulsive symptoms. Thus, all people who function badly in our society suffer from this difficulty, but none of them expresses it as clearly and as directly as the lawbreaker.

All the effort in the world to discover why a child is irresponsible and breaks the law won't change the fact that he is irresponsible. Neither will all the treatment we can muster, unless this treatment is from the start concerned with guiding the patient toward becoming a more responsible person right now. This is why we claim that diagnosis based on detailed studies is meaningless; however superficial or deep the explanation may be, the ultimate fact remains that the person involved is not acting or thinking in a responsible manner.

In the traditional process of looking for explanations and diagnoses, a reason for deviant behavior will often seem clear. For example, the psychotherapist may find out that a homosexual girl is afraid of men because her father was both brutal and seductive, so she turns toward women for gratification. When he understands this, and even when *she* understands this, he is in a poor position to help her because he has advanced a reasonable cause for her behavior. Dr. Harrington and I do not believe, as the traditional therapist does, that this understanding will allow her to relate to a man who is not her father. We believe that all she will understand is that the situation is just as she feared—men can be brutal and so it is much safer to remain homosexual. The psychotherapist's initial efforts have, in a sense, only made the girl's trouble more reasonable. She now has an excuse to stay the way she is. In fact, everyone is looking for an excuse for her behavior.

But our job is to make her behavior less reasonable, to help her take the responsibility she must take as a woman in order for her to turn away from this deviant approach to sex. Our job is not to discuss her father (who may or may not have been brutal) but to relate to her now so that she can feel that men are human beings with whom she can make emotional contact.

Therefore, if we want to face reality, we must admit that we can never rewrite a person's history. No matter how much we can understand about the cruel and unusual circumstances which led to his behavior, his neurosis, his ulcer, his depression, or his drug addiction, there is nothing this information can do for us or for him except reinforce the concept that indeed he has a reason to break the law and excuse this transgression on the ground that he is "sick." Therefore we emphasize what traditional therapy tries to ignore: No matter what happened to him, he still has the responsibility for what he does.

If we continue to accept the offender's irresponsibility because of his traumatic history, we become trapped from a therapeutic standpoint. With noncriminal psychiatric problems, we often avoid facing this trap directly. A man with a neurosis can come for traditional treatment indefinitely or a psychotic patient can be locked up for years in a mental hospital; neither exerts great pressure on anyone because his irresponsibility primarily hurts himself.

When a man breaks the law, however, we have to help him because, unless he becomes more responsible, he endangers us. Either we must help him to become more responsible or we must lock him up indefinitely. It is unrealistic to keep him locked up once he has demonstrated that he has gained responsibility. It is not up to us in correction to advance explanations for irresponsibility, but to recognize that individual responsibility must be the goal of our treatment.

Treatment, Not Punishment. At this point, many will think that I just want to return to the old Mosaic concept of "an eye for an eye" to punish the wrongdoer severely. Nothing could be further from my intention. What I advocate is treatment, not punishment. Until an offender can accept the fact that he is responsible for what he did, there can be no treatment in our field. If, as in the first example, the girl prostituted, both she and those who treat her must understand that she did it voluntarily and that better possibilities were open to her than prostitution. Until this is established, there is no treatment. I do not consider it punishment to confront her with her wrongdoing. She has to face both her lack of responsibility and the implication that this is not the way she has to be. She must see that we think she can do better.

From a treatment standpoint, exactly what a person did is of little importance. What matters is in how many areas of his present life he is responsible. The more we find, the easier he is to treat and the better his prognosis. (This is why in many cases it is easier to rehabilitate a murderer than any other criminal. Except for the single grossly irresponsible act, many murderers are fairly responsible people.) Thus, the crux of our theory of reality therapy is personal responsibility.

Describing the Offender. Under our concept, a helpful description of a young female offender might consist of a phrase such as "chronic runaway with minor sex delinquency but moderately responsible" and a brief outline of the areas in which she is responsible and those in which she is not. This description would give everyone working with her some basis for what to expect from her. It would indicate where we should work and where not too much effort is needed. It might further indicate, if she were a fairly responsible older girl, that she would be a good candidate for self-parole. We might, on the other hand, describe a narcotics addict as a young man who takes no responsibility for his behavior and lives only for the feeling that narcotics bring him. He can then be periodically reevaluated and treated until he can take more responsibility in important areas of his life.

The theory can be used by the judge, the probation or parole officer, and the psychiatrist, as well as by the nonprofessional correctional personnel because it can be easily understood without the use of such nebulous jargon as "insight," "conflict resolution," or "transference work-through."

Happiness—a Stumbling Block. In addition to coming to grips with his irresponsible behavior, the offender must also face the question of that ill-defined term, happiness. From a treatment standpoint, happiness can be a huge stumbling block. Most children who get into trouble do so in the pursuit of what they conceive to be happiness—"kicks" to escape boredom, to "feel high." The big obstacle in treatment is that upon inquiry into the life of the young offender, we generally find a wealth of material to indicate that he was unhappy. We then wrongly conclude that unhappiness leads to delinquency. When we find the mountains of misery that these children carry on their shoulders, our first human reaction is to do something to make them happy. So we try to change their environment, find them a good foster home, feed, clothe, and provide for their recreation. Then we wonder why they are not happier after we have done so much. After our good treatment why do they return to their old habits? We are puzzled because we haven't been taught that we can't make people happy, that unhappiness is the result, not the cause, of irresponsibility.

Therefore, in reality therapy, we ignore the unhappy past, but provide the offender with an opportunity to benefit himself in a responsible way. When a girl at Ventura comes to me and says she is unhappy, I won't sympathize. I'll listen, and then I'll suggest that she herself could do something about her problems. I'll further suggest what she might do. I'm a compassionate human being who wants to teach her better ways, but I'm not a crying towel. I don't promise to produce happiness or alleviate misery; it's not my job as a psychiatrist. That is up to her. In the same vein, I'll never do anything to keep her from taking responsibility, no matter how initially upsetting this may be. I'll never change the rules, no matter how much she begs, and I won't give her tranquilizers which promise her happiness without responsibility. Only when she becomes more responsible will she be in a position to find some lasting happiness.

Past—Nonessential to Treatment. A final part of the theory is our belief that what happens to a person now is more important than anything which happened in the near or remote past. One has to assume that everything a person thinks and does in the present is a sum total of his past, that each present action carries with it roots from his whole existence. Although few psychiatrists will argue against this statement, most will nevertheless draw conclusions far different from the ones Dr. Harrington and I propose. The precept traditionally accepted and taught as essential to therapy is that a person cannot understand or change his present behavior unless he is able to tie it clearly to roots in the past. Logically, however, this view becomes redundant if one accepts the previous statement that the present is already a summation of the past. This redundancy, the crux of traditional therapy, is what causes the fruitless historical journeys, diagnostic studies, and unending psychotherapy which lead to excusing the offender's present actions as an unfortunate culmination of his history.

Our view of this assumption is much different. The present as the sum of the past is all that's really important. If a delinquent boy can understand that what he has been doing is irresponsible and can modify his present behavior, then his pathological past is effectively nullified. The object of our treatment is to replace his past experiences with what goes on between him and his various reality therapists. The boy will be willing and ready to accept reality therapy because he realizes it was his present behavior that resulted in his being locked up, and the indirect cause—his father's rejection of him, let us say—is forever beyond his or our control. In attempting to relate to the reality therapist, he must overcome the obstacles of reality, not run from them. Although this course is harder for both, he will readily accept it if it is presented in a firm but compassionate way. Reality therapy treats the youngster as a potentially responsible adult rather than as an unfortunate child. On the other hand, traditional psychiatry, by dragging him back into his forgotten past, blocks his progress and excuses his behavior, thereby leaving him exactly where he was before—or worse.

THE THERAPIST

All psychiatric theory is meaningless unless there is a therapist who knows how to use it to help the young offender. One therapist may know theory from A to Z and still be unable to provide the warmth and strength needed to make contact, while another who has these essential qualities may have no knowledge of theory whatever and still do some good. No one, delinquent or not, can become responsible without some warm human involvement with a strong mature person who cares about him. It takes human contact alone to initiate treatment. Books, movies, records, music, poetry, or lectures all will help make a responsible person more responsible, but he will be powerless to use these cultural advantages unless he has had good human relationships to start with.

The reality therapist has to assume that in the life of the young offender no one was close enough to enable him to feel worthwhile enough to take responsibility for himself. Unless we can provide this person, we will fail. The more people we can provide, the greater chance we have in succeeding. One caution, however: the delinquent youngster must be seen in a situation where his behavior can be controlled before a therapist can make progress. Merely sending the young offender to a psychiatrist while placing no control over the rest of his life is rarely successful. Without some external control, few therapists can provide enough firm contact in the brief time allotted to have a practical effect on their patient.

Abiding by the Rules. Expensive, well-designed, fully staffed institutions will have little effect unless each staff member takes a personal interest in the inmates. But "personal interest" does not mean condoning poor behavior. It means rigorous enforcement of the rules and realistic praise. No matter how bad his offense, we must show belief that the offender can become more responsible.

Never missing an opportunity to praise present responsible behavior, we must become as involved as possible with his strong points, his interests, his hopes, his fears—anything not tied up with his irresponsible past. If he wants to talk about his escapades, we should show little interest because he is testing us. If we are real friends, we should not be interested in his wrongdoing. If we are interested in it, then he has gained our attention through harming himself, and when he leaves will do so again. Our interest must emphasize the positive, never reinforce the negative aspect.

Just what do we, the reality therapists, do in an actual situation? Suppose, for example, the youngster runs away. What should be done with him once he's found? If the institution rules say he must be locked up securely for a few weeks, then the rules must be followed. This does not mean, however, that we reject him personally because of it. We're both sorry for the act but we go on from there. We do not ask him *why* he ran away, but we show him how his doing so has caused him to suffer.

Although this sort of treatment may sound rigid, we have so very little time that what we might overlook in more responsible people we have to be on guard for with the young people in our charge. Ventura School is one of the strictest institutions in California, yet most of the girls are happy and anyone is free to come in and talk with any girl at any time. No matter how strict we get, the girls always tell us we are too lenient, that we ought to tighten up.

Each person in an institution must function in his own framework. The cook is not a psychiatrist, the psychiatrist is not a cook. All persons in contact with the young offender must stick to their own skills and help in their areas of competence. The mechanics instructor should expect high standards of work performance from the young men assigned to him: he should not become their counselor because that would be false. The boys and girls have met many phonies in the world who feign deep interest in their problems but who, by their excessive willingness to listen to their tales of wrongdoing, are—at best—unwillingly evading their responsibility of guiding them toward a better life or—at worst—living vicariously through the children's misdeeds.

Too much listening to problems is one of the best ways of remaining detached and uninvolved because the young person knows that you can do nothing about his troubles. Listen for a short time, then offer him your skills. Accept him at your level, not his.

REALITY THERAPY IN PRACTICE

I would like to describe an ideal reality therapy situation— something we try very hard to approximate at Ventura School. But even what I describe as ideal for this institution has inherent shortcomings because when the young offender is apprehended it is usually late in his career. In many cases the school authorities, his parents, and others were aware of his delinquent potential well before he was arrested. With this in mind, let us look at realistic treatment of the young offender.

Let us suppose that tonight at 11 p.m. a police officer apprehended a sixteen-year-old boy who has just wrecked a stolen car in his effort to escape pursuit. In custody, he should first be given a careful physical examination and be checked to see whether he is under the influence of narcotics or alcohol. Police questions should be fair but brief. His parents should be notified and asked to cooperate, and he should be informed about his legal rights. The police should let him know the charge and ask him, in an unthreatening manner, whether he wants to make a statement. No attempt should be made to obtain a long statement that night. When questions are mandatory, they should concern the circumstances of, not the reasons for, his offenses. Open-end questions, such as "Why did you do it?" should be avoided. If he wishes, his story should be recorded without comment and he should be locked up, preferably alone, for the night. From a treatment standpoint, it's best, at first, to engage him in little conversation or questioning but to allow him time to think over his behavior.

Even if he is to be released in the morning, he should spend one night by himself in custody because now, more than at any other time, he may begin to think that he has done something wrong and that he has some responsibility for it. Too much questioning, too much initial conversation, gives him the opportunity to make excuses, to feel antagonistic toward authority, to justify in his mind that what he did was not very wrong or, if wrong, not really his fault. As soon as possible and throughout reality therapy, we must give him a chance to compare his values to his behavior, because ultimately the strength of this comparison will determine his future.

In the morning, assuming that he is to be kept, he should be taken to the detention home, where the rules should be carefully explained to him, whether or not he has been there before. We can never assume that the youngster already knows the rules, for, if he breaks one of them, this assumption allows him to blame us for not carefully explaining them.

An experienced staff member—a counselor, caseworker, or psychologist—should work with him until his case is decided in court. This counselor should see him as soon as possible and at regular intervals during his detention. In the interviews, he should put the boy at ease (allowing him to smoke if necessary), reread the charge along with the boy's statement, and ask him whether he wants to add or subtract anything. This should be done in a friendly, unaccusing way, but the situation should be reviewed so that the boy knows definitely what he is charged with.

Discussion should continue until the boy understands that he is being locked up because he broke the law. When this point has been reached (hopefully, during the first interview), the counselor should tell the boy that he would like to help him keep out of further trouble. If the boy is hostile or uncooperative, the counselor should tell him to think about it. The counselor should never return his hostility and never pressure him with "help." He should continue to see the boy regularly, but make no further issue over treatment.

The remainder of the counseling situation should be a discussion of the following three points:

1. Has the boy done anything else illegal or wrong? This is a short, factual discussion, not a case history. Hence the question of right and wrong will probably arise, as will the question of the boy's own values and standards. The counselor should ask the boy what his parents or relatives think of his offense. How do their values compare to his? Is he ashamed of what he has done? Does he feel guilty? If he does, this is good; he should. (The counselor should never lighten the guilt; it is the most powerful weapon we have. This does not mean he should add to it, but he should not attempt to reduce it.) The therapist should also ask the boy what he has done that he considers responsible, something he can be proud of.

2. How is he getting along in the detention home right now? Does he feel that anything is unfair? If he has any complaints or he feels unjustly treated, the realities of life in a detention home should again be clarified.

3. Subsequent interviews should dwell more and more on his future plans. The counselor should review the various possibilities that will be decided in court—release to parent, probation, or training school. The therapist should be open with the boy, keep nothing secret from him. Both have to face the reality of the disposition. Does the boy have a home to go to? Does he *want* to go home? What does he think is the best place for him? Does he want to go to school, to work, to be trained for a vocation? A long discussion of his future will help him begin to feel responsibility for himself, the goal of reality therapy.

The counselor must never discuss causes—just or unjust—for the boy's actions or imply that he was emotionally disturbed. Our job is to help him, not convince him he's deeply maladjusted.

Further conversations can inquire about his friends. Whom would he like to visit him? The counselor should encourage the boy to write to the people he likes. The boy should not be made to feel that he would be better off without anyone he considers near or dear to him—even if the counselor feels these people are not a good influence. Attempts to sever close attachments will usually produce more trouble than benefits. Above all, the counselor should never imply that the boy's family or anyone is in any way responsible for his predicament. The boy's responsibility is to be a better person, and doing so may cause his parents and society to improve their attitudes toward him.

The counselor's report to the court should sum up the degree of responsibility and maturity found in the boy. Does he have a workable set of standards or values which he can use when not closely supervised? How much of what he says is just talk and how much does he really mean? Is he somewhat *over*willing to admit irresponsibility (which is another way of saying, "I'm so mixed up I don't know what I'm doing")? Will someone enjoy working with him? What kind of person would work best with him? What is the best treatment for him in view of the material gathered?

When the report is completed and the recommendation made, it should be read and discussed with the boy so he knows where he stands and what will be brought up in court.

In court, the judge should again review the charges and the report. This repetition, though monotonous, is extremely important to the boy. It means we care. The boy's parents should be present and be given a chance to make a statement. If the judge, on the counselor's recommendation, decides to send the boy to a training school, he should state exactly where the boy will go, the approximate length of his stay, and what he can expect to do there. This means that the judge himself should have an accurate idea of the program at that school. The judge will also want to discuss how often the parents may visit and what responsibility they will take for their son while he is away. The judge then should take the boy aside, wish him luck, and perhaps tell him of other boys who have succeeded after going through training school. This extra personal touch from an authoritative power can often make a great impression on young people in trouble who, despite appearances, are as impressionable about good things as they are about the bad.

The boy leaves the court with the idea that a better future is up to him, not us, but that we'll help as much as we can. He arrives at the training school understanding that what was done has been for him, not to him. Once there, he should be assigned a primary counselor trained in reality therapy who can continue what has been started, usually in group therapy. Here again, the charge is reviewed and the rules carefully explained. As soon as possible, he should participate in a training program conducted by staff who do not "counsel" but who point out what he is doing wrong and show him better ways.

What constitutes a good training program is, of course, another subject in itself. Briefly, I think it should be a program that teaches a youngster something useful for at least eight hours a day. Idleness and make-work are deadly.

A youngster's progress should be praised, but if he breaks the rules he should suffer reasonable consequences. Discipline for serious breaches should be complete isolation from the main program, followed by isolation from the recreational aspects of the program, and finally return to full program. This will be adequate punishment, however, only if the program is attractive enough to be missed. Corporal punishment is never justified.

Gradually, the youngster should be given more responsibility. He should be permitted week-end visits home in order to become acclimated to the place where he will live when he leaves the school. This is preferable to a sudden shift from school to parole.

The therapist who becomes involved with a boy's life cannot help feeling a little hurt and angry when the boy breaks the rules or gets into trouble in the school. If there is real feeling between them, the boy will always have the ability, in a sense, to hurt the therapist; but the therapist should always point out that when he is hurt, the boy is the real loser. The counselor who shows no emotion really isn't involved in treating this particular boy.

When the boy is discharged, treatment should be continued by the parole officer until a responsible adjustment at work, at school, or at home is made.

Reality therapy is much more than this brief introductory article can possibly explain. It is, in our opinion, the only kind of psychiatric treatment which works for behavior problems. When employed by everyone in the institution it works extremely well, and the positive results can be easily seen.

Young delinquents want the mature, responsible treatment that we offer and they are young and flexible enough to be helped quickly. Where this therapy is employed, there is no schism between treatment and custody.

Because reality therapy works so well in both large and small group therapy situations, it is especially suited for institutional practice. It does away with the need for expensive testing, record keeping, and numerous time-consuming speculative conferences. The only records needed are occasional notes about what has occurred that shows increased responsibility. If the boy fails, the reason is that we were not able to help him become responsible enough to live in society. We need no detailed record of this failure to explain why. The fact that the boy failed speaks for itself. We are human enough to admit that extenuating circumstances are of solace to us as therapists, but they are meaningless to the child whose parole is revoked. If all the time spent in keeping records and conferring about why we or our patients failed were devoted to doing reality therapy, there would be far fewer failures in correctional psychiatry.

8

AN INFORMAL DISCUSSION
OF BIOCENTRIC THERAPY

Nathaniel Branden, Ph.D.

Let me begin by explaining why I characterize my approach to psychology and psychotherapy as "biocentric."

"Biocentric" means: life-centered. So a biocentric psychology is one that approaches the study of human beings from a biological or a life-centered perspective. What does this mean?

A human being is an organism—a living entity. Like all other organisms, he has needs and capacities. And like all other organisms, his primary task is to exercise his capacities so as effectively to satisfy his needs, to preserve and enhance his well-being. The way in which an individual deals with this task is the key to his psychology.

It is characteristic of the state of contemporary thought that if one speaks of advocating a biologically oriented or biocentric psychology, the listener is very likely to assume that one intends to study man with his head omitted, i.e., without reference to his mind or his power of conceptual thought. Yet the behavioristic or physicalistic or "guillotine" approach to man is profoundly antibiological. In the study of a living species, the biologist is vitally interested in learning the nature of that species' distinctive means of survival, since he recognizes that such information constitutes an indispensible key to the species' behavior. In the case of man, it is clear that *his* distinctive way of dealing with reality, of coping with his environment—of maintaining his existence—is through the exercise of his conceptual faculty. All of his unique attainments—scientific knowledge, technological and industrial achievements, art, culture, social institutions, etc.,—

This paper is a revised version of a lecture given at the Psychological Clinic, Rutgers University, September 21, 1973.

proceed from and are made possible by his ability to think. It is upon his ability to think that his life depends. A biocentric approach requires that one grant prime importance to man's conceptual faculty in the study of behavior (Branden, 1969).

Thus I want to emphasize that when I speak of man's needs and capacities, I am not speaking merely of his *physical* needs and capacities. As a being who exhibits a conceptual form of consciousness, man has distinctive *psychological* needs and capacities, firmly rooted in his biological nature; to cite two prime examples: he has a need of self-esteem—and he has the capacity to think (which includes the capacity to judge and evaluate his own behavior).

THE CONCEPT OF PSYCHOLOGICAL WELL-BEING

From a biological point of view, the basic function of human consciousness is *awareness*—and, collaterally, the regulation of behavior.

If a person is to act effectively, if he is to maintain and further his life, he requires a knowledge of his environment and of his own state—of external reality and of internal reality—of the world and of self. In order to function successfully, a person needs to be in contact with the universe in which he acts—and with his own needs, feelings, desires, frustrations, capabilities and goals. To the extent that his awareness is blocked, to the extent that he is blind to facts about the world or about himself which, in the absence of his blocks, would be available to him, his life and well-being are impaired.

A human being is free to seek awareness or to avoid it. To the extent that contact with reality is his goal, and to the extent that he is unblocked and unobstructed, a person tends to maintain a free, natural, spontaneous flow of awareness back and forth between the outer world and the inner, as circumstances require. An individual's needs, interests, goals and general context, at any given moment, determine the aspects of external reality that will be drawn into the forefront of awareness.

A blindness concerning important aspects of self leads to a blindness concerning important aspects of the environment. For instance, a person who denies the presence of a need may be oblivious to opportunities to satisfy that need. A person who denies the reality of his pain will be blind to the source of the pain and may continually re-expose himself to new hurt. A person who guiltily disowns certain of his own desires may, via projection, falsely attribute them to others. We deal here with a profoundly important law of psychological functioning: *awareness moves freely in both directions—or it moves freely in neither.*

Thus, a person's psychology is biologically adaptive, a person is "mentally healthy," to the extent that the functioning of his consciousness is unimpeded by blocks; his psychology is biologically maladaptive, he is "mentally unhealthy," to the extent that blocks obstruct the functioning of his consciousness.

To express this thought a bit differently: a person is "psycho-biologically adaptive" or "mentally healthy" to the extent that he is in good contact with the outer world, and with his inner world, and with the relationship between them.

A central goal of psychotherapy is to remove obstructions to awareness and thus to restore the integrative power of the mind.

REASON AND EMOTION

If one does not dichotomize mind and body, reason and emotion, thinking and feeling—if one recognizes that a human being is an organismic unity—one is led to a realization of the importance of unblocking disowned or repressed feelings in restoring the individual to effective functioning. This is only one aspect of psychotherapy, but it is a vital one.

Emotions are implicit value-responses; they reflect subconscious, super-rapid appraisals of "for me or against me," "good for me or harmful," "to be pursued or to be avoided," and so forth. His emotional capacity is a person's automatic barometer of what is for him or against him, within the context of his knowledge, beliefs, values and past experiences. Emotions reflect the value-meaning that different aspects of reality have for the perceiver. Emotions are psychophysical embodiments of value-judgments. I define "emotion" in the following way: an emotion is the psychophysical form in which a person experiences his estimate of the beneficial or harmful relationship of some aspect of reality to himself.

To cease to know what one feels is to cease to *experience* what things mean to one—which is to be cut off from one's own context.

Thus, every blocked emotion is at the same time a blocked thought—a blocked value-judgment. Contrary to the notion that one must repress one's emotions in order to think clearly, it is repression that makes clear thinking impossible, in the areas affected by the repression. So the formula of the Biocentric approach is: Feel deeply, feel honestly, to think clearly. (There are emergency situations in which, *momentarily*, one might have to suppress some of one's feelings in order to act effectively, but that is a different matter.)

In Biocentric Therapy, great importance is attached to releasing blocked feelings; the goal of such work is that of enabling an individual to re-experience and re-own repressed needs, desires, emotions, frustrations and longings—so that blocks to awareness are removed and assimilation and integration are facilitated. To this end a variety of means are applied: my own sentence-completion experiments (which I will illustrate later), breathing techniques, neo-Reichian body work, fantasy exercises, forms of psychodrama, and so forth.

Aside from the utilization of certain original technical procedures, I believe that what distinguishes the Biocentric approach in this area is the integration of the emotional and the cognitive, the practice of constantly moving back and forth between the experiential and the conceptual. This is not a matter of a single technique but rather reflects a basic attitude, a philosophy, expressed through an interrelated multiplicity of techniques, directed toward specific problems. I will give examples of this later.

It is easy enough to pay lip service to the ideal of integrating thought and feeling, mind and body, in the course of doing therapy. It is unlikely that any psychotherapist would dispute the desirability of this ideal. However, psychologists who emphasize the intellect, cognition, reason, tend to take a disparaging attitude toward emotions, though few of them will admit it; often their attitude is implicit rather than explicit. I think the work done in Rational-Emotive Therapy, Transactional Analysis and in Reality Therapy reflect this tendency. On the other hand, psychologists who emphasize emotions and specialize in emotional-release types of therapy tend to be hostile to reason and the intellect—though, again, few of them will admit it. I think this trend is clearly discernible in Reichian Therapy, Bioenergetic Therapy and Gestalt Therapy; it is screamingly obvious in Primal Therapy. In sum, most psychotherapists seem to encounter great difficulty in achieving a true integration of the rational and the emotional, the cognitive and the experiential, the intellectual and the organismic—just as their clients or patients do.

When an individual in effect decides—or is (implicitly) encouraged by his therapist—to disown his emotions in order to function effectively in reality, he sabotages his ability to think. When an individual in effect decides—or is (implicitly) encouraged by his therapist—to disregard objective reality in order to be "true" to his feelings, the predominant feeling left to him tends to be anxiety.

If an individual is to function effectively and to achieve that state of integration which psychological well-being requires, he must learn to function on two levels: to preserve contact with external reality *and* with internal reality—with the objective requirements of any given situation *and* with its emotional meaning to him; with the facts *and* with his appraisal of the facts; with what he may have to do *and* with what he feels about what he may have to do.

To communicate this method of functioning, to inculcate a respect for reason, reality, objectivity, on the one hand and a respect for the client's own experience, on the other, is one of the prime goals of Biocentric Therapy (Branden, 1972).

THE SURVIVAL VALUE OF NEUROTIC BEHAVIOR

I spoke earlier of the fact that psychological well-being or biologically adaptive functioning relate to an absence of blocks, an absence of obstructions (constrictions and distortions) to awareness.

The repression of feelings is the avoidance of awareness; to disown feelings is to avoid consciousness. This perspective is basic to the Biocentric approach to emotional-release aspects of psychotherapy.

Without denying that catharsis and abreaction are often inherently valuable, inherently healing, the primary focus in Biocentric Therapy is on the expansion of awareness, the facilitation of cognitive integration, that results from cathartic-abreactive experiences.

Perhaps there is no universal formula that will encompass all instances of neurosis. But the evidence seems overwhelming that the main root of neurosis is the process of disowning, of repressing important aspects of one's own experience, repressing needs, emotions and perceptions.

We know that the disowning process begins very early in life. Many parents *teach* children to repress their feelings. A little boy falls and hurts himself and is told sternly by his father, "Men don't cry." A little girl expresses anger at her brother, or perhaps shows dislike toward an older relative, and is told by her mother, "It's terrible to feel that way. You don't really feel it." A child bursts into the house, full of joy and excitement, and is told by an irritated parent, "What's wrong with you? Why do you make so much noise?" Thus a child learns to disconnect from—and soon not to recognize—his own feelings.

But beyond that, a child may find himself in an environment that is frightening or even terrifying, frustrating, bewildering, perhaps excruciatingly painful. In effect, he feels himself trapped in a nightmare. His basic needs are not fulfilled. Intolerable emotions threaten to overwhelm him and to render him incapable of functioning. How is he to protect himself, to preserve his sanity, to preserve his ability to function? That is the problem he confronts. He generates a solution, and within the limits of his knowledge it may be the only solution he can produce: he learns to disconnect from his own emotions, to block his feelings, to become alienated from his own body—and perhaps to deny and disown certain of his perceptions. (It is possible that we are dealing here with an evolutionary problem; perhaps human beings have simply not evolved to the point where they are yet able to generate a better solution to stresses of this kind.) Later in life, the child's repression, if it is severe, becomes the foundation of psychological problems. If he does not learn to reconnect with his feelings, to discover his needs, and to remain loyal to his perceptions, his functioning will inevitably be impaired. But here is the point: as a child *his repression had survival value.* In a special sense, one can say it was adaptive. Or the child *felt* it was because he could see no alternative.

Whether I am dealing with a child or an adult, my first question about a piece of neurotic behavior is: What purpose does it serve? What is its *felt* or *experienced* survival value? Objectively, neurotic behavior reflects self-destructive processes; but *subjectively* in the context of the individual's own experience and development, it usually represents an attempt at self-preservation, protection against pain, protection of sanity or self-esteem—above all, of self-esteem.

As I see it, the environment presents the growing individual with a problem: pain, terror, frustration, bewilderment, feelings of helplessness, a threat to his sense of control, a threat to his sense of personal worth—and to deal with this problem the individual generates a solution: his symptoms, i.e., his neurotic behavior. I believe this is the most common pattern of symptom formation.

When attempting to build an understanding of neurotic behavior, I invite the client to consider: What is or was the problem to which your symptom represents an attempted solution? If your "solution" harms and diminishes your life, are you willing to experiment with alternative ones?

NEUROSIS AND SELF-ESTEEM

The goal-directed character of neurotic symptoms cannot be adequately understood without an appreciation of a human being's need of self-esteem and the profound role this need plays in his development. The theory of self-esteem and its role in human behavior stands at the center of Biocentric Therapy.

Self-esteem has two interrelated aspects: a sense of personal efficacy and a sense of personal worth. It is the conviction that one is competent to live and worthy of living.

The conviction that one is *competent* to live means: confidence in the functioning of one's own mind; confidence in one's own ability to understand and judge the facts of reality (within the sphere of one's interests and needs); intellectual self-reliance. The conviction that one is *worthy* of living means: an affirmative attitude toward one's right to live and to be happy; a self-respect derived from the conviction that one is functioning in the manner one's life and well-being require (Branden, 1969).

On the conceptual level of consciousness, the distinctively *human* level—the level that goes beyond the sensory-perceptual mode of awareness human beings share with animals—the level of abstractions, principles, explicit reasoning and self-consciousness—on this level, an individual has to direct and regulate his mind's activity. The *capacity* of conceptual functioning is innate, but the *exercise* of this capacity is volitional. On the conceptual level, a person has the ability to strive for increasing clarity, intelligibility, understanding—and he has the ability to suspend his right. He is able to think and he is able to avoid thinking. He is able to be aware and he is able to avoid awareness. The reasoning process does not function automatically, like the beating of his heart; purposeful thought is an activity that a person must *choose* to set in motion.

Further, having formulated principles of proper action, he is able to act in accordance with them—and he is able to act in defiance of them. *Hypocrisy* is a distinctively human possibility; it is not a characteristic possible to animals; neither is *integrity*.

Thus a human being carries a special kind of responsibility known to no other living species. *His need to know that he carries this responsibility properly, that his method of functioning is appropriate to reality, to the requirements of his own survival and well-being, is his need of self-esteem.*

There is no value-judgment more important to a person than the estimate he passes on himself. This is a fact that anyone can verify introspectively. And it is easy for the clinician to see that the nature of a person's self-evaluation has profound effects on the person's thinking processes, emotions, desires, values and goals.

One of the tragedies of human development is that many of a person's most self-destructive acts are prompted by a blind, misguided, and often subconscious attempt to protect his sense of self—to preserve or strengthen his self-esteem.

When a person disowns certain of his thoughts and memories, because he regards them as immoral or humiliating, he disowns a part of himself—in the name of protecting his self-esteem. When a person disowns certain of his emotions, because they threaten his sense of control or conflict with his notion of "strength" or "maturity" or "sophistication," he disowns a part of himself—in the name of protecting his self-esteem. When a person disowns certain of his desires, because he cannot tolerate the anxiety of wondering whether or not he will attain them, an anxiety that makes him feel helpless and ineffectual, he disowns a part of himself—in the name of protecting his self-esteem. When a person disowns certain aspects of his personality which seem incompatible with the standard of his "significant others," because he has tied his sense of personal worth to the approval of those "others," he disowns a part of himself—in the name of protecting his self-esteem. When a person disowns certain of his legitimate needs, because their frustration leaves him feeling impotent and defeated, he disowns a part of himself—in the name of protecting his self-esteem.

When a young child represses a pain that he experiences as intolerable, he does so not only because pain is intrinsically a disvalue, but also because it threatens his sense of control, it causes him to feel impotent and incapable of functioning; it nullifies his sense of efficacy. In later years, his block against reconfronting that pain serves the same purpose as in childhood: to maintain his equilibrium, to protect his sense of efficacy, of control, of self-esteem.

In doing psychotherapy, I am always concerned with the question: In what way is the client's behavior aimed at strengthening feelings of control, efficacy, self-esteem, *or* of avoiding feelings of helplessness, inefficacy, powerlessness, worthlessness?

Even expressions of guilt and self-condemnation can reflect this quest. "I'm no good, so expect nothing of me. Then I won't have to suffer the humiliation of failing." "I'm no good—I said it first, so I don't have to wait in terror for you to say it." "I'm no good—so I don't have to try. I don't have to struggle, there's no point in struggling, since I'm worthless anyway. That's my secret strength, that's my secret core of control, that I call myself worthless and thereby avoid the responsibility of action at the risk of failure and of being reproached."

Sometimes, when a child is ill-treated by his parents, he consoles himself by telling himself that he's "bad," that it's his fault, even if he doesn't understand how. That makes the universe more sane, more comprehensible. It offers him the hope that if he can somehow learn to act differently, he can win his parents' love; that puts him back in control, in a manner of speaking. As a child, it may feel too terrifying to regard himself as innocent, in view of how his parents treat him; to regard himself as innocent would mean that he is at the helpless mercy of monsters. So it might be said, in such a situation, that the child makes himself neurotic in order to avoid becoming psychotic.

THE CASE OF BETH: SURVIVAL THROUGH HELPLESSNESS

Rather than talk further about theory, I would prefer now to offer two examples of practice. They are not complete case histories, but only fragments excerpted from an on-going therapeutic process.

The first of these examples involves a twenty-two year old married woman—Beth—who sought therapy because of unhappiness associated with her marriage. She was generally passive, withdrawn and somewhat vague. At her first group session, Beth was entirely silent; she rarely looked at anyone. The incident I shall describe took place at her second session.

A few minutes before this second session was to end, she said in a tone of muted intensity, "Nathan, I have to work." Then, in a flat, unemotional manner she proceeded to declare that sometimes she was unable to perceive objects as objects, that they became only meaningless shapes to her, and that this frightened her.

At this point, there was a rustle of tension among the other members of the group.

I saw that she was watching me intently for a reaction and I chose to respond in a casual, almost nonchalant manner by saying that I could understand her fear but that I did not find her experience ominous. Sometimes, I explained to her and to the group, when a person feels the emergence within himself of unacceptable feelings that provoke anxiety, the person defends himself by cutting off from his own feelings so severely that a sense of depersonalization and unreality can result. In non-technical terms, I explained the phenomenon of dissociation.

She indicated that she understood, but in a manner that communicated that she felt acutely frustrated, which is what I had intended, and she then proceeded to make her next "move."

"Yes," she said, "but the thing is . . . I feel I am in my present incarnation . . . and I can't get out . . . and it disturbs me very much. . . ." She stopped, again obviously waiting for my reaction. I said, almost enthusiastically, "Oh, that's interesting. Can you say more about it?" In boxing, one would call the strategy I was adopting: breaking your opponent's rhythm. This strategy was employed by me throughout the encounter. (I trust this remark will be taken in the spirit in which it is meant and no one will conclude that I regard a client as my "opponent.")

She was obviously taken aback and was a bit confused by my manner, but she proceeded as follows: "Well, I feel as if I'm trapped in my present incarnation." Again she stopped and waited expectantly. "Go on," I said pleasantly. She stated, more emphatically and somewhat annoyed, "Well, what bothers me is the thought that there is a power controlling my life, intervening, manipulating me, taking over. . . ."

By now the other members of the group had become rather uneasy. I do not work with the severely disturbed, and some of the group members were wondering, as they later told me, if we had a borderline psychotic in the room.

"Oh, I see," I said to her in a relaxed, business-like manner. "That's fine. I'd like you to try an experiment. On your feet, my sweet!" She stood up, now utterly bewildered. I went on: "We're going to work with open-ended sentences. I will give you an open-ended sentence: you'll go around to each person in the group, make eye contact with that person, really see him, then repeat my open-ended phrase and conclude it any way you want, without worrying whether what you say is true or false, reasonable or unreasonable. Are you willing to do that?" "Yes," she replied, a bit dazed.

She positioned herself in front of the first person in the circle and waited for further instructions. I said, "Let's begin with the phrase: 'When I speak of living in my present incarnation what I really mean is—' "

Moving from person to person, without any hesitation whatsoever, she proceeded as follows: "When I speak of living in my present incarnation, what I really mean is—my marriage. When I speak of living in my present incarnation, what I really mean is—my whole way of life. When I speak of living in my present incarnation, what I really mean is—the way I've always lived."

As she was speaking, her posture was subtly straightening, her eyes were becoming more alive and her face was becoming more animated; her breathing had visibly become deeper.

I said to her, "Now we'll go on to another item. 'When I speak of being trapped in my present incarnation, what I really mean is—' "

And continuing to move around the circle from person to person, she went on: "When I speak of being trapped in my present incarnation, what I really mean is—I don't know whether or not I want to leave my husband. When I speak of being trapped in my present incarnation, what I really mean is—I don't want to stay and I'm afraid to leave."

I said to her, "Now let's work with the phrase: 'When I speak of being controlled by a power, what I really mean is—' "

She said, "When I speak of being controlled by a power, what I really mean is—my own feelings of helplessness. When I speak of being controlled by a power, what I really mean is—my own feelings of inadequacy. When I speak of being controlled by a power, what I really mean is—I want someone to tell me what to do."

I then said to her, as if what I was asking was the most natural thing in the world, "Now let's try the phrase: 'The good thing about pretending to be crazy is—' "

A slight, almost undiscernible convulsion flickered through her body, then she went on: "The good thing about pretending to be crazy is—I won't have to experience my own pain. The good thing about pretending to be crazy is—people will know I need help. The good thing about pretending to be crazy is—people will take my problems seriously. The good thing about pretending to be crazy is people will do something. The good thing about pretending to be crazy is—people will feel sorry for me. The good thing about pretending to be crazy is—people will know I'm in trouble."

I then said to her, " 'If I couldn't pretend to be crazy—' "

And Beth went on, "If I couldn't pretend to be crazy—how would people know I needed help? If I couldn't pretend to be crazy—people wouldn't feel sorry for me. If I couldn't pretend to be crazy—I would have to start being responsible for my own life. If I couldn't pretend to be crazy—I would have to start making my own choices and decisions and take the consequences."

Then Beth turned to grin at me sheepishly; she seemed utterly relaxed, in good contact with me, with the room and with herself.

I asked her to sit down and I said to her, not casually but solemnly, "Now listen. I want you to know that I hear you. I take your fear very seriously. I take your pain very seriously. Everything you're feeling is important. I respect that. Do you understand?" "Yes," she answered. "Do you believe me?" "Yes," she answered. "That being the case," I went on, "it really isn't necessary for you to pretend to be crazy and—" I indicated the others in the group—"and scare all my friends here." She began to laugh, relieved.

As it turned out, rather predictably, in a subsequent session, one of the frightening feelings against which she was blindly seeking to defend herself was murderous rage against her husband.

As a very young child Beth had learned the technique of what I call "survival through helplessness," by which I mean a strategy of parading feelings of helplessness in order to manipulate others into taking care of one, thereby using helplessness as a technique of mastery and control.

Again, confronting the difficulties in her marriage, her flight from reality into some rather bizarre symptoms represents a twisted and misguided struggle for self-preservation.

Human beings destroy themselves every day—in the name of assuring their survival. *Neurosis might almost be defined as the attempt to protect one's self-esteem and assure one's survival by self-destructive (reality-avoiding) means.*

I think this will be evident in the next case I wish to cite.

THE CASE OF SAM: SURVIVAL THROUGH SUFFERING

Sam was a man in his middle twenties—highly intelligent, sensitive, but very passive, very timid, very soft-spoken, very withdrawn and very self-pitying. He was holding down a fairly meaningless job, meaningless, that is, relative to his intellectual potential. He couldn't seem to get his life started. He complained of not having any friends and of not knowing how to relate to other people. He projected a quality of forlorn helplessness and hopelessness.

One day, in group, he said that he wanted to work on the problem of why he wasn't getting anywhere in his life.

I asked him to begin with what I call "the death-bed exercise" (Branden, 1972)—which meant that I asked him to lie on the floor, to close his eyes, and to imagine that he was in a hospital room bed and that he was dying. His life was over; he had only a few more hours to live; all of his chances had been used up. Then I asked him to look up, in imagination, and see his father—who was a Lutheran Minister—standing by the side of his bed, "There is so much that you have never said to him," I suggested, "so much that you've kept locked up inside of you. If ever your father would want to hear you, it would be now. If ever it would be possible to reach him, it would be now. Talk to him. Tell him what it was like to be his son." The "death-bed exercise" is one of my favorite techniques for exploring the childhood origins of emotional problems.

Slowly and reluctantly Sam began to talk to his father and to describe various childhood incidents that had been very painful or frightening. He spoke about ways in which he felt his father had been cruel to him—neglecting him in order to be free to do "good works" in the community, and so forth. But his manner was very cerebral, he was obviously disconnected, cut off from his emotions: his words were without feeling. One could see, from looking at him, that he was tensing his body and making himself numb to hold back an immense amount of rage that he felt he dared not express. I knew we couldn't get anywhere until he could release, express and confront that rage.

I asked him to stop, and shifted into a different exercise. I asked him to remain lying on the floor, to begin shaking his head from side to side, and to say "No!" as he did so. When a person is angry and is holding that anger back, he tenses up the muscles in his back and shoulders—the very muscles that would be mobilized should the anger be released. By having him move his head from side to side, I was making it impossible for his neck muscles to lock completely, and thereby I was hoping to facilitate the release of feeling. Gradually his "Nos" became stronger and angrier—until he was stamping his feet, pounding his fists, and shouting "No!" at the top of his lungs.

Then I asked him to re-enter the hospital fantasy and to talk to his father again. He was emotionally connected now and he began to scream and to cry and to rage and to tell his father about the many hurts and frustrations that he had endured at his father's hands.

When I began the first exercise, I did so on the hypothesis that his relationship with his father was relevant to his problem; but I did not have a firm conviction as to the direction in which the work was going to take us. Now, suddenly, I had a hunch—an idea struck me—and I asked him to stay in contact with his father in fantasy and simply to say to his father, over and over again, "But I'm getting back at you!"

Sam began shouting this sentence and as he did so his rage kept climbing to higher and higher peaks of intensity. Then I switched to still another exercise; I asked him to do sentence-completions beginning with the phrase: "I'm getting back at you by—"

He screamed, "I'm getting back at you by—being unhappy! I'm getting back at you by—sitting in my room all day alone! I'm getting back at you by—crying all the time! I'm getting back at you by—making a mess of my life! I'm getting back at you by—holding stupid, senseless jobs that don't lead anywhere! I'm getting back at you by—not having any friends! I'm getting back at you by—never letting myself be happy! I'm getting back at you by—never for a minute forgetting how much you hurt me! I'm getting back at you by—keeping my anger for you alive! I'm getting back at you by—never giving you anything to be proud of!"

So what he was put in contact with was that his self-defeating behavior had two immediate goals: it was an act of revenge, a way of inflicting pain on his father—and, at the same time, a scream for help, a way of signaling to his father: "See what you've done to me? See how unhappy I am? *Now* will you be a father to me and satisfy my needs?"

Now why was he unwilling to accept the past and put it behind him? Why was he unwilling to say, in effect, "Okay, I had a rotten, miserable, frustrating childhood. But I'm not a child any longer. So what am I going to make of my life?"

Those questions were dealt with in subsequent sessions.

Part of the reason was that Sam had never adequately dealt with this childhood pain, never got it out of his system; he had frozen himself emotionally in order to avoid feeling it—and it paralyzed himself intellectually in the process. So additional work was needed to allow him to fully confront and experience that denied childhood pain. But also involved was his longing to remain a child—in the hope that somehow those frustrated childhood needs would be fulfilled by someone. To put the past behind him would mean to accept the fact that those needs were never going to be fulfilled, that it was too late, that there is nothing more to be done, except to get on with his life. He couldn't or wouldn't tolerate that.

In the end, we were dealing here with the issue of a person's willingness or unwillingness to assume full responsibility for his own existence. To assume full responsibility for one's own existence is to put one's self-esteem on the line, as it were; the choice of many people is to so arrange their lives that they never have to face this problem—or they think they don't.

In the process of growing up and meeting the increasingly complex challenges of life, an individual can basically adopt one of two strategies: he can strive always to grow in the direction of increasing awareness, increasing contact with the environment, increasing effectiveness, increasing mastery—which is the creative approach to life—the approach out of which self-esteem is born; or he can struggle to shrink his environment to a range in which he will feel safe and comfortable and unchallenged and unthreatened.

Of course, human beings do not move entirely in one direction or the other; perhaps everyone represents a mixture of the two, and what we are talking about is dominant trends.

ASPECTS OF THERAPY

I think of my therapy groups (I work exclusively in groups, although I do not consider that essential to my method) as, in effect, personal growth seminars. They are *experiential* seminars, as contrasted with *didactic* seminars. Explicit teaching does play a part in my therapy, but the heavier emphasis is on working with different types of exercises or experiments. I don't think so much in terms of therapy as I do in terms of growth, of helping the individual to discover and release his potential, intellectually, creatively, emotionally, sexually.

Although I use a variety of technical procedures, and keep experimenting with new ones, I am very partial to my sentence-completion work as a basic therapeutic tool. I have many different versions of this technique. One version is discussed at length in

The Disowned Self. But there are many other ways of working with sentence-completion that I have developed, such as are evidenced in the two cases I cited.

One of the things I like about the technique, in any of its variations, is that, when the client is properly into the exercise and working well, it becomes simultaneously a cognitive and emotional experience for him, sometimes a very explosive one. It is not an issue of my "interpreting" his motivation, or "explaining" a client to himself; rather it is a matter of what he confronts and discovers himself, discovers intellectually and organismically, discovers with the unmistakable authenticity of first-hand knowledge. In some circumstances this exercise is sufficient, by itself, to stimulate dramatic changes in a person, to eliminate neurotic symptoms and inspire radical improvement in behavior.

The chief breakthrough in psychotherapy seems to occur when the client discovers, in terms personally meaningful to himself, that alternative, more satisfying ways of functioning are possible to him. In a sense, all techniques aim at this goal.

Any description of what goes on in the process of doing therapy is inevitably going to be over-simplified. But I see therapy as moving along four major lines:

1. Explicit teaching; the providing of information. While I do not believe that a therapist can lecture a client into psychological well-being, neither do I believe that the information-providing aspect of psychotherapy can be ignored. Teaching is valuable insofar as it is personal and relevant to immediate emotional situations; it tends to be ineffective insofar as it is impersonal, formally didactic, oblivious to the emotional needs of the moment. To teach without "preaching" is one of the greatest skills a psychotherapist has to master.

2. Leading the client to attain insight or understanding. Such insight concerns (a) *what* the client does to sabotage his effective functioning (for example, he freezes mentally when faced with a difficult problem); (b) the *means* by which he does it (for example, he tenses certain muscles to block off his anxiety, he tells himself he is incapable, and induces a sense of passivity and helplessness); (c) the *purpose* for which he does it (for example, to avoid the pain of trying and failing); (d) and (sometimes, but not always) the *historical context* in which he first practiced self-sabotaging behavior and in which it first felt plausible and/or necessary (for example, when presented with expectations and demands on the part of his parents that he experienced as overwhelming and beyond

his abilities).

3. Emotional release work; unblocking repressed needs, feelings, desires, painful and frightening emotions, and so forth. Neo-Reichian body-work is sometimes especially helpful in this area.

4. Encouraging the client to experiment with changes in his behavior, to experiment with new ways of responding to and dealing with various situations; to break out of the rut of habitual patterns of self-sabotaging behavior. Sometimes, in teaching this, I may use role-playing, rehearsal, or a variety or other such teaching techniques.

Almost everything I try to communicate in therapy is contained in four basic concepts with which I work constantly: self-awareness, self-acceptance, self-responsibility, self-assertiveness. What do these concepts mean?

Self-awareness. Awareness of what? Awareness of feelings, awareness of bodily states, awareness of needs, awareness of desires, emotions, ideas, evaluations and behavior. Therapy begins with teaching clients how to be self-aware, how to know what they are feeling and what they are doing.

Self-acceptance. Acceptance of what? Acceptance of all the items I have just named. Acceptance of the fact that all of these feelings, ideas, behavior and so forth are expressions of the self *at the time they occur.* Self-acceptance entails a refusal to disown any of these aspects of the self, any of these instances of self-expression. Not necessarily to approve of all of them, but to accept them as real and as one's own. Acceptance of the reality of one's own being, of one's inner experience and one's behavior. Self-acceptance literally means: full realism applied to the realm of inner experience as well as to behavior. We all know that people can verbally or intellectually acknowledge their feelings or reactions or behavior while denying them emotionally and psychologically, refusing to accept and integrate them. Self-acceptance means more than merely verbal acknowledgment; it means integration.

Self-responsibility. Responsibility for what? Responsibility for being the cause of one's choices and one's acts. Not responsibility in the sense of moral blame, but responsibility in the sense of recognizing one's self as the chief causal agent in one's life and behavior. Further, self-responsibility means: acceptance of responsibility for one's own existence. Acceptance of one's basic—metaphysical—aloneness. Acceptance of responsibility for the attainment of one's own goals. (This last is extremely important. This is a theme I hit again and again in therapy. No one plays the "helplessness game" on a desert island; we can tell ourselves and others that we are helpless only if we expect someone to pick up the responsibility we have dropped.)

Self-assertiveness. Assertiveness of what? Of one's desires and judgments. Of one's needs. Of one's right to exist and to be happy. Sometimes, as an exercise, I will ask a client to face the group and simply say, again and again, "I have a right to exist." For many clients, this is very difficult. It is interesting to observe what happens. First, the statement may be made hesitantly and tearfully; later, it may be made angrily; then eventually, it is made firmly and with conviction. One can see the whole posture and demeanor of the person has changed: he has released his own power; he experiences his own strength; he asserts his own existence.

The consequence of these four principles applied in action is self-esteem—and the enhancement of self-esteem is the central theme of Biocentric Therapy.

REFERENCES

Branden, N. *The Psychology of Self-Esteem.* Los Angeles: Nash Publishing, 1969.

Branden, N. *The Disowned Self.* Los Angeles: Nash Publishing, 1972.

9

DIRECT DECISION THERAPY

Harold Greenwald, Ph.D.

This article is about the role of decision in psychotherapy and in life in general. When I first started working with these ideas I thought I had found an effective approach to psychotherapy As I continued to work with these ideas and to speak about them to various groups of professionals and nonprofessionals, I became aware that I was also dealing with a philosophy of living, with a way of being in the world. The name I have chosen for this approach is Direct Decision Therapy.

I was close to forty when I discovered I was a failure. I had a job working at a resort hotel, and was supposedly in charge of building a golf course. I was supervising a group of partially dried-out alcoholics. A man I knew came up to me. I don't know what his real name was, but everyone called him "Mike the Plumber." Mike and I had been talking for a while when he asked: "How old are you?" I said I was in my late thirties and he demanded, "When are you going to do something, when will you get yours?"

At that point I realized that in many ways I was a failure. I was aware that I had many abilities and a high I.Q.; I was married to a remarkable wife, and had two great children. Many things were O.K. Except that I had had so many awful jobs—more than sixty of them—that some of the anger and annoyance and disgust with myself about my jobs had spilled over and affected my family feelings.

Then and there, speaking to Mike the Plumber, I had a moment

Reprinted, with a few editorial changes, with the permission of the author and the publisher, from Chapter 1, pp. 3-26, of *Direct Decision Therapy* (San Diego: Edits, 1973).

of realization. I said to myself, "I'm going to do something."

Within one month, I had the best job I've ever had: I had become an executive in a good-sized manufacturing company, and within two years as a result of reading a book by Theodor Reik about his being a psychoanalyst and not being a physician—I had also decided to become a psychologist. That was the big decision I made.

The payoff has been quite remarkable. A few years after that conversation with Mike the Plumber, I found myself with a Ph.D. and a full psychoanalytic practice. I wrote a book, based in part on my doctoral dissertation, which sold about a million copies and was made into a movie. I was being invited to speak about my work, and I had a very different feeling about myself. My modicum of success, having come so late in life, has been all the sweeter. So that for me the payoff of decisions is neither an abstract idea or something I use only for patients, but something I know very well from my own experience, my own life.

I would like to tell you how I came to formulate Direct Decision Therapy. After having been a therapist for about twenty years, I was invited to Norway as a Guest Professor for a year. While I was in Norway, I was asked to prepare a seminar for psychologists and psychiatrists from various parts of the country. During the seminar I covered various therapies now being practiced: active psychoanalytic psychotherapy, hypnotherapy, behavior modification, and rational-emotive therapy. At the end of two days of lecturing, I was supposed to present a summary of the whole thing. During the seminar I also did demonstrations with different persons to illustrate the four techniques I had covered. When I came to summarize, it suddenly became clear to me that everything I had been doing in all those cases with people I had been treating could be explained in one way: I was helping these people to *make a decision to change*. That's how I presented the summary. That is, I expressed the view that the only thing that happens in therapy—regardless of the methods or techniques used—is that the person you're working with is helped to make a *decision to change*, and then is helped to carry out the decision. As will be seen later, even the most difficult problems—homosexuality, addiction to drugs, and various forms of compulsive or destructive behavior—respond remarkably favorably to this kind of therapy, once a *wish* to change had led to a *decision* to change.

I had been teaching therapists and lecturing about psychotherapy for at least eighteen years, and every once in a great while someone would come up and say, "You know, I once heard you explain something that I found helpful with one of my patients." After I got through with the seminar and my summary on decision in Norway, I had a whole new experience. Eight out of the forty people attending came up to me and remarked, "What you said about decisions helped me with my *personal* problem." These were all people who had had psychoanalysis or psychotherapy, people who had already had a therapeutic experience. Obviously, with that kind of feedback, I wasn't going to let the idea go, so I began to develop the entire area of personal decision-making. Since then, I have had similar experiences in various parts of the world whenever I have spoken on the subject.

While I am organizing it as therapy, I'm really talking about more than therapy as practiced in an office, because this is something that many people can apply for themselves, and I think that people reading this article will have a chance to *use* some of the insights I will share here. You might consider yourself the patient as I describe the method. Whether you're a professional or not, the best way to learn therapy is to go through the therapeutic experience yourself. The most valuable part of my training was my own psychoanalysis. If you want to use Direct Decision Therapy, it would be useful to apply it to yourself as you read about it.

One of the steps I took in developing Direct Decision Therapy was to review my experiences with patients, and I saw how many times the crucial event that had happened was that they had made a decision. Then I came across a book called *Decision Making*. which really deals with decision-making as applied to economics. This was also helpful in my thinking.

I don't think anybody's theory can be fully appreciated without seeing a relationship to his personal life. If you cannot apply it to your own life, what good is it? Obviously, a lot of my own experiences influenced my theory and I am therefore including an autobiographical section which may help explain why Decision Theory is so compatible and so sympathetic to me. This is not to say that I am so good at decisions. If I were, I probably would never have thought of the entire theory.

In any therapeutic approach, I try to remember certain things. One, which has almost been talked to death, is to be authentic, to be myself. I would like to define this a little more operationally than it usually is: that is, as a therapist, I should try to be the same as I am in my nonprofessional life. I'll tell you a story about how I did that in one aspect of my life and how that has been very useful to me ever since. I've been a public speaker since I was four years old, when I was pushed onto a soap box in Brooklyn and made a speech before an adult audience all about World War I. Later I won medals for public speaking in elementary school, high school and community centers. At college I was on the debating team. One of the ways that helped me to make the transition to becoming a psychologist was a job I had lecturing about psychology to the guests at the same hotel (the Concord in Kiamesha Lake, New York) where I had formerly worked on the golf course.

One time, after I had finished speaking at the hotel, and was on my way home, a friend who was driving back with me asked me some questions about my lecture, and when I got through answering them, he said, "Why don't you talk as simply as this when you talk to an audience?"

I said, "It had to be larger than life; you have to get their attention." But then I thought about it and made a decision to try it: I would speak to any audience the way I speak to anybody else in ordinary conversation. I really had to work at it. It was much easier to go off into oratory.

Well, it's hard work, if you are a therapist, to speak in an informal way. You have the mantel on you, and you think you have to carry a lot of things with you, but authenticity pays off. For me, that is one of the most important preconditions to successful therapy.

The other one is empathy. Achieving empathy takes a certain amount of effort. When I first meet a person who has come to me for help, I try to forget everything I know about psychology. That was very difficult at the beginning, when I didn't know very much. It's much easier now, when I think I know a lot. I try to look at the person, try to look at the problem, in a completely new and different way. I try to forget everything I know about neurosis, psychosis, transference and dynamics. I ask myself, "What's this person telling me?" As far as possible, I try to see what he is telling me through his own eyes; I try to put myself in his place.

If a therapist doesn't like people and doesn't have some feeling about them, no matter how awful they seem to be, he is not in the right field. There's not enough money in psychotherapy to make it worthwhile unless he can get gratification from it. Maybe it's a wish for power, maybe it's compassion. Whatever it is, if one is not really committed to the people one works with, if one doesn't get a good feeling out of doing something helpful for them, it's better not to be a therapist, because it can become too difficult, too painful and boring.

The first question I ask a person who comes to see me is, "What's your problem?" You can ask yourself right now—"What problem do I have?"

Get that stated as clearly as possible. One of the problems today is that people don't describe a problem as they experience it, but rather as it has been defined *for* them. "I am very self-destructive; I can't find meaning in life; I want to actualize myself; I want to be more authentic."

I remember asking a young woman who told me all these things, "What do you really mean? What do you really want?"

She answered, "I'd like to find a husband." She had explained her inability to find one when she used those general terms, but it's necessary to define the problem as specifically as possible in order to find out what kind of help is wanted.

There are, in a sense, two kinds of problems. Of course there are many more, but let's divide them into two simple categories. One is a very specific situational problem: "I have an unhappy marriage." "I have a fear of heights." "I am anxious when I speak in public." These are very specific problems. More frequently, a professional therapist sees people whose problems have been called "characterlogical": "I am unhappy." "I can't be assertive." "I am very passive in many situations." Their problems become, not specific symptoms, but their whole way of being in the world.

One of the most common problems I get is the one Thoreau described so perceptively when he said, "The mass of men lead lives of quiet desperation." A lot of the people I work with are trapped in unhappy, bitter marriages; terrible jobs they hate; wearing themselves out with imaginary illnesses which are not experienced as imaginary—these kinds of long-continuing problems. The insight that I have found extremely valuable is to look upon all of these problems as choices and to ask myself, "Is this the person's choice?" To me, it is extremely important not to start with a prejudgment of the situation.

If a person is depressed or angry all the time, this is either the way he chooses to be or is the result of decisions he has made. And so after he presents the problem, I search for the past decision which is behind the present problem.

Let me give you some examples of what I call "life choices" or "life decisions." There are many people whose decision at some point was that they were going to be perfect; that they would do everything in such a way as to be absolutely perfect without any errors. Others have made the decision to be so accommodating, so kind, so good, so non-threatening, so agreeable, that the whole world will love them. I have a friend who, every time I wanted to have lunch with her or talk with her, told me, "I can't. I gotta run an errand for Fred." She was always so busy doing things for people that a friend, a comedienne, once said to her, "Listen, one more present and you're going to get it right in the teeth. I'm sick and tired of your presents." This woman had made a decision to be loved by everybody.

Then there are those who make the decision to be "different." They study how the rest of the world is, and act in the opposite way. If everyone has short hair, they have long hair; and if everyone has long hair, they have short hair. I had an uncle like that. In the labor unions in the 1920s there was a fierce struggle between the right wing and the left wing. While the right wing was in power, he was an ardent leftist. Then the left wing took control of his particular union and he became a rightist. He joined a temple in order to fight against the administration there, even though he didn't believe in religion. As soon as he led a group out of that place, he immediately went on the outs with his followers. His decision was to be different, to be in constant and total rebellion. Many people make the kind of choice—to be different, to call attention to themselves, to be conspicuous.

Then there are people who have made the decision to suffer. They have the capacity, like many mothers, to snatch disaster out of every victory. Every event can be turned into a catastrophe, and they know how.

Another type (I owe this term to someone at a seminar where I was working) I call the "silent gotchas." These are people whom professionals call "passive-aggressive." They try to do everything pleasantly and never disagree until they've "gotcha." Maybe that sounds a little implausible, so I'll give an example. I was working with one of the brightest psychologists I've ever known. He was in graduate school, and he was at the difficult stage of having completed all his degree work except for writing his dissertation. Several years had passed, and we talked about the way he was putting off this final task. He explained that his father and mother wanted him to get his Ph.D., his wife wanted him to get it and even his girlfriend would sometimes ask, "When am I going to be able to call you doctor?"

Then he got me involved, too. At first I would respond with,

"Well, it's up to you." But then he started bringing in his research proposals to me. I would make some suggestions, and then he would make it all more complicated. Months passed and he couldn't get his proposal accepted by his faculty committee. One day he came to me and said, "Well, I'll never be able to get a doctorate at this university. If I want one, I'll have to start all over again." And then, to my astonishment, he smiled triumphantly, because he had "got" me. He was willing to sacrifice everything to "get" everybody through his failure, his defeat. This is the kind of self-defeating behavior to which a lot of people dedicate their lives.

What I'm describing are different kinds of life decisions that people make, different ways of operating. These are some of the ones that cause problems. There are, of course, other decisions which are valuable, like the decision a person makes to be assertive; to be kind; to be cooperative; to improve the world.

I was talking to a young man recently whom I have known for many years. It used to be very difficult to speak with him because whatever the subject of the discussion, he would smile in a superior way and nod his head and tell you how much more he knew about it than you did. Recently I discovered I could talk to him. Now he is interested, asks me questions and wants to know my opinion. The change was so noticeable that I commented on it, and asked him, "How did it happen?" And he remembered making the decision when he was working on a project with his wife. No matter what he said, she wouldn't listen to him. She knew another way to do it, or she knew why it wouldn't work. At that point he realized how similar this was to the way he had been operating. Once he realized that, he said to himself, "That's stupid," and he started to listen to others. The result was that a number of very nice things began to happen to him; the payoff was favorable.

One of the most important things in working with people is to find out the context in which the former decision was made—the decision that is now causing trouble, the one that is no longer functional. I have found that if I really understand the context in which that decision was made, no decision is completely stupid or irrational. That's why it's very helpful for me to get into the mind of the other person, so I can figure it out, how he made his decision, no matter how bizarre it may appear to me.

Let me give you an example. A young man refuses to do any work. He goes to school, but doesn't do any of the necessary work. He drops out and gets a job. When someone tells him to do something, he says, "You can take this job and shove it."

He absolutely refuses to do anything.

This is obviously not a functional decision. It's not helpful to him. I try to find out the context. I'll ask him, "When did you start doing this?" I'll try to find out how he got into this pattern of behavior; how did he come to make the decision to refuse to do what is expected of him? I discover that when he was a child and was asked to do anything, he used to be eager to comply and was happy to be given a chore to do, but he remembers that he never could do it right. Whatever he did, it seemed to him that all he got was criticism, and—what's even harder for a child to take—he was made fun of, laughed at: "Look how he brings that milk bottle. Did you ever see anyone bringing the milk bottle that way? He's a real loser."

Remarks of this kind and sometimes anger and punishment followed his acts. When he would undertake something, he found he could never carry it through as well as his perfectionist parents and the rest of his family demanded. Well—sensibly enough, given that context—he made the decision never to attempt anything. Because if he didn't do anything, he couldn't be criticized or laughed at. Within the context of his life, that seemed like a rational decision, an appropriate response.

A man comes to me and complains that he cannot be close to anyone. He feels that there's a wall, or he sometimes describes it, he feels there is a "pane of glass between me and other people, and I can see them but I can't feel any direct contact." He tells me that he finds this very painful. So I ask, "Is it possible that this is your choice?" He thinks about it and says, "Yes, I was very close to my mother. I loved her. I had a wonderful time. When I was four years old, she left. Somebody said, 'Oh, she went out for a walk.' But she never came back. She had gone to the hospital and died. And then there was a whole series of relatives I was farmed out to. I made up my mind. No more: I'll never be close again." At that early age he could remember making up his mind, "No more, never again will I let myself get so close to somebody and experience that pain again." That's not an unusual cause with people who have problems with closeness.

Another way I find out the context of a decision is to ask when somebody complains about something, "What's the advantage; what's the payoff?" For instance, a woman complains that she's very depressed. Here the therapist must probe gently, because if he questions the person in a disapproving way, what he's saying is, "You're a faker."

That is not so. She is really suffering. So say, "Look, I know you're suffering, but is it possible that there's some payoff for this suffering, some advantage? Have you ever thought of the possible advantage? After discussion, this woman was able to see that her depression was a self-defeating expression of a loneliness she was able to take decisive measures to correct.

Frequently the depression will lift immediately if I have simply asked the proper question, and the patient will tell me the payoffs. Not all the time, of course, and only when I can question that patient in such a way that I am not experienced as being judgmental. That would kill it. If I ask my questions in such a way as to give the feeling what I am saying, "I think you're a faker; you don't have to suffer," I am in trouble and they're in trouble. I must explore whether there is any possible advantage to this behavior, and yet continue to show I am sympathetic. That's what I mean about being able to get into the person's head and show him that I am there. Then he will be able to tell me, rather than feel I am doing this only to collect evidence against him.

Some therapists are always playing Mr. District Attorney: "Why are you doing a thing like that?"—trying to "get" the patient. Such therapists ought to display a sign warning, "Everything you say will be used against you." That's not a productive attitude. The attitude has to be very much of trying to understand the payoffs for past decisions. And this can take a long time or it can take a very short time. The ways of getting this information can be as varied as the schools of therapy. One can use an encounter group, Gestalt therapy, the free association of psychoanalysis, or a completely nondirective way. Whatever the method, "Tell me about yourself" is a good way to start.

Then, after the person has described how he has lived, what the choices were which caused him to live this way and what the payoffs were for these choices within the context in which they were made, I ask, "Well, would you like to change?"

Many people don't necessarily want to change. It's not up to me to decide that they could change. Many times people are not ready to change. I try not to push them, because that would just make it more difficult for them to change when they are ready. If I push, I would just postpone the moment of decision, postpone their moment of change. I don't push them because most people have been pushed enough in life. So I just ask, "Do you want to change?"

You can ask yourself, if you find that you are doing something that displeases you, "Do I want to change this? There are payoffs to my procrastinating, to my depression, to my overeating, to my drinking too much, to my just hanging around." There are a lot of payoffs to all this and you have to ask yourself, "Do I want to give this up?" It's essential to find this out.

Now, one of the ways you can decide whether you want to change is to ask a very important question: "What are the alternatives to my present behavior?" There are always alternatives. One of the problems that most people I see have is that they don't recognize the alternatives or they see only two choices. We have a great tendency to perceive everything as either-or; either black or white; either yes or no. Many of us look at life only with such limited alternatives.

I remember a woman who came to see me saying, "What shall I do—continue to live with this horrible monster who's making life so impossible for me, or shall I commit suicide?" Obviously there were other alternatives, but she couldn't see any at the time.

Sometimes people see no alternative at all to the way they are. "I'm stuck with a husband I hate. I feel myself falling apart, the work is just too much; I can't stand it; I have to take care of the children and I get no help from him, only difficulties which he puts in my way, but what can I do? I have no alternative." They never even think of looking for alternatives.

It's very important to ask people whether there are any alternatives to the way they are living. Once in a while they are so stuck and have such blind spots about their lives, that they can't see any alternative, any other way of living. Sometimes it's important to start exploring the other possibilities. I tend to believe that the greatest growth in an individual, the best development and the best chance of his not having these kinds of problems again come if I let him find the other choices rather than try to sell him on another choice. It is very easy to become an evangelist for another choice. I might, for example, say that a person should be monogamous or I might say he shouldn't be. Either way, I'd be pushing him. The decision he arrives at *himself* is the most valuable for the individual, because one of the things I'm trying to help people learn is not just to deal with their immediate problems, but a whole way of dealing with life in general. That's the difference between psychoanalysis and behavior modification. Psychoanalysis has as its goal a way of dealing with problems in general, whereas behavior modification aims only to teach one how to deal with a specific problem. What I am trying to do is develop a method of dealing with problems in general; that's why selling people on a solution or alternatives is not helpful, but having them get the practice of looking for a variety of solutions *is* helpful.

Suppose after you've allowed yourself enough time for examining possible alternatives, you choose one. At this point, again, it becomes important to examine the possible payoffs and consequences of the one you've chosen and how they compare with the payoffs and consequences of the previous choice. This is the essence of the decision process. All systems of decision-making deal in terms of what the payoffs are. How does this one compare with the other one? Most people can project a little into the future, and see what is the advantage of the payoff.

Well, suppose a person finally decides. I try not to be in a hurry to be a cheerleader, not to say "good work," not to play coach. It's more important that he arrive by his own determination. Because he is going to have to do the work, not I. I can't be with him all the time. I can't lend him my ego, so it's *his* decision and he's approaching it completely from his own point of view.

A person says, for example, "Well, I want to give up dope." I ask, "Well, why?" It's a good question. "Why do you want to give it up? After all, with dope you have a tremendous way of dealing with anxiety." No method we know will get rid of anxiety as quickly as taking heroin—unfortunately. It's not that it doesn't work. It works very well. I make sure to present the advantages which I have got from listening to him, from his previous way of being. "Why do you want to give up suffering? As long as you're suffering you can control your whole family. You can tell your wife and she will do everything that needs to be done, if you suffer enough. Don't forget, cry and the world cries with you. Laugh and you laugh alone."

Many people really don't believe they have any alternative. Now, what we could say (and what many therapists have been saying for years) when a patient says, "I can't do this" is, "You don't *want* to do it." When someone says, "I can't do that," I try to look at it from the context of his life; not from an "outside" attitude of "he doesn't want to do it." He wants to do it, some part of him wants to do it, but at this point the payoffs for the present behavior are greater than the payoffs for a changed behavior, or the fear of change is too great.

Now, one very important payoff for the present behavior may be reduction of anxiety. Suppose somebody is suffering because he can never assert himself. Everybody walks all over him. He feels like a "dish-rag, like a doormat, like shit." And he says he can't change, no way he can change. "Well," I say, "this is your choice." But to just put it that way is not enough. If I start with, "What are the advantages to that? What are the payoffs to that?" if I really study with them what the payoffs are, there are still people who will say that they can't change. Therefore I try not to put the emphasis on their changing. To me, this is not manipulation because I believe with my value system that the emphasis should be on awareness. All I ask is that people be aware of their choices. They don't *have* to change. Once I insist on change, I am back in the same kind of relationship they have had in the past, which often led to the trouble to begin with. Because usually if I study the context of their lives, it seems to me someone wanted them to act in a certain way and they wanted to act in a different way. That's why they had to develop all kinds of methods of opposition which we label neurotic.

Let's look at some of the kinds of problems people come to me with. When a person comes in with something that appears to be completely outside his choice, say a very painful tic, I could certainly use behavior modification or one of the learning-theory techniques to deal with that, but before using anything I would ask, "Are you sure you want to get rid of it?" What are the advantages? Does it attract attention to him, set him apart? Even though I'm eventually going to use some other technique, I still deal first with having him study the payoff, because too often when I have used techniques that have been very effective in other cases, they weren't helpful because I had skipped a step, hadn't dealt first with the payoffs.

Now, when somebody has made a decision, the next job is to help him carry it through. For one thing, many people think that once they've made the decision, that's it. Unfortunately, it's not so. In many cases much more than one decision is required because some decisions deal with long-ingrained habits. Somebody who makes a decision to stop smoking still needs a lot of help in stopping because that is a habit with rewards of its own, principally the relief of tension. So he has to make his decision every time he is faced with the thought of picking up a cigarette. When I decide to lose weight, I can't just decide it once. I have to decide it every time I sit down to eat. I have to ask, "Do I want this food or do I want to be slim and beautiful?" "Do I want to eat the steak with the baked potato, the sour cream and the chives, the salad with roquefort dressing, apple pie with ice cream and the cocktails beforehand, and the wine with it and the brandy after-wards? Or do I want to be slim and beautiful?" In my case I decide that I'm not going to be narcissistic so I eat the potato and the pie and the ice cream. You really have to decide many of these things over and over again.

Let's use the example of the diet again. Very often, like many people who diet all the time, I go out and have a big meal and say to myself, "There goes the diet," and I forget all about dieting. Well, that's not necessary. It's too bad I had the big meal, but I can go back to carrying out the decision the next day. Since I know this, I break my diet rules all the time.

Say a man makes the decision not to be homosexual anymore—and then he meets a very groovy young lad with a very round ass, and loses himself. He doesn't have to continue to be homosexual just because he did that once. So in this case the therapist has to remind him that 1) the decision has to be made constantly, and 2) just because he slipped, it doesn't mean that it's all over. Another consideration to keep in mind is that even when someone doesn't carry through a decision, the very making of it can be a valuable experience. It's helpful for any person to guide him into a "no lose" situation. Many people have been in "no win" situations all their lives. So I try to help them into a "no lose" situation.

One man I had been working with made a decision to stop drinking. Months went by and he didn't take a drink, and then one night he got drunk. But when he got drunk this time he knew he was doing it as a conscious choice. He didn't claim, "I was led to drink by evil companions" anymore, or some other excuse. He knew he had made the choice, and because he knew this, he was able to tell me the context within which he had made the choice. He had trained himself always to examine the context in which he made a choice, so he knew the payoffs. What he recognized was that whenever he was out with a very attractive woman, he would get drunk. And he had been out with such an attractive woman. He then remembered all the feelings of anxiety he experienced when other men looked enviously at him for having this attractive woman—his fear that she would leave him, his fear that he would be made a fool in that situation. He realized that he chose drinking as a way of dealing with those fears. It seemed to me that in that one session when we discussed this incident he got a great deal more insight than we would have had in many months of traditional, free-associational, uncovering therapy. I have found that focusing on what happens when people do not carry out a decision can be very productive in arriving at understanding. I deal with the question of payoffs; that is, I stick over and over with the payoffs for which they decided not to stick with their decisions. This particular drinker, while he had not managed to stick to his decision, had nevertheless discovered that he had the guts to make it, and to make it again.

This is a simplified description of my method. But one of the hopeful things about this approach is that it sees human beings as having some control over what they are, rather than seeing them as victims of their biology or their history or their learning or their glands. Yet I don't believe that we have complete and total choice over our lives. Obviously, we don't.

A young man tells me the story about the time he wanted to kill himself. He is driving his car and comes to a bridge, and he figures, "Here's my perfect chance. There's a curve in the bridge and if I don't make that curve, I go off the bridge." So he rolls down the windows and steps on the gas and goes zooming up the bridge, and he runs out of gas. No gas, no suicide. Fortunately, this young man had a sense of humor, which should not be underestimated as a therapeutic tool.

Obviously, there are situations in which we don't have choices: our biology, our body, whether we'll be tall or short. We don't have a choice about the kind of world we're born into or about many of the experiences we have. We accept those limitations. But we do have a certain amount of choice. I remember listening to Konrad Lorenz, the eminent biologist and ethnologist, speaking about this matter. He was asked: "Do you believe in causality or in choice?" And he answered: "As a scientist speaking objectively, of course everything is causal. But as a human being, my experience tells me that I make decisions all day long." It is the area of choice which I think is the proper area for psychotherapy to concern itself with; that's the area where you can make the greatest amount of improvement.

Sometimes you have to change the milieu, that's true. That's another approach. Sometimes you have to change the chemical composition of a disturbed person with drugs or diet; that's another approach. But for a psychotherapist, somebody who has an interest in an individual's growth, his capacity to deal with life, it is helpful to deal with the matter of choice. Both from my clinical experience and from reading biography, I see over and over the crucial role played by the choices people make.

One of the most important partial techniques that I use frequently when somebody says he's unhappy and depressed, and makes a decision that he doesn't want to be depressed anymore, is to say, "Then, act as if you're happy"—using the James-Lange theory that we are happy because we laugh, and not that we laugh because we're happy. I suggest to a person that he act as if he *is* the way he wants to be. If he is not assertive, I suggest he act as if he *were* assertive. I give him homework and say, "Okay, you want to be assertive. What are some special places where you can act as if you're an assertive person?" And if he can't think of any, I have a whole bunch. Very simple things like having someone walk into a restaurant and not order food and just use the bathroom. Ask for matches without buying cigarettes; or ask a very handsome man you're interested in how to get someplace. Or I tell someone who can't speak in class, "The next time you go to class, prepare three questions you're going to ask." I work out with him things he can do to "act as if" he were the way he wants to be—the chosen desired behavior—and then I say, "Okay, let's see if you can be that way." In addition to acting "as if," I also ask people to imagine themselves the way they would like to be. If a woman is overweight I might ask her to imagine herself slim and attractive in a lovely bikini.

One of the problems in dealing with decisions is finding out which one is operative. Usually there is a whole hierarchy of decisions and every decision you have made influences every future decision. A woman gets up at a meeting where I am speaking. She says she wants help in carrying through a decision not to see a young man anymore. When we speak longer, we find out why she is seeing him. It becomes clear that the reason she continues to see him and says "yes" is that she doesn't know anyone else who can give her such a hard time. Her choice, as it turns out, is to suffer. So it is often important to get behind a decision. In this case the decision in front was not to see the man. The crucial one was whether she wished to suffer.

I decided to write this book on *Direct Decision Therapy*, or thought I had decided to write it, two years ago, but I hadn't been able to carry it out. So the other day I finally had the good sense to say to myself, "Now, let's see, what are the decisions that are interfering with this?" And I came up with some interesting ones. One decision I had made a long time ago was that everything should be easy for me. I was defined at the age of three as a genius, and therefore I decided that everything I do should be easy. When I sit down to write, I can't sit still and struggle with an outline because that would cast doubt upon my status of genius. I should be able to sit down and write, and all my thoughts should spring full-blown out of my brow, like Minerva out of the brow of Jupiter. So that was one crazy decision I had made, not to work like a mere mortal! Once I realized that this was one of my problems, I sat down and, for the first time, prepared a detailed outline, which I am now working from. It was necessary to become aware of a decision I had made. Actually, there was a whole series of decisions that I had to examine—not just the decision to write the book, but all the decisions which were interfering with this one.

If you learn to do this kind of self-questioning some of you will be able to apply it much better than I can, because it's notorious that everyone picks up a theory in the area where he has trouble. Many therapists who call themselves existential and talk about closeness and intimacy are among the coldest herrings you ever met. These are people who are incapable of live interactions for the most part. Obviously, if I chose to write a book about decisions, this is where I have had the greatest problem. And problems we have solved for ourselves are often the ones we can best solve for others.

The process of helping people with decisions starts the first moment I see them. One of the first things I ask is, "How long do you want to come for therapy?" We agree on the length of time it should take, with, of course, the provision that we not be inflexibly bound to a timetable. Very often in my experience, because a lot of my patients have come looking for classical psychoanalysis, the problem was to convince them that they didn't have to come for so long.

10

THE ESSENCE OF RATIONAL-EMOTIVE THERAPY

Albert Ellis, Ph.D.

It is the central theme of rational-emotive therapy (RET) that several basic irrational ideas, and many corollaries to which they normally lead, cause most emotional disturbances. For once humans believe the kind of nonsense included in these notions, they will tend to become inhibited, hostile, defensive, guilty, anxious, ineffective, inert, uncontrolled, or unhappy. If, on the other hand, they become thoroughly released from these kinds of illogical thinking, it would be difficult for them to become intensely emotionally upset, or at least to sustain their disturbance for any extended period.

Does this mean that all the other so-called basic causes of neurosis, such as the Oedipus complex or severe maternal rejection in childhood, are invalid and the the Freudian and other psychodynamic thinkers of the last sixty years have been barking up the wrong tree? Not necessarily. It means, if the main hypotheses of this approach are correct, that these psychodynamic thinkers have been emphasizing secondary causes or results of emotional disturbances rather than truly prime causes.

Let us take, for example, an individual who acquires, when he is young, a full-blown Oedipus complex: that is to say, he lusts after his mother, hates his father, is guilty about his sex desires for his mother, and is afraid his father is going to castrate him. This person, when he is a child, will certainly be disturbed. But, if he subsequently surrenders the basic illogical ideas we have been discussing he will not *remain* disturbed.

For this individual's disturbance, when he is a child, does not consist of the *facts* of his Oedipal attachment to his mother but of his *attitudes* — his guilt and his anxiety — about these facts. He is not guilty, moreover, *because* he lusts after his mother, but because *he thinks it is criminal and awful* for him to lust after her. And he is not anxious *because* his father disapproves of his sexual attachment to his mother, but because *he thinks it is horrible* to be disapproved by his father.

It may be very "natural" — meaning *quite common* — for a child to think himself a criminal when he lusts after his mother; but there is no evidence that he is born with this idea or that he *has* to acquire it. In fact, considerable autobiographical and clinical evidence regarding individuals reared even in our own very anti-incestuous society shows that many boys are able to lust after their mothers quite consciously and openly without becoming guilty about their lusting or terribly fearful of their father's opposition.

So Oedipal *attachments* do *not* have to result in Oedipal *complexes.* Even if, in a given case, a boy does become disturbed about his sexual feelings for his mother, he does not, as the Freudians stoutly and erroneously contend, have to remain neurotic in his adult life. For if he is reared (as, alas, he rarely is in our society) to be truly rational, he will not, as an adult, be too concerned if his parents or others do not approve all his actions, since he will be more interested in *his own* acceptance than in *their* approval. He will not believe that his lust for his mother (even should it continue to his adolescent and adult years) is wicked or villainous, but will accept it as a normal part of being a fallible human whose sex desires may easily be indiscriminate. He will realize that the actual danger of his father castrating him is exceptionally slight, and will have few fears on that account. And he will not feel that because he was *once* afraid of his Oedipal attachment he need *forever* remain so.

If this individual, when he is adult, still believes that it would be improper for him to have sex relations with his mother, instead of castigating himself for even thinking of having such relations, he will merely resolve not to carry his desires into practice and will stick determinedly to his resolve. If (by any chance) he weakens and actually has incestuous relations, he will again refuse to castigate himself mercilessly for being weak but will keep showing himself how self-defeating his behavior is and will actively work and practice at changing it.

Under these circumstances, if this individual has a truly rational approach to life, he will take an equally sane approach to Oedipal feelings. How, then, can he possibly *remain* disturbed about any Oedipal attachment that he may have?

Take, by way of further illustration, the case of a woman who, as a child, is continually criticized by her parents, who then feels loathsome and inadequate, who refuses to take chances at trying and possibly failing at difficult tasks, and who comes to hate herself more for being evasive and cowardly. Such a person, during childhood, would of course be disturbed. But how would it be possible to *sustain* her disturbance if she began to think, later in life, in a truly rational manner?

For if this person begins to be consistently rational, she will stop being overconcerned about what others think and will care primarily about what *she* wants to do in life. Consequently, she will stop avoiding difficult tasks and, instead of blaming herself for making mistakes, will say to herself something like: "Now this is not the right way to do things; let me stop and figure out a better way." Or: "There's no doubt that I made a mistake this time; now let me see how I can benefit from making it, so that my next performance will be improved."

This person, if she thinks straight in the present, will not blame defeats on external events, but will realize that she is causing them by inadequate or incompetent behavior. She will not believe that it is easier to avoid than to face difficult life problems, but will see that the so-called easy way is usually the harder and more idiotic procedure. She will not think that she needs someone greater or stronger than herself on whom to rely, but will independently buckle down to hard tasks. She will not feel, because she once defeated herself by avoiding doing things the hard way, that she must always continue to act in this self-defeating manner.

How, with this kind of thinking, could originally disturbed people maintain and continually revivify their emotional upsets? They wouldn't. Similarly, the spoiled brat, the worry-wart, the egomaniac, the autistic stay-at-home — all these disturbed individuals would have the devil of a time indefinitely prolonging their neuroses if they did not continue to believe utter nonsense: namely, the kinds of basic irrational postulates listed in rational-emotive writings.

Will not people's experiences during early childhood frequently *make* them think illogically, and thereby cause disturbance? No, not exactly. For even during childhood, humans *accept* the ideas that are pounded into them, and *need* not (at least technically speaking) automatically take them over. They *can* choose to reject these notions.

Thus, it is statistically probable that the great majority of children, if taught that they are monstrous if they do not behave well, will accept the idea that this is true, and will come to despise themselves for their misdeeds. But all children *need* not accept this belief; and a few, at least, do not seem to do so. These few, apparently, can and do challenge the notion that they are worthless, and somehow manage to grow up thinking of themselves as acceptable, even though their parents or others teach them the contrary.

Moreover, even when young children tend to accept parent-inculcated irrational thinking, they are quite able, in many instances, to challenge and contradict these views during their adolescence and adulthood, and to think otherwise — just as they are able to give up the religious views of their parents at this time. It is certainly *difficult* for adolescents or young adults to disbelieve the nonsense about themselves (or about religion) that their parents teach. But it is hardly mpossible! Childhood training, then, is an exceptionally strong influence in helping individuals to think irrationally. But it is not a fatal or irrevocable influence.

Neurosis, in sum, seems to originate in and be perpetuated by some fundamentally unsound, irrational ideas. People come to adopt unrealistic, impossible, often perfectionistic goals — especially the goals that they should be approved by everyone who is important to them, should do many things perfectly, and should never be frustrated in any major desires. Then, in spite of considerable contradictory evidence, they refuse to surrender these anti-empirical beliefs.

Why do so many millions of intelligent, well-educated, potentially rational people act in such a "nutty" manner today? A full answer to this question will eventually be given in a volume of its own. Part of this answer is summarized in the final chapter of my book, *Reason And Emotion In Psychotherapy* (1962). Suffice it to say here that even the most intelligent and capable persons in our society tend *also* to be, because of their biological tendencies, amazingly suggestible, unthinking, overgeneralizing, and strongly bound to the low-level kinds of ideation which it is so easy for them to become addicted to as children; and, perhaps more importantly, we bring up our citizens so that, instead of counteracting their normal tendencies toward irrationality, we deliberately and forcefully encourage them to keep thinking in childish, nonsensical ways.

By innate predisposition, therefore, as well as by powerful social propaganda (especially that promulgated by our families, schools, churches, and governmental institutions), even the brightest human beings often tend to become and to remain disturbed — that is, to behave stupidly and self-defeatingly when they are potentially able to behave more sanely and constructively.

Some "crazy" philosophies, such as the idea that people should be approved or loved by all the significant people in their lives, are not entirely inappropriate to childhood; but they are decidedly inappropriate to adulthood. Since most irrational ideas are specifically taught by our parents and other social agencies, and since these same irrational notions are held by the great majority of others in our community, let's acknowledge that neurotics tend to be *statistically* normal. In many respects, they have what may be called a cultural or philosophic rather than a psychiatric disturbance (Paul Meehl and William Schofield, personal communications). As Victor Frankl (1966) has pointed out "neurosis" today is usually "noetic" — that is, related to *value* inconsistencies and falsehoods.

Ours, in other words, is a generally neuroticizing civilization, in which most people are more or less emotionally disturbed partly because they are brought up to believe, and then to internalize and to keep reinfecting themselves with, arrant nonsense which leads them to become ineffective, self-defeating, and unhappy. Nonetheless, it is not absolutely *necessary* that humans believe the irrational notions which, in point of fact, most of them seem to believe today; and the task of psychotherapy is to get them to disbelieve their irrational ideas, to change their self-sabotaging attitudes.

This, precisely, is the task rational-emotive therapists assume. Like other therapists, they frequently resort to some of the usual techniques of therapy which I have outlined elsewhere (Ellis, 1955a, 1955b) — including the techniques of relationship, expressive-emotive, supportive, and insight-interpretative therapy. But they view these techniques, as they are commonly employed, largely as preliminary strategies, designed to gain rapport with clients, to let them express themselves fully, and to show them that they have the ability to change.

Many therapeutic techniques, in other words, wittingly or unwittingly show clients *that* they are illogical and how they presumably *originally* became so. But they fail to show how they are presently *maintaining* illogical thinking and precisely what to do to change it and replace it with more rational philosophies of life. And where many therapists passively or indirectly show clients that they are behaving illogically, the rational therapist goes beyond this point to make a forthright, unequivocal *attack* on clients' irrational ideas and to try to *induce* them to adopt more rational views.

Rational-emotive psychotherapy makes a concerted attack on self-defeating positions in two main ways: (a) The therapist serves as a frank counter-propagandist who directly contradicts and denies the self-defeating propaganda and superstitions which clients learned and are now self-instilling. (b) The therapist encourages, persuades, cajoles, and directs clients to engage in some activity (such as doing something they are afraid to do) which itself will serve as a forceful counter-propaganda agency against the nonsense they believe.

Both these main therapeutic activities are consciously performed with one main goal in mind: namely, that of finally inducing clients to internalize a rational philosophy of life just as they originally learned and internalized irrational views.

The rational therapist, then, assumes that clients somehow imbibed irrational modes of thinking and literally *made* themselves disturbed. It is the therapist's function not merely to show clients that they have these low-level thinking processes but to encourage them to change and substitute more efficient cognitions.

If, because clients are exceptionally upset when they come to therapy, they are first to be approached in a cautious, supportive, permissive, and warm manner, and sometimes allowed to ventilate feelings in free association, abreaction, role playing, and other expressive techniques, that may be an effective part of effective therapy. But the rational therapist is not deluded that these relationship-building and expressive-emotive methods are likely to really get to the core of irrational thinking and induce clients to cogitate more rationally.

Occasionally, this is true: since clients may, through experiencing relationship and emotive-expressive aspects of therapy, come to see they are acting illogically; and may therefore resolve to change and actually work at doing so. More often than not, however, illogical thinking will be so ingrained from constant self-repetitions and will be so inculcated in motor pathways (or habit patterns) by the time they come for therapy, that simply showing them, even by direct interpretation, *that* they are illogical

174

will not greatly help. They will often, for example, say to the therapist: "All right: now I understand that I have castration fears and that they are irrational. But I *still* feel afraid of my father."

Therapists, therefore, had usually better keep pounding away, time and time again, at the illogical ideas which underlie clients' fears and hostilities. They'd better show clients that they are afraid, really, not of their father, but of being blamed, of being disapproved, of being unloved, of being imperfect, of being failures. And he'd better convincingly demonstrate how and why such fears (for some of the reasons explained in other rational-emotive writings) *are* irrational and will lead to dreadful results.

If the therapist, moreover, merely tackles the individual's castration fears, and shows how ridiculous *they* are, what is to prevent this person's showing up, a year or two later, with some *other* illogical fear — such as the horror of his being sexually impotent? But if the therapist tackles his *basic* irrational thinking processes, which underlie *all* kinds of serious anxiety, it is going to be most difficult for this client to turn up with a new neurotic symptom some months or years hence. For once an individual truly surrenders ideas of perfectionism, of the horror of failing at something, of the dire need to be approved by others, of the world's owing him a living, and so on, what else is there to be severely anxious or disturbed about?

To give some idea of precisely how the rational-emotive therapist works, it might be well to outline an illustrative case.

Mervin Snodds, a 23-year-old male, came into his therapeutic session a few weeks after he had begun therapy and said that he was very depressed but did not know why. A little questioning showed that this severely neurotic client, whose main presenting problem was that he had been doing too much drinking during the last two years, had been putting off the inventory-keeping he was required to do as part of his job as an apprentice glass-staining artist. "I know," he reported, "that I should do the inventory before it keeps piling up to enormous proportions, but I just keep putting if off and off. To be honest, I guess it's because I resent doing it so much."

"But why do you resent it so much?"

"It's boring. I just don't like it."

"So it's boring. That's a good reason for *disliking* this work, but is it an equally good reason for *resenting* it?"

"Aren't the two the same thing?"

"By no means. Dislike equals the belief, 'I don't enjoy doing

175

this thing and therefore I don't want to do it.' And that's a perfectly sane sentence in most instances. But resentment is the belief, *'Because* I dislike doing this thing, I shouldn't *have* to do it.' And that's invariably a very crazy belief."

"Why is it so crazy to resent something that you don't like to do?"

"For several reasons. First of all, from a purely logical standpoint, it just makes no sense at all to say to yourself, 'Because I dislike doing this thing, I shouldn't *have* to do it.' The second part of this sentence just doesn't follow in any way from the first part. For the full sentence that you are saying actually goes something like this: 'Because *I* dislike doing this thing, *other people* and the *universe* should be so considerate of me that they should never make me do what I dislike.' But, of course, this belief doesn't make any sense: for why *should* other people and the universe be that considerate of you? It might be nice if they were. But why the devil *should* they be? In order for your belief to be true, the entire universe, and all the people in it, would really have to revolve around and be uniquely considerate of you."

"Am I really asking that much? It seems to me that all I'm asking, in my present job, is that I don't have to do the inventory-keeping. Is that too much to ask?"

"Yes, from what you've told me, it certainly is. For the inventory-keeping *is* an integral part of your job, isn't it? You *do* have to do it, in order to keep working at your present place, don't you?"

"Yes. I guess I do."

"And you do, from what you told me previously, want to keep working at this place, for your own reasons, do you not?"

"Yes. As I told you before, in my field I must have an apprenticeship for at least a year. And they agreed to take me on as an apprentice, if I'd work pretty long hours and do the work —"

"— including the inventory-keeping? —"

"Yes, including the inventory-keeping. If I did that and worked long hours, they'd take me on for the year I'd need toward the apprenticeship."

"All right, then. Because *you* wanted to learn the art of glass-staining and *you* can only learn it by having a year's apprenticeship, *you* decided to take on this job, with all its onerous aspects, especially including inventory-keeping. You had, in other words, a logical choice between graciously accepting this job, in spite of the onerous parts of it, or giving up trying to be a glass-stainer. But then, after presumably taking the first of these alternatives, you're now resentful because you can't get the second alternative without this onerous first part."

"Oh, but it isn't the work itself that I resent, in toto; but just the inventory-keeping part."

"But that still doesn't make sense. For the work, in toto, *includes* the inventory-keeping; and your choice of accepting the work in toto obviously includes accepting this part of it, too. So, again, instead of selecting one of two logical alternatives — doing the onerous work, including the inventory-keeping, or giving up trying to be a glass-stainer — you are resentfully and grandiosely refusing the first of these and yet insisting that you should not *have to* give up the second one, too. You are thereby actually insisting, as I said before, that the universe and the people in it should really revolve around *your* wishes rather than be what it and they actually are."

"It sounds, the way you're putting it, like I really haven't got a leg to stand on logically. But what about the fact that my boss *could,* if he wanted to be really fair to me — since I do quite a bit of work for him at a very low rate of pay — get someone else to do the inventory-keeping? After all, he knows perfectly well how I feel about it; and it is *not* work that is necessary for my glass-staining apprenticeship."

"True. Your boss *could* arrange matters differently and *could* let you off from this work that you so abhor. And let's even assume, for the moment, that he is wrong about *not* arranging things more this way and that any decent kind of boss would let you, say, do more glass-staining and less inventory-keeping work."

"Oh, that would be fine! Then I wouldn't gripe at all."

"No, probably you wouldn't. But even assuming that your boss *is* completely in the wrong about this inventory-keeping matter, your resenting him for *being* wrong still makes no sense."

"Oh? How come?"

"Because, no matter how wrong he is, every human being has the right to be wrong — and you're not giving him that right."

"But why does every human being have the right to be wrong?"

"Simply because he *is* human; and, because he is human, is fallible and error-prone. If your boss, for example, is wrong about making you do this inventory work — and let's still assume that he is dead wrong about it — then his wrongdoing would obviously result from some combination of his being stupid, ignorant, or emotionally disturbed; and he, as a fallible human being, has every

177

right to be stupid, ignorant, or disturbed — even though it would be much better, perhaps, if he weren't."

"He has a right, you say, to be as nutty or as vicious as he may be — even though I and others might very much like him to less nutty or vicious?"

"Correct. And if you are blaming him for being the way he is, then you are denying his right to be human and you are expecting him — which is certainly silly, you'll have to admit! — to be superhuman or angelic."

"You really think that that's what I'm doing?"

"Well, isn't it? Besides, look again at how illogical you are by being resentful. Whether you boss is right or wrong about this inventory deal, resenting him for being, in your eyes, wrong is hardly going to make him be any righter, is it? And your resentment, surely, is not going to do *you* any good or make you feel better. Then what good is it — your resentment — doing?"

"No good, I guess. If I take the attitude that — well, it's too bad that inventory-keeping is part of my job, and that by boss sees it this way, but that's the way it is, and there's no point in resenting the way it is, I guess I'd feel a lot better about it, wouldn't I?"

"Yes, *wouldn't* you? On still another count, too, your resentful attitude doesn't make sense."

"On what ground is that?"

"The ground that no matter how annoying the inventory-keeping may be, there's no point in making it still *more* irksome by your continually telling yourself how *awful* it is. As we consistently note in rational-emotive therapy, you're not merely being annoyed by the inventory-keeping job itself, but you're making yourself annoyed *at* being annoyed — and you're thereby creating at least two annoyances for the price of one. And the second, the one of your own creation, may well be much more deadly than the first, the one that is being created by the circumstances of your job."

"Because I'm refusing to gracefully *accept* the inherent annoyingness of doing the inventory, I'm giving myself an even harder time than *it* is giving me — is that right?"

"Quite right. Where the inventory-keeping is a real pain in the neck to you, you are a much bigger pain in the neck to yourself."

"Yeah. And since I have to do this kind of clerical work anyway, since I know darned well that the boss is not going to take it away from me, I would be doing myself much more good if I calmly and quickly got it out of the way, instead of making this terrible to-do about it."

"Right again. Can you see, then, the several points at which your resentment is thoroughly illogical in this situation, even though your dissatisfaction with doing the bookkeeping procedure may well be justified?"

"Let's see, now. First, I make a decision to take the job, in spite of its disadvantages, because I really want to be an apprentice, and then I try to go against my own decision by refusing to accept these disadvantages that I had first presumably accepted."

"Yes, that's illogical point number one."

"Then, second, I go to work for a human being, my boss, and then I refuse to accept him as human, and insist that he be a goddam angel."

"Exactly. That's illogical point number two."

"Third — let's see — I get quite wrapped up in my resentment, and give myself a start on an ulcer, when it's not likely at all to get my boss to change his mind or to do me any good."

"Right."

"And fourth. Now what was fourth? I don't seem to remember?"

"Fourth: you make yourself annoyed at being annoyed and put off doing work that you'll have to do, sooner or later, anyway, and with your annoyed-at-being-annoyed attitude, almost certainly make that work become considerably *more* onerous than it otherwise doubtless would be."

"Oh, yes. To my real annoyance I add to and imagine up a fake annoyance. And I make an unpleasant job more unpleasant than ever."

"Yes. Now can you see, not just in this case, but in every case of this kind, how your resenting someone is highly irrational?"

"Hm. I think so. But how can I stop being resentful? Just by seeing that it doesn't pay for me to be so?"

"No, not exactly. That's too vague. And too easy. More concretely, track down the exact sentences which you are saying to yourself to cause your resentment; and then question and challenge these sentences, until you specifically see how silly they are and are prepared to substitute much saner sentences for them."

At this point, I helped this client to see that he was telling himself sentences like these in order to be upsetting himself: "My boss makes me do inventory-keeping . . . I do not like to do this . . . There is no reason why I have to do it . . . He is therefore a blackguard for making me do this kind of boring, unartistic work.

179

So I'll fool him and avoid doing it . . . And then I'll be happier."

But these beliefs were so palpably foolish that Mervin could not really believe them, so he began to finish them off with sentences like this: "I'm not really fooling my boss, because he sees what I'm doing. So I'm not solving my problem this way . . . I really should stop this nonsense, therefore, and get the inventory-keeping done . . . But I'll be damned if I'll do it for him! . . . However, if I don't do it, I'll be fired . . . But I still don't want to do it for him! . . . I guess I've got to, though . . . Oh, why must I always be persecuted like this? . . . And why must I keep getting myself into such a mess? . . . I guess I'm just no good . . . And people are against me . . . Especially that son-of-a-bitch boss of mine . . . Oh, what's the use?"

Employing these irrational beliefs, Mervin soon became depressed, avoided doing the inventory-keeping, and then became still more resentful and depressed. Instead, I pointed out to him, he could tell himself quite different sentences, on this order: "Keeping inventory is a bore . . . But it is presently an essential part of my job . . . And I also may learn something useful by it . . . Therefore, I'd better go about this task as best I may and thereby get what *I* want out of the job, and later what *I* want out of the profession of glass-staining."

I also emphasized that whenever Mervin found himself intensely angry, guilty, or depressed, he was thinking irrationally and could immediately question himself as to what was the irrational element in his thinking, and set about replacing it. I used his current dilemma — that of avoiding inventory-keeping — as an illustration of his general disturbance, which largely took the form of severe alcoholic tendencies. He was shown that his alcoholic trends, too, resulted from his trying to do things the easy way and from his resentment against people, such as his boss, who kept making him toe the line and blocking his easy-way-out patterns of response.

Several previous incidents of irrational thinking leading to emotional upheaval in Mervin's life were then reviewed, and some general principles of rational thought were discussed. Thus, the general principle of self-damnation was raised and he was shown precisely why it is illogical for one person to damn anyone else (or himself) for anything.

The general principle of inevitability was brought up, and Mervin was shown that when a frustrating or unpleasant event is inevitable, it is only reasonable to accept it uncomplainingly instead of dwelling on its unpleasant aspects. The general principle of hostility was discussed, and he was shown that accepting oneself and trying to do what one is truly interested in doing in life is far more important than being obsessed with others' behavior and resentfully trying to get back at them.

In this manner, by discussing with Mervin some of the general rules of rational living, I tried to go beyond his immediate problem and to help him devise a generalized mode of thinking or problem solving that would enable him to deal effectively with almost any future similar situation that might arise.

After 47 sessions of RET (mainly in group), spread out over a two-year period, Mervin was able to solve his work problems, to finish his apprenticeship, and to go on to high-level activity in his profession. More importantly, he cut out almost all drinking and restricted himself to a half dozen glasses of beer a week. His hostilities toward his bosses and his other associates became minimal, and for the first time in his life he became "popular." Three and a half years after the close of therapy, he was maintaining his gains and was reasonably unescapist and unhostile.

Rational therapists, then, are frank re-educators who believe in a rigorous application of the rules of logic, of straight thinking, and of scientific method to everyday life. They ruthlessly uncover the most important elements of irrational thinking in clients' experience and energetically direct them into more reasonable channels of behaving. In so doing, they do not ignore or eradicate the clients' emotions. On the contrary, they help change emotions, when they are disordered and self-defeating, through the same means by which they commonly arise in the first place – that is, by thinking and acting. Through exerting consistent interpretive and philosophic pressure on clients to change their thinking and actions, the rational therapist gives them a specific impetus toward achieving mental health without which it is not impossible, but quite unlikely, that they will move very far.

Man and woman are uniquely suggestible as well as uniquely rational animals. Other animals are to some degree suggestible and reasoning, but peoples' better equipped cerebral cortex gives them unusual opportunities to talk themselves into *and* out of many difficulties.

The rational therapists hold that although humans' possession of a high degree of suggestibility and negative emotionality (such as anxiety, guilt, and hostility) may possibly have been adequate or advantageous for primitive survival, they can get along much better today when they become more rational and less suggestible. Perhaps it would be more realistic to say that since suggestibility seems to be an almost ineradicable human trait, we should not aim at destroying but at modifying it so that men and women become more *intelligently* suggestible.

In other words: people act in certain ways because they *believe* that they should or must act in these ways. If they are irrationally suggestible, they believe that they should act in intensely emotional, self-defeating ways; and if they are more rationally suggestible, they believe that they should act in less negatively emotional, less neurotic ways. In either event, the deeds in which they believe they tend to actualize. As Kelly (1955) has noted, an individual's difficulty frequently "arises out of the intrinsic meaning of his personal constructs rather than out of the general form which they have assumed. A person who believes that punishment expunges guilt is likely to punish himself."

The main problem of effective living, then, would seem to be not that of eradicating people's beliefs, but of changing them so that they become more closely rooted to information and to reason. This can be done, says the rational therapist, by getting people to examine, to question, to think about their beliefs, and thereby to develop a more consistent, empirically based, and workable set of constructs than they now may possess.

Rational-emotive psychotherapy is by no means entirely new, since some of its main principles were propounded by Dubois (1907) and many pre-Freudian therapists. Unfortunately, these therapists for the most part did not understand the unconscious roots of emotional disturbance, and it was Freud's great contribution to stress these roots. But although Freud, in his first book with Josef Breuer (*Studies in Hysteria,* 1895), was willing to go along with the notion that "a great number of hysterical phenomena, probably more than we suspect today, are ideogenic," he later often talked about emotional processes in such a vague way as to imply that they exist in their own right, quite divorced from thinking.

Because he came to believe that neurosis originates in and is perpetuated by unconscious "emotional" processes, and because he (and his leading followers) never defined the term "emotional" very accurately, Freud held that neurotic symptoms only can be thoroughly understood and eradicated through an intense emotional relationship, or transference relationship, between the client and the therapist. He and his psychoanalytic followers have used cognitive, or interpretive, therapeutic techniques to a considerable degree. But they still mainly stress the importance of the transference encounter in therapy.

In this emphasis, the psychoanalysts are at least partly correct, since many borderline and psychotic individuals (whom Freud himself often mistakenly thought were hysterical neurotics) are so excitable and disorganized when they come for therapy that they can mainly be approached by highly emotionalized, supportive or abreactive methods.

Even these severely disturbed individuals, however, are often surprisingly and quickly responsive to logical analysis of their problems and to philosophic reeducation if this is adequately and persuasively done. And the run-of-the-mill, less disturbed neurotics who come to therapy are usually quite reactive to rational therapeutic approaches and have little or no need of an intensely emotionalized transference relationship (including a transference neurosis) with the therapist.

That cognitive and rational processes can be important in understanding and changing human behavior has become increasingly acknowledged in recent years. Thus, Robbins (1955) notes that "cure is change; cure is the development of rational consciousness." Sarnoff and Katz (1954), in listing four major modes of changing human attitudes, put first the attacking of the cognitive object and frame of reference in which it is perceived, or the rational approach. Cohen, Stotland and Wolfe (1955) point out that, in addition to the usual physical and emotional needs of the human organism, "a need for cognition may exist, and . . . it may be a measurable characteristic of the organism, and . . . it may operate independently of other needs."

Bruner, Goodnow and Austin (1956) note that "the past few years have witnessed a notable increase in interest in and investigation of the cognitive processes. . . . Partly, it has resulted from a recognition of the complex processes that mediate between the classical "Stimuli' and 'responses' out of which stimulus-response learning theories hoped to fashion a psychology that would bypass anything smacking of the 'mental.' The impeccable peripheralism of such theories could not last long. As 'S-R' theories came to be modified to take into account the subtle events that may occur between the input of a physical stimulus and the emission of an observable response, the old image of the 'stimulus-response bond' began to dissolve, its place being taken by a mediation model. As Edward Tolman so felicitously put it some years ago, in place of a telephone switchboard connecting stimuli and responses it might be more profitable to think of a map room where stimuli were sorted out and arranged before every response occurred, and one might do well to have a closer look at these intervening 'cognitive maps.' "

Mowrer (1960a) even more strongly makes the point that the old S-R behaviorism has to be replaced by neobehaviorism which includes a liberalized view of perception. He notes that "the relevance of *cognitive* as well as *affective* processes is being recognized in systematic theory; and the solution to the problem of response selection and initiation hinges, quite specifically it seems, upon the reality of *imagery* (or *memory*), which is a cognitive phenomenon, pure and simple."

Even the Freudians have in recent years given much attention to "ego psychology," which is a distinct emphasis on the cognitive processes and how they make and can unmake human emotional disturbance. Freud himself noted, in *The Future of An Illusion* (1927): "We may insist as much as we like that the human intellect is weak. . . . But nevertheless there is something peculiar about this weakness. The voice of the intellect is a soft one, but it does not rest until it has gained a hearing. Ultimately, after endlessly repeated rebuffs, it succeeds." Modern psychoanalysts, such as Hartmann, Kris, and Loewenstein (1947, 1949), French (1952-1960), and Menninger (1958), have gone far beyond Freud, and beyond Anna Freud's (1937) pioneering work in ego psychology, and have helped make psychoanalytic technique radically different from its early ways and means.

In the field of modern psychology, Bartlett (1958), Berlyne (1960), Brown (1960), Brunswik (1952), Church (1961), Hovland and Janis (1959), Johnson (1955), Piaget (1952, 1954), in addition to the above-mentioned Bruner, Goodnow, and Austin (1956), have pioneered in the study of cognitive processes; and Leon Festinger (1957) has devised a theory of cognitive dissonance to explain much human normal and abnormal behavior. The work of these thinkers and experimentalists has sparked literally scores of studies that are adding to our knowledge in this area and showing how tremendously important cognitive and rational processes are in human affairs. As Arnold (1960) has appropriately noted in this connection, the emphasis of the orthodox Freudians on unconscious thinking and emotional affect may well have been an excellent corrective against the one-sided mentalistic views of the nineteenth century. But the fact remains that "in deliberate actions (and they comprise the large majority of our daily activities) we must depend on a judgment that is not intuitive to arouse an impulse to do something that may or may not be pleasant. Whatever may be the explanation for such rational judgments and deliberate actions, it is such judgments and actions that distinguish man from the brute."

It may also be glancingly noted that preoccupation with language and the cognitive processes has been most prevalent in recent years in many semi-psychological areas of knowledge, such as communication theory (Shannon, 1949; Wiener, 1948); the theory of games and economic behavior (Marschak, 1950; Von Neumann and Morgenstern, 1944); philosophy (Ayer, 1947; Morris, 1946); and literature and semantics (Burke, 1950, 1954; Korzybski, 1933, 1951). In fact, it is difficult to think of any major social science where an absorbing interest in the cognitive-rational processes has not become pronounced in the last several decades.

Friedman (1955) contends that Pavlovian conditioning consists largely of laws of unconscious biological learning and does not by any means cover the whole field of human adaptability. Rather, there also exists "learning at a conscious level with little involvement of dominant biological activities" and this cognitive type of learning "may well follow principles that are quite different from those found by Pavlov." Fromm (1950) insists that "to help man discern truth from falsehood in himself is the basic aim of psychoanalysis, a therapeutic method which is an empirical application of the statement, 'The truth shall make you free.' " Flew (in Feigl and Scriven, 1956) contends "that the fundamental concepts of psychoanalysis are distinctly human because they can only be applied to creatures possessed of our unique capacity to employ a developed language; that these are precisely the notions which rational agents employ to give account of their own conduct and that of other rational agents *qua* rational agents; that their place in psychoanalysis necessarily makes this a peculiarly rational enterprise. . . ."

Modern anthropological thinking, as Voget (1960) shows in an important recent paper, has also swung away from the concepts of the early 1900's which emphasized man's dependency upon and subservience to cultural processes or to his own unconscious emotions. Today, says Voget:

"It is apparent that judgment in human action is admitted and the individual no longer is conceived to be a habituated social unit or subject wholly to unconscious feeling states. The trend moved cautiously in the direction of Grace de Laguna's (1949) assertion that:

"... Man's rationality is not a higher faculty added to, or imposed upon, his animal nature. On the contrary, it pervades his whole being and manifests itself in all that he does well as in what he believes and thinks. Men may rationalize more often than they think objectively, but it is only because they are fundamentally rational beings that they are capable of rationalizing or feel the need of it. Man is rational in all his acts and attitudes, however unreasonable these may be; he is rational also in his feelings and aspirations, in his unconscious desires and motivations as well as in his conscious purposes, and his rationality shows itself in the very symbolism of his dreams. Men could not act and feel as they do if they could not form concepts and make judgments, but neither could they make use of concepts and engage in the ideal activity of thinking if they had not developed their innate capacity for the 'idealized' modes of behavior and feeling characteristic of human beings."

By direct statement and by implication, then, modern thinkers are tending to recognize the fact that logic and reason can (and damned well better!) play an important role in overcoming human disturbance. Eventually, they may be able to catch up with Epictetus in this respect, who wrote — some nineteen centuries ago — that "the chief concern of a wise and good man is his own reason."

Since I presented my first formulations on rational-emotive psychology in 1956, literally hundreds of controlled studies have appeared that almost unanimously show that the basic assumptions of RET — especially the assumption that changing human thinking significantly changes emoting — are empirically confirmed. In addition, scores of research studies have shown that (1) RET is clinically effective; (2) disturbed individuals have irrational ideas; (3) RET-type homework assignments are one of the most efficient forms of psychological treatment; (4) RET's educational forms of training can be efficiently used with many different kinds of groups of children, adolescents, and adults; (5) cognitive instruction and training improves the efficacy of behavior therapy. These and many other rational-emotive hypotheses keep acquiring increased empirical confirmation (Ellis, 1973a, 1973b, 1974a,

186

1974b, 1974c; Ellis and Budd, 1974).

REFERENCES

Arnold, Magda. *Emotion and Personality*. 2 vols. New York: Columbia University Press, 1960.

Ayer, A. J. *Language, Truth and Logic*. New York: Dover Publications, 1947.

Bartlett, Frederick. *Thinking*. London: Allen & Unwin, 1958.

Berlyne, D. E. *Conflict, Arousal and Curiosity*. New York: McGraw-Hill, 1960.

Brown, Roger W. *Words and Things*. New York: Basic Books, 1960.

Bruner, Jerome S.; Goodnow, Jacqueline J.; and Austin, George. *A Study of Thinking*. New York: Wiley, 1956.

Brunswik, E. *The Conceptual Framework of Psychology*. Chicago: University of Chicago Press, 1952.

Burke, Kenneth. *A Rhetoric of Motives*. New York: Prentice-Hall, 1950.

Burke, Kenneth. *A Grammar of Motives*. New York: Prentice-Hall, 1954.

Church, Joseph. *Language and the Discovery of Reality*. New York: Random House, 1961.

Cohen, Arthur R., Stotland, Ezra, and Wolfe, Donald M. An experimental investigation of need for cognition. *Journal of Abnormal and Social Psychology*, 1955, 51, 291-294.

Dubois, Paul. *The Psychic Treatment of Nervous Disorders*. New York: Funk & Wagnalls, 1907.

Ellis, Albert. *New Approaches to Psychotherapy Techniques*. Brandon, Vermont: *Journal of Clinical Psychology*, 1955a.

Ellis, Albert. Psychotherapy techniques for use with psychotics. *American Journal of Psychotherapy*, 1955b, 9, 452-476.

Ellis, Albert. *Reason and Emotion in Psychotherapy*. New York: Lyle Stuart, 1962.

Ellis, Albert. *Humanistic Psychotherapy: The Rational-Emotive Approach*. New York: Julian Press, 1973a.

Ellis, Albert. Rational-emotive therapy. In Corsini, Raymond (Editor) *Current Psychotherapies*. Itasca, Illinois: Peacock, 1973b. Pp. 167-206.

Ellis, Albert. Empirical validation of rational-emotive psychotherapy. *Counseling Psychologist*, In press, 1974a.

Ellis, Albert. The rational-emotive theory of personality. In Burton, A. (Editor) *Theories of Personality.* New York: Brunner-Mazel, 1974b.

Ellis, Albert. *Growth Through Reason.* New York: McGraw-Hill Paperback, 1974c.

Ellis, Albert, and Budd, K. *A Bibliography of Rational-Emotive Therapy and Cognitive-Behavior Therapy.* New York: Institute for Rational Living, 1974.

Feigl, Herbert, and Scriven, Michael (Editors) *Minnesota Studies in the Philosophy of Science.* Vol. I. Minneapolis: University of Minnesota Press, 1956.

Festinger, Leon. *A Theory of Cognitive Dissonance.* Evanston, Illinois: Row, Peterson, 1957.

Frankl, Victor. *Man's Search for Meaning.* New York: Washington Square Press, 1966.

French, Thomas M. *The Integration of Behavior.* 4 vols. Chicago: University of Chicago Press, 1952-1960.

Freud, Anna. *The Ego and the Mechanisms of Defense.* London: Hogarth, 1937.

Freud, Sigmund. *The Future of an Illusion.* London: Hogarth, 1927.

Freud, Sigmund, and Breuer, Josef. *Studies in Hysteria.* New York: Basic Books, 1895, 1957.

Friedman, Ira. Phenomenal, ideal and projected conceptions of self. *Journal of Abnormal and Social Psychology,* 1955, 51, 611-615.

Fromm, Erich. *Psychoanalysis and Religion.* New Haven: Yale University Press, 1950.

Hartmann, Heinz; Kris, Ernest; and Loewenstein, Rudolph M. Comments on the formation of psychic structure. *Psychoanalytic Studies of the Child,* 1947, 2, 5-30.

Hartmann, Heinz; Kris, Ernst; and Loewenstein, Rudolph M. Notes on the theory of aggression. *Psychoanalytic Studies of the Child,* 1949, 3, 9-36.

Hovland, Carl I., and Janis, Irving L. *Personality and Persuasibility.* New Haven: Yale University Press, 1959.

Johnson, D. M. *The Psychology of Thought and Judgment.* New York: Harper, 1955.

Kelly, George. *The Psychology of Personal Constructs.* New York: Norton, 1955.

Korzybski, Alfred. *Science and Sanity.* Lancaster, Pa.: Lancaster Press, 1933.

Korzybski, Alfred. The role of language in the perceptual process. In Blake, R. R., and Ramsey, G. V. (Editors) *Perception.* New York: Ronald, 1951.

Marschak, J. Rational behavior, uncertain prospects and measurable utility. *Econometrica,* 1950, 18, 111-141.

Menninger, Karl. *Theory of Psychoanalytic Technique.* New York: Basic Books, 1958.

Morris, C. W. *Signs, Language, and Behavior.* New York: Prentice-Hall, 1946.

Mowrer, O. H. *Learning Theory and Behavior.* New York: Wiley, 1960.

Piaget, Jean. *The Language and Thought of the Child.* New York: Humanities Press, 1952.

Piaget, Jean. *The Moral Judgment of the Child.* Glencoe, Illinois: Free Press, 1954.

Robbins, Bernard S. The myth of latent emotion. *Psychotherapy,* 1955, 1, 3-29.

Sarnoff, Irving, and Katz, Daniel. The motivational bases of attitude change. *Journal of Abnormal and Social Psychology,* 1954, 49, 115-124.

Shannon, C. E. *The Mathematical Theory of Communication.* Urbana: University of Illinois Press, 1949.

Voget, Fred W. Man and culture. *American Anthropology,* 1960, 62, 943-965.

Von Neumann, J., and Morgenstern, O. *Theory of Games and Economic Behavior.* Princeton: Princeton University Press, 1944.

Wiener, Norbert. *Cybernetics.* New York: Wiley, 1948.

11

EXISTENTIAL PSYCHOLOGY—WHAT'S IN IT FOR US?

A. H. Maslow, Ph.D.

I am not an existentialist, nor am I even a careful and thorough student of this movement. There is much in the existential writings that I find extremely difficult, or even impossible, to understand and that I have not made much effort to struggle with.

I must confess also that I have studied existentialism not so much for its own sake as in the spirit of, "What's in it for me as a psychologist?" trying all the time to translate it into terms I could use. Perhaps this is why I have found it to be not so much a totally new revelation as a stressing, confirming, sharpening, and rediscovering of trends already existing in American psychology (the various self psychologies, growth psychologies, self-actualization psychologies, organismic psychologies, certain neo-Freudian psychologies, the Jungian psychology, not to mention some of the psychoanalytic ego psychologists, the Gestalt therapists, and I don't know how many more).

For this and other reasons, reading the existentialists has been for me a very interesting, gratifying, and instructive experience. And I think this will also be true for many other psychologists, especially those who are interested in personality theory and in clinical psychology. It has enriched, enlarged, corrected, and strengthened my thinking about the human personality, even though it has not necessitated any fundamental reconstruction.

First of all, permit me to define existentialism in a personal way, in terms of "what's in it for me." To me it means essentially a radical stress on the concept of identity and the experience of

---

Reprinted, with permission, from *Existential Psychology*, edited by Rollo May, (New York: Random House, 1961), Chapter II, pp. 52-60.

identity as a sine qua non of human nature and of any philosophy or science of human nature. I choose this concept as *the* basic one partly because I understand it better than terms like essence, existence, and ontology and partly because I also feel that it can be worked with empirically, if not now, then soon.

But then a paradox results, for the Americans have *also* been impressed with the quest for identity (Allport, Rogers, Goldstein, Fromm, Wheelis, Erikson, Horney, May, *et al*). And I must say that these writers are a lot clearer and a lot closer to raw fact, that is, more empirical than are, e.g., the Germans Heidegger and Jaspers.

1. Conclusion number one is, then, that the Europeans and Americans are not so far apart as appears at first. We Americans have been "talking prose all the time and didn't know it." Partly, of course, this simultaneous development in different countries is itself an indication that the people who have independently been coming to the same conclusions are all responding to something real outside themselves.

2. This something real is, I believe, the total collapse of all sources of values outside the individual. Many European existentialists are largely reacting to Nietzsche's conclusion that God is dead and perhaps to the fact that Marx also is dead. The Americans have learned that political democracy and economic prosperity do not in themselves solve any of the basic value problems. There is no place to turn but inward, to the self, as the locus of values. Paradoxically, even some of the religious existentialists will go along with this conclusion part of the way.

3. It is extremely important for psychologists that the existentialists may supply psychology with the underlying philosophy that it now lacks. Logical positivism has been a failure, especially for clinical and personality psychologists. At any rate, the basic philosophical problems will surely be opened up for discussion again, and perhaps psychologists will stop relying on pseudo-solutions or on unconscious, unexamined philosophies that they picked up as children.

4. An alternative phrasing of the core (for us Americans) of European existentialism is that it deals radically with that human predicament presented by the gap between human aspirations and human limitations (between what the human being *is*, what he would *like* to be, and what he *could* be). This is not so far off from the identity problem as it might at first sound. A person is both actuality *and* potentiality.

That serious concern with this discrepancy could revolutionize psychology, there is no doubt in my mind. Various literatures already support such a conclusion, e.g., projective testing, self-actualization, the various peak experiences (in which this gap is bridged), the Jungian psychologies, various theological thinkers.

Not only this, but they raise also the problems and techniques of integration of this twofold nature of man, his lower and his higher, his creatureliness and his Godlikeness. On the whole, most philosophies and religions, Eastern as well as Western, have dichotomized them, teaching that the way to become "higher" is to renounce and master "the lower." The existentialists however, teach that both are simultaneously defining characteristics of human nature. Neither can be repudiated; they can only be integrated. But we already know something of these integration techniques— of insight, of intellect in the broader sense, of love, of creativeness, of humor and tragedy, of play, of art. I suspect we will focus our studies on these integrative techniques more than we have in the past. Another consequence for my thinking of this stress on the twofold nature of man is the realization that some problems must remain eternally insoluble.

5. From this flows naturally a concern with the ideal, authentic, or perfect, or Godlike human being, a study of human potentialities as *now* existing in a certain sense, as current knowable reality. This, too, may sound merely literary, but it is not. I remind you that this is just a fancy way of asking the old, unanswered questions, "What are the goals of therapy, of education, of bringing up children?"

It also implies another truth and another problem that calls urgently for attention. Practically every serious description of the "authentic person" extant implies that such a person, by virtue of what he has become, assumes a new relation to his society and, indeed, to society in general. He not only transcends himself in various ways; he also transcends his culture. He resists enculturation. He becomes more detached from his culture and from his society. He becomes a little more a member of his species and a little less a member of his local group. My feeling is that most sociologists and anthropologists will take this hard. I therefore confidently expect controversy in this area.

6. From the European writers, we can and should pick up their greater emphasis on what they call "philosophical anthropology," that is, the attempt to define man, and the differences between man and any other species, between man and objects, and between

man and robots. What are his unique and defining characteristics? What is as essential to man that without it he would no longer be defined as man?

On the whole, this is a task from which American psychology has abdicated. The various behaviorisms do not generate any such definition, at least none that can be taken seriously. (What *would* an S-R man be like?) Freud's picture of man was clearly unsuitable, leaving out as it did his aspirations, his realizable hopes, his Godlike qualities. The fact that he supplied us with our most comprehensive systems of psychopathology and psychotherapy is beside the point, as the contemporary ego psychologists are finding out.

7. The Europeans are stressing the self-making of the self, in a way that the Americans do not. Both the Freudians and the self-actualization and growth theorists in this country talk more about discovering the *self* (as if it were there waiting to be found) and of *uncovering* therapy (shovel away the top layers and you will see what has been always lying there, hidden). To say, however, that the self is a project and is *altogether* created by the continual choices of the person himself is almost surely an overstatement in view of what we know of, e.g., the constitutional and genetic determinants of personality. This clash of opinion is a problem that can be settled empirically.

8. A problem we psychologists have been ducking is the problem of responsibility and, necessarily tied in with it, the concepts of courage and of will in the personality. Perhaps this is close to what the psychoanalysts are now calling "ego strength."

9. American psychologists have listened to Allport's call for an idiographic psychology but have not done much about it. Not even the clinical psychologists have. We now have an added push from the phenomenologists and existentialists in this direction, one that will be *very* hard to resist, indeed, I think, theoretically *impossible* to resist. If the study of the uniqueness of the individual does not fit into what we know of science, then so much the worse for the conception of science. It, too, will have to endure re-creation.

10. Phenomenology has a history in American psychological thinking, but on the whole I think it has languished. The European phenomenologists, with their excruciatingly careful and laborious demonstrations, can reteach us that the best way of understanding another human being, or at least *a* way necessary for some purposes, is to get into *his Weltanschauung* and to be able to see *his*

world through *his* eyes. Of course such a conclusion is rough on any positivistic philosophy of science.

11. The existentialist stress on the ultimate aloneness of the individual is a useful reminder for us not only to work out further the concepts of decision, of responsibility, of choice, of self-creation, of autonomy, of identity itself. It also makes more problematic and more fascinating the mystery of communication between aloneness via, e.g., intuition and empathy, love and altruism, identification with others, and homonomy in general. We take these for granted. It would be better if we regarded them as miracles to be explained.

12. Another preoccupation of existentialist writers can be phrased very simply, I think. It is the dimension of seriousness and profundity of living (or perhaps the "tragic sense of life") contrasted with the shallow and superficial life, which is a kind of diminished living, a defense against the ultimate problems of life. This is not just a literary concept. It has real operational meaning, for instance, in psychotherapy. I (and others) have been increasingly impressed with the fact that tragedy can sometimes be therapeutic and that therapy often seems to work best when people are *driven* into it by pain. It is when the shallow life does not work that it is questioned and that there occurs a call to fundamentals. Shallowness in psychology does not work either, as the existentialists are demonstrating very clearly.

13. The existentialists, along with many other groups, are helping to teach us about the limits of verbal, analytic, conceptual rationality. They are part of the current call back to raw experience as prior to any concepts or abstractions. This amounts to what I believe to be a justified critique of the whole way of thinking of the Western world in the twentieth century, including orthodox positivistic science and philosophy, both of which badly need reexamination.

14. Possibly most important of all the changes to be wrought by phenomenologists and existentialists is an overdue revolution in the theory of science. I should not say "wrought by," but rather "helped along by," because there are many other forces helping to destroy the official philosophy of science or "scientism." It is not only the Cartesian split between subject and object that needs to be overcome. There are other radical changes made necessary by the inclusion of the psyche and of raw experience in reality, and such a change will affect not only the science of psychology but all other sciences as well. For example, parsimony, simplicity,

precision, orderliness, logic, elegance, definition are all of the realm of abstraction.

15. I close with the stimulus that has most powerfully affected me in the existentialist literature, namely, the problem of future time in psychology. Not that this, like all the other problems or pushes I mentioned up to this point, was totally unfamiliar to me, nor, I imagine, to *any* serious student of the theory of personality. The writings of Charlotte Buhler, of Gordon Allport, and of Kurt Goldstein should also have sensitized us to the necessity of grappling with and systematizing the dynamic role of the future in the presently existing personality, e.g., growth and becoming possibly necessarily point toward the future, as do the concepts of potentiality and hoping and of wishing and imagining; reduction to the concrete is a loss of future; threat and apprehension point to the future (no future = no neurosis); self-actualization is meaningless without reference to a currently active future; life can be a gestalt in time, etc., etc.

And yet the *basic and central* importance of this problem for the existentialists has something to teach us, e.g., Erwin Strauss's paper in Existence (Rollo May, 1958). I think it is fair to say that no theory of psychology will ever be complete that does not centrally incorporate the concept that man has his future within him, dynamically active at this present moment. In this sense, the future can be treated as an historical in Kurt Lewin's sense. Also we must realize that *only* the future is *in principle* unknown and unknowable, which means that all habits, defenses, and coping mechanisms are doubtful and ambiguous because they are based on past experience. Only the flexibly creative person can really manage future; *only* the one who can face novelty with confidence and without fear. I am convinced that much of what we now call psychology is the study of the tricks we use to avoid the anxiety of absolute novelty by making believe the future will be like the past.

I have tried to say that every European stress has its American equivalent. I do not think that this has been clear enough. I have recommended to Rollo May a companion American volume to the one he has already turned out. And of course most of all this represents my hope that we are witnessing an expansion of psychology, not a new "ism" that could turn into an antipsychology or into an antiscience.

It is possible that existentialism will not only enrich psychology. It may also be an additional push toward the establishment of another branch of psychology, the psychology of the fully evolved and authentic self and its ways of being. Sutich has suggested calling this onto-psychology.

Certainly it seems more and more clear that what we call "normal" in psychology is really a psychopathology of the average, so undramatic and so widely spread that we do not even notice it ordinarily. The existentialist's study of the authentic person and of authentic living helps to throw this general phoniness, this living by illusions and by fear, into a harsh, clear light which reveals it clearly as sickness, even though widely shared.

I do not think we need take off seriously the European existentialists' harping on dread, on anguish, on despair, and the like, for which their only remedy seem to be to keep a stiff upper lip. This high I.Q. whimpering on a cosmic scale occurs whenever an external source of values fails to work. They should have learned from the psychotherapists that the loss of illusions and the discovery of identity, though painful at first, can be ultimately exhilarating and strengthening.

REFERENCE

May, Rollo, *et al.* (Eds.) *Existence.* Basic Books. New York, 1958.

12

FAMILY INTERACTION, FAMILY HOMEOSTASIS AND SOME IMPLICATIONS FOR CONJOINT FAMILY PSYCHOTHERAPY

Don D. Jackson, M.D.

In a paper entitled *The Question of Family Homeostasis* presented at the 1954 annual meeting of the American Psychiatric Association, I focused on the upset that can occur within a family when one of its members undergoes intensive psychotherapy. Since then, I have continued to be interested in family interaction and family psychotherapy and would like to describe a way of viewing the family and some of the implications this system has for psychotherapy. These ideas stem mainly from two year's experience in seeing families in conjoint psychotherapy, listening to tapes of family interviews conducted by others, and occasionally studying sound movies of familial interactions. Recently our group has had the opportunity of serving as observers during the conjoint therapy of families of delinquents.[1] This experience has provided some valuable contrast data to our own studies which have been mainly concerned with the families of schizophrenics.

Our approach to understanding family interaction stems from certain biases. We favor communication theory because it lends itself to the descriptive study of tape recordings and sound movies. It avoids the necessity of imputing effects to the subjects and allows outside observers more opportunity to see if the data war-

Reprinted from Therapy, Communication, and Change. *Human Communication, 2:* 185-203. Edited by Don D. Jackson, Palo Alto: Science & Behavior Books, 1968 with the permission of the publishers.

[1] Courtesy of Dr. Charles Fulweiler.

rant the conclusions.[2] A second bias is our assumption that there is no "not caring"; that is, the family member is only relatively independent, and whether he admits it or not, is continually responding to reflected appraisals from others in his family. Third, along with Maier, Halstead, the Russells and others we feel that the characteristic of frustrated behavior is its stereotypy or compulsivity, whereas motivated behavior is characterized by flexibility. In the study of family interaction, stereotypy may be indicated by the absence of behavior in certain areas as well as by inexorable, inflexible and characteristic transactions. Thus the absence of family arguments can be a pathologic sign, but to the superficial observer might be considered evidence of good adjustment.

METHODOLOGY

Given these biases there still remains the problem of how to collect data, what data to collect and how to process the data collected. Our approach has favored the group situation over collaborative data because although collaborative psychotherapy has established its worth, as a methodology for research it has certain serious drawbacks:

1. The most obvious is simply the flow of information. It is dependent upon the therapists' relaying data, and therapists tend to react to each other as well as to form coalitions with their particular patient.

2. In collaborative therapy, time sequences may be puzzling. Reactions in therapy may be of a linear nature; that is, from A to his therapist to B's therapist, to B. But these may also be out of phase reactions like the song that says: "I Can't Get Used To The You That Got Accustomed To Me." In short, it is difficult for the therapists to know if A is reacting because B was hostile, or because B was so nice A couldn't stand it!

3. It is nearly impossible to introduce planned interventions for experimental reasons in collaborative therapy. If you wish to see what parameter A does to the family interaction you cannot drop it into the family pool and study the ripples. There is the time problem already mentioned, and the fact that each therapist will

---

[2]It is of interest that Dysinger, studying family interaction at the National Institute of Mental Health, came to a similar conclusion. Dysinger, Robert H. The action dialogue in an intense relationship. Presented at the American Psychiatric Association Annual Meeting, Chicago, Illinois, May 1957.

drop a slightly different pebble in a slightly different manner.

4. There is an economic aspect to collaborative therapy which is not relevant here except as it pertains to the enormous difficulty in getting the therapists together to spend a significant amount of time going over their material.

Seeing a married couple together, the patient and his parents, or the whole family as a group does not completely overcome the above objections to collaborative therapy, but does offer some advantages as a scientific tool. Suppose, for example, one wished to study the kind of transactions that result in a homeostatic shift in the family. It is possible to get the family to play a game while being filmed. The game might consist of each member, in turn, introducing an idea much as he would play a card. The next member can add to the idea, trump it, or play a different suit, as it were. The therapist for his turn introduces the idea: "who is the boss in this family?" One family appeared stunned, gazed uneasily at each other, and then the mother came through brilliantly with, "the cook!"

Although the therapist in conjoint therapy is on the scene and thus tends to correct the "time problem" of collaborative therapy, he has a huge problem in handling the manifold transferences and counter reactions. Recording or filming the sessions and supervision are important checks. Another possibility has been introduced by Fulweller.[3] He views the family interaction from behind a one-way mirror and steps into the room only to make an intervention or interpretation. Unless you have observed this technique, it is difficult to picture how the therapist's resolute detachment forces the family members to turn to each other. Our group plans to employ this technique, as well as having the therapist present during the sessions.

PROCESSING THE DATA

Once one has collected tapes or films or simple impressions, the problem of what to do with the data arises. As a background for that I would like to emphasize that in studying the homeostatic mechanisms of the family it is useful to make a distinction between variables and parameters. If a thermostat is set at 68 degrees there

---

[3]Personal communication.

are constant oscillations which turn the furnace on and off in order to maintain a relatively steady state. The better the thermostat, the wider the range of variables that can be handled without a new set being necessary. When the thermostat is moved to 70 degrees we have a new parameter and a new level of homeostasis. If the neighbors buy a new car there are apt to be oscillations in the family around the point of what it takes to make them happy. However, in some families such a variable may require a new parameter being introduced; for example, the concept of how lovely it is not to be mercenary. It might seem that the introduction of a new parameter could be treated like a simple learning experience, that is, if we are frustrated by our own not having a new car we make up a rule that says we wouldn't want one anyway. Actually new parameters are apt to be of the order of learning to learn. This is because in a family we do not have just a linear system where A affects B who is affected by C which alignment augments or diminishes A's effects. Family interaction is a system in which A can also anticipate an effect on B, and this modifies his subsequent behavior, and B in turn modifies his response in anticipation of what he thinks A anticipates. When C and perhaps some little Ds and Es are thrown into the picture one is faced with a problem that Univac is unprepared to handle.

Many of you perhaps remember the game, "paper, scissors and rock," or one of its many modifications. Paper covers rock, rock breaks scissors and scissors cut paper. You are playing the game and about to make the sign for paper when you think, "My opponent thinks I'm going to make paper so he'll make a scissors. I'll fool him and make a rock." Meanwhile your opponent is thinking. "He thinks that I think he's going to make paper so that he'll make a rock and break my scissors so therefore I'll make paper." In such games of two, with dedicated players, there are no random moves. The dedicated player discerns what system his opponent will use in anticipation of such and such a move on his own part and, in addition, at a higher level he anticipates what changes his opponent will make in response to having his system unveiled. In such a game of two, one possibility for successful gamesmanship occurs when a player randomly varies his play; that is, ignores that the other is an opponent who changes his system of systems. This does not seem a possible gambit in the family unless one of the members has outside experiences which increase his independence to the point that he ignores the moves of the other members. As I will mention later, this is one possible explanation of why psychotherapy for one member can upset the whole family. Or conversely, why progress in psychotherapy may be impossible for one member if the rest of the family is left out.

To return to the thermostat analogy, it is obvious that oscillation can be detected by the clustering of oscillations around a new point. In the family, because of the inexact state of behavioral science currently, we are faced with a variety of measures or units. Such units as anxiety, dependency processes, and role-playing have been utilized but it has seemed to us that they have disadvantages some of which our own system avoids. The system we use might be labelled "control theory." In essence, it is the belief that *all persons implicitly or explicitly are constantly attempting to define the nature of their relationships.* "Control" in this sense does not mean anything as simple as one individual explicitly telling another what to do. Rather, it refers to the fact that every communication can be seen as a report and a command and the command may be of a higher order of messages than the explicit message. Thus A may use a "one down" play to influence B to take care of him. B would thus appear to be in control, but as far as A is concerned, he is determining the nature of the situation.

Evidence for the attempt to define the nature of the situation can be inferred from the individual's communication when context, verbal and non-verbal communications are all regarded as capable of modifying each other. Rather complex possibilities occur when as in a recent *New Yorker* cartoon, the boss says with a smile, "But, Jones, I don't want you to agree with me because I say so, but *because you see it my way.*" This is as confusing a ploy as the mother who orders the child not to be so obedient. The communicative behavior that we view as an attempt to define the nature of the relationship consists of labelling a relationship or aspects of a relationship in one of two ways: complementary or symmetric. A complementary relationship consists of one individual giving and the other receiving. In a complementary relationship the two people are of unequal status in the sense that one appears to be in the superior position, meaning that he initiates action and the other appears to follow that action. Thus the two individuals fit together or complement each other. The most obvious and basic complementary relationship would be the mother and the infant.

A symmetric relationship is one between two people who behave as if they have equal status. Each person exhibits the right to initiate action, criticize the other, offer advice and so on. This type of relationship tends to become competitive; if one person mentions that he has succeeded in some endeavor the other person mentions that he has succeeded in an equally important endeavor. The individuals in such a relationship emphasize their equality or their symmetry with each other. The most obvious symmetric relationship is a pre-adolescent peer relationship.

This simple division of relationship into two types applies to all two person systems. No relationship between two people will consistently be of one type in all circumstances. Mature relationships, we label "parallel" since there are frequent complementary and symmetric crossovers. In the ideal husband and wife relationship each defines areas in which he determines the nature of the relationship, in which he typically behaves in a symmetric or complementary manner. The determination of areas of control obviously are determined by cultural factors as well as by special skills such as the fact that the woman is the only one who can have a baby.

In a pathologic relationship, we see rather than areas of control a constant sabotaging or refusing of the other's attempts to define the relationship. The communication methods used to refuse, negate or sabotage the other's attempt to define the nature of the relationship may range from a simple, direct "no" to complex multi-level messages in which a covert denial is further obscured by itself being denied. This is the essence of the "double bind" situation which our group has described (Bateson, et al, 1956).

A pathologic situation may also be evident because there is a direction in the two person system. Consider the following examples. The husband, in a culturally acceptable complementary maneuver says to his wife, "I'll take you to a movie." The wife (not accepting his benevolence) states, "There's nothing good playing." The husband replies (not accepting her denial of his benevolence), "Are you sure? Where's the newspaper?" Whereupon the wife responds: "Besides I have a headache." The husband running into a rather impervious ploy states, "Okay, I guess I'll watch some TV." The wife responds: "Fine. There is a program I wanted to see."

We would expect in this situation where the wife increasingly appears to define the nature of the relationship, that the husband will resort increasingly to withdrawal techniques thus increasing the wife's apparent control of the relationship. The relationship will thus exhibit a tendency, a direction rather than a healthy oscillation.

Every child begins life in the secondary position of a complementary relationship since someone must take care of him. However, as the child grows older, in the normal family situation he is encouraged more and more to determine the nature of his own activity, and ultimately he is able to behave with his parents as one equal to another. From the moment the child is old enough to "assert himself" he begins to learn to make symmetric maneuvers. When he insists on walking by himself or tying his own shoes he is learning to act with others in a symmetric way. In the normal situation his parents let him behave in this way. They are willing to encourage him to tie his own shoes, and they are willing to tie his shoes for him if he requests a complementary maneuver on their part. Within a general framework of taking care of their child, the parents encourage him to experiment and to learn to behave as an equal in preparation for that time when he leaves his complementary context and achieves symmetric relations with other people. The child also learns to make these maneuvers in fantasy prior to the time he is capable of making them in reality. Such practice often takes place during play. For example, the child may ride on his father's back and treat the father like a beast of burden who must be directed in his activities. Thus the child assumes in play the superior end of a complementary relationship. Of course, daddy knows that he really isn't a horse and he can show this at any time by bucking the child off, which he may do to end the game.

Obviously, the adult's ability to interact in different types of relationships can be inhibited by the ways his family encourages or discourages his maneuvers during childhood. For example, a mother who resents taking care of her child may make it unpleasant for him to accept the secondary position in a complementary relationship. The child will learn that he should not maneuver her to take care of him because this provokes punishment. As an adult he could not accept the secondary position in a complementary relationship. When ill he might insist on continuing his own activities and refuse to let anyone take care of him. Although he might be capable of competing with others, he would be unwilling to be dependent on others. Similarly, a child might be discouraged from learning to behave in a symmetric way. If he behaved as an equal, for example, by trying to tie his own shoes, his mother might punish him by withdrawal, and the child learns that he must let her tie them for him. These problems are complicated by the fact that *a child not only learns to respond to his parents, but learns to use them as a model for how to respond.* If a mother resents taking care of her child, the child will not only avoid requests that she take care of him, but he has before him a model of how he should take care of others. Because of that model, he might only be capable of resentfully taking care of others, as well as being inhibited in letting others take care of him.

Each individual in a relationship is constantly commenting on his definition of the relationship implicitly or explicitly. Every message exchanged (including silence) defines the relationship implicitly since it expresses the idea, "This is the sort of relationship where this sort of message may be given." There are also relationship messages (or maneuvers, or ploys) in which the purpose of the message is to test the other's acceptance of one's definition of the relationship. The obvious relationship messages are requests, commands or suggestions but in a more important way relationship messages can also consist of letting the other individual define the relationship. For example, one individual might act passively in order to force the other to take over. Such a ploy may not appear to be defining the relationship and thus may be acceptable to the other person, but the introduction of a new parameter may reveal the ploy and cause an upheaval. Thus a wife might behave in a helpless fashion and her husband accept the role of the strong one. However, if he takes to bed with a cold and she says, "I'd love to take care of you, dear, but I feel so terrible myself," the horrible thought may intrude on the husband's consciousness that "she's been doing this to me right along."

CATEGORIES OF FAMILIES

Since relationship messages are constantly being exchanged, it is likely (within certain limits) that a family can be characterized by the maneuvers used. The extent to which relationship messages are implicit (e.g., symptoms of various kinds), explicit, commands, helpless or "one-down" ploys, will vary from family to family. It is possible to classify families or relationships into four types on the basis of the transactions used to define the nature of the relationship.[4] These four categories are: stable satisfactory, un-

[4]Apology is made here for the fact that "complementary" and "symmetric" are mainly useful in describing two-person systems. In describing a family, we can use two-person terms since it is possible to talk about alliances, coalitions, disalliances, etc.; however, a three- or four-person terminology would be far more appropriate. Unfortunately, we have not yet developed it.

stable satisfactory, stable unsatisfactory and unstable unsatisfactory.

These categories may be used to describe a phase of a relationship, a relationship that has perduring features or a family that shows a predominant trend. A couple may have an unstable satisfactory relationship until their first child, and by their third have settled down to a stable unsatisfactory existence. The range, or richness of maneuvers, makes a certain amount of prediction possible as to the relationship tendencies; however, fate, acts of God and one thing and another make accurate prediction unlikely. One of our families went through an unstable period with much overt battling between father and mother until the father developed tuberculosis and was more or less out of the home for four years. After he returned the family situation jelled into a stable unsatisfactory state.

I would like briefly to describe each type of family and to emphasize that this description is temporal, and no attempt has been made to relate these types to socio-economic classes.

A stable satisfactory relationship can be defined as one where both parties can explicitly reach agreement that one or the other is in control of the relationship or in control of areas within the relationship. A person defined as being in control of the relationship is the one who initiates action, decides what action will be initiated or establishes what areas within the relationship shall be controlled by the other person. Note the emphasis on "explicitly." In this type of relationship, it is possible for each person to discuss the relationship and comment on the effect of the other person's behavior on him. Thus the stability is maintained by the possibility of reinstituting a stable state when the relationship becomes unstable through a disagreement. "Stable" does not mean an entirely smooth functioning of the relationship and implies brief periods of instability. Further, it is not implied that discussing the relationship means psychiatrizing. The fact that one may comment on the relationship may mean that no comment is necessary.

An unstable satisfactory relationship differs from the stable satisfactory relationship only in the length of the periods of instability. It occurs when two people are working out their definition of the relationship during a time when internal or external forces are creating frequent unstable periods which are stabilized with difficulty. These periods occur frequently enough to make the relationship unstable, yet the stable periods are satisfactory to both parties.

For example, mother and daughter may begin to reach an unstable but satisfactory relationship when pubertal forces plus the behavior of her friends encourage the girl to seek more independence and more adventures as a female rather than a child. The mother may at the same time feel reluctant to see her daughter growing up, feel competitive as the daughter becomes a woman, or fear the criticism of her friends if her daughter doesn't behave. The issue immediately becomes one of who is in control of the relationship as the daughter seeks to define it along the line of a relationship between two equal women and the mother tries to define it as a mother and child relationship. The girl may stay out too late on a date as a maneuver to show that she is defining the relationship in her way, and the mother may restrict the girl to the house for a week to prove that she is defining it in her way. The relationship can continue to be satisfactory only if mother and daughter explicitly deal with the relationship and eventually reach compromises. Explicit, I must point out again, does not necessarily refer to verbal processes. In the example above, neither the mother nor the daughter need speak to each other about their definitions. They might interact with the father in such a way that he eventuates a set of apparently new rules that result in a compromise.

The unstable satisfactory type of relationship is characteristic of any new or changed relationship since it must be progressively defined by the parties until a shared definition of the relationship is worked out. For example, a newly married couple must go through unstable but satisfactory periods in their relationship until the question of who is in charge of particular areas of the relationship is agreed upon. The introduction of parameters like toilet training and sexual intercourse into a relationship are bound to produce at least temporary instability. If the mother feels the child does it on the potty because she said to, and the child feels, "It's my feces so I don't mind doing what she says," then stability can return because areas have been agreed upon. It is quite another matter if the child feels vaguely that mother makes his bowels move.

An unstable unsatisfactory relationship is one where no explicit or implicit agreement is reached upon the question of who is in control of the relationship or areas within it. It is characterized by the need to redefine the relationship the moment it becomes defined so that stable periods are brief, and unstable periods are long. *The discussion that takes place between the parties is apt to be not at a relationship level, but at a level of details.* Each party tends to take the behavior of the other party as a challenge at a relationship level without this ever being discussed. Maneuvers to control the relationship are made with simultaneous denials that these are maneuvers. Often psychosomatic or hysterical symptoms are used as ways of defining the relationship *since they are messages which can be denied as messages.* A wife may get a headache whenever she is with her husband, yet both can discuss how unfortunate it is that she has headaches. Having the headache may permit her to control an area of the husband's behavior without any need to take explicit responsibility for defining the relationship. Thus, she can ask that he leave her alone because she has a headache rather than defining the relationship explicitly as one where she has the right to be alone if she wishes to be.

The unstable unsatisfactory relationship is often characterized by "helpless" maneuvers to control the relationship. Neither party can say, "I'm the boss," nor can they say, "You're the boss." Thus transactions are apt to consist of *complementary maneuvers* which are redefined as soon as they are accepted by the other individual. Or to put it another way, there is competition over dependency as well as alleged independency.

The mother and the daughter in this type of relationship might quarrel about whether a blue dress is prettier than a pink one or whether someone else is allowed to stay out until one o'clock instead of twelve. The quarrels would not explicitly deal with whether the mother has a right to define the limits of the daughter's behavior or whether the daughter has the right to define her own limits. The mother cannot let the daughter choose her time to come home because this would mean the daughter was boss in the relationship. Similarly, she cannot set a time for the daughter to come home and insist that her instructions be followed because this would mean that she was defining their relationship. The result is the setting of a time by the mother which the daughter either ignores, or complies with by indicating she was tired and wanted to come home anyway. Should the daughter truly comply, the mother would indicate concern over her submissiveness. In this type of relationship rebellion by the daughter might be handled by hurt and helpless maneuvers on the mother's part so that the daughter constantly feels she must volunteer to do things which would please her mother. That is, she must initiate action in response to indirect commands by her mother, but since such actions appear to put her in charge of the relationship they must be sabotaged by the mother. *Neither mother nor daughter can overtly and explicitly take responsibility for the action nor assume the initiative in setting the limits of the relationship.* The relationship thus never becomes stabilized because mother or daughter becomes panicked or hurt if discussion is threatened at the relationship level.

We have been impressed by the virtual absence of completed transactions in the unstable unsatisfactory family. As soon as agreement is apparently reached by two members the issue is reopened either by the participants or a third party.

In an interview with such a family, the mother arrived drunk in order to be able to tell the therapist that her daughter had to change her ways or leave home. The daughter, who had begun to define her relationship to her mother as symmetric, stated she would be glad to leave home. The therapist tried to force father to state his opinion but he allowed mother to speak for him. The therapist then stated he had found a rather ideal place for the daughter to stay and perhaps she should move out of the house for awhile. The mother ended the session stating the therapist should find a place for her also because she was leaving her husband!

A stable unsatisfactory relationship is one where the parties have agreed never to make an issue of who is in charge of the relationship nor of areas within it. Neither party dares signal dissatisfaction with the relationship nor dares recognize such signals from the other party. The relationship is stable in the sense that those problems which might make it unstable are avoided, yet it is unsatisfactory since there is so little giving or receiving. Typically, this is a withdrawn, distant kind of relationship although the "stability" may make it appear to the outsider as more satisfactory than it is. Both Lidz (1958) and ourselves (Jackson, 1957) have mentioned it may be several months before the therapist sees the underlying pathology. This is particularly true because of the initial "united front" of the parents, or their "pseudo-mutuality" as Lyman Wynne and his co-workers have called it. (Wynne, et al, 1958).

The stable unsatisfactory relationship is characterized by tremendous inflexibility and compulsivity. Cultural and social rules such as religious principles are important because they involve outside authority and thus apparently free the family from conflict over who is determining the nature of the relationship. Role playing may be stressed for much the same reason; thus "mother" has certain agreed upon rights and privileges that go with the title. There may be gigantic distortions of ordinary social definitions in order to impersonalize the actions of the individual. The lack of contact with people outside the family aids this process.

A problem arises for these families on the rare occasions when they encounter a psychotherapist. In order to show agreement and cohesion, the parents especially may apologize for, or explain, each other. In doing so they are making a symmetric maneuver and it may be rebuffed by the spouse. A mother, wanting to account for the father's being away from home a great deal, but not wanting to imply that it related to his feeling toward her, stated that he was a very hard worker. The father retorted that he didn't work "that hard"; thus giving the therapist an opening to inquire about what he did do with his time.

John Weakland and I recently reported on a patient from a stable unsatisfactory family (Weakland and Jackson, 1958). His psychotic break occurred at the point when he had to separate long letters from short letters on his post office job. The "in-betweens" proved too much; he was unable to define explicitly which should go in which pile. When a co-worker told him he looked ill, he realized he felt sick and went home.

In our experience, the stable unsatisfactory family is difficult to get into therapy and nearly impossible to keep in therapy. If they produce a schizophrenic, current hospital practices in the handling of relatives protect them from coming under scrutiny, and the patient remains *the patient*.

THE PSYCHOTHERAPEUTIC APPROACH

The three categories of families from which patients come—namely, unstable satisfactory, unstable unsatisfactory, and stable unsatisfactory—present different problems in terms of optimum psychotherapeutic intervention. While no hard and fast rules obtain, since the dividing lines between these categories are arbitrary, it does seem that an appraisal of the kind of family interaction aids the therapist in planning his treatment. Thus a young schizophrenic from a stable unsatisfactory family probably could not recover while living at home if he were seen only in individual therapy, or if the family were seen only once a week. I would like to give an example or two of psychotherapeutic experiences with each category of families, while emphasizing that our knowledge of tailored techniques is very limited.

The unstable satisfactory family. Obviously the most joyful results come from this group. If the spouses are seen together there is usually enough mutual regard between them to withstand some fairly straightforward intervention on the therapist's part. The presenting complaint can usually be traced to an event or happening—a new parameter. Occasionally, it is as obvious as the couple who felt they were in love until they made it legal. Sometimes it is a concatenation of events that crystallizes into a gestalt that the psychiatrist can help clarify.

A young man was sent to the psychiatrist by his wife because of three recent episodes of infidelity. It became apparent during the interview that 1) he had become successful recently after some years of working toward it in dubious battle; 2) his wife had recently had their third child, a boy, and the patient was the third child in his family. The wife had a younger brother who was the favorite in her family and who was referred to as "a juvenile delinquent"; 3) the wife was unbelievably naive or else she was pushing the patient toward his extracurricular activity, 4) the patient did all that one can do and still managed to remain unaware of it in order to signal his wife that he was being unfaithful.

The patient was told to bring his wife to the next visit since his cure lay largely in her hands. This was done since it was obvious that she felt unimportant and also felt uninvolved in his sins in the typical manner of the injured party. Although she came initially with the attitude of "anything to help George get over this nasty business," by the end of the second session she was able to accept the comment that her finger was also in this particular pie. They were seen together for only nine sessions with two follow-up visits and made remarkable progress. The brevity of the therapy was partly financial, and partly because of the amount of work they did together between sessions.

I would say that the danger in the unstable satisfactory category lies in overestimating the extent of family fracture and not utilizing positive forces present. If one member is focused upon as the sick individual, and if he is closeted away from the others with his private therapist and instructed not to blab about his therapy, the richness of the situation is largely ignored. A case in point was the subject of a recent paper (Liebermann, 1957). It concerned a little girl with *Pavor nocturnus* who did not respond to therapy until the psychiatrist got the whole family together and discovered that the real patient was an older sister who was calculatingly mean enough to be whispering horror stories into the little girl's ears after the lights went out.

The *unstable unsatisfactory* family probably comprises the large bulk of what the psychiatrist or social worker would immediately spot as a sick family. We feel that many of the serious psychosomatic disorders and possibly psychoses of rather acute onset come from this group. How terribly unsatisfactory things are for the family members need not be immediately apparent. This is because medical practice usually dictates that the sick one be removed from the household and the label helps keep other members from speaking their piece. Then when the sick member returns home and falls ill again it is all the more apparent that he is the rotten apple in this particular barrel. After several bounces back into the hospital, he adds a layer of institutionalization to his difficulties, and that is usually that.

What I am trying to say is that current mores regarding mental illness may seriously complicate locating and diagnosing both the unstable and the stable unsatisfactory families even though the former's difficulties are much easier to ferret out than is the case with the stable unsatisfactory group.

We have found in our limited experience with the unstable unsatisfactory families in conjoint therapy that the patient's recovery poses a serious threat to the parents and occasionally to a sibling. We have seen, without any doubt, many patients who have sacrificed themselves and returned to the hospital rather than upset the family.

Such an incident occurred in the therapy of a young woman who had improved during the family sessions and was to be released from the hospital. She came home for a trial visit prior to her release and the mother and father had a serious fight. The patient and the mother left and went to a nearby town. The patient called the father to let him know where they were, and he joined them and made up with the mother whereupon the patient "misbehaved" and both parents joined in chastising her. At the next session the mother announced that the patient could not live at home and that she was becoming upset by having her around. It was interesting that during her description of the way the patient bothered her she used almost the exact words of the patient's delusions in her initial breakdown. That is, she spoke of the patient sitting in her room alone thinking evil thoughts about the mother, spying on her, being full of hate, and so on. The patient's initial delusions contained exactly similar references about the neighbors. The patient returned to the hospital, promptly threw a tray of food on the floor and was put in a locked ward and was given electro-shock therapy. The patient knew the hospital and her particular physician well enough to know that acting up was regarded as worthy of punishment.

The unstable unsatisfactory family is a classic example of not being able to live with someone and not being able to live without him. Considering the terrible struggles that go on within the walls, it is surprising that so many of these families stick together. Some investigators had hoped to demonstrate that schizophrenia comes from fractured families without taking sufficiently into account that *clinging together can be a particularly vicious malady*. As Clausen and others have shown, the socio-economic group also plays a part in whether an unstable family continued to stick together or falls apart (Clausen and Kohn, 1956).

We feel we have been having some success in the treatment of these families. Our main focus has been on aiding the parents to realize how self-depriving they are and thus to avoid the guilt and blame that are strewn about. It follows from our theory that we hope to enable them to make symmetric maneuvers and this in turn will allow the patient to do the same.

A husband was hinting that his wife relaxed in the afternoon by taking a few drinks and was also covertly complaining that by the time he got home she was no company at all. The therapist asked her if she was not offended by the husband's delicacy in handling the topic whereupon the whole issue came out into the open. His light touch on a touchy topic was a maneuver defining the nature of their relationship and she would not accept it.

Although in the few families we have treated, the mother had been the more dominant figure, it appears to be something of a relief for her if the therapist can help her husband to be more assertive. At some level, the mother recognizes her intense self-depriving ways and longs to be taken care of. This fact becomes the therapeutic toe hold.

Our dealings with the *stable unsatisfactory family* have to date not been encouraging. There are several such families at whom we are currently chipping away but movement is very slow. The family is so aligned toward keeping the patient sick, and the patient himself so willing to accept the role that therapists can easily despair. On the other hand, if some movement is made, it can be quite upsetting to the group since *the cardinal rule of such families is that no one must comment on the nature of the other's behavior.* There is no tolerating of symmetrical behavior. The following incident illustrates rather tragically this fact.

During a family interview the patient's brother encouraged by his relationship to the therapist tentatively ventured that his mother might be a little hypocritical in her dealings with the patient. The father, with a liberal sprinkling of alibis for her, agreed with the son and his wife quietly accepted the verdict but with an air of "that's what I get for trying my best." Unfortunately, the therapist had the impression that the mother was accepting the comment and since it was near the end of the session nothing further was done with it.

Early the following morning the mother was taken to the hospital for an emergency cholecyctectomy although she had had no previous history of gall bladder distress nor stones. Upon her return home the father was hospitalized for a coronary attack and in the midst of this psychosomatic melee the brother, who had initially introduced the damaging remark, had three automobile accidents all of a similar nature. He simply crashed into the rear end of the car ahead. At this point the family decided that they could no longer afford our expert help and placed the patient in a state hospital.

THE RELEVANCE OF COMMUNICATION THEORY AND FAMILY HOMEOSTASIS FOR CONJOINT FAMILY THERAPY

It is one of my private notions that the method of description presented above has practical uses for the psychotherapist interested in the family. His appraisal of interfamily communication will help him establish how the patient got to be the patient, and how serious consequences might be for other family members if the patient alone is treated.

As the therapist notes the families' communication behavior he should pay special attention to how messages are qualified or labelled. Are messages labelled congruently; that is, the context, nonverbal communication, etc., is appropriate to the message and does not deny, conceal or alter it but affirms the message. The most serious form of incongruent message has been described by our group as the double bind (Clausen & Kohn, 1956). In this situation, two incongruent messages are accompanied by a prohibition against noting their incongruence. If no one in the family can deal with double bind statements, we would suspect serious pathology and would suspect that one member's receiving psychotherapy might seriously upset the family since incongruence will become more apparent to him with the therapist's help.

A rather typical situation occurred in the family of a hospitalized schizophrenic the session following one in which his mother urged him to participate in hospital activities. The patient announced he was on the baseball team and that they were going to an air field some miles away to play a game. His mother beamingly replied, "Oh good, they'll have doctors there too!"

If one considers the context, which includes the mother's instructions the previous week, this is a deadly statement. Were the patient able, as he was not, to say, "Mother dear, how come you refer to doctors and my being sick just at the point I'm doing what you asked me to?" the mother would reaffirm her interest and love and the patient would realize he was a cur for doubting. However, the therapist can ask the mother (if he's not too angry) if she notices anything at all peculiar about her remark and can judge the depth of her unawareness.

In families who tend toward incongruent statements, the therapist can judge the effect of a symmetric maneuver; that is, a defining of the relationship statement that is not handled incongruently. The patient mentioned above once, appropriately enough, sent his mother a beautiful card on Mother's Day. However, the card stated majestically across its colorful surface, "For Someone Who Has Been Just Like a Mother to Me." When he was confronted by her at the next therapy session, he was able to make a simple, quiet, symmetric statement, "Look Ma, maybe I meant to sting you a little bit," and, under the increasing pressure of his parents' attack, stated the maneuver was linked to feeling she hadn't been as good a mother as she might have been. The cat being out of the bag called for heroic measures on mother's part and she was up to them. By threatening abandonment, and with an assist from father, she soon had the patient declaring he didn't know what was on the card, he didn't remember sending it, he could obtain no other card, and there was a Communist inspired plot to plant such cards to get boys like himself into trouble.

The forty-five minutes of the interview were a tribute to the effect of a symmetric statement in such a family. Not only did the parents' defensive techniques cause the patient to back down, but at each step of the way his psychotic processes were reinforced. For example, while crying, he stated, "I don't even remember what the thing was," and his mother replied triumphantly, "Well, that's all I wanted to know!"

As the patient improved, he began to label the incongruencies in his parents' messages. Conforming to our experience with other schizophrenic families, he began with the father.[5] The difference in his responses not only upset the parents, but produced strife between them. It is not entirely safe to notice that the Emperor is not wearing a fine new set of clothes.

CONCLUSION

I have tried to demonstrate a method of thinking about family interaction and family therapy. The emphasis has been on theory rather than on technique because we have had so little experience that comments on therapy are rather premature. In spite of this, our group has a definite feeling that conjoint family therapy has some advantages over collaborative therapy. It may be that the peculiar pathologic sticking together that these families demonstrate can be used to keep them in therapy. Perhaps our therapy should be called homeopathic family therapy since we proceed on the notion that the particular communication devices the family uses can be in turn used against them for therapeutic purposes as in the homeopathic idea that "like cures like."

REFERENCES

Bateson, G., Jackson, D. D., Haley, J., and Weakland, J. Toward a communication theory of schizophrenia. *Behav. Sci., 1*:1, 1956. Reprinted in Don D. Jackson (Ed.), *Communication, Family, and Marriage.* Vol. 1, Human Communication Series, Science and Behavior Books, Palo Alto, California, 1968.

Clausen, J., and Kohn, M. Parental authority behavior and schizophrenia. *Orthopsychiatry, 26*:300, 1956.

Jackson, D. D. A note on the importance of trauma in the genesis of schizophrenia. *Psychiatry, 20*:181-184, 1957. Reprinted in Don D. Jackson (Ed.), *Communication, Family, and Marriage.* Vol. 1, Human Communication Series, Science and Behavior Books, Palo Alto, California, 1968.

----

[5]Dr. Murray Bowen confirms this observation (personal communication).

Liebermann, L. P. Joint interview technique: an experiment in group psychotherapy. *Brit. J. Med. Psychol., 30* (Part 3):202, 1957.

Lidz, T. Schizophrenia and the family. *Psychiatry, 21*:21-27, 1958.

Weakland, J., and Jackson, D. D. Therapist's and patient's report of circumstances surrounding a psychotic break. *Arch. Neurol. Psychiat., 79*:554-574, 1958.

Wynne, L., et al. Pseudo mutuality in the family of the schizophrenic. *Psychiatry 21*:205-220, 1958.

13

MINIMUM CHANGE THERAPY

Leona E. Tyler, Ph.D.

I have some misgivings about the problem we are considering today. Any attempt we make to limit the duration of counseling, though we may think of it as a purely quantitative change, may turn out to have large qualitative effects. One of our ground rules, so basic that we seldom even state it explicitly, is that a person is worth whatever amount of time and trouble it takes to help him. We do not measure concern and kindness in hours or dollars. It would be as though a mother should say to herself: "Let's see. I can afford to devote 10 years of my life primarily to the nurture of these children. That means that the total amount of time that each of them can claim is 10,000 hours." Instead of thinking in this fashion, a mother naturally assumes that she must give whatever the task demands, without rationing it. An increasing mass of evidence is showing that the optimal growth of a human being requires just this kind of unlimited commitment on somebody's part. Under favorable circumstances, a person has had enormous amounts of love and care devoted to him by the time he reaches maturity.

The experience of having someone really care about him is such an indispensable part of what counseling means for a client that we must be especially careful never to jeopardize it. It is for this reason that I am inclined to doubt the wisdom of setting arbitrary time limits. If what the client understands by the arrangements we make is: "You are worth spending 10 hours on, but no more," an

Reprinted from the *Personnel and Guidance Journal,* 1960, 38:475-479, with the permission of the author and the American Personnel and Guidance Association.

experience he might otherwise have had simply will not occur. It has always seemed to me that there is a big difference psychologically, between limits that are inevitable and obviously necessary, such as those resulting from the end of a school term or the illness of the therapist and those that are arbitrary or unexplained.

However, after all this has been said, the fact remains that to prolong counseling contacts unnecessarily does not do a client any good and may even hamper his further development. And our own full schedules make it imperative that we try to avoid this type of error. Thus we do need to give some thought to the matter of how this can best be done.

CHANGE OR UTILIZATION

My approach to this and other counseling problems has been to attempt to clarify the nature of the task itself. Elsewhere during the last year I have tried to distinguish between two kinds of helping process. Therapy generally has as its goal personality change; counseling attempts to bring about the best possible utilization of what the person already has. It is a distinction similar to the one Tolman years ago introduced into learning theory, the difference between learning and performance.

The only trouble with simple, clear-cut classifications like this is that they don't seem to fit a lot of the tasks and situations with which we are confronted. Certainly most of the work we do in facilitating occupational choices and educational decisions can be classified as utilization rather than as change. But what of the client with major or minor personality problems? Is the treatment we offer in such cases therapy or counseling? Is it perhaps really therapy, but called counseling in order to make it more palatable to him or to the community? It would not be so important what label we used, except that the ambiguity spreads out over our own thinking about what we call therapeutic counseling. And because we are not at all sure what we are trying to accomplish, we never know just when we are through.

What I have been questioning in my own mind more and more is the assumption that therapy should attempt to bring about as much personality change as possible. Could it be largely because of the enormous prestige psychoanalysis has acquired that we tend to assume that personality reorganization is the goal toward which we should strive? Is it really true that the therapy that produces the most changes is the best therapy? Would it not be possible to make the opposite assumption and deliberately set as our goal "minimum-change" therapy? This would be a kind of undertaking that would fit in well with the rest of the activities that go on under the name of counseling. We would try in each case to help the person discover some unblocked path in which he could move forward, develop his unique personality, and thus transcend rather than delve into the anxieties and conflicts in which he is now enmeshed.

I picture this process in terms of a change of direction rather than in terms of distances or amounts. The difficulties a client is experiencing can be thought of as indications that he is headed in a direction that is wrong for him or that he has at some former time made a wrong turn into a blind alley. All of this may have occurred without conscious awareness, of course. Counseling can create a situation in which a person may become aware of the directional shifts that are possible for him and in which he can be sure someone will see him through what may be a difficult "rotation of his axis." In pursuing the implications of this geometric analogy a little further I calculated that a directional shift of only 10 degrees makes a difference of 170 miles in where one comes out if his journey is 1,000 miles long—enough to make a considerable difference in terrain and landscape. Similarly, a relatively minor shift in the psychological direction in which a person is moving may well change his life considerably over a long period of years.

This is what I mean by "minimum-change therapy." It has made it possible for me to see how in principle therapeutic counseling could be shortened considerably without making it any less valuable. It involves no great change in the procedures we use, but some aspects of the complex counseling situation need to be emphasized or even modified to some extent.

EMPHASIS ON STRENGTH

In the first place, it implies that more emphasis than one ordinarily finds be placed on *positive* diagnosis. By and large, our diagnostic thinking rests on concepts taken over from psychopathology. We try to ascertain where a person's weak spots are. Many psychologists, especially in recent years, have criticized this approach and advocated the diagnosis of strengths. In minimum-change therapy we pay no attention to personality weaknesses that are adequately controlled or neutralized. We all have areas like this. It is only the difficulties that are actually blocking the person's forward movement that we must attempt to deal with. And as suggested in the previous section, it is quite possible that these may be by-passed rather than attacked. A person who knows his real strengths and is clear about his basic values may be able to turn away from anxieties about aspects of his life that would be very difficult to change.

Though there is a widespread current interest in ego processes and positive personality traits, we do not as yet have tests we can count on for this sort of diagnostic task. We are more likely to become aware of a person's strengths by observing things he does than by asking him questions. Some of this meaningful behavior occurs in the interview situation itself. For example, when Mary Hart flashes a sudden smile as she is struck with the amusing aspects of a particularly humiliating social experience she is re-counting, we know that she possesses an asset that may be of considerable use to her. Call it a defense if you will, but in social situations and personal emotional adaptation to the vicissitudes of her life her ability to laugh at her own predicament will be a valuable asset. Other assets frequently showing up even in inter-views where hostility, doubt, guilt, and anxiety are the main themes include moral principles of which the person is absolutely certain, demonstrated courage in the face of adversities, loyalty to those he loves. Whether or not it is advisable for the counselor to reflect or interpret such expressions at the time they occur is another question. But he can make a mental note of them.

We are more likely to become aware of a client's personality assets if we have some knowledge of his life outside the counseling room. In small or moderate-sized colleges, the counselor is likely to encounter his clients here or there—on the street, in the student union, at concerts, plays, or games. The growing practice of placing psychologists on the wards in mental hospitals serves the same purpose of permitting the kind of observation that positive diagnosis is based on. Conversations with a client's family or friends is another resource, but I am strongly of the opinion that it should not be used without the person's knowledge or permission. It is the characteristics he knows you have had a chance to observe—the things you can talk over together—that are grist for counseling's mill. In the last analysis, it is the client himself who must make the positive diagnosis we have been talking about if it is to be effective in his life.

COUNSELING STRUCTURE

A second point of emphasis in minimum-change therapy is the way in which the situation is structured for the client. We must take into account *his* expectations and goals as well as our own. To a person profoundly dissatisfied with the way his life has been going, the only thing that really looks good is change—complete change. What he may have read about psychotherapy in popular magazines or seen in movies leads him to expect or at least hope that some fundamental change will occur. True, the experience of countless therapists has shown that such a person will hang on to his unconscious defenses and fight every sort of change at every step of the way. But if anyone tells him at the beginning that small shifts of direction rather than larger changes in total pattern are to be expected he is likely to reject the whole undertaking. He thinks he wants to be made over.

It is in this connection that some explicit verbal distinction between counseling and therapy may be useful. Instead of trying to fight the person's wishful dreams about miraculous effects of therapy, I can simply explain that I am a counselor rather than a psychoanalyst and that my job is to help a person find out what his personality is like and decide how he can use the assets he has and get rid of the obstacles that are blocking his progress. If he accepts the situation on these terms, therapeutic counseling can proceed within the framework of the very broad general question "What kind of person are you?" Anything the person wishes to bring up can be considered, but we have not committed ourselves to an analysis of all his problems and innumerable childhood experiences out of which they may have arisen.

NECESSARY SUPPORT

A third essential feature of minimum-change therapy is the use of the counseling relationship to reduce the client's anxiety enough to allow him freedom to consider new possibilities. This, of course, is nothing new or at all peculiar to therapy of this type. It seems to be the one common denominator linking together all sorts of diverse procedures. I suppose many workers in the psychotherapeutic vineyard would classify the approach I have been presenting as just another variety of supportive therapy. I would have no quarrel at all with that idea were it not that we are so prone to discredit support and to think of it as a superficial palliative measure to be used when more powerful methods are impractical. The idea of support should not be devalued in this way. Obviously by support I do not mean inspirational pep talks, shallow reassurance, or the encouragement of dependence. What I do mean is the act of lending one's own strength to the client for the period during which he needs it, so that he can be certain that his world is not going to fall apart if he moves. I have an idea that this is by far the most important thing we do for our clients, whatever our special theoretical predilections are. It is the crucial factor that enables his own development processes to operate.

I suspect that it would be possible in many cases to furnish this firm support much more economically than we now do if we were willing to use it without working for insight or drastic restructuring of self-concepts. Once a client has established new direction for himself, it may well be that regularly scheduled interview hours a month apart may be enough to maintain his courage and confidence. It is the quality of the relationship rather than the amount of time spent in the counselor's presence that constitutes support.

THE CLOSING PHASE

This brings us to the last point I wish to make about minimum-change therapy. Its intensive phase is brought to a close as soon as a clear direction has been established in the client's life, even though there are many emotional complexes still unexplored, many interpersonal problems still unsolved. Here again, as in the preliminary diagnosis, evidence from outside the interview room can be combined with what comes up during therapy sessions in judging whether a change of direction has been stabilized. A client may mention casually, without apparently attaching any importance to the remark, something that marks such a significant movement. Mr. Eldridge, for example, may speak of having had a long talk with his wife the night before, an action unprecedented in his previous experience. Gwen Riley, who has always been an anxious, perfectionistic procrastinator, may say that she has handed in, on time, an assigned paper for a course she is taking. Or the counselor may note the change in the incidental observation we discussed earlier. When he sees Bill Laraway having a coke with a girl, he knows that Bill has taken the first step toward overcoming the paralyzing shyness of which he has been complaining. A newspaper item stating that Mr. Bellingham has given a talk before the Active Club indicates to the counselor that this client's inferiority feelings are being surmounted. I know that, taken alone, such examples sound trivial. But remember, it is these ten-degree or even five-degree changes in direction that we are trying to facilitate. A small change in the direction of closer emotional ties with one's family or greater willingness to assume responsibility is the kind of shift that has a profound effect on later development. When it is clear that this shift has occurred it is time to think about the termination of formal therapy interviews.

One way of characterizing this kind of therapeutic counseling is to say that its basic premises come from the psychology of development and individual differences rather than from the psychology of adjustment. Its most fundamental assumption is that there are many different ways of living an individual life richly and well, and that it is natural for a person to continue to develop throughout his life in his own unique way. We work with nature instead of fighting or ignoring it.

I have often been struck by the fact that almost any personality trait one can think of may be either an asset or a liability, depending on how it is used. Touchy oversensitiveness to slights and insults is not really basically different from tact and social awareness. Aggression can lead to high achievement as well as murderous rage. Timidity and reasonable caution, compulsiveness and constructive orderliness are opposite sides of the same coins. Instead of bewailing our heredity and the mistakes that were made in bringing us up, perhaps we can learn to turn what we have to good account.

I have been thinking a good deal about the way in which therapeutic counseling of this sort might be evaluated. It is an intriguing thought that the very failure to obtain clear evidence for personality change as a result of therapy may be construed as success rather than failure if we reverse our basic assumption—namely, that maximum change is what we are after. It may even be that Eysenck is right and that no kind of therapy produces change that is greater than that which time and the processes of nature would ultimately have brought about by themselves. The therapist may make a contribution only to the extent that he facilitates or speeds up this natural process. The kind of evaluation I should like to see would be designed to show whether our therapeutic efforts do in fact accomplish this facilitation, so that individuals find their way with less suffering and wasted time with therapy than without. And if so, we need to know what aspects of the help we give contribute most toward this end.

To come back at the end to the topic of this symposium, the point I have been trying to make is that we can best control the duration of counseling contacts by adopting consistently an attitude of respect for what each individual client now is and lending him support and understanding while he comes to terms with this unique self of his. Whether it takes him two hours or two hundred, if he succeeds the effort will have been very much worthwhile.

14

RADICAL APPROACHES TO THERAPY

Breffni Barrett, Ph.D.

Our task here is to explore some of the ideas and values inherent in radical therapy and radical approaches in working with people. There are some basic assumptions made by most who are writing about and talking about radical therapy. These assumptions may be summarized as follows:

— A commitment to change rather than adjustment
— To better the quality of life
— Personal freedom exists only when other people are free
— Individual struggles are most often related to societal issues and oppression
— The goal of the therapist needs to be to work herself out of a job.

In the end, Radical Therapy is a massive re-thinking of our basic ideas about reality and human freedom.

The concept of Radical Therapy is an amorphous one. When we talk about it we must bear in mind that it is not a new psychotherapeutic formula for how to do things or how to help people. Rather, it is an awareness—a new way for therapists to understand and deal with human suffering. There are no formulas that can be described here which, if practiced, will allow one to become a radical therapist. The radical therapist questions his own biases, assumptions, and values. She is aware of the limitations of her training. The primary purpose of most training institutions is to perpetuate the procedures and techniques of diagnosis and labeling of pathology. When the process of helping people is dealt with in training (and this is most often not the case in our training institutions), the concern is usually intrapsychic and the concepts mystifying. Change and innovation are discouraged in our training institutions and maintenance of the status quo rewarded (probably due to the obsessional character of therapists and Freud's pessimism).

The therapist can view human suffering through three perspectives. These perspectives are all relevant to human behavior and feeling and affect both. They may be viewed as different related levels to be addressed in therapy. The three levels are:

Intra-psychic
Inter-relational
Societal

As mentioned above, the primary focus of therapy has been the intra-psychic, and as therapists, we have been trained to view patients as favorable candidates for psychotherapy if they have insight into their "illness"—that is, they accept their problems as internal. The evolution of radical approaches to therapy begins with the awareness that certain groups in our society have been and continue to be oppressed (put down) in our society.

There are people in our society who are oppressed because of their age, sex, race, life style, sexual preference, income level, political preference and education. This should not be surprising; but what is astonishing is that as therapists, we have primarily helped people to adjust to this oppression. The role of the radical therapist is to be aware of oppression and to work for change rather than adjustment. This working toward change in radical approaches to therapy includes all three levels of human interaction: intra-psychic, inter-relational, and societal.

Different groups of radical therapists have emerged in the past several years addressing the concept of change in therapy. An overview of the apparent direction and emphasis of three of these different "schools" of radical approaches to therapy is presented here.[1]

There seem to be three emerging approaches to radical therapy which may be represented by the Berkeley Radical Psychiatry Center, the Rough Times group in Massachusetts, and Jaffe and

---

[1] This delineation of differing philosophies into "schools" is this author's conspectus and should not be construed to mean that the three groups see themselves this way.

Clark in their work *Toward a Radical Therapy* (1972), which explores new ways of perceiving youth and deviant behavior and alternative agency approaches to human care services.

BERKELEY RADICAL PSYCHIATRY CENTER

The therapists at the Radical Psychiatry Center call themselves psychiatrists because psychiatry is the art of soul healing and anyone who practices the art is a psychiatrist. Claude Steiner, formerly at the Radical Psychiatry Center, has posited some principles of radical psychiatry among which are:

1. In the absence of oppression, human beings will live in harmony with nature and each other.

2. Alienation is the essence of all psychiatric conditions.

3. Alienation is the result of oppression about which the oppressed has been mystified or deceived.

This group of therapists rely heavily on the early theories of Eric Berne (not transactional analysis). The primary focus seems to be inter-relational when working with people who want help. The problems experienced by people may be seen as:

$$Oppression + Mystification = Alienation$$

If you're oppressed and know what is going on—you're angry. (Examples of this abound and the reader is referred to the *Radical Therapist* and *Rough Times* for further elucidation.)

The treatment may be outlined as:

$$Awareness + Contact = Action$$

Thus, awareness of one's oppression together with contact with other people who, united, will move against the oppression is seen as the successful treatment. Emphasis is placed on contracts between client and therapist to equalize responsibility for treatment and to avoid collusion with the powerlessness which often accompanies alienation. Finally, radical psychiatry is seen as best practiced in groups to enhance contact and awareness.

The Radical Psychiatry Center, as any innovative and revolutionary group, is inconstant. The focus seems at present to be to work with specific oppressed groups such as women and gays, with emphasis on group process and inter-relational skills with less consideration for other societal issues. There seems to be a trend toward utilization of body and energy techniques and a moving away from the earlier stated assumption about freedom. The stance of feeling in touch with one's body and energy flow and inter-relations and saying so becomes a political statement. This is a far more limiting approach than the following group where there is much more emphasis on political and revolutionary tactics to effect change and gain freedom for all people.

ROUGH TIMES GROUP

This group of therapists started out in North Dakota and eventually moved to West Somerville, Massachusetts, where a collective was formed which now publishes a journal titled, *Rough Times.* The focus of the Rough Times group seems to be moving more toward a revolutionary stance wherein the class struggle in a capitalist and imperialist society is recognized. The journal is an organizing tool for oppressed people in mental hospitals, prisons and the armed forces as well as an excellent source of information for therapists and others interested in raising their consciousness in regard to the mental health movement.

The charges against the traditional therapeutic model are multitudinous and include the abusiveness of chemical therapy, lobotomies, ECT, prisons and mental hospitals. Therapy has become one of the largest industries in the United States—two million people a year in out-patient clinics and over a million a year enter mental hospitals occupying half the country's hospital beds. Another one-half million people are in private therapy and larger numbers visit clergymen, counselors, and welfare workers. This mental health system is costly—about $4 billion a year, and almost 75 percent of it for outdated hospital services (Glenn and Kunnes, 1973).

In attacking therapy and therapists today, the *Rough Times* points that the entire structure of therapy supports the ruling class of this country. Exploiting others and keeping clients helpless and dependent (through drugs, ECT, hospitalization, etc.) becomes part of the entire therapy structure and a means of social control. Therapists have the power to put people away, to use drugs to control deviant or unwanted behavior, to keep women "in their place," to call gay people "sick," to reinforce the family and its values and to see and define problems as personal (intra-psychic) rather than political.

Society today is filled with unhappy, lonely, depressed, anxious, angry, frustrated people. Therapy has become part of this social malady and if it is to be useful at all—therapy and treatment must be part of changing this society. Therapists today, to make therapy an effective treatment modality, must begin to change the way things are in our society and in the profession at the roots. We must become committed to social change.

JAFFE AND CLARK

The book *Toward A Radical Therapy* (1973) addresses the problems of one of this society's largest oppressed groups—young people. The authors examine (a) how society can remain flexible while dealing with social change, and (b) how society can effectively deal with deviant behavior in ways which protect and develop human potential. Our institutions which were designed to discourage deviant behavior are known to actually teach and perpetuate it (e.g., prisons and mental hospitals). The use of social control has been the means utilized to ameliorate deviance and delinquency. The authors re-evaluate the common view of deviant behavior and see deviance as a way of expanding constrictive and rigid social boundaries. They suggest that many forms of deviant behavior need to be supported rather than controlled.

Repression by police, schools, and society distort and force underground the more open deviant (rebeller) who is likely to conform to society in other ways. The result of this repression of our young is that the positive potential for social change in school demonstrations, controlled drug use and experimentation, and open exploration of sexuality becomes suppressed. The suppression brings about a determination wherein drug use becomes random and uncontrolled and is often used destructively; resistance to school takes the form of vandalism and rioting, and sexuality becomes exploitive and irresponsible. Currently, deviant and illegal behavior is common among young people in virtually every community, regardless of class distinctions; furthermore, the amount of deviant and illegal behavior (e.g., dope smoking, sexual experimentation, vandalism) among white middle-class youth has increased dramatically.

The radical therapist must understand the ways in which the

basic institutions of our society (family, school, and community) act together to limit and mystify attempts at independence or change. Oppression of adolescents is the frustration of being—the prevention of selfhood. One of the first indications of oppression of young people is their identification with other oppressed groups, i.e., women, blacks, poor, elderly. The usefulness of therapy for youth comes through its ability to assist in their struggles for liberation. Jaffe and Clark call their work therapy because they begin by concentrating on a difficulty an individual is experiencing—but it might well be called education, growth, or community organizing.

This is a brief overview of the three emerging "schools" of radical approaches to therapy and there are more. Groups of radical therapists as well as self help groups (mental patients and prisoners liberation) are being formed all over the country. A word of caution, however, may be in order. We have radical treatment approaches such as bioenergetics, psychedelic therapy, psychosynthesis, meditation, psychodrama, energy sharing and the human potential movement. Radical therapy has the ever pervasive potential for becoming another packaged commodity whose appeal makes it marketable to large numbers of new and fledgling therapists. The humanist movement, the "sugar water" humanists, growth centers, touchy-feely therapies, have had a profound impact on the therapy movement. The perils of humanistic psychology must be recognized. Mario Fantini, one of the founders of the humanistic psychology movement, has pointed out that it has become a refuge for navel contemplators. The spectre of all these people seeking personal pleasure while fellow human beings are starving is ironic and obscene. Contemporary humanism belongs to the middle class—greeting one another as brother or sister is closer to real humanism than seeking actualization in hot baths and massages. Radical therapy may get caught up in rhetoric, become the "in thing" to do and lose its potential for redefining and changing the therapy establishment.

The importance of the therapist, whether he be radical or not, recognizing and being able to relate to the client's present circumstances cannot be over-emphasized. Some of the people we see are being oppressed by the various institutions of our society and some are not. One of the skills of the radical therapist is cutting through the propaganda we hear from each other in our profession and listening to those whose lives we affect. We cannot send hurting people away with the idea that therapy is useless.

The development of awareness is essential to separate political oppression from internalized oppression because they are two different issues. Mass political and social movements are needed for the former and the latter internalized oppression is changed on an individual basis.

The three perspectives on human behavior become even more important in this view. The client we see may be alienated or oppressed on an intra-psychic, inter-relational, or societal level, or perhaps all three or some other combination. Our skills and theories must be adaptable so that we are always in a position to understand the client and his or her struggle for change. We must be prepared to assume an advocacy role so that we are "healers" in a way that is helpful and creates a climate for change rather than adjustment, advocacy rather than resignation, enabling rather than limiting for all those with whom we work.

REFERENCES

Agel, J. *Rough Times.* New York: Balantine Books, 1973.

Agel, J. *The Radical Therapist.* New York: Balantine Books, 1971.

Alinsky, S. *Rules For Radicals.* New York: Random House, 1971.

Anderson, W. *Politics and the New Humanism.* California: Goodyear Publishing, 1973.

Barrett, B. Decision therapy and the de-mystification of psychotherapy. *Marriage and Family Counselors Quarterly,* 1973, *8:* 22-28.

Brown, P. *Radical Psychology.* New York: Harper and Row, 1973.

Glenn, M., & Kunnes, R. *Repression or Revolution.* New York: Harper and Row, 1973.

Halleck, S. *The Politics of Therapy.* New York: Science House, 1971.

Hampden-Turner, C. *Radical Man.* New York: Doubleday and Co., 1970.

Jaffe, D., & Clark, T. *Toward a Radical Therapy.* New York: Gordon and Breach, 1973.

Laing, R. D. *The Politics of Experience.* New York: Pantheon Books, 1967.

15

SOCIAL AND HISTORICAL DETERMINANTS OF PSYCHOTHERAPEUTIC SYSTEMS

Nathan Adler, Ph.D.

"Innovations" in counseling and psychotherapy have been among the enthusiastically hailed products of the counter-culture. They are another expression of attack on the academy and the establishment with the concurrent repudiation of role, commitments, and institutions by a restless generation seeking new channels of access to status and power. The new therapies, instead of serving elites, affirm the problems and thrust toward upward mobility of fringe groups struggling out of their marginality who are anti-academy and anti-establishment only so long as they are denied access to status and role positions. These innovations have been expressed in many forms; as group and family therapies, behavioral reinforcement techniques, sex engineering, and other fundamental modifications in values, techniques, and ideologies such as those asserted by the gestalt and radical therapies. In institutions like Esalen which have proliferated rapidly throughout the nation, spiritual exercise, meditation, body massage, breathing techniques, encounter groups, and naked marathon therapies have been commercialized or packaged as do-it-yourself manuals and tapes. Congregations like Erhard's Sensitivity Training, the more frankly religious groups like the "Jesus freaks," the Sufi dervishes, and the Astrodome Festival gurus, have been some of the new agencies and roles generated

This paper has been presented at the staff conference, Psychology Clinic, University of California, Berkeley; a colloquium at the Department of Psychology, University of California, Santa Cruz; a symposium entitled "Innovations in Counseling and Psychotherapy," State University of California at San Francisco, June 1, 1974; and at a symposium of The Psychotherapy Institute, Berkeley, California, September 28, 1974.

to express and channel the values of this new life style.

Is radical innovation really involved in these technologies and institutions? Do they represent fundamental breakthroughs in knowledge for the behavioral and social sciences? Or are they a reoccurrence of nostrums and remedies which have been known at other times and places?

Under the canopy covering these innovations are a facile commercial exploitation of the popular, side by side with a critical reassessment of the urban and industrial revolution, and the assumptions of imminent progress and evolution.

For example, let us look at an announcement of a meeting aimed at a group of Berkeley businessmen introducing them to Transcendental Meditation. Is this really the marriage of East and West; the wisdom of the Orient penetrating the Chamber of Commerce? These businessmen are offered an "effortless mental technique, easily learned and practiced, bringing great benefits for executives and employees alike, practical for today's life," and an understanding of the mechanics of creativity and intelligence which will develop the full potential of the individual. The announcement goes on to say that the practice, involving concentration or contemplation, is easy and restful even in sleep. In a similar way est promises in one easy weekend to develop growth and change in the individual in procedures reminiscent of sales meetings or evangelical jamborees. That agency packages for a mass market suggestion and conversion procedures, the insights of Zen Buddhism, and encounter assault therapies. The scientific legitimation of some of these innovative procedures is augmented by new hardware systems that demonstrate and condition brain waves, an authoritative sanction for technocracy's children.

We cannot, however, dismiss these products merely as fads and fashions of a changing market place. I believe there is a theoretical framework within which we can account for these procedures, explain their emergence at particular times, and predict the context and regular occurrence of the values they affirm.

When the world is consistent and reliable, when roles and relationships are expressed in customary and predictable ways, then institutionalized procedures deal with disease, define deviance, and structure the ways to cope with tension. There are characteristic ways in which people are excluded or reinstated into a community. What it means to be a person is a shared and acknowledged experience. At such times one speaks of therapy as we spoke of it in the recent past, accounting for socialization, change, and therapeutic transactions solely in terms of learning theory and the stages of socialization.

In a time of flux when institutions are discredited and expectancies are not confirmed, learning models no longer serve as useful or effective explanations. In the counter-culture, we have seen the centripetal and diffusing ethos of a nihilistic relativism which asserts, "you do your thing; I'll do mine." Hesse became the poet laureate of a generation; Castaneda's three volumes became its best selling manual, demonstrating that world and self are constructs, and that one can be either the slave or the master of categories which organize events and experience. Castaneda transformed phenomenology into a popular lore. After Castaneda one needs no abstruse philosophy to demonstrate that in interacting in the world we manipulate constructs, filtered through norms and categories, mediated by paradigms. We make our reality through those models we assume and accept as self-evident.

The new therapies express the flight from repudiated categories, the improvisation and experimentation with new ones, and the specific adaptive activities that attend the derangement and reorganization of personality. During the past decade the ultimate sententious dismissal was, "That's merely a value thing," as if statements ever flowed free of value. The more erudite pointed out that talk of good versus evil and right versus wrong set up dualistic models which were culture-bound. They preferred the ultimate truth in the teachings of the Eastern mystics. Talk of dualism as contrasted to Eastern philosophies disregards the dialectic in Heraklitos, Hegel, Schopenhauer, and Nietzsche and reveals more about the repudiation of allegiances than it does about understanding. The counter-culture confuses cultural relativism with a nihilistic sanction which justifies the aphorisms "you do your thing and I'll do mine," and "take your own trip." A standard no longer exists by which to measure, evaluate, and consensually validate facts and events.

Implicit in the new therapies are models of man and society. Nihilism itself is a paradigm, one which invokes a diffuse rather than a discrete structure, opts for release rather than control, and centers upon the self rather than the community. In the world of physics the use of different procedures and instruments produce different data. So the new therapies using different models, categories, and values, produce alternative views of man, society, and reality. Instead of insisting in futile polemic on the truth value of one system as opposed to another, we should attempt to account for the ground out of which they develop.

The unusual and the abnormal are neither irregular nor unlawful. Granted that values and meanings are culture bound, it is possible to establish the social contexts in which kinds of personalities, pathologies, and therapies recur.

In what follows I propose to present a transformational model to demonstrate the interrelation of structure and process and to elucidate the settings for the development of both personality systems and their associated therapies. Levi-Strauss (1967) defines transformational models as a group of models of the same type which have the characteristics of a system and in which the several elements cannot change without effecting change in all the other elements. In ordering a series of transformations it should be possible to predict how the model reacts if one or more of the elements are modified. Such transformational models make intelligible all of the observed facts, and promote an interdisciplinary convergence since they override the traditional boundaries of the disciplines.

Transformational model demonstrating
structure and process for personality
therapeutic systems and social settings.

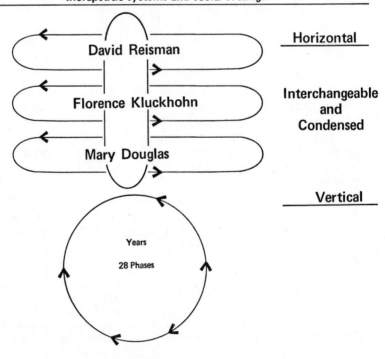

238

Social and Historical Determinants of Psychotherapeutic Systems

The group of models[1] which I wish to order and superimpose upon each other are those developed by David Reisman (1950), Florence Kluckhohn (1961), and Mary Douglas (1970). Some years ago Reisman developed a model for the relationship of character structure and social setting. He correlated the relative stability of a society's goals with the individual's self-orientation. The self can be seen as unique, isolated, and self-contained, or it can be construed as merely a part of the collective totality. For example, in the Chinese language the word for individual, translated literally, means "a part of the whole." If one differentiates an individual versus a collective self, and correlates these with the stability of a society's goals, one has the following distribution of personality orientations:

Goal Stability	Collective Self	Individual Self
Permanent Goals	Tradition-Directed	Inner-Directed
Fluid Goals	Millenarian	Other-Directed

In Western society there have been times when the self is seen as agent, separate and apart from the outside world. At other times the sense of separateness disintegrates and the self is seen as agency or as fused with the world about it. "Not I, but the wind that blows through me," sings the poet of such an age. Those who used marijuana, LSD, and other drugs widely available this last decade, found that these drugs disrupted the models and categories by which our culture is construed. The effect of the drug experience was not to get the individual out of the "little boxes," but, in

---

[1]Elsewhere I propose to superimpose upon these models the complex paradigm elaborated by William Butler Yeats in *A Vision*. Despite its occult and astrologic metaphors I believe it explicates a profound psychology and as a further elaboration of this transformational model, develops more precisely differentiated character and role structures, the dialectic reciprocals of the drives in which they are articulated, and the settings in which they occur. The completed transformational model, constructed as a globe and working like a color wheel will unify a complex set of variables, demonstrate their structural components as well as their functional modifications over time and changing settings.

terms of our fourfold table, to place him into a different set. Drugs made possible a shift in anchorage moving the orientation of the self from its inner direction and an internal orientation to an other-directedness and an external anchorage.

Confronting relatively permanent goals, in a society that maintains a stable group reference, the individual is field-dependent, externally oriented, and tradition directed. When the goals become labile rather than enduring, and the individual is aware of turbulence and flux, then though he remains externally oriented, the commitment to tradition is replaced by millenarian and utopian drives. It is at such times that apocalyptic movements arise heralding the end of the world or the New Jerusalem.

In an individually oriented system, the frame of reference is internal and expressed as guilt rather than shame. When goals are enduring, an individuated self postpones immediate gratification, and has a Puritan conscience. On the other hand, when the individual faces unstable and no longer legitimated goals and loses his commitments, desublimation leads him to an outer-directed orientation and to sensate values.

Stress is expressed in many ways; as alienation and depersonalization where the universe is perceived as empty and absurd, or as ego inflation when, instead of withdrawing boundaries from the world, one over-cathects it. Then ego expansion is expressed as the pathetic fallacy, endowing neutral physical objects with human affect, or in ideologies of vitalism and animism. In such manic conditions the boundaries between self and universe are annihilated and psychokinesis and extra-sensory perception become modes of knowing and acting upon the world. Occult mystifications become popular. Body and beyond are seen as one. There are reports of living and acting outside the body. Otherness and objectivity are denied. As a snake swallows a mouse, or, as in the mandala, his own tail, men cope with threat by incorporating the universe. It is ironic that such views seek a scientific legitimacy and try to account for mediation in physicalistic terms rather than in gnostic modes or symbolic interaction. It is an odd spiritualism that justifies itself in the crude physicalisms of auras, poltergeist pranks, psychokinesis, celestial fluids, orgone boxes, mesmeric rods and tubs, and the hardware of brainwave conditioning machines.

In the classic model, particularly in its psychoanalytic form, psychotherapy served elite clients in a commercial and industrializing society. Its procedures enabled patients to examine the norms in terms of which they lived. They were enabled to step aside and scrutinize these constructs and, through a disciplined reassessment of their behavior and through membership in a new sub-community of the elect, the "well analyzed," modify their activities and beliefs so that they could continue to function in a world of tension.

Opposed to such a psychotherapy of stoic endurance and tension binding, contemporary spiritual exercises, transcendental meditation, massage, and sex engineering design a therapy of discharge, desublimation, and immediacy. These new therapies retrain the individual for life in the mass society which is coming. They induce the procedures for accommodation and adjustment to an automated, mass society. They teach man to fit in standardized and interchangeable roles in a world on the move. Changes in residence, in rate of movement, and in mobility have their consequences. They induce the need for amplification of sensory input to locate and maintain the self and its boundaries. It is such operations that constitute the core of the new therapies. These models, introduced in the name of greater individualism, self-expression and self-actualization are more meaningful as emergency exercises in the face of the disintegration of the self's supports.

These models are derived from different axiomatic systems and embody disparate assumptions about human nature, habitat, and about ascribed roles, and memberships in the community. They assume different body images, relating the self to the body and its organs and functions, and the self to the world, in dissimilar ways. Instead of seeing the body as a boundary over against alien objects, distinctions are blurred and fusion and expansion are encouraged. Instead of acting as a selective filter for stimuli, the body becomes an insatiable sponge.

Different therapies determine disparate points at which to intervene in behavior, name other initiating stimuli, and terminal responses, distinguish different configurations as illness or as deviance, and ascribe to different internal or external loci etiologic significance. They differ as to whom they grant absolution and reprieve, a visa for that limbo where, like passengers in transit, patients are permitted to dwell. They nominate different candidates for expulsion and excommunication.

The distinction between deviance and disease, though both often share functional equivalence, depends upon whether the individual is perceived as agent or agency, whether the locus of control is assigned inside or outside, whether the individual acknowledges the legitimacy of the community or challenges and abdicates from it. This differs from the radical therapies which see man as innocent and society as evil, or for those that deem aggression and sadism to be primary rather than secondary. It implies different assumptions for the sex therapy technologists than it does for the advocates of sublimation.

All societies must come to terms with a basic set of parameters of meaning and value, implicitly construing answers which define man, his world, his time perspective, and his community membership. These answers are formulated by Florence Kluckhohn in the following modalities.

Man	*Good*	*Evil*	*Neutral*
Relation to nature	In harmony with nature	Mastery over nature	Subjugated to nature
Time Perspective	Present	Future	Past
Activity	Being	Doing	Becoming
Interpersonal Configurations	Collateral	Fragmented, Atomistic, Individualistic	Lineality, Chain of being through time

At different times and places man is assigned varying roles. Man may be seen as active or passive; as agent or agency. Since the Romantic Revolution in the West, man has seen himself as "master of his fate, and captain of his soul." The medieval world did not assert such independence. He may be seen as the noble savage, innocent until corrupted by society, or as born in original sin, in Rousseau's image of man or that of Hobbes. Man may be construed as maker and shaper, dominating, exploiting, and transforming the environment, or as the helpless victim subjugated by an overwhelming and indifferent fate. At some periods he is seen in a congruent, benign relationship with nature. The latter view is most clearly expressed in some of the ideological formulations of the current ecology movement, most notably in Buckminster Fuller's formulation of the concept of Spaceship Earth.

A crucial habitat in which man lives, a variable both in the organization of the self and the modalities of therapy, is his time perspective. He may seek the Golden Age in a lost Atlantis or look forward to its coming. From these orientations toward time, flow not only alternative value systems, but differing disease patterns and syndromes; obsessional striving toward the future, or ritualistic undoing of the past, depressive rumination, amnesic fugues. They all involve assumptions about time. Simone de Beauvoir says, old age comes when suddenly one is aware that there is only now and that one can no longer live in terms of an extended future. What shall we make of a generation and of a therapeutic system which clamors and affirms the here and now?

Paradigms define, not only the nature of man, world, and time, but ascribe as well the structure and quality of the community; see it as sacred or profane, men linked in a great chain of being or isolated, fragmented, swarming atoms. It is thus that self and world are mediated by a framework of orientations and values out of which models are elaborated. Stimulus-response models organize behavior in terms of mechanics or, in the age of McLuhanism, communication models account for behavior in terms of information theory. The personality can be viewed as a telephone exchange, as a binary digital computer, as a cybernetic feedback system, as a radar system searching out reward potentials, striving for constancy or homeostasis, or as a thermodynamic system running down toward death. Our age chooses technological metaphors, other ages spoke of the shepherd and his flock, the angel and the Devil. Personality has also been stratified into departments of Id, Ego, and Superego, and in political metaphors, assigned roles of rebellious mob, instrumental, reasonable parliament, or tyrannical king. Topological models formulate levels of consciousness, primary and secondary behavior, or invoke hydraulic metaphors of flowing and dammed libido. Too often we fall into the trap of treating these pedagogic devices as actual and more than names, instead of examining them to discover the values they reveal and their social and historical context.

One way to order the range of social and personal values of these treatment modalities is to classify them as systems of release and discharge or inhibition and control — release and control to be understood in the context of the values dominant in a particular society. The behavioral technologies are a prime example of a control therapy, an orientation which accepts as given the values of the culture, and wishes to tune the organism to its assumptions. Gestalt therapy deliberately intends to disrupt such assumptions. Transcendental meditation, and other forms of spiritual exercises, are specific procedures of derangement and reorganization. Elsewhere I have described the ways in which activities such as dancing, massage, awareness exercises, the rituals of encounter groups, etc., are procedures which manipulate the boundaries and motility of the self. Sexual therapies and the bio-feedback techniques similarly can be explained as procedures which lower or raise thresholds, and shift the range and boundaries of the self.

Conduct organization and conduct change have been institutionalized throughout man's history. Therapy does not begin with Kraepelin, Charcot, or Freud. The models change and now invoke secular or scientific metaphors but the underlying operations in Saint Bonaventura's or in Saint Ignatius' spiritual exercises reveal the same communalities of operations. At all times and in all societies internal and external sources of information are both necessary and used since the self is a product of both internal and external milieus. But, the ratios of this equation, as they change in time and place, make for different ways of construing the self and ordering its interactions in the world.

If on the models of Reisman and Kluckhohn we superimpose a model first suggested by Mary Douglas, it is possible to shift from a structural view to one that can demonstrate structure as process. Structure is a stop-camera statement, a schematization that exhibits the instant but, the categorical abstraction condenses only upon one point of the continuum. Beneath it, time, process, and change continue.[2] Drawing upon data from preliterate society, as well as from the contemporary world, and other epochs, she demonstrates the characteristic and recurring patterns of personal relations and values. These she correlates with the structure of groups and their methods of social control.

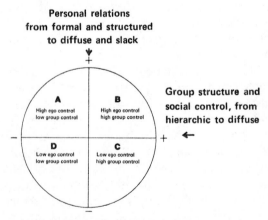

---

[2] Douglas' four-fold table should, ideally, be presented within a circle to emphasize further the continuous and processional characteristics, pointing to states as phasic stages through which one moves.

A: High Ego Controls Low Group Controls	B: High Ego Controls High Group Controls
Ego belongs to bounded group but is constrained by internal controls	Sharp discrete boundaries for both ego and group Control is external
Dominated by things rather than persons	Role definitions maximum, fixed social positions, relationships hierarchical and differentiated
Ritualistic, private magic	Society exalted over self, personal elements attenuated
Success cosmology	Sharp distinctions between inside and outside, smooth hair, formal costume
Potential millenialism	
Banality of rituals and roles	Ritualism high and formal, condensed symbol systems
	Complex, regulative cosmos

D: Low Ego Controls Low Group Controls	C: Low Ego Controls High Group Controls
Low social constraints for both ego and group	Sharply defined group boundaries and reference, status positions insignificant
Diffusion of controls, confusion of internal and external	
Role definitions minimal, relationships loose, optional, and interpersonal	Control is external. Individual confronts warring forces of good and evil and sees himself as dominated by witches and magical rituals.
Role confusion, stress on intimacy and familiarity	
Self and society seen as dichotomy, ideology of self-actualization	
Personalistic religions	
Expressive values emphasized, e.g., effervescence, spontaneity, syncretistic fusion	
Rejection of established systems, theories and professionals	
Weakly condensed symbol systems	
Unstructured cosmos	

Religious and Therapeutic Systems	
High Structure *(e.g., Skinner, Mowrer)*	*Low Structure* *(e.g., Laing)*
Future orientation	Present orientation
Value placed on consciousness and control of individual behavior	Social categories devalued, individual exalted. Ideology of self-actualization.
Sublimation stressed	Lack of role differentiation resulting in symmetrical, therapeutic relationships, e.g., co-counseling.
Stern morality	Rejection of specialists, intellectualism, formalism and theory.
Vigilant control of body	Desublimation valued. Philosophy of joy, spontaneity, and intimacy.
Trances and psychotic breakthroughs treated as dangerous	Body disassociation favored, trances, trembling, ecstasy, and psychotic breakthroughs valued and induced.
	Erotic millenarianism.

Groups in early stages have low structure; later they tend to congeal into denominations and sects.

This model is a scheme which locates and predicts the reoccurrence of ritualized societies and circumscribed, rigorously-defined roles, as well as pointing to the contrasting location of loosely structured, informal societies, in which role diffusion, and release replace strategies of control.

It extends Reisman's model since it is both more highly differentiated, and points to processes rather than to a dichotomy. It locates the occurrence of discrete, sharply bounded relationships and roles, elaborate, formal rituals, and of a complex regulative cosmos and also locates the setting for deregulation and desublimation when relationships become loose and role-definition minimal. In such a world one moves, in Piaget's term, toward a diffuse animism. The world becomes pregnant with self-reference. It is both non-reflexive and non-reflective: non-reflexive in that one denies any sense of mediation between self and world, and non-reflective in that one is committed to immediacy.

The highly structured systems of the upper right quadrant in

Douglas' model, locate therapies and religions of control which affirm a high value to consciousness. Trances are deemed dangerous, disruptive behavior, psychotic breakthrough is a danger to be averted. There is a vigilant control of body boundaries.

Contrary to this orientation, is the one in which the legitimacy of status positions is repudiated and roles are diffused. There is a move away from hierarchic relations. In Durkheim's phrase, "effervescence" and enthusiasm replace rituals. Theory and systems are repudiated. Formalism is denounced as irrelevant. Trances and talking in tongues express the diffuse, global, undifferentiated affect which displaces earlier precise denotation.

If we apply Douglas' scheme to therapeutic modalities, we find that highly structured systems assume an asymmetrical therapy with differentiated relations between patient and therapist. The contrary system moves toward symmetrical roles, toward encounter groups, co-counseling, toward participatory dyads, and rejection of specialists and professional training. Instead of sublimation, psychotic breakthroughs are held to be good and constructive. Therapies of joy, intimacy, and communion become emphasized. All the familiar exercises of group trust and touch displace vision and objectification.

Frenetic activity restores the sense of coherence and unity. Temporary improvised communities make up for the loss of gratification no longer supplied by family, job, and social institutions. The new therapeutic modalities provide a haven and a reference group for a highly mobile society and offer a new ground for a synthesized solidarity and identity.

It is in this way that we can understand the rediscovery and reversion to abreaction and catharsis models, the ideology of openness and trust, manifested in the belief systems of contemporary psychotherapy. To maintain that these are cyclic phenomena which have specific determinants implies no notion of an eternal return. It does imply that as a human organism with a limited range of sensory and perceptual modalities, structured in specific cognitive modes, man's activity is a characteristic response to specific social and historical conditions. I do, in fact, hypothesize that the cycles of economic activity identified as the Kondratieff cycle, which measure both economic upswings and declines, correlate with changes in cognitive and gnostic modalities, with antinomian movements, with the resurgence of transcendental and mystic, and animistic value systems. Such correlations need not be in a single, dominant pattern, but may involve many-stranded and complex movements which intersect, cross and parallel one another.

I could cite instances from Pythagoras to the Anabaptists, from the anchorites to today's drop-outs, from the Quakers and Diggers to contemporary intentional communities and extended families to demonstrate such correlations and phase activity.

Permit me to elaborate two instances as historical examples, the development of Mesmerism, reminiscent in so many ways of the Reichian systems now popular, and the events in the Burned-Over District in the early 1800s in America.

Toward the end of the Enlightenment, in the decade preceding the French Revolution, there was an absorbing interest in animal magnetism. Therapeutic cults became concerned with procedures for massaging the body's poles, inducing cataleptic and somnambulistic trances, welcoming convulsions, and searching for ways to restore the harmony of man and nature. Like orgone boxes today, mesmeric tubs and rods provided a new scientific hardware for procedures intended to induce crisis. In the context of Benjamin Franklin's demonstrations of electricity and Newton's theory of gravity, at the time in 1783 when marvelous gases proved the possibility of flight through the air by balloons, it seemed that animal magnetism must be as real as phlogiston, as real as ether, as real as the homunculi "discovered" in sperm on microscope slides. Mesmerists described their activity as a modern scientific version of the mystic views of the Illuminists and Jansenists. Ardent upper-class coteries expressed the Enlightenment's faith in reason and the opposing thrust toward Romanticism. After 1785, the movement became peripheral, its activities being displaced by active political pamphleteering. On the eve of the French Revolution, in a strange melange of Newton and Astrology, soirees of Mesmerists communicated with ghosts, tried to contact astro-intelligences on remote planets, or in extra sensory ways to contact each other over great distances. In somnambulistic trances, they viewed their own insides. They manipulated cabalistic magic numbers, and deciphered hieroglyphics.

It was a movement that challenged the authority of the church and the academy and replaced the conventional medicine of the time, a medicine of purgative potions and bleeding, with therapeutic procedures that located the hostile agent outside, rather than inside, man. It defended humanity against the academicians, encouraged non-professional activity, and mixed it with radical politics. The Mesmerists were associated with Rosicrucians, Swedenborgians, with alchemists, and cabalists. They achieved diagnosis through the sensations felt by the mesmerizer, who, much like today's Kirillian photographers, saw colored auras around his patients.

With their emphasis on harmony, such movements encourage and sanction political quietism, provide access to social mobility, and make a platform for the proclamation of apocalyptic concerns. The extraordinary weather of the mid 1780s, a summer of heavy fogs, earthquake and volcanic eruptions, followed by a winter of sixty-nine days of extremely severe freezing temperatures which resulted in numerous deaths from exposure, and followed by catastrophic spring floods, was read as an augury of the Mesmerist revolution. The entire globe, it seemed, was preparing itself for physical changes and the extraordinary weather was explained in elaborate theories about the unequal distribution of electric and phlogistic fluids which were preparing the convulsions of the earth. It is in such characteristic ways that affect is invested externally, as in our time the real dread of the hydrogen bomb overdetermines the ideology of the ecology movement.

Ultimately, the movement deteriorated into table rapping seances. It had, however, long term consequences for the development of both hypnotism and Christian Science, as well as the work of Charcot and Freud. It is also in the line of direct descent to those today who speak of good vibes and auras, and to the est emphasis on maintaining eye contact. It offered a platform both to those who criticized the Establishment in the name of the Revolution and, to those mystic and conservatives who spoke for the Holy Alliance.

Let me offer a second example. The Burned-Over district is an area so designated because between 1815 and 1837 it was swept by contagions of enthusiasm like forest fires. It is in New York west of the Catskill and Adirondack Mountains and extends west to Lake Ontario. During the years of 1815 to 1837 in that area Seventh Day Adventism and Mormonism both were founded. It offered a stage for the epidemic revival of Swedenborgians and Mesmerists. Phrenology and Spiritualism also became mass movements. The area became the center for major commune colonies, for experiments in celibacy and spiritual wifery, for the repudiation of the single family and its replacement by group marriage. It offered platforms for significant breakthroughs in women's liberation and suffragism. It rejected reason and regulation in favor of inspiration, enthusiasm, and visions. The groups at that time promoted mass prayer meetings and evangelical sessions as great as the festivals at Altamont and Woodstock. It was a time of flux, of self-examination, and inner emigration, a time of a radical shift in what people construed to be the nature of things.

How can we account for the emergence of such behavior at that time? By 1815 the promise of the American Revolution had dissolved into disillusion. Those who were not successful in Boston moved west to the frontier of stoney Vermont and, when they failed there, continued on into western New York. In the year 1800, 80 percent of the population of Vermont was under the age of twenty-five. Talk of a youth explosion and a youth consciousness! The Burned Over District was the California Bay Area of 1965. The war of 1812, a shattering, dirty, little war, was over. An economic depression was under way. In Europe, Napoleon had been defeated and, after the Congress of Vienna it seemed reaction was back in the saddle. There was a loss of belief in the future. At that time, too, a cholera epidemic threatened and a strange new comet appeared in the evening sky. Many prepared for the end of the world and even named the date in 1837.

The construction of the Erie Canal and the shift from a rural to a manufacturing economy based on water power threatened the status and power relations of the small town aristocracy. Catholic immigrants, Irish, and German intruders, displaced the native Americans. In the ensuing struggle between the small town and the new manufacturing cities, a nativist Know-Nothing party like the current Wallace populism reacted politically to their threatened loss of status and downward mobility. In ten years Albany's population increased 96 percent; Utica, 183 percent; Syracuse, 282 percent; Buffalo, 314 percent, and Rochester, 512 percent. The Burned-Over District now is an area of resorts and ghost towns. Between 1825 and 1830 its population was greater than in the years 1920 to 1960. Then it was the great frontier of turbulence and change. In that setting, with the breakdown of old institutions, new intentional groups flourished. They experimented with telepathy, exorcism, astrology, and macrobiotic diets to purify the spirit and subdue matter, saying through the body, in terms of food and sex, what they wanted to say about their society.

One needs no "vibes," no auras, no celestial fluids, to account for events and bind interaction. We need no fantasies of influence at a distance or of relationship mediated in reductionist physical terms by orgone boxes, mesmeric tubs and rods, by massage, or breathing techniques, to explain what happens whenever the fabric of meaning and values that binds a people is shredded. When the events of daily life lose their value and cease to serve as an anchorage and a frame of reference, "innovations" in belief systems, whether they are formulated in millenial, religious, or therapeutic metaphors, inevitably recur.

REFERENCES

Adler, N. *The Underground Stream: New Life Styles and the Antinomian Personality*, New York: Harper and Row, 1972.

Braudel, Fernand. *The Mediterranean and the Mediterranean World in the Age of Phillip the II*, Vol. 2, New York: Harper and Row Publishers, 1972, pp. 892-900.

Castanada, Carlos. *The Teachings of Don Juan: A Yaqui Way of Knowledge; A Separate Reality: Further Conversations With Don Juan; Journey to Ixtlan: The Lessons of Don Juan*, New York, Simon and Schuster.

Cross, Whitney. *The Burned Over District,* Ithaca, New York: Cornell University Press, 1951.

Darnton, Robert. *Mesmerism and the End of the Enlightenment in France,* New York: Schocken Books, 1970.

Douglas, Mary. *Natural Symbols,* Pantheon Books, New York: Random House, 1970.

Gutmann, David. "The new mythologies and premature aging in the youth culture," *Social Research,* 72 or 73.

Kluckhohn, Florence and Strodtbeck, F. L. *Variations in Value Orientations,* Evanston, Ill.: Row Peterson, 1961.

Koch, Sigmund. "Reflections on the State of Psychology," in *Social Research,* Vol. 38, No. 4, Winter 1971, pp. 669-709.

Levi-Strauss, Claude. *Structural Anthropology,* New York: Anchor Books, 1967, p. 272.

London, Perry. "The end of ideology in behavior modification," *American Psychologist,* Vol. 27: No. 10, pp. 913-920.

Nelson, B. "Self images and systems of spiritual direction in the history of European civilization," in *The Quest for Self-Control: Classical Philosophies and Scientific Research.* Edited by Klausner, S.Z., New York: Free Press, 1965, pp. 49-103. 49-103.

Reisman, David. *The Lonely Crowd: A Study of the Changing American Character;* in collaboration with Reuel Denney and Nathan Glazer. New Haven: Yale University Press, 1950.

Sarbin, T. R. and Adler, N. "Self-Reconstitution processes: a preliminary report," in *The Psychoanalytic Review*, Vol. 57, No. 4, 1970-1, pp. 599-619.

Wilden, Anthony. Marcuse and the Freudian Model: energy, information, and phantasie in *Salmagundi, a Quarterly of the Humanities and the Social Sciences*, Skidmore College Fall 1969 — Winter 1970, No. 10-11, pp. 196-245.

Yeats, William Butler. *A Vision*, New York: The Macmillan Company, 2nd edition, 1956.

SECTION II

ISSUES

It is good to rub and polish our brain against that of others.

Montaigne
Essays, Book I, Chapter 24

16

THE THERAPIST AS A PERSON
(OR: THE COMPLEAT COUNSELOR)

Ben N. Ard, Jr., Ph. D

What sort of a *person* should a good therapist or counselor be? What are the characteristics of the "compleat" counselor? In what follows I would like to discuss some ideas centering around these basic questions.

Some theorists have suggested that a good therapist is just a good human being (with the implication that a good therapeutic relationship is merely an ideal human relationship) (Moustakas, 1956; Rogers, in this text; Schofield, 1964, as representatives of this point of view).

Lists of the proper characteristics of a good therapist or counselor have been proposed and they seem, at times, to be describing super-humans rather than mere mortals (Bugental, 1964). It seems, according to some writers, as if therapists must be all things to all people.

When one reads these lists of the required characteristics of the therapist as a person, one might get the impression that to be a successful counselor one should be, practically, at least a Methodist minister, if not a saint. And, at the same time, know all the Masters and Johnson sex techniques and also be able to be completely relaxed leading a nude marathon—not a mean feat! (Ard, 1974). If this sounds a bit far-fetched to a prospective therapist or counselor, that is the beginning of an important insight.

One theorist, after considering the personal characteristics which are thought to be prerequisite to being a good counselor, came to

This is an expanded, revised version of an article by the same title which appeared in *Marriage Counseling Quarterly*, Vol. 6, No. 4, pp. 1-5; Summer, 1971.

the conclusion that "the counselor is a *woman*" (Farson, 1962). That is, all the characteristics wanted in a counselor (e.g., warmth, compassion, tenderness, understanding, gentleness, perceptiveness, closeness, receptiveness, caring, thoughtfulness, loving, kindliness, intuitiveness, social skills, and an angelic air of patience and forebearance, as well as forgiveness, etc.) seem to be, in our culture, attributes usually associated with women rather than men.

As a matter of fact, good counselors (even the male counselors) score higher on the feminine side of the masculine-feminity scales in some of the reported research. Does this mean that homosexuals make better counselors than other men? Not necessarily. These so-called "feminine" characteristics are *cultural*, not biological traits.

And, lest the women's liberation element begin to cheer too loudly about the counselor being a woman (assuming, perhaps, that at last they have at least one profession sewed up for women), other factors around this issue need to be critically examined. "Women are expected to be the other-directed members of our society, always on the look-out for the feelings of others, and finally more dependent than anyone else on the good opinion of others" (Sykes, 1962, p. 226). And yet we must never forget that very basic insight that "It is a definition of insecurity to depend on someone else's approval" (Sykes, 1962, p. 226). This very fundamental idea or assumption in our culture (that everyone "needs" the approval of others) may contribute to the fact that most psychiatric patients are women.

Some writers say that it is even harder for women than for men to complete their private revolutions and become self-reliant (Sykes, 1962, p. 226). And, of course, all women suffer seriously when social pressures insist that they remain eternally young. So even though women in our culture have traditionally been assumed to have had the characteristics which might help them become good counselors, they have cultural pressures which bring problems and difficulties, and which may hinder them from becoming effective counselors unless they resist the self-defeating acculturation trends in our culture.

Sometimes the professional training a therapist or counselor receives gives him or her what might be called a "professional deformity," i.e., their professional theoretical orientation gets in the way of their effective functioning as counselors or therapists, specifically of their seeing, hearing, and thinking things which are necessary to their effective performance as therapists or counselors.

They might be said to have "blinders" on, like some mules wear, and it seems to increase their mulishness, or at least contribute to some "tunnel vision."

A good way to begin overcoming such a handicap is to ask oneself what new ideas, new approaches, etc., one has adopted *since* one ended one's professional training. Even Carl Rogers has commented on this theoretical "blindness" by saying: "I am distressed at the manner in which small caliber minds immediately accept a theory—almost any theory—as a dogma of truth" (this text).

One of the concepts in this whole area of what the compleat counselor should be is one at which I would like to take a critical look with you. That concept is that the compleat counselor should be a "model" for his clients. There is some value to this concept, that is, one would hope that the counselor would be more mentally healthy than his clients, more able to solve problems, more congruent, more rational, more in touch with reality, less anxious, less tense, more knowledgeable in some areas relevant to therapy, etc. But some authorities have even said that "The life style of the counselor is perhaps as important as his competencies " (Hobbs, 1962, p. 53).

Yet I have some hesitation when I hear that the compleat counselor should be a "model" for his clients, particularly in the model he himself provides in his own life (Hobbs, 1962, p. 49). Too many marriage counselors, for example (as well as therapists in general), come from backgrounds that have to be categorized as WASP in character (i.e., white, anglo-saxon, Protestant), with the attendant middle-class values that accompany this sort of background. Now not all middle-class values are bad from the point of view of a therapist or counselor (Ard, 1972, and reprinted in this text). But some of the traditional middle-class values are the ultimate causes of many of the problems that clients bring to counselors and therapists. Unless the counselor or therapist overcomes much of this background of experience (even though it fits in with traditional measures of "success" in marriage), he or she will not be able to perform the necessary tasks of therapy.

Rather than emphasizing the counselor's personal life style, I would like to urge that the counselor in his professional work, at least, should learn to get beyond his own personal experience, or the limitations thereof. The counselor needs a broad, cross-cultural perspective. This can be accomplished in various ways, through classes, travel, practicums and internships in different settings, counseling experience with people from various walks of life and different backgrounds from the counselor, reading books, comparing notes through listening to tape recordings of cases, etc.

The compleat counselor "should have a long view of things, a product of his habit of reflection, and he should appreciate that we must be concerned not only with the preservation of our society but with the question of what kind of society we want to preserve" (Hobbs, 1962, p. 50). For some thoughtful discussions of what the future might hold for us, the reader may profitably dip into Roderic Gorney's *The Human Agenda* (1972) and Abraham Maslow's *The Farther Reaches of Human Nature* (1971).

Put another way, the compleat counselor is not merely a "well-adjusted" person. Adjustment can be a blind alley, a form of conformity that is detrimental to good mental health (Linder, 1956). The counselor must live independently from society. This must be because the therapist has to be free to do whatever is necessary to effect constructive change in the client. This sometimes means going against the prevailing cultural standards. The therapist helps the client to be free and creative, whether or not the particular social system or sub-culture wishes the client to be free and creative. The compleat counselor does not feel bound by the notion that counseling and psychotherapy are dedicated solely to helping the individual to adjust to society (Carkhuff & Berenson, 1967, pp. 225-226).

If some of the currently prevailing ideas in our culture are basically irrational and self-defeating, then we can say today that our society is indeed sick (or irrational); but *we* need not be as counselors or therapists, and we can work to see that our clients are not, either. It is difficult but not impossible to live a rational life in this irrational world (Ellis & Harper, 1961). We can be the self-reliant few, the "hidden remnant" in our society today (Sykes, 1962).

Sometimes the quality of "openness" or "genuineness" is mentioned as an important characteristic of the person who is an effective therapist. In many ways these may be helpful traits. However, a recent trend has seemed to encourage the expression of hostility or aggression. But "genuineness" must not be confused, as is so often done, "with free license for the therapist to do what he will in therapy, especially to express hostility. Therapy is not for the therapist" (Carkhuff & Berenson, 1967, p. 29). The sources and consequences of rage, hate, hostility, and agression are discussed with clarity and perceptiveness by Leon Saul in his book

The Therapist as a Person (Or: The Compleat Counselor)

The Hostile Mind (1956). Murray Straus, in an article: "Leveling, Civility, and Violence in the Family," systematically attacks one of the most popular premises of contemporary theories of mental health and interpersonal competence. On the basis of the review Straus made of previous research, including his own, one can conclude that much of the new therapy and advice in the literature, especially much current encounter group activity, is almost exactly opposite to what the scientific evidence suggests is appropriate for reducing physical aggression and bringing about satisfying interpersonal relationships (1974).

The compleat counselor has to have the courage to risk himself in the helping relationship. He has to be willing to confront the client with the client's self-defeating patterns of thought and behavior. "The therapist who is willing to take the responsibility of confrontation needs to know, at his deepest level, that he is a constructive human being *who wants life for the client because he has chosen life for himself*" (Carkhuff & Berenson, 1967, p. 177).

The traditional or orthodox psychoanalytic view that the therapist should be a "blank screen" upon which the client projects his transference problems seems to be falling out of favor of late. Hiding behind a couch is also disappearing as a pattern in favor of face-to-face sessions. The therapist today can be a human being with real, live traits and qualities (maybe even faults and frailties?), as long as these do not interfere with therapy.

As psychotherapists and counselors, some have said, we must be able to accept love and to offer love to our clients (Farson, 1962, p. 45). If you agree with this concept, you are in for some moving, troublesome, and problematic experiences (Wheelis, 1958). If you are going to give out love to your clients, I hope you do not have an empty bucket, or even a hole in your bucket, because eight or ten clients a day can be very draining if your own supply gets depleted. This is another good reason for setting one's own house in order *before* going into counseling and psychotherapy as a profession. If you are not getting enough of that wonderful stuff (love and affection, including sex), it may interfere with the practice of your helping profession. Try to make arrangements for your supply basically from outside your practice; it may help you in the long run.

It just may be possible to be an effective therapist without loving all your clients. If you think you can help people you do not even like, that provides another interesting aspect of this most fascinating of relationships: the helping profession.

The Therapist as a Person (Or: The Compleat Counselor)

In these days of emphasis on feelings, one gets the impression from some of our theorists that it is id to id that is important (Whitaker & Malone, 1953). It is the gut reactions that are stressed as important in much of our recent literature. Now obviously feelings will always be a basic part of the materials presented to the therapist in his work. But I sometimes get the idea that a compleat counselor these days has no head, or at least no cerebral cortex. Much recent theory ignores or deprecates ideas, philosophies, thinking, reasoning, logic, and problem-solving, for example. And yet, I would like to suggest that thinking, reasoning, and problem-solving are a necessary part of the compleat counselor. A therapist cannot just deal with feelings and complete the job of therapy (Ard, 1969). In addition to using his guts, bowels, heart or feelings, the compleat counselor needs to use his head or cerebral cortex at least as much if not more (Ellis, 1962, 1973).

In conclusion, I would like to leave you with a comforting thought from Carl Rogers" . . . Imperfect human beings can be of therapeutic assistance to other imperfect human beings" (this text). So you do not have to be "perfect," even if you are a therapist or a counselor.

REFERENCES

Ard, Ben N., Jr. A rational approach to marriage counseling, in Ard, Ben N., Jr. & Ard, Constance C. (Eds.). *Handbook in Marriage Counseling.* Palo Alto: Science & Behavior Books, 1969, pp. 115-119.

Ard, Ben N., Jr. In my opinion: Are all middle-class values bad? *The Family Coordinator.* Vol. 21, pp. 223-224, April, 1972.

Ard, Ben N., Jr. *Treating Psychosexual Dysfunction.* New York: Jason Aronson, 1974.

Bugental, J. F. T. The person who is the psychotherapist. *Journal of Consulting Psychology.* Vol. 28, No. 3, pp. 272-277, 1964.

Carkhuff, Robert R. & Berenson, Bernard G. *Beyond Counseling and Therapy.* New York: Holt, Rinehart & Winston, 1967.

Ellis, Albert. *Reason and Emotion in Psychotherapy.* New York: Lyle Stuart, 1962.

Ellis, Albert. *Humanistic Psychotherapy: The Rational-Emotive Approach.* New York: Julian Press, 1973.

Ellis, Albert & Harper, Robert A. *A Guide to Rational Living.* Hollywood: Wilshire Books, 1961.

Farson, Richard E. The counselor is a woman, in McGowan & Schmidt (Eds.). *Counseling: Readings in Theory and Practice.* New York: Holt, Rinehart & Winston, 1962, pp. 43-45.

Gorney, Roderic. *The Human Agenda.* New York: Simon & Schuster, 1972.

Hobbs, Nicholas. The compleat counselor, in McGowan & Schmidt (Eds.). *Counseling: Readings in Theory and Practice.* New York: Holt, Rinehart & Winston, 1962, pp. 45-54.

Lindner, Robert. *Must You Conform?* New York: Rinehart, 1956.

Maslow, Abraham H. *The Farther Reaches of Human Nature.* New York: Viking, 1971.

Moustakas, Clark E. (Ed.) *The Self.* New York: Harper, 1956.

Rogers, Carl R. A theory of therapy as developed in the client-centered framework, pp. 31-64 in this text.

Rogers, Carl R. The necessary and sufficient conditions of therapeutic personality change, pp. 281-298 in this text.

Saul, Leon J. *The Hostile Mind.* New York: Random House, 1956.

Schofield, William. *Psychotherapy: The Purchase of Friendship.* Englewood Cliffs, New Jersey: Prentice-Hall, 1964.

Straus, Murray. Leveling, civility, and violence in the family. *Journal of Marriage and the Family.* Vol. 36, No. 1, pp. 13-29, February, 1974.

Sykes, Gerald. *The Hidden Remnant.* New York: Harper, 1962.

Whitaker, C. A. & Malone, T. P. *The Roots of Psychotherapy.* New York: Blakiston, 1953.

17

THE FUSION OF DISCIPLINE AND COUNSELING IN THE EDUCATIVE PROCESS

E.G. Williamson, Ph.D.

Of the many opposite and contradictory concepts to be found in the literature of education, discipline and counseling are perhaps most sharply separated.

Discipline is characterized as:	*Counseling is described as:*
Repressive	*Growth producing*
Regulatory	*Ego strengthening*
Forced conformity	*Self-regulating*
Law abiding	*Affect integration*
Orderliness	*Confidence development*
Imposed	*Self-initiated*
Forced control	*Self-centered*

Discipline and counseling differ sharply in other respects:

Discipline is imposed by external restraining authority of parents, teachers, fellow pupils, community mores, law authorities, or principals. It is not requested by pupils in elementary school and least of all by high school students whose idea of a pure democracy is a society of adolescents with no adults anywhere in the vicinity.

Counseling long has been a self-initiated relationship at the adolescent age and a seemingly wanted one at the child level. It is centered not on the community, school or group but upon the

---

This paper originally appeared in *Discipline and the Guidance Program* (1953 Potsdam Guidance Conference). Reprinted by permission of the author and the *Personnel and Guidance Journal*, 1955, *34*: 74-79.

individual and his own unique problems—as though he were more important than everyone else in the home, school, and community. This centering of counseling upon the isolated individual pupil has been characterized recently as an instance of individual relativism as opposed to cultural relativism.

Discipline is a "public" matter in two respects: It is imposed conformity to other persons, and there is nothing private or confidential about it. One either conforms voluntarily publicly to group requirements or else one is compelled to do so by social pressures, punishment, or some other means of regulation.

Counseling is highly personal and confidential. Except for certain persons who are motivated to be abnormal publicly, most persons desire to discuss their intimate adjustments with one counselor at a time. This is the reason that the highly prized confidentiality of counseling is a necessity—the pupil desires it, profits most through it, and suffers relapses when it is dissipated. From the viewpoint of a counselor, the absence of privacy and confidentiality are among the four most devastating weaknesses in most programs of discipline. The ineffective use of punishment for rehabilitation is a third weakness, and the fourth is the inhuman, impersonal manner in which human beings often are handled and processed, sometimes even in education.

Discipline, as I am now using the term, is a discordant note in that type of education designed to stimulate the growth of individuality—social, moral, and intellectual. Indeed, forcing conformity in behavior is often an indication that other educational methods have failed and that in desperation we have abandoned efforts to persuade and have turned to the use of superior authority. It needs to be re-emphasized, however, that many times we face situations in which too much damage to morale has been done to permit persuasion to have any effect. In such cases, we must use compulsion, but we must not deceive ourselves that we are using an educational method. And we ought to return to persuasion as soon as we can.

Let me continue my contrast of discipline and counseling. I am leading up to a re-definition of discipline achieved by fusing the two into a new type of relationship between teacher and administrator, on the one hand, and pupils and students, on the other.

In a distant university, a teacher of counseling is said to have told his trainees: No counselor should have anything to do with registration of students in subjects or with discipline. Presumably, in such a school, unruly and destructive behavior would be handled by the principal or superintendent, and they, harassed by many other pressures and crises, quickly would be forced to dispose of disciplinary cases by assigning penalties, once guilt had been established. As one result of such "drum head" justice, resentment would be added to conflict and the pupil would make a test case to determine who was boss. Such conflict psychology of relationship would often preclude rehabilitation.

Moreover, the counselor, in such a school, would be freed from such conflict so that he could deal with the "behaving" students about their personal problems. Thus the delinquents, who most desperately need clarification of their own chaotic emotions, would often turn to stronger misbehavior as a substitute of counseling.

And counseling, by avoiding such disciplinary responsibilities, would become limited in its usefulness since it takes place only with "good" citizens in the school or home, requires voluntary seeking of counseling, and is of no help in dealing with the pupils who rebel against conformity. These consequences might not be a serious matter if we were content to dismiss delinquency and disciplinary cases by asserting that they are caused by pure cussedness, moral depravity, and other uncontrollable factors and that "nice" persons don't behave that way.

But we now know that misbehavior occurs in some pupils who are otherwise fine persons and quite capable of good citizenship. It is to discover the correctible causes of misbehavior that I believe discipline must be infused with counseling. Discipline as punishment is no corrective of misbehavior unless it is a part of a consequence of a counseling relationship. Alone, punishment is repressive and growth arresting. With counseling, it can become educative, corrective, and growth producing.

This is my thesis, and I now turn to a defense of it.

Many counselors are willing to be used as consultants in exploring the deeper motivations underlying misbehavior, but they understandably do not wish to play any role whatsoever when it comes to imposing restrictions and "punishment" upon the offending student. They wish to be completely without authority and to be perceived by the client as having no possible authority which could be a threat to him. Rather do they wish to serve as his advocate and friend even to the extent of pleading his case with the school authority.

In terms of its effectiveness in maintaining counseling relationships, such a course of action is necessary. But the principal is thus segregated and symbolized with all the trappings of "harsh" authority and is often perceived by the counselor and misbehaving student alike as being a repressive and threatening authority symbol. In my opinion, the counselor does not play his full and proper counseling role in an educational institution when he thus completely segregates and separates himself from such an authority symbol.

It seems to me that, in addition to the consultant role, there are three other functions that counselors properly have in disciplinary situations: first, counseling as active rehabilitation of misbehaving offenders; second, the prevention of misbehavior through counseling to achieve normal development in inner-control of self; and, finally, counseling as a way of aiding students to perceive and to accept that external authority which influences inner development and modifies unbridled individualism.

Counseling as Rehabilitation. My point is best illustrated by quoting from the field of child psychology. In her delightful book, *New Ways in Discipline*, Baruch (1949) has illuminated the major revolution that has taken place in the home with respect to the parental-child relationship, now reconstructed so that counseling techniques, emphasis, and points of view are built into the changed normal relationship of parent and child. Baruch's book is replete with insightful transposing reorientation guidelines, such as: "If a child *misbehaves*, we'll recognize that he must have *unsatisfied emotional needs* . . . we'll try to satisfy it all we can." And again, "When unwanted *negative feelings* have been emptied out sufficiently then—warm and good *positive feelings* flow in." And again, "All children need release and acceptance of 'mean' feelings. All children have 'mean' feelings that need to be released." The logic of therapy as rehabilitation in disciplinary cases is thus made clear. Misbehavior stems from the repression of "mean" feelings, and if the "mean" feelings are aired, brought up to the level of conscious communication, then the basic drive for misbehavior is lessened, if not eliminated. Rehabilitation consists, therefore, of straightforward therapy in which the individual finds substitute channels for his repressed feelings of aggression and disappointment.

So far so good. But it is one thing for the parent-child to restructure the relationship within the imposition of the home in which the child is scarcely willing or able to reject the parent, except symbolically; it is quite another thing for an adolescent, with some degree of possible freedom to reject a non-parental relationship, to be given that kind of release therapy which he does not want because he does not see the necessity of correcting his misbehavior or of being rehabilitated through counseling relationships. Here we run squarely into the complex problem of imposed counseling relationships. Counseling as rehabilitation in a disciplinary situation seems to work well when it is accepted by the counselee, but when it is not thus accepted, such voluntary counseling obviously will not be operative—according to the assumption of current therapists. Our experiences lead us to question the generalization that in all instances and in all respects, imposed counseling relationships are ineffective as well as "bad." I shall return to this point below.

There is a second way in which counseling can serve as the rehabilitation of offending students, and that way is through the transposition of points of view, techniques, and emphases from the customary one-to-one relationship of the counseling interview to the entire school situation. In much the same way as parent-child relationships in the home are now being restructured according to counseling generalizations and experiences, likewise the entire school atmosphere and the relationships between teachers and students, principals and students, and teachers and parents may be restructured with the counseling interview serving as a model. In many schools, such a revolution is well under way, but there are many counselors who do not accept this opportunity to extend the influence of counseling far beyond the one-to-one counseling interview.

Prevention of Misbehavior through Counseling. I come to my second point, the use of counseling techniques and emphases to facilitate the achievement of normal development of self-control and self-discipline. Every counselor understands some phases of the process by means of which warm and positive feelings become a normal part of the child's development through the maintenance of satisfying affective relationships with others and with adults. Optimum development of the individual is indeed achievable, as far as affect is concerned, through the emotional climate of the school and home in which the child is encouraged, assisted, and permitted to grow up with a minimum of repression and negative attitudes and feelings.

Baruch (1949) summarizes this generalization with respect to misbehavior and behavior when she says, "The more we accept a child's FEELINGS, the more will he accept our RULES." It is quite true that if the relationships of the home and school are satisfying, affectively, to the child, then there seems to be little motivation for misbehaving; that is, the child thus achieves satisfaction through conforming to the requirements of his social environment, and there is no desire or motivation to do otherwise. He is, in this sense, a normally developing individual, and he does not experience the necessity of conflicting or warring with his environment because the environment thwarts him. Thus developing effective school situations provides another opportunity for counselors to prevent misbehavior.

Counseling as an Aid to Perception and Acceptance of External Authority. I turn to my third point, counseling as a process of reorientation to the reality of external authority. As a facilitator of normal development, the school counselor enters the disciplinary situation, or at least can enter it, in a new and in many ways more important role, as an educator-counselor who seeks to help the misbehaving student perceive and accept the role of authority as it impinges upon his own "autonomous" inner life and behavior. Within the friendly home, the consequences of misbehavior are soon forgotten, and there is frequently no external legal authority acting for society to impose consequences, restrictions, and limitations upon the autonomy of the individual in the light of or as a result of his misbehavior. In most home-centered misbehavior, all is soon forgiven, and certainly the term "punishment" has no long-term connotation. But as a child grows into adolescence and begins to misbehave away from home, all is not so readily forgiven and forgotten. Consequences flow from misbehavior and are sometimes legally imposed in the form of punishment as retribution following upon the heels of misbehavior. It is at this point that the counselor can play a very significant role in helping the individual to learn to live in a universe in which his autonomy is hedged about and "infringed" upon by external authority and to understand how the role of the forgiving parent, who generates positive feelings and warmth, is often set aside in many instances by a harsh, repressive, and sometimes vengeful authority symbol-role.

I am not advocating that a counselor enter into partnership with such a vengeful authority. But I feel certain that a counselor can play a significant role in helping the individual to perceive, and to accept emotionally, the inevitability of authority in some form or another acting as a restrictive agency upon the individual's free play of self-directed freedom. This learning is a profound one and most necessary in a democratic society of cooperative and interrelated individual persons. To be sure, it is not easy to teach such a generalization to an individual who has come into conflict with that society, or even in conflict with other individuals in a small, restricted club or school. Such an individual has already alienated himself from other individuals and from authority by his misbehavior. How then can he be aided to accept that which he has flaunted? As Kurt Lewin (1948) so cogently states:

"We can now formulate the dilemma which re-education has to face in this way: How can free acceptance of a new system of values be brought about if the person who is to be educated is, in the nature of things, likely to be hostile to the new values and loyal to the old?

Re-education influences conduct only when the new system of values and beliefs dominates the individual's perception. The acceptance of the new system is linked with the acceptance of a specific group, a particular role, a definite source of authority as new points of reference. It is basic for re-education that this linkage between acceptance of new facts or values and acceptance of certain groups or roles is very intimate and that the second frequently is a prerequisite for the first."

At this point counselors can and should, I believe, pioneer in testing Lewin's hypothesis by searching for counseling techniques that will aid a misbehaving individual to learn and to like the "imposed" role and the new values required of him as a member of a group, his home, and his school.

I have now stated what I mean by the fusion of discipline and counseling in an educative process—discipline becomes not "forced" conformity or punishment, but a type of re-education designed to aid the individual to so understand his emotions and feelings and to so redirect them into new behavior channels that he no longer wants to or is forced to misbehave as an unsuccessful attempt to rid himself of external authority. Parenthetically, it escapes the attention of some counselors that the state of individualistic autonomy that some students seek is, in its extreme form, self destructive or at least not a full measure of self fulfillment in the case of human beings.

There are, I repeat, two arguments for attempting such a fusion of discipline and counseling: Counseling is our present chief prospect for changing discipline from punishment to rehabilitation; and counseling as a form of growth-producing and morale building human relationship will aid the individual to achieve that degree of self-control and self-restraint so necessary in all members of an inter-dependent democratic society. And I borrow the words of a cultural anthropologist who describes the way in which one individual can achieve his individuality through, and not in spite of, the imposed discipline of membership in a society:

> . . . to belong to a society is to sacrifice some measure of individual liberty, no matter how slight the restraints which the society consciously imposes. The so-called free societies are not really free. They are merely those societies which encourage their members to express their individuality along a few minor and socially acceptable lines. At the same time they condition their members to abide by innumerable rules and regulations, doing this so subtly and completely that these members are largely unconscious that the rules exist. If a society has done its work of shaping the individual properly, he is no more conscious of most of the restrictions it has imposed than he is of the restraints which his habitual clothing imposes on his movements (Linton, 1945).

Let me quote my summary of a recent conference on discipline and counseling:

> To achieve full personal development, each pupil must learn to live mutually helpfully with others in group life.
>
> This means that each individual must learn self control or at least develop in the direction of that ideal of our democracy.
>
> It follows that the individual cannot grow toward self control in a social vacuum of rampant and selfish individualism.
>
> And that aspect involves the school (and counselor) in helping (and insisting) that the individual "conform" to the requirements of group living involving the needs of other pupils. Such a concept bothers those who feel guilty about "imposing" any restrictions from the outside upon the inner growth processes of the individual. Nevertheless, it is clear that both types of discipline (self and group) must be fused in the personality of the individual if he is to avoid disintegration and self conflict.
>
> The crux of the matter is the methods the school and the counselor use to achieve this self control adjusted to group conformity. And rigid regimentation involving sharp punishment for deviation from official pathways of behavior is an ineffective way. Conversely, the maintenance of a friendly school atmosphere and the offering of a rich variety of growth-producing experiences in learning self control are effective ways of teaching self discipline.
>
> If we redefine "discipline" as a constructive life-style of living as a human being involving the maintaining of human relationships with others, we then see new ways in which counseling can play a

significant role in discipline.

But, and this is a troublesome spot, many individuals deviate in their learning and some deviate destructively to self and to others. It is at this point that the legal authorities step in, both in the school and community, and force conformity as well as "punish" deviation.

Up to this point, counselors participate in discipline through their normal activities of helping the individual to achieve optimum growth and also by insisting upon accommodation to standards required by membership in society. In this sense, the counselor does not permit unbridled self-growth of any kind that is destructive of self or other selves.

In the conflict state of disciplinary situations, the counselor becomes a teamwork consultant to the "authorities," participating within school and community in rehabilitating the "offender." It follows that he must make clear to the student that he, the counselor, is on the side of morality and "law and order." He is not neutral in such a situation. He also makes it clear that part of the student's behavior which is destructive of the "right" kind of self control is balanced in counseling between the needs and rights of other individuals within the group (Williamson, 1954).[1]

I can sum up my point of view about the fusion of discipline and counseling by quoting a wise psychiatrist who played a major role in the conference referred to above. Dr. Carson of Potsdam, New York, capsuled the point in these words: "Discipline must be given a matrix of love." All human beings, and especially children and adolescents, have great "affect hunger" and misbehaving children and adolescents have greater need. If their misbehavior erupts out of affect hunger and resentment from rejection in home or community, then the school and especially the counselors must substitute affection for that hunger. Punishment will not completely fill such a deep void, but the humanized relationship of counseling will be effective. Therefore, in the area of behavior (as contrasted with "inert" knowledge of the classroom), human relationships in the school will often prove to be effective in helping pupils to achieve maturity, social, moral, intellectual, and other kinds. It is not unreasonable to restructure schools so that human

---

[1]The above nine paragraphs are taken from my article, "Discipline and Counseling," *Education*, 1954, *74:* 513-516.

beings are related to each other in a way characterized as humane.

In this way, self-control discipline is cultivated by the very personal relationships of the persons in the school, and this is one of the most important goals of counseling. Discipline then becomes restructured through the adoption of counseling methods and points of view as substitutes for discipline by inhuman punishment.

REFERENCES

Baruch, Dorothy W. *New Ways In Discipline*. New York: McGraw-Hill, 1949.

Lewin, K. *Resolving Social Conflicts*. New York: Harper, 1948.

Linton, R. *The Cultural Background of Personality*. New York: Appleton-Century-Crofts, 1945.

Williamson, E. G. *A Conference Summary: Counseling in a Disciplinary Situation*. 1953 Potsdam Guidance Conference, State Univer. Teachers College, Potsdam, New York.

Williamson, E. G. Discipline and counseling. *Education,* 1954, *74:* 513-516.

18

SHOULD ALL COUNSELORS BE CLASSROOM TEACHERS?

Ben N. Ard, Jr., Ph.D.

Many people in education feel that all counselors should be classroom teachers. As Gerald Kushel has put it (in the words of a teacher who may speak for many), "It would seem to me that every guidance counselor ought to teach one or two classes. They should be guidance 'teachers' in the full sense of the word. They should be teaching at the same time" (1967, p. 99).

Even in some school systems where counselors may devote their full time to counseling, many administrators will not hire a counselor who has not been a teacher (i.e., who does not hold a teaching credential). Perhaps the predominant view in the field of education today is that "all counselors should be classroom teachers."

But to defend the thesis that "all counselors should be classroom teachers" is to deny, ultimately, that counselors serve any necessary function distinct from teachers. If all counselors should be classroom teachers, this amounts to saying, in effect, that *only* classroom teachers should be trained to be counselors. It is also implied in this position that teachers should be trained as counselors, too; that is, that counseling (ideally, according to this view) should be provided by the classroom teachers. Some authorities in the field have said as much. For example, Francis P. Robinson, in his *Principles and Procedures In Student Counseling*, has said, "Every teacher needs to be guidance-minded if he is to teach effectively, and many teachers can also carry on certain types of personnel activity" (1950, p. ix).

This is a much expanded version of an earlier paper by the same author, reprinted with the permission of the publisher, from *Guidance Journal,* Vol. VI, No. 2, pp. 279-282, Fall, 1967.

However, this same authority has also pointed out that there has been a tendency to differentiate between the work of the teacher and the work of the student personnel specialist or counselor (Robinson, 1950, pp. viii-ix). This distinction must necessarily be made, it would seem, if the different, separate, and distinct functions of both teachers and counselors are to be clearly recognized, respected, and fostered. As Robinson has stated, "the wide range of aims in education and the needs of individual students require that schools use many kinds of specialists, e.g., not only administrators, teachers, and janitors, but also well-trained counselors, specialists in activities, test experts, registrars, and placement workers" (1950, p. ix).

Robert Rossberg, after citing evidence in his article "To Teach or Not To Teach: Is That The Question?" concluded that there are many in the field of counselor education who are not convinced that teaching experience is the *sine qua non* of counselor preparation (1967, p. 191). But many administrators still will not hire counselors who have not had teaching experience.

Part of the slowness in adopting counseling services in more of our schools may be due to the thinking which underlies those who might defend the thesis that "all counselors should be classroom teachers." The other side of this coin is revealed in the phrase often heard in educational circles: "Every teacher is a counselor" (Froehlich, 1950, p. 16). However, as Froehlich has candidly commented on this statement, "It is a trite phrase, and has little basis in fact" (1950, p. 16). He went on to say, "Let us be realistic about it. Every teacher is not trained as a counselor, nor is it likely that he will be in the near future" (1950, p. 16).

Nevertheless, since a counselor is an educational worker, "he must in most states meet state requirements for a teacher's certificate valid at the level on which he is employed" (Froehlich, 1950, p. 52). This means, in effect, that counselors must have been classroom teachers (or at least practice teachers) before they can take positions as counselors. Specifically, as one minimum requirement, prospective counselors must usually have completed a required number of credit hours in supervised practice teaching experience in order to qualify for a teacher's certificate in most states.

Yet, as Strowig has concluded in his article ". . . And Gladly Teach (That I May Counsel)"

". . . in the case of requiring teaching experience of counselors I believe we make the questionable assumption that experience in the one career is most appropriate for success in another career—the same error we make in requiring teacher certification of counselors."

Strowig also concluded,

"I know of no evidence, just opinion, which suggests strongly that counselors who have taught are more effective as counselors than are counselors who have had no teaching experience, or even no experience of any kind" (Strowig, 1967, p. 185).

The basic position taken in the present paper may be explicitly stated as follows: while it may prove helpful to have had some classroom teaching experience, it is *not* absolutely necessary for a counselor to have had such experience in order to perform his counseling duties effectively.

In fact, too much emphasis on this matter of insisting that all counselors should be (or at least should have been) classroom teachers has had an unfortunate effect upon the quality of counselors. As Robinson has pointed out: "Many present-day counselors are inadequately trained for their work. One reason for this is the tendency to appoint teachers as counselors because they 'like pupils,' have kept out of trouble, and show promise of keeping students out of trouble" (1950, p. 290). These would seem rather poor, insufficient reasons for making a person a counselor.

There are several reasons why classroom teachers should *not* be selected to be made into counselors. We may agree with Lester Sands in that "Though we adhere to the ideal that the teacher should be the intimate guide of the student, we find that teachers may not always be trusted with confidential information pertaining to children's backgrounds. Teachers are prone to gossip and distribute interesting data regarding students" (Sands, 1952, p. 341).

Some of the basic reasons why teachers are frequently not suitable to become counselors may be found in some of the conditions surrounding their jobs. "Their concentration on academic matters and the pressure of parents for a continuing emphasis on the fundamentals also prevents them from making subsurface inquiries into the thinking of pupils" (Sands, 1952, pp. 341-342).

There are even further reasons why classroom teachers should not always be recruited for counseling positions. "The vast majority of teachers, even with special training, are not fully fitted for the work. Furthermore, the attitudes of teachers toward educational experiences is such that personal guidance of the child is practically excluded from consideration" (Sands, 1952, p. 341). Finally, Lester Sands has summed up his position on this matter as follows: "Unfortunately, there has not been enough professional training and growth among teachers generally to warrant their being considered effective personnel counselors of students" (1952, p. 341).

The foregoing reasons would not necessarily preclude any teacher from becoming a counselor, given sufficient training, if the particular teacher did not evidence the limitations mentioned above. We could conclude then that while *some* teachers might become good counselors, *all* counselors *need not* be classroom teachers, nor *need not* necessarily have even *been* classroom teachers.

Ultimately, the principle reason why counselors should *not* be classroom teachers is because the *nature of the relationship* to the student-client must necessarily be different from that of the teacher to the pupil. This would not be admitted, perhaps, by all the workers in the field. For example, Carl Rogers and E. G. Williamson would evidently differ with the view just stated. These two men, while usually at opposite ends of the non-directive versus directive counseling continuum, at least appear on the same side of the fence on this matter of the ideal counseling and teaching relationship, it would seem. For an example of Rogers' viewpoint, see his chapter on "Student-Centered Teaching" in his book *Client-Centered Therapy* (1951). For an example of Williamson's viewpoint, see the previous chapter on "The Fusion of Discipline and Counseling in the Educative Process" (in the present text).

Thorne has criticized Williamson's view that discipline and counseling be fused by saying that Williamson's conception of "counseling should more properly be called "management," since the activities described are conducted within a plainly authoritarian judgmental framework which can hardly be perceived as anything else by the students (Ard, 1966, pp. 24-25). That is, the basic operational framework is not primarily therapeutic, but rather is regulatory and administrative.

The present writer would maintain that pupils usually experience the *relationship with counselors* as "safer" than that relationship usually experienced with their *teachers*. That is, the pupil usually feels that he can "say more" with impunity in the counselor-client relationship than in the teacher-pupil relationship.

Some evaluation is obviously necessary even in counseling (and by the way, even in non-directive or client-centered counseling), but the quality and quantity of it (particularly as experienced by the pupil) is quite a bit different from teaching. This differentiation between the two roles is basic.

Shertzer and Stone, in discussing this issue or question of should the ranks of teachers constitute the sole source of counselor supply, cite the fact that experienced counselor educators frequently note the difficulties encountered in altering teacher-oriented attitudes which are detrimental to counseling. In some instances, it might be easier to start with students in a counseling program who did not have to unlearn previous attitudes picked up in teaching (1974, pp. 447-448).

The counselor can adopt the client's frame of reference (for a while during the interview at least), whereas this is not as feasible for the teacher who has to function in another frame of reference, usually (for no other reason than because there are thirty or more additional pupils in the room at the same time). The classroom situation cannot usually function as even a group therapy session in most instances.

The pupil *experiences* the *counselor* in a different way than he does the *teacher*. The counselor is not "authority" in the same way the teacher is, since the counselor does not operate as a disciplinarian (ideally speaking), whereas the teacher necessarily does have to function as a disciplinarian. The counselor is not experienced by the pupil as "threatening," whereas the teacher may be experienced as very threatening (perhaps because of the teacher's judgmental and disciplinarian functions).

Norman Gilbert, in his study of "When the Counselor Is A Disciplinarian," reached the following conclusions:

"Most experts in the field point out the inadvisability of combining responsibility for discipline with that of counseling. Common among the reasons cited are the following: 1) Utilization of the counselor as a disciplinarian represents a misunderstanding of the counselor's appropriate function in the school setting; 2) it is difficult, if not impossible, to establish an adequate counseling relationship under circumstances in which the counselor possesses either the authority or responsibility for carrying out disciplinary measures; . . ." (Gilbert, 1967, pp. 122-131).

The *expectations* pupils have of counselors are different from those they have of teachers. The counselor has more empathic identification with the pupil than the teacher does (i.e., the counselor may be perceived by the pupil as more "on his side" than the teacher, usually). Consequently the counselor usually has more understanding of the pupil than the teacher does, certainly at least with regard to the "whys" of his behavior (since the counselor's *function* is to delve into the "whys," while the teacher does not have time to do this with all his pupils).

After considering what various authorities in the field have had to say on this matter, and some observations on the *distinctive roles* and *functions* of counselors and teachers, we arrive at the conclusion that *all* counselors should *not* be classroom teachers.

REFERENCES

Froehlich, C. P. *Guidance Services in Smaller Schools.* New York: McGraw-Hill, 1950.

Gilbert, Norman S. When the counselor is a disciplinarian, in C. H. Patterson (Ed.). *The Counselor in the School: Selected Readings.* New York: McGraw-Hill, 1967, Chap. 16, pp. 122-131.

Kushel, Gerald. *Discord in Teacher-Counselor Relations.* Englewood Cliffs, New Jersey: Prentice-Hall, 1967.

Robinson, Francis P. *Principles and Procedures in Student Counseling.* New York: Harper, 1950.

Rogers, Carl R. *Client-Centered Therapy.* Boston: Houghton-Mifflin, 1951.

Rossberg, Robert H. To teach or not to teach: Is that the question? in C. H. Patterson (Ed.). *The Counselor in the School: Selected Readings.* New York: McGraw-Hill, 1967, Chap. 24, pp. 188-192.

Sands, Lester B. The administration of special services, in John T. Wahlquist, et al. *The Administration of Public Education.* New York: Ronald Press, 1952.

Shertzer, Bruce & Stone, Shelley C. *Fundamentals of Counseling.* Boston: Houghton-Mifflin, 2nd edition, 1974.

Strowig, R. Wray. . . . And gladly teach (that I may counsel), in C. H. Patterson (Ed.). *The Counselor in the School: Selected Readings.* New York: McGraw-Hill, 1967, Chap. 23, pp. 182-188.

Thorne, Frederick C. Critique of Recent Developments in personality counseling theory, in Ben N. Ard, Jr. (Ed.). *Counseling and Psychotherapy: Classics on Theories and Issues.* Palo Alto: Science & Behavior Books, 1966, Chap. 2, pp. 13-31.

Williamson, E. G. The fusion of discipline and counseling in the educative process,

19

THE NECESSARY AND SUFFICIENT CONDITIONS OF THERAPEUTIC PERSONALITY CHANGE

Carl R. Rogers, Ph.D.

For many years I have been engaged in psychotherapy with individuals in distress. In recent years I have found myself increasingly concerned with the process of abstracting from that experience the general principles which appear to be involved in it. I have endeavored to discover any orderliness, any unity which seems to inhere in the subtle, complex tissue of interpersonal relationship in which I have so constantly been immersed in therapeutic work. One of the current products of this concern is an attempt to state, in formal terms, a theory of psychotherapy, of personality, and of interpersonal relationships which will encompass and contain the phenomena of my experience. What I wish to do in this paper is to take one very small segment of that theory, spell it out more completely, and explore its meanings and usefulness.

THE PROBLEM

The question to which I wish to address myself is this: Is it possible to state, in terms which are clearly definable and measurable, the psychological conditions which are both necessary and sufficient to bring about constructive personality change? Do we, in other words, know with any precision those elements which are essential if psychotherapeutic change is to ensue?

Before proceeding to the major task let me dispose very briefly

---

Reprinted by permission of the author and *Journal of Consulting Psychology*, 1957, *21*:95-103.

of the second portion of the question. What is meant by such phrases as "psychotherapeutic change," "constructive personality change"? This problem also deserves deep and serious consideration, but for the moment let me suggest a common-sense type of meaning upon which we can perhaps agree for purposes of this paper. By these phrases is meant: change in the personality structure of the individual, at both surface and deeper levels, in a direction which clinicians would agree means greater integration, less internal conflict, more energy utilizable for effective living; change in behavior away from behaviors generally regarded as immature and toward behaviors regarded as mature. This brief description may suffice to indicate the kind of change for which we are considering the preconditions. It may also suggest the ways in which this criterion of change may be determined.[1]

THE CONDITIONS

As I have considered my own clinical experience and that of my colleagues, together with the pertinent research which is available, I have drawn out several conditions which seem to me to be *necessary* to initiate constructive personality change, and which, taken together, appear to be *sufficient* to inaugurate that process. As I have worked on this problem I have found myself surprised at the simplicity of what has emerged. The statement which follows is not offered with any assurance as to its correctness, but with the expectation that it will have the value of any theory, namely that it states or implies a series of hypotheses which are open to proof or disproof, thereby clarifying and extending our knowledge of the field.

Since I am not, in this paper, trying to achieve suspense, I will state at once, in severely rigorous and summarized terms, the six conditions which I have come to feel are basic to the process of personality change. The meaning of a number of the terms is not immediately evident, but will be clarified in the explanatory sections which follow. It is hoped that this brief statement will have much more significance to the reader when he has completed

---

[1]That this is a measurable and determinable criterion has been shown in research already completed. See Rogers and Dymond (1954), especially chapters 8, 13, and 17.

the paper. Without further introduction let me state the basic theoretical position.

For constructive personality change to occur, it is necessary that these conditions exist and continue over a period of time:

1. Two persons are in psychological contact.

2. The first, whom we shall term the client, is in a state of incongruence, being vulnerable or anxious.

3. The second person, whom we shall term the therapist, is congruent or integrated in the relationship.

4. The therapist experiences unconditional positive regard for the client.

5. The therapist experiences an empathic understanding of the client's internal frame of reference and endeavors to communicate this experience to the client.

6. The communication to the client of the therapist's empathic understanding and unconditional positive regard is to a minimal degree achieved.

No other conditions are necessary. If these six conditions exist, and continue over a period of time, this is sufficient. The process of constructive personality change will follow.

A Relationship

The first condition specifies that a minimal relationship, a psychological contact, must exist. I am hypothesizing that significant positive personality change does not occur except in a relationship. This is of course an hypothesis, and it may be disproved.

Conditions 2 through 6 define the characteristics of the relationship which are regarded as essential by defining the necessary characteristics of each person in the relationship. All that is intended by this first condition is to specify that the two people are to some degree in contact, that each makes some perceived difference in the experiential field of the other. Probably it is sufficient if each makes some "subceived" difference, even though the individual may not be consciously aware of this impact. Thus it might be difficult to know whether a catatonic patient perceives a therapist's presence as making a difference to him—a difference of any kind—but it is almost certain that at some organic level he does sense this difference.

Except in such a difficult borderline situation as that just mentioned, it would be relatively easy to define this condition in operational terms and thus determine, from a hard-boiled research point of view, whether the condition does, or does not, exist. The simplest method of determination involves simply the awareness of both client and therapist. If each is aware of being in personal or psychological contact with the other, then this condition is met.

This first condition of therapeutic change is such a simple one that perhaps it should be labeled an assumption or a precondition in order to set it apart from those that follow. Without it, however, the remaining items would have no meaning, and that is the reason for including it.

The State of the Client

It was specified that it is necessary that the client be "in a state of incongruence, being vulnerable or anxious." What is the meaning of these terms?

Incongruence is a basic construct in the theory we have been developing. It refers to a discrepancy between the actual experience of the organism and the self picture of the individual insofar as it represents that experience. Thus a student may experience, at a total or organismic level, a fear of the university and of examinations which are given on the third floor of a certain building, since these may demonstrate a fundamental inadequacy in him. Since such a fear of his inadequacy is decidedly at odds with his concept of himself, this experience is represented (distortedly) in his awareness as an unreasonable fear of climbing stairs in this building, or any building, and soon an unreasonable fear of crossing the open campus. Thus there is a fundamental discrepancy between the experienced meaning of the situation as it registers in his organism and the symbolic representation of that experience in awareness in such a way that it does not conflict with the picture he has of himself. In this case to admit a fear of inadequacy would contradict the picture he holds of himself; to admit incomprehensible fears does not contradict his self concept.

Another instance would be the mother who develops vague illnesses whenever her only son makes plans to leave home. The actual desire is to hold on to her only source of satisfaction. To perceive this in awareness would be inconsistent with the picture she holds of herself as a good mother. Illness, however, is consistent with her self concept, and the experience is symbolized in this distorted fashion. Thus again there is a basic incongruence between the self as perceived (in this case as an ill mother needing attention) and the actual experience (in this case the desire to hold on to her son).

When the individual has no awareness of such incongruence in himself, then he is merely vulnerable to the possibility of anxiety and disorganization. Some experience might occur so suddenly or so obviously that the incongruence could not be denied. Therefore, the person is vulnerable to such a possibility.

If the individual dimly perceives such an incongruence in himself, then a tension state occurs which is known as anxiety. The incongruence need not be sharply perceived. It is enough that it is subceived—that is, discriminated as threatening to the self without any awareness of the content of that threat. Such anxiety is often seen in therapy as the individual approaches awareness of some element of his experience which is in sharp contradiction to his self concept.

It is not easy to give precise operational definition to this second of the six conditions, yet to some degree this has been achieved. Several research workers have defined the self concept by means of a Q sort by the individual of a list of self-referent items. This gives us an operational picture of the self. The total experiencing of the individual is more difficult to capture. Chodorkoff (1954) has defined it as a Q sort made by a clinician who sorts the same self-referent items independently, basing his sorting on the picture he has obtained of the individual from projective tests. His sort thus includes unconscious as well as conscious elements of the individual's experience, thus representing (in an admittedly imperfect way) the totality of the client's experience. The correlation between these two sortings gives a crude operational measure of incongruence between self and experience, low or negative correlation representing of course a high degree of incongruence.

The Therapist's Genuineness in the Relationship

The third condition is that the therapist should be, within the confines of this relationship, a congruent, genuine, integrated person. It means that within the relationship he is freely and deeply himself, with his actual experience accurately represented by his awareness of himself. It is the opposite of presenting a facade, either knowingly or unknowingly.

It is not necessary (nor is it possible) that the therapist be a paragon who exhibits this degree of integration, of wholeness, in every aspect of his life. It is sufficient that he is accurately himself in this hour of this relationship, that in this basic sense he is what he actually is, in this moment of time.

It should be clear that this includes being himself even in ways which are not regarded as ideal for psychotherapy. His experience may be "I am afraid of this client" or "My attention is so focused on my own problems that I can scarcely listen to him." If the therapist is not denying these feelings to awareness, but is able freely to be them (as well as being his other feelings), then the condition we have stated is met.

It would take us too far afield to consider the puzzling matter as to the degree to which the therapist overtly communicates this reality in himself to the client. Certainly the aim is not for the therapist to express or talk out his own feelings, but primarily that he should not be deceiving the client as to himself. At times he may need to talk out some of his own feelings (either to the client, or to a colleague or supervisor) if they are standing in the way of the following two conditions.

It is not too difficult to suggest an operational definition for this third condition. We resort again to Q technique. If the therapist sorts a series of items relevant to the relationship (using a list similar to the ones developed by Fiedler (1950, 1953) and Bown (1954), this will give his perception of his experience in the relationship. If several judges who have observed the interview or listened to a recording of it (or observed a sound movie of it) now sort the same items to represent *their* perception of the relationship, this second sorting should catch those elements of the therapist's behavior and inferred attitudes of which he is unaware, as well as those of which he is aware. Thus a high correlation between the therapist's sort and the observer's sort would represent in crude form an operational definition of the therapist's congruence or integration in the relationship, and a low correlation, the opposite.

Unconditional Positive Regard

To the extent that the therapist finds himself experiencing a warm acceptance of each aspect of the client's experience as being a part of that client, he is experiencing unconditional positive regard. This concept has been developed by Standal (1954). It means that there are no *conditions* of acceptance, no feeling of "I like you only *if* you are thus and so." It means a "prizing" of the person, as Dewey has used that term. It is at the opposite pole from a selective evaluating attitude—"You are bad in these ways, good in those." It involves as much feeling of acceptance for the client's expression of negative, "bad," painful, fearful, defensive, abnormal feelings as for his expression of "good," positive, mature, confident, social feelings, as much acceptance of ways in which he is inconsistent as of ways in which he is consistent. It means a caring for the client, but not in a possessive way or in such a way as simply to satisfy the therapist's own needs. It means a caring for the client as a *separate* person, with permission to have his own feelings, his own experiences. One client describes the therapist as "fostering my possession of my own experience . . . that [this] is *my* experience and that I am actually having it: thinking what I think, feeling what I feel, wanting what I want, fearing what I fear: no 'ifs,' 'buts,' or 'not reallys.' " This is the type of acceptance which is hypothesized as being necessary if personality change is to occur.

Like the two previous conditions, this fourth condition is a matter of degree,[2] as immediately becomes apparent if we attempt to define it in terms of specific research operations. One such method of giving it definition would be to consider the Q sort for the relationship as described under Condition 3. To the extent that items expressive of unconditional positive regard are sorted as characteristic of the relationship by both the therapist and the observers, unconditional positive regard might be said to exist. Such items might include statements of this order: "I feel no revulsion at anything the client says"; "I feel neither approval nor disapproval of the client and his statements—simply acceptance"; "I feel warmly toward the client—toward his weaknesses and problems as well as his potentialities"; "I am not inclined to pass judgment on what the client tells me"; "I like the client." To the extent that both therapist and observers perceive these

---

[2]The phrase "unconditional positive regard" may be an unfortunate one, since it sounds like an absolute, an all or nothing dispositional concept. It is probably evident from the description that completely unconditional positive regard would never exist except in theory. From a clinical and experiential point of view I believe the most accurate statement is that the effective therapist experiences unconditional positive regard for the client during many moments of his contact with him, yet from time to time he experiences only a conditional positive regard—and perhaps at times a negative regard, though this is not likely in effective therapy. It is in this sense that unconditional positive regard exists as a matter of degree in any relationship.

items as characteristic, or their opposites as uncharacteristic, Condition 4 might be said to be met.

Empathy

The fifth condition is that the therapist is experiencing an accurate, empathic understanding of the client's awareness of his own experience. To sense the client's private world as if it were your own, but without ever losing the "as if" quality—this is empathy, and this seems essential to therapy. To sense the client's anger, fear, or confusion as if it were your own, yet without your own anger, fear, or confusion getting bound up in it, is the condition we are endeavoring to describe. When the client's world is this clear to the therapist, and he moves about in it freely, then he can both communicate his understanding of what is clearly known to the client and can also voice meanings in the client's experience of which the client is scarcely aware. As one client described this second aspect: "Every now and again, with me in a tangle of thought and feeling, screwed up in a web of mutually divergent lines of movement, with impulses from different parts of me, and me feeling the feeling of its being all too much and suchlike—then whomp, just like a sunbeam thrusting its way through cloudbanks and tangles of foliage to spread a circle of light on a tangle of forest paths, came some comment from you. [It was] clarity, even disentanglement, an additional twist to the picture, a putting in place. Then the consequence—the sense of moving on, the relaxation. These were sunbeams." That such penetrating empathy is important for therapy is indicated by Fiedler's (1950) research in which items such as the following placed high in the description of relationships created by experienced therapists:

The therapist is well able to understand the patient's feelings.

The therapist is never in any doubt about what the patient means.

The therapist's remarks fit in just right with the patient's mood and content.

The therapist's tone of voice conveys the complete ability to share the patient's feelings.

An operational definition of the therapist's empathy could be provided in different ways. Use might be made of the Q sort described under Condition 3. To the degree that items descriptive of accurate empathy were sorted as characteristic by both the therapist and the observers, this condition would be regarded as existing.

Another way of defining this condition would be for both client and therapist to sort a list of items descriptive of client feelings. Each would sort independently, the task being to represent the feelings which the client had experienced during a just completed interview. If the correlation between client and therapist sortings were high, accurate empathy would be said to exist, a low correlation indicating the opposite conclusion.

Still another way of measuring empathy would be for trained judges to rate the depth and accuracy of the therapist's empathy on the basis of listening to recorded interviews.

The Client's Perception of the Therapist

The final condition as stated is that the client perceives, to a minimal degree, the acceptance and empathy which the therapist experiences for him. Unless some communication of these attitudes has been achieved, then such attitudes do not exist in the relationship as far as the client is concerned, and the therapeutic process could not, by our hypothesis, be initiated.

Since attitudes cannot be directly perceived, it might be somewhat more accurate to state that therapist behaviors and words are perceived by the client as meaning that to some degree the therapist accepts and understands him.

An operational definition of this condition would not be difficult. The client might, after an interview, sort a Q-sort list of items referring to qualities representing the relationship between himself and the therapist. (The same list could be used as for Condition 3.) If several items descriptive of acceptance and empathy are sorted by the client as characteristic of the relationship, then this condition could be regarded as met. In the present state of our knowledge the meaning of "to a minimal degree" would have to be arbitrary.

Up to this point the effort has been made to present, briefly and factually, the conditions which I have come to regard as essential for psychotherapeutic change. I have not tried to give the theoretical context of these conditions nor to explain what seem to me to be the dynamics of their effectiveness. Such explanatory material will be available, to the reader who is interested, in the document already mentioned.

I have, however, given at least one means of defining, in operational terms, each of the conditions mentioned. I have done this in order to stress the fact that I am not speaking of vague qualities which ideally should be present if some other vague result is to occur. I am presenting conditions which are crudely measurable even in the present state of our technology, and have suggested specific operations in each instance even though I am sure that more adequate methods of measurement could be devised by a serious investigator.

My purpose has been to stress the notion that in my opinion we are dealing with an if-then phenomenon in which knowledge of the dynamics is not essential to testing the hypotheses. Thus, to illustrate from another field: if one substance, shown by a series of operations to be the substance known as hydrochloric acid, is mixed with another substance, shown by another series of operations to be sodium hydroxide, then salt and water will be products of this mixture. This is true whether one regards the results as due to magic, or whether one explains it in the most adequate terms of modern chemical theory. In the same way it is being postulated here that certain definable conditions precede certain definable changes and that this fact exists independently of our efforts to account for it.

THE RESULTING HYPOTHESES

The major value of stating any theory in unequivocal terms is that specific hypotheses may be drawn from it which are capable of proof or disproof. Thus, even if the conditions which have been postulated as necessary and sufficient conditions are more incorrect than correct (which I hope they are not), they could still advance science in this field by providing a base of operations from which fact could be winnowed out from error.

The hypotheses which would follow from the theory given would be of this order:

If these six conditions (as operationally defined) exist, then constructive personality change (as defined) will occur in the client.

If one or more of these conditions is not present, constructive personality change will not occur.

These hypotheses hold in any situation whether it is or is not labeled "psychotherapy."

Only Condition 1 is dichotomous (it either is present or is not), and the remaining five occur in varying degree, each on its continuum. Since this is true, another hypothesis follows, and it is likely that this would be the simplest to test:

If all six conditions are present, then the greater the degree to which Conditions 2 to 6 exist, the more marked will be the constructive personality change in the client.

At the present time the above hypotheses can only be stated in this general form—which implies that all of the conditions have equal weight. Empirical studies will no doubt make possible much more refinement of this hypothesis. It may be, for example, that if anxiety is high in the client, then the other conditions are less important. Or if unconditional positive regard is high (as in a mother's love for her child), then perhaps a modest degree of empathy is sufficient. But at the moment we can only speculate on such possibilities.

SOME IMPLICATIONS

Significant Omissions

If there is any startling feature in the formulation which has been given as to the necessary conditions for therapy, it probably lies in the elements which are omitted. In present-day clinical practice, therapists operate as though there were many other conditions in addition to those described, which are essential for psychotherapy. To point this up it may be well to mention a few of the conditions which, after thoughtful consideration of our research and our experience, are not included.

For example, it is *not* stated that these conditions apply to one type of client, and that other conditions are necessary to bring about psychotherapeutic change with other types of client. Probably no idea is so prevalent in clinical work today as that one works with neurotics in one way, with psychotics in another; that certain therapeutic conditions must be provided for compulsives, others for homosexuals, etc. Because of this heavy weight of clinical opinion to the contrary, it is with some "fear and trembling" that I advance the concept that the essential conditions of psychotherapy exist in a single configuration, even though the client or patient may use them very differently.*³*

It is *not* stated that these six conditions are the essential conditions for client-centered therapy, and that other conditions are essential for other types of psychotherapy. I certainly am heavily influenced by my own experience, and that experience has led me to a viewpoint which is termed "client centered." Nevertheless my aim in stating this theory is to state the conditions which apply to *any* situation in which constructive personality change occurs, whether we are thinking of classical psychoanalysis, or any of its modern offshoots, or Adlerian psychotherapy, or any other. It will be obvious then that in my judgment much of what is considered to be essential would not be found, empirically, to be essential. Testing of some of the stated hypotheses would throw light on this perplexing issue. We may of course find that various therapies produce various types of personality change, and that for each psychotherapy a separate set of conditions is necessary. Until and unless this is demonstrated, I am hypothesizing that effective psychotherapy of any sort produces similar changes in personality and behavior, and that a single set of preconditions is necessary.

It is *not* stated that psychotherapy is a special kind of relationship, different in kind from all others which occur in everyday life. It will be evident instead that for brief moments, at least, many good friendships fulfill the six conditions. Usually this is only momentarily, however, and then empathy falters, the positive regard becomes conditional, or the congruence of the "therapist" friend becomes overlaid by some degree of facade or defensiveness. Thus the therapeutic relationship is seen as a heightening

---

*³*I cling to this statement of my hypothesis even though it is challenged by a just completed study by Kirtner (1955). Kirtner has found, in a group of 26 cases from the Counseling Center at the University of Chicago, that there are sharp differences in the client's mode of approach to the resolution of life difficulties, and that these differences are related to success in psychotherapy. Briefly, the client who sees his problem as involving his relationships, and who feels that he contributes to this problem and wants to change it, is likely to be successful. The client who externalizes his problem, feeling little self-responsibility, is much more likely to be a failure. Thus the implication is that some other conditions need to be provided for psychotherapy with this group. For the present, however, I will stand by my hypothesis as given, until Kirtner's study is confirmed, and until we know an alternative hypothesis to take its place.

of the constructive qualities which often exist in part in other relationships, and an extension through time of qualities which in other relationships tend at best to be momentary.

It is *not* stated that special intellectual professional knowledge—psychological, psychiatric, medical, or religious—is required of the therapist. Conditions 3, 4, and 5, which apply especially to the therapist, are qualities of experience, not intellectual information. If they are to be acquired, they must, in my opinion, be acquired through an experiential training—which may be, but usually is not, a part of professional training. It troubles me to hold such a radical point of view, but I can draw no other conclusion from my experience. Intellectual training and the acquiring of information has, I believe, many valuable results—but becoming a therapist is not one of those results.

It is *not* stated that it is necessary for psychotherapy that the therapist have an accurate psychological diagnosis of the client. Here too it troubles me to hold a viewpoint so at variance with my clinical colleagues. When one thinks of the vast proportion of time spent in any psychological, psychiatric, or mental hygiene center on the exhaustive psychological evaluation of the client or patient, it seems as though this *must* serve a useful purpose insofar as psychotherapy is concerned. Yet the more I have observed therapists, and the more closely I have studied research such as that done by Fiedler (1953) and others, the more I am forced to the conclusion that such diagnostic knowledge is not essential to psychotherapy.[4] It may even be that its defense as a necessary prelude to psychotherapy is simply a protective alternative to the admission that it is, for the most part, a colossal waste of time. There is only one useful purpose I have been able to observe which relates to psychotherapy. Some therapists cannot feel secure in the relationship with the client unless they possess such diagnostic knowledge. Without it they feel fearful of him, unable to be empathic, unable to experience unconditional regard, finding it necessary to put up a pretense in the relationship. If they know in *advance* of suicidal impulses they can somehow be more acceptant of them. Thus, for some therapists, the security they perceive in

---

[4]There is no intent here to maintain that diagnostic evaluation is useless. We have ourselves made heavy use of such methods in our research studies of change in personality. It is its usefulness as a precondition to psychotherapy which is questioned.

diagnostic information may be a basis for permitting themselves to be integrated in the relationship, and to experience empathy and full acceptance. In these instances a psychological diagnosis would certainly be justified as adding to the comfort and hence the effectiveness of the therapist. But even here it does not appear to be a basic precondition for psychotherapy.[5]

Perhaps I have given enough illustrations to indicate that the conditions I have hypothesized as necessary and sufficient for psychotherapy are striking and unusual primarily by virtue of what they omit. If we were to determine, by a survey of the behaviors of therapists, those hypotheses which they appear to regard as necessary to psychotherapy, the list would be a great deal longer and more complex.

Is This Theoretical Formulation Useful?

Aside from the personal satisfaction it gives as a venture in abstraction and generalization, what is the value of a theoretical statement such as has been offered in this paper? I should like to spell out more fully the usefulness which I believe it may have.

In the field of research it may give both direction and impetus to investigation. Since it sees the conditions of constructive personality change as general, it greatly broadens the opportunities for study. Psychotherapy is not the only situation aimed at constructive personality change. Programs of training for leadership in industry and programs of training for military leadership often aim at such change. Educational institutions or programs frequently aim at development of character and personality as well as at intellectual skills. Community agencies aim at personality and behavioral change in delinquents and criminals. Such programs would provide an opportunity for the broad testing of the hypotheses offered. If it is found that constructive personality change occurs in such programs when the hypothesized conditions are not fulfilled, then the theory would have to be revised. If how-

---

[5]In a facetious moment I have suggested that such therapists might be made equally comfortable by being given the diagnosis of some other individual, not of this patient or client. The fact that the diagnosis proved inaccurate as psychotherapy continued would not be particularly disturbing, because one always expects to find inaccuracies in the diagnosis as one works with the individual.

ever the hypotheses are upheld, then the results, both for the planning of such programs and for our knowledge of human dynamics, would be significant. In the field of psychotherapy itself, the application of consistent hypotheses to the work of various schools of therapists may prove highly profitable. Again the disproof of the hypotheses offered would be as important as their confirmation, either result adding significantly to our knowledge.

For the practice of psychotherapy the theory also offers significant problems for consideration. One of its implications is that the techniques of the various therapies are relatively unimportant except to the extent that they serve as channels for fulfilling one of the conditions. In client-centered therapy, for example, the technique of "reflecting feelings" has been described and commented on (Rogers, 1951, pp. 26-36). In terms of the theory here being presented, this technique is by no means an essential condition of therapy. To the extent, however, that it provides a channel by which the therapist communicates a sensitive empathy and an unconditional positive regard, then it may serve as a technical channel by which the essential conditions of therapy are fulfilled. In the same way, the theory I have presented would see no essential value to therapy of such techniques as interpretation of personality dynamics, free association, analysis of dreams, analysis of the transference, hypnosis, interpretation of life style, suggestion, and the like. Each of these techniques may, however, become a channel for communicating the essential conditions which have been formulated. An interpretation may be given in a way which communicates the unconditional positive regard of the therapist. A stream of free association may be listened to in a way which communicates an empathy which the therapist is experiencing. In the handling of the transference an effective therapist often communicates his own wholeness and consequence in the relationship. Similarly for the other techniques. But just as these techniques *may* communicate the elements which are essential for therapy, so any one of them may communicate attitudes and experiences sharply contradictory to the hypothesized conditions of therapy. Feeling may be "reflected" in a way which communicates the therapist's lack of empathy. Interpretations may be rendered in a way which indicates the highly conditional regard of the therapist. Any of the techniques may communicate the fact that the therapist is expressing one attitude at a surface level, and another contradictory attitude which is denied to his own awareness. Thus one value of such a theoretical formulation as we have offered is that it may assist therapists to think more critically about those elements of their experience, attitudes, and behaviors which are essential to psychotherapy, and those which are nonessential or even deleterious to psychotherapy.

Finally, in those programs—educational, correctional, military, or industrial—which aim toward constructive changes in the personality structure and behavior of the individual, this formulation may serve as a very tentative criterion against which to measure the program. Until it is much further tested by research, it cannot be thought of as a valid criterion, but, as in the field of psychotherapy, it may help to stimulate critical analysis and the formulation of alternative conditions and alternative hypotheses.

SUMMARY

Drawing from a larger theoretical context, six conditions are postulated as necessary and sufficient conditions for the initiation of a process of constructive personality change. A brief explanation is given of each condition, and suggestions are made as to how each may be operationally defined for research purposes. The implications of this theory for research, for psychotherapy, and for educational and training programs aimed at constructive personality change, are indicated. It is pointed out that many of the conditions which are commonly regarded as necessary to psychotherapy are, in terms of this theory, nonessential.

REFERENCES

Bown, O. H. An investigation of therapeutic relationship in client-centered therapy. Unpublished doctor's dissertation, University of Chicago, 1954.

Chodorkoff, B. Self-perception, perceptual defense, and adjustment. *J. Abnorm. Soc. Psychol.*, 1954, *49*: 508-512.

Fiedler, F. E. A comparison of therapeutic relationships in psychoanalytic, non-directive and Adlerian therapy. *J. Consult. Psychol.*, 1950, *14*: 436-445.

Fiedler, F. E. Quantitative studies on the role of therapists' feelings toward their patients. In O. H. Mowrer (Ed.), *Psychotherapy: Theory and Research*. New York: Ronald, 1953.

Kirtner, W. L. Success and failure in client-centered therapy as a function of personality variables. Unpublished master's thesis, University of Chicago, 1955.

Rogers, C. R. *Client-Centered Therapy*. Boston: Houghton Mifflin, 1951.

Rogers, C. R., and Dymond, Rosalind F. (Eds.). *Psychotherapy and Personality Change*. Chicago: University of Chicago Press, 1954.

Standal, S. The need for positive regard: a contribution to client-centered theory. Unpublished doctor's dissertation, University of Chicago, 1954.

20

REQUISITE CONDITIONS
FOR BASIC PERSONALITY CHANGE

Albert Ellis, Ph.D.

Are there any necessary and sufficient conditions which an emotionally disturbed individual *must* undergo if he is to overcome his disturbance and achieve a basic change in his personality? Yes and no—depending upon whether our definition of the word "conditions" is narrow or broad.

Carl Rogers (1957), in a notable paper on this subject, stuck his scientific neck out by listing six conditions that, he hypothesized, must exist and continue to exist over a period of time if personality change is to be effected. I shall now stick out my own scientific neck by contending that none of his postulated conditions is necessary (even though they may all be desirable) for personality change to occur.

For purposes of discussion, I shall accept Rogers' definition of "constructive personality change" as consisting of "change in the personality structure of the individual, at both surface and deeper levels, in a direction which clinicians would agree means greater integration, less internal conflict, more energy utilizable for effective living; change in behavior away from behaviors regarded as immature and toward behaviors regarded as mature." In my own terms, which I believe are a little more specific, I

This chapter consists of an expanded version of a paper read at the workshop on psychotherapy of the American Academy of Psychotherapists, held in Madison, Wisconsin, August 9, 1958, and subsequently published in *J. Consult. Psychol.,* 1959, 23: 538-540. Reprinted by permission of the author and publisher from Albert Ellis. *Reason and Emotion in Psychotherapy.* New York: Lyle Stuart, 1962.

would say that constructive personality change occurs when an individual eliminates a significant proportion of his needless, unrealistically based self-defeating reactions (especially intense, prolonged, or repeated feelings of anxiety and hostility) which he may consciously experience or whose subsurface existence may lead him to behave in an ineffective or inappropriate manner (Ellis, 1957a, 1958a).

According to Rogers, the six necessary and sufficient conditions for constructive personality change are as follows: 1) Two persons are in psychological contact. 2) The first (the client or patient) is in a state of incongruence, being vulnerable or anxious. 3) The second person, the therapist, is congruent or integrated in the relationship. 4) The therapist experiences unconditional positive regard for the patient. 5) The therapist experiences an empathic understanding of the patient's internal frame of reference and endeavors to communicate this experience to the patient. 6) The communication to the patient of the therapist's empathic understanding and unconditional positive regard is to a minimal degree achieved.

Let us now examine each of these six conditions to see if it is really necessary for basic personality change.

Two persons, says Rogers, must be in psychological contact. This proposition, I am afraid, stems from a kind of therapeutic presumptuousness, since it ignores thousands, perhaps millions, of significant personality changes that have occurred when a single individual (a) encountered external experiences and learned sufficiently by them to restructure his philosophy and behavior patterns of living, or (b) without being in any actual relationship with another, heard a lecture, read a book, or listened to a sermon that helped him make basic changes in his own personality.

I am reminded, in this connection, of many individuals I have read about, and a few to whom I have talked, who narrowly escaped death and who were significantly changed persons for the rest of their lives. I am also reminded of several people I have known who read books, ranging from Mary Baker Eddy's idiotic mishmash, *Science and Health, with Key to the Scriptures,* to my own *How to Live with a Neurotic* or my collaborative effort with Dr. Robert A. Harper, *A Guide to Rational Living* (1961), who immediately thereafter significantly changed their unconstructive behavior toward others and themselves.

I am not saying, now, that having dangerous life experiences or reading inspirational books is likely to be the most effective or frequent means of personality reconstruction. Obviously not—or psychotherapists would quickly go out of business! But to claim, as Rogers does, that these non-relationship methods of personality change never work is to belie considerable evidence to the contrary.

Rogers secondly contends that for personality change to occur the patient must be in a state of incongruence, being vulnerable or anxious. Incongruence he later defines as "a discrepancy between the actual experience of the organism and the self picture of the individual insofar as it represents that experience." Here again, although he may well be correct in assuming that *most* people who undergo basic personality changes are in a state of incongruence before they reconstruct their behavior patterns, he fails to consider the exceptions to this general rule.

I have met several individuals who were far above the average in being congruent and basically unanxious and yet who, as I said above, improved their personalities significantly by life experiences or reading. I have also seen a few psychologists, psychiatrists, and social workers who were distinctly congruent individuals and who came to therapy largely for training purposes or because they had some practical problem with which they wanted help. Most of these patients were able to benefit considerably by their therapy and to make significant constructive personality changes—that is, to become more congruent and less anxious. I often feel, in fact, that such relatively congruent individuals tend to make the *most* constructive personality changes when they come to therapy— largely because they are best able to benefit from the therapist's placing before them alternative philosophies of life and modes of adjustment which they had simply never seriously considered before.

It should be remembered, in this connection, that there are often *two* main reasons why an individual comes to and stays in therapy: 1) he wants to be healed, and 2) he wants to grow. Once he has been healed—that is, induced to surrender most of his intense and crippling anxiety or hostility—he still can significantly grow as a human being—that is, reevaluate and minimize some of his less intense and less crippling negative emotions, and learn to take greater risks, feel more spontaneously, love more adequately, etc. Frequently I find that group therapy, in particular, is an excellent medium for individuals who have largely been healed in a prior (individual and/or group) therapeutic process, but who still would like to know more about themselves in relation to others, and to grow experientially and esthetically. And I find that relatively healed individuals, who are what Carl Rogers would call congruent persons, can still grow and make basic personality changes in themselves in some form of therapy.

The third requisite for constructive personality change, says Rogers, is "that the therapist should be, within the confines of this relationship, a congruent, genuine integrated person. It means that within the relationship he is freely and deeply himself, with his actual experience accurately represented by his awareness of himself. It is the opposite of presenting a facade, either knowingly or unknowingly." Here, once again, I feel that Rogers is stating a highly desirable but hardly a necessary condition.

Like most therapists, I (rightly or wrongly!) consider myself a congruent, genuine, integrated person who, within my relationships with my patients, am freely and deeply myself. I therefore cannot be expected to quote a case of my own where, in spite of my own lack of congruence, my patient got better. I can say, however, that I have seen patients of other therapists whom I personally knew to be among the most emotionally disturbed and least congruent individuals I have ever met. And *some* of these patients—not all or most, alas, but *some*—were considerably helped by their relationship with their disturbed and incongruent therapists.

In saying this, let me hasten to add that I am definitely not one of those who believes that a therapist is most helpful to his patient when he, the therapist, is or has been a victim of severe disturbance himself, since then he is supposedly best able to empathize with and understand his patients. On the contrary, I believe that the therapist who is least disturbed is most likely to serve as the best model for, and be able to accept without hostility, his severely disturbed patients, and I am consequently in favor of discouraging highly incongruent therapists from practicing. I distinctly agree, therefore, with Rogers' contention that congruence on the part of the therapist is very desirable. That such congruence is in all cases necessary, however, I would dispute.

Rogers next lists as a necessary condition for personality change the therapist's experiencing unconditional positive regard for the patient—by which he means "a caring for the client, but not in a possessive way or in such a way as simply to satisfy the therapist's own needs." Here, with almost nauseating repetition, I must insist that Rogers has again turned a desideratum of therapy into a necessity.

I have recently been in close contact with several ex-patients of a small, and I think highly unsavory, group of therapists who do not have any real positive regard for their patients, but who deliberately try to regulate the lives and philosophies of these patients for the satisfaction of the therapists' own desires. In all cases but one, I would say that the ex-patients of this group whom I have seen were not benefited appreciably by therapy and were sometimes harmed. But in one instance I have had to admit that the patient was distinctly benefited and underwent significant constructive personality change—though not as much as I would have liked to see him undergo—as a result of this ineffective and in some ways pernicious form of therapy. I have also seen many other ex-patients of other therapists who, I am quite certain, were emotionally exploited by their therapists, and some of them, surprisingly enough, were considerably helped by this kind of an exploitative relationship.

The fifth condition for constructive personality change, says Rogers, "is that the therapist is experiencing an accurate, empathic understanding of the client's awareness of his own experience. To sense the client's private world as if it were your own, but without ever losing the 'as if' quality—this is empathy, and this seems essential to therapy." This contention I again must dispute although I think it is perhaps the most plausible of Rogers' conditions.

That the therapist should normally understand his patient's world and see the patient's behavior from this patient's own frame of reference is highly desirable. That the therapist should literally feel his patient's disturbances or believe in his irrationalities is, in my opinion, usually harmful rather than helpful to this patient. Indeed, it is precisely the therapist's ability to comprehend the patient's immature behavior without getting involved in or believing in it that enables him to induce the patient to stop believing in or feeling that this behavior is necessary.

Even, however, when we strictly limit the term "empathy" to its dictionary definition—"apprehension of the state of mind of another person without feeling (as in sympathy) what the other feels" (English and English, 1958), it is still doubtful that this state is always a necessary condition for effective therapy. I have had, for example, many patients whose problems I have been able to view from their own frame of reference and whom I have shown exactly how and why they have been defeating themselves and what alternate modes of thinking and behaving they could employ to help themselves. Some of these patients have then dogmatically and arbitrarily indoctinated their friends or relatives with the new philosophies of living I have helped them acquire, without their ever truly understanding or sympathizing with the private world of these associates. Yet, somewhat to my surprise, they have occasionally helped their friends and relatives to achieve significant personality changes with the non-empathic, dogmatic technique of indoctrination.

Similarly, some of the greatest bigots of all time, such as Savonarola, Rasputin, and Adolf Hitler, who because of their own severe emotional disturbances had a minimum of empathy with their fellow men, frequently induced profound personality changes in their adherents, and at least in a few of these instances the changes that occurred were constructive. This does not contradict the proposition that to empathize with another's private world usually helps him become less defensive and more congruent, but it throws much doubt on the hypothesis that empathically motivated therapy is the only kind that is ever effective.

Roger's final condition for constructive personality change is "that the client perceives, to a minimal degree, the acceptance and empathy which the therapist experiences for him." This proposition I have disproved several times in my own therapeutic practice. On these occasions, I have seen paranoid patients who, whether or not I was properly empathizing with their own frames of reference, persistently insisted that I was not. Yet, as I kept showing them how their attitudes and action, including their anger at me, were illogical and self-defeating, they finally began to accept my frame of reference and to make significant constructive personality changes in themselves. Then, after they had surrendered some of their false perceptions, they were able to see, in most instances, that I might not have been as unempathetic as they previously thought I was.

In one instance, one of my paranoid patients kept insisting, to the end of therapy, that I did not understand her viewpoints and was quite wrong about my perceptions of her. She did admit, however, that my attitudes and value systems made a lot of sense and that she could see that she'd better adopt some of them if she was going to help herself. She did adopt some of these attitudes and became more understanding of other people and considerably less paranoid. To this day, even though she is making a much better adjustment to life, she still feels that I do not really understand her.

In the light of the foregoing considerations, it may perhaps be legitimately hypothesized that very few individuals significantly restructure their personalities when Rogers' six conditions are all unmet, but it is most dubious that *none* do. Similarly, it is equally dubious that no patients make fundamental constructive improvements unless, as Freud (1924-1950) contends, they undergo and resolve a transference neurosis during therapy; or, as Rank (1945) insists, unless they first have a highly permissive and then a strictly limited relationship with the therapist; or, as Reich (1949) claims, unless they loosen their character armor by having it forcefully attacked by the therapist's psychological and physical uncoverings; or, as Reik (1948) notes, unless they are effectively listened to by the therapist's "third ear"; or, unless as Sullivan (1953) opines, they undergo an intensive analysis of the security operations they employ with the therapist and with significant others in their environment. All these suggested therapeutic techniques may be highly desirable, but where is the evidence that any of them are necessary?

Are there, then, any other conditions that are absolutely necessary for constructive personality change to take place? At first blush, I am tempted to say yes, but on second thought, I am forced to restrain myself and say no, or at least probably no.

My personal inclination, after working for the last several years with rational-emotive psychotherapy, is to say that yes, there is one absolutely necessary condition for real or basic personality change to occur—and that is that somehow, through some professional or non-professional channel, and through some kind of experience with himself, with others, or with things and events, the afflicted individual must learn to recognize his irrational, inconsistent, and unrealistic perceptions and thoughts, and change these for more logical, more reasonable philosophies of life. Without this kind of fundamental change in his ideologies and philosophic assumptions, I am tempted to say, no deep-seated personality changes will occur.

On further contemplation, I nobly refrain from making this claim, which would so well fit in with my own therapeutic theories, for one major and two minor reasons. The minor reasons are these:

1. Some people seem to make significant changes in their personalities without concomitantly acquiring notably new philosophies of living. It could be said, of course, that they really, unconsciously, do acquire such new philosophies. But this would be difficult to prove objectively.

2. Some individuals appear to change for the better when environmental conditions are modified, even though they retain their

old childish views. Thus, a person who irrationally hates himself because he is poor may hate himself considerably less if he inherits a fortune. It could be said that the security he receives from inheriting this money really does make him change his childish, irrational views, and that therefore he has had a philosophic as well as a behavioral change. But again; there would be difficulty in objectively validating this contention. It could also be alleged that this individual really hasn't made a constructive personality change if he can now be secure only when he is rich. But how, except by a rather tautological definition, could this allegation be proven?

Which brings me to the major and I think decisive reason for my not contending that for constructive personality change to occur, the individual must somehow basically change his thinking or his value system. Granted that this statement may be true—and I am sure that many therapists would agree that it is—it is largely tautological. For all I am really saying when I make such a statement is that poor personality integration consists of an individual's having unrealistic, self-defeating ideological assumptions and that to change his personality integration for the better he must somehow surrender or change these assumptions.

Although descriptively meaningful, this statement boils down to the sentence: in order to change his personality the individual must change his personality. Or: in order to get better he must get better. This proves very little about the "necessary" conditions for personality change.

Again: rational psychotherapy significantly differs from virtually all other theories and techniques in that, according to its precepts, it is desirable not merely for the therapist to uncover, understand, and accept the patient's illogical and unrealistic assumptions which cause him to remain immature and ineffective, but it is usually also required that he forthrightly and unequivocally *attack* and *invalidate* these assumptions. Is this desideratum of psychotherapy necessary?

Most probably not: since some patients and non-patients (although relatively few, I believe) seem to have significantly improved in spite of their not having the benefit of a competent rational therapist to help them understand how they acquired, how they are currently sustaining, and how they can and should forthrightly attack and annihilate their basic irrational attitudes and assumptions.

The conclusion seems inescapable, therefore, that although basic constructive personality change—as opposed to temporary symptom removal—seems to require fundamental modifications in the ideologies and value systems of the disturbed individual, there is probably *no* single condition which is absolutely necessary for the inducement of such changed attitudes and behavior patterns.

Many conditions, such as those listed by Freud, Rank, Reich, Reik, Rogers, Sullivan, and other outstanding theorists, or such as are listed in this book, are highly desirable, but all that seems to be necessary is that the individual somehow come up against significant life experiences, *or* learn about others' experiences, *or* sit down and think for himself, *or* enter a relationship with a therapist who is *preferably* congruent, accepting, empathic, rational, forceful, etc. Either/or, rather than this-and-that, seems to be the only realistic description of necessary conditions for basic personality change that can be made at the present time.

The basic contention of this book *Reason and Emotion in Psychotherapy*, then, is not that RT is the *only* effective method of therapy. It is, rather, that of all the scores of methods that are variously advocated and employed, RT is probably one of the most effective techniques that has yet been invented. Certainly, in my twenty years as a counselor and psychotherapist, it is far and away the best method that I have found, and an increasing number of my professional colleagues are finding it unusually efficient in their own practices. Even when it is only partially employed, along with other basic therapeutic methods, it often produces fine results. And when it is consistently and thoroughly used, the results seem to be still better.

REFERENCES

Ellis, A. *How To Live with a Neurotic.* New York: Crown, 1957.

Ellis, A. Neurotic interaction between marital partners. *J. Counsel. Psychol.*, 1958, *5:* 24-28.

Ellis, A., & Harper, R. A. *A Guide to Rational Living.* Englewood Cliffs, New Jersey: Prentice-Hall, 1961.

English, H. B., & English, Ava C. *A Comprehensive Dictionary of Psychological and Psychoanalytical Terms.* New York: David McKay, 1958.

Freud, S. *Collected Papers.* London: Hogarth, 1924-1950.

Rank, O. *Will Therapy and Truth and Reality.* New York: Knopf, 1945.

Reich, W. *Character Analysis.* New York: Orgone Institute Press, 1949.

Reik, T. *Listening with the Third Ear.* New York: Rinehart, 1948.

Rogers, C. R. *Client-Centered Therapy.* Boston: Houghton Mifflin, 1951.

Sullivan, H. S. *The Interpersonal Theory of Psychiatry.* New York: Norton, 1953.

21

THE ETHICS OF COUNSELING

G. Gilbert Wrenn, Ph.D.

In November, 1950, Dr. L. E. Drake and I worked as a team in the first oral examinations administered by the American Board of Examiners in Professional Psychology. We were responsible for examining the candidates in the areas of research and of ethics and it became embarrassingly apparent at that time that there was no generally understood code of ethics upon which to examine the candidates. Drake and I agreed upon certain principles and raised what we considered crucial questions but we worked in something of a fog. It was at that time that I determined to discuss this topic with the Division of Counseling and Guidance at the 1951 meetings.

For some years counselors have been concerned with confidential information that is transmitted within the counseling relationship. There has been some discussion of just what is confidential and what is not and thought has been given as to just how to record information considered confidential. More recently has arisen the question of the legal position of the counselor who possesses information given to him in counseling. If this information suggests that the client is a law breaker, a violator of mores, or contemplates harm to others is the counselor legally obligated to reveal this information? Beyond this, under what conditions can he be legally required to disclose information given to him by a client while the two were in a counseling relationship to each other?

Presidential address before the Divison of Counseling and Guidance of the American Psychological Association, Chicago, Illinois, September 30, 1951. Reprinted by permission of the author and *Educational and Psychological Measurement*, 1952, 12:161-77.

The Ethics of Counseling

During the year 1951, section 3 of the very important formulations of the APA Hobbs' Committee on Ethical Standards for Psychology was made available in the February and May issues of *The American Psychologist*. (The revised version of these standards is given in the Appendix, page 471). The present paper is built upon this published statement of ethics in clinical and consulting relationships, soon to become the official code of the APA. I can claim little originality therefore, although my self-confidence was strengthened by comparing my notes of last November for this paper with the codified statement of the official committee. Perhaps I should not have been surprised at the degree of agreement because the code was built upon the problems supplied by hundreds of operating psychologists throughout the country. It is an operational code, not one spun out of gossamer abstractions. It is a statement of principles that grew out of the experiences of many practicing psychologists. Since I am one such psychologist, it might be expected that the ethical problems that seem significant to me also seem important to others.

This discussion is, therefore, concerned with the implications for counselors of the proposed code. I have selected some of the more significant principles for comparison and application and have occasionally added one that I thought should be considered by counselors. There is one important conflict in counseling ethics that will be carefully explored but before engaging that issue allow me to state briefly two or three other considerations.

WHY A CONCERN FOR ETHICS

First of all, why this greatly increased interest in the ethics of counseling? There are, perhaps, two major reasons. Counseling is becoming a profession and as such is at once concerned with its dual obligation to society and to the client. For generations the concept of a profession has been linked with that of service to society. Roscoe Pound defines a profession very simply in these terms—"(it is) an organized calling in which men pursue a learned art and are united in the pursuit of public service" (Pound, 1936). If people generally are to regard counseling with respect because counselors consider themselves to be professional men, then the members of this profession must have a clear understanding of its social purpose and obligation. So long as the counseling function is merely an arm or a projection of some institution there is little problem, for under these conditions it tacitly adopts the principles and procedures of its parent organization. If, however, counseling is to operate independently or is to have professional independence within an institution then its status as an independent profession demands a clear understanding of its ethical obligations. One of the generally accepted criteria of a profession—or so Darley and I stated in 1947 (Wrenn and Darley, 1947, pp. 283-284)—is the development and adoption of a code of ethics by the members of that occupational group. Counseling—and psychology in general—is all too tardy in this respect.[1]

A further consequence of arriving at professional status is the closer relationship between professional skill and professional ethics. As a body of professional knowledges and skills develops, it becomes an ethical concern if a counselor attempts to operate without these skills. The statement "I didn't know" is no longer an excuse if there exists a body of knowledge that he *should* know. Still another outgrowth of professional status is the need for defining our relationships with the members of other professions. We must know clearly the conditions under which a counselor discloses client information to a member of another profession. We must also know what is ethically sound in receiving and using client information from others. There are questions of *both skill and ethics* in referring a client to a colleague either within or without the counseling profession.

A second reason for our growing interest in ethics—and perhaps a more compelling one—is the changing emphasis in counseling itself. The shift is in the direction of more self-information being disclosed in counseling, more of the client's attitudes, emotions, and self concepts being shared with the counselor. There is still, and will continue to be, concern about information that should be given to the client, and concern about the quality of the counselor's judgment in introducing interpretations or in discussing outcomes of projected action. These are interview elements that are *outside* the client, relating to his environment or to the attitudes of the counselor. It is still true that both counselor and client may be guilty of serious misinterpretations of personality unless they give full recognition to the cultural influences that shape their concepts

---

[1]Note the published codes of ethics of 133 professions and businesses in Heermance, 1924; see also the very complete code for the medical profession, "Principles of Medical Ethics," 1945.

of themselves and of others (Ichheiser, 1943).

Regardless of these considerations the trend of our knowledge of personality dynamics leads the counselor to emphasize that which happens within the client, leads him to encourage the client to explore his own attitudes and feelings. In doing this the client discloses much that is very vitally a part of him—he gives to the counselor a part of himself and in that disclosure places a heavy burden of responsibility upon the counselor. This burden of knowledge is one which the counselor sometimes wishes he did not have, but it is one which he cannot avoid. The ethics of dealing with the intimate self-stuff of a counseling interview takes both personal discernment and professional standards of behavior. Without a code of carefully conceived ethical principles a counselor may unwittingly injure himself in the eyes of both his client and his professional colleagues.

LEGAL POSITION OF COUNSELOR

The counselor's concern for his legal position was earlier mentioned and perhaps an expansion of this point belongs also in our prologue. Upon several occasions I have had law professors in this field of law speak to seminars in personnel work. The counselor has more legal leeway than he may recognize. For example, he does not have to release any personnel or counseling records merely upon the request of an officer of a court, a state, or the Federal government. In fact he probably should *not*, for the client can sue the counselor for failing to protect his interests. A warrant for the release of the records is necessary. Furthermore, the counselor may keep confidential notes on his clients in the form of personal memoranda and since these do not become part of the official records of the institution or of his office they do not have to be released when the personnel records of an individual are taken into custody.

In states where a psychologist has no "privileged communication" status by law he is not under obligation to reveal that which he considers confidential *unless* he is under oath before a grand jury or a court of law. The mere request for specific or general information about a client, even though made by a person in uniform or with an imposing title, does not obligate a counselor to reveal information that he considers confidential unless he is under oath. If he refuses to answer when under oath he *may* be cited for contempt of court. What would actually happen if such a situation arose we do not know for no precedent exists. I have been told that there is no assurance at all that a counselor would be cited for contempt of court if he refused to answer giving as his reason that to do so would be violating the confidential nature of his relationship with his client. Lawyers, physicians, and ministers are in most states protected by "privileged communication." Counselors and clinical psychologists should seek the same type of protection. But a precedent would be set by a court *acknowledging* privileged status if some counselor, with legal aid, pled for recognition of his professional ethics and refused to disclose interview information.

This is a fascinating subject because so little exists in print which acknowledges the professional nature of the client-counselor relationship, but the counselor still has certain privileges in law. (See Fowerbaugh, 1945.) It should be noted, for example, that information given to a counselor by a client is almost always "hearsay" evidence and therefore not admissible in court. For example, the counselor did not see the client injure someone else, he merely heard him tell about it. For the purpose of proving the fact of injury this statement to the counselor is hearsay evidence and not admissible over objection in most instances. Certainly much that is told in an interview is "hearsay" in every sense of the word. We seldom have more evidence than what the client said.

Here is another point. The possession of information that a client gave in an interview to the effect he *said* that he violated a law or a social convention does not make the counselor legally liable to disclose this information to any official or officer of the law. He has an ethical problem on his hands but no legal one until he is under oath. Certainly lawyers, ministers and physicians are frequently recipients of information indicating criminal behavior upon the part of their client but they are not obligated to reveal this information. As a matter of fact they are under ethical compulsion *not* to do so. So is the counselor. He differs from the members of these other professions only when he is under oath, for then he does not know what is his legal right with regard to "privileged communication" as they do.

Nothing of what has been said here should be interpreted as suggesting that counselors should not cooperate with an officer of the law or of any other agent of society. We are citizens and obligated to uphold the duly constituted law of the state or nation. What I have tried to suggest is that when questions of ethics arise, particularly those regarding the disclosure of information transmitted in an interview, the counselor has some discretion even in states where he is not legally recognized as a member of a profession. He is not obligated to "tell all" merely because some one requests him to do so and, as a matter of fact, he is professionally obligated to his client *not* to tell. This dilemma of client versus society is given further attention a little later.

LITERATURE ON ETHICS IN COUNSELING

It is a sad commentary on the maturity of our profession that the published literature on ethics in counseling can be discussed quite briefly. Reference has been made to one published report of the currently operating Committee on Ethical Standards of APA, that on Ethics in Clinical and Consulting Relationships, but not to the report of the Sub-Committee on the Distribution of Psychological Tests that was published in the November 1950 *American Psychologist.* Aside from the work of this Committee the literature on ethics in counseling is generalized and discursive.[2] The Committee on Ethical Practices of the National Vocational Guidance Association has, during the past five years, developed a published statement and working standards regarding the counseling done in vocational guidance agencies. The latest directory of approved guidance agencies[3] is a marked contribution to professional and ethical practices in counseling and in vocational guidance in general. Its two chairmen during the five-year period, Albert Harris and Nathan Kohn, and the chairman for the succeeding year, Robert Kamm, are members of this Division, as have been several members of the Committee—Daniel Harris, Donald Super, Henry McDaniel, and myself. The extent of my personal concern for ethics in vocational guidance is suggested in an address I gave

---

[2] One must of course note that the literature contains reference to several smaller groups of psychologists, in the United States and elsewhere, who have adopted ethical codes. Illustrative is the recently adopted Code of Ethical Standards of the New York State Psychological Association which is based upon Section 3 of the APA code, and the Code of the Victorian Group of the Australian Branch of the British Psychological Society, cited in *The American Psychologist*, May, 1951, p. 176.

[3] *1951 Directory of Vocational Counseling Services.* Ethical Practices Committee of the National Vocational Guidance Association, Box 64, Washington University, St. Louis, Missouri.

before NVGA in 1947. At the conclusion of a review of trends in this field I stated a kind of personal creed for counselors which contained the following two paragraphs:

I will respect the integrity of each individual with whom I deal. I will accord to him the same right to self-determination that I want for myself. I will respect as something sacred the personality rights of each person and will not attempt to manipulate him or meddle in his life.

I will define my personal and ethical responsibility to my client as well as my legal and vocational responsibility to my organization and to society. I work for both the group to which I am responsible and for each individual that I serve as a client. This dual responsibility must be defined and understood by my employers and by myself (Wrenn, 1947).

The Committee on Professional Ethics of the National Education Association is in the process of preparing a revision of the N.E.A. code which has been in effect for 21 years. The revision, which will be completed in 1952, is based upon 1,309 teachers' reports of what are considered to be ethical problems. It is cited here because it will contain some reference to the nature of confidential realtions between teachers and pupils and to the ethics of professional relations among teachers themselves (*School and Soc.*, 1950).

Some of the recent textbooks dealing with counseling give passing attention to the question of ethics—two pages in Watson's *Readings* book, one in Robinson's text on counseling procedures, one or two in my book on college personnel work. Thorne's book has one chapter (Thorne, 1950) on "Problems of Professional Responsibility," dealing with the counselor's responsibility to society, family or friends, the profession, and himself, as well as his administrative responsibilities. It is the best and most complete textbook treatment of the ethics of counseling, although somewhat closely tied in with medical ethics and with ethical problems that arise with psychotics and severe neurotics. The professional relation of the psychologist to the medical man is appropriately emphasized since Thorne himself is both an M.D. and a psychologist.

The periodical literature is not very rewarding. There is great need for a thoughtful paper on the place of the psychologist in our society and the ethical implications of that societal responsibility. During the coming year someone should write such a paper.

Someone should also write a paper on our legal position that is the result of a study of state laws and court decisions. One remarkable series of journal articles on ethics in psychotherapy and in counseling deals with the basic issue raised in this paper—client versus society. This series of four articles in four successive volumes of the *Journal of Abnormal and Social Psychology* (Sutich, 1944; Sargent, 1945; Bixler and Seeman, 1946; Meehl and McClosky, 1947) is probably known to most readers. It was started by Anthony Sutich in 1944 with an extensive statement of 51 duties and rights of counselors who practice within a "democratic counseling relationship." The 51 statements of the code were grouped under such headings as psychologists' duties and rights, third party duties and rights, client's rights, and interprofessional responsibilities that are suggestive of the divisions of our present code. The publication was a pioneer effort of considerable significance but its reception was influenced by the fact that the code was postulated upon Sutich's particular modification of the non-directive point of view. It was, in a sense, an exposition of a philosophy of counseling.

Helen Sargent in 1945 published a reply that expressed agreement in general with Sutich but took him to task at two points: 1) where he departs from simple non-directive theory with his "democratic counseling relationship," and 2) where his code becomes so detailed and didactic that it must be explained formally to the client. The succeeding year, 1946, saw a contribution by Ray Bixler and Julius Seeman in an urgent plea for a code under the three headings of 1) Responsibility to the individual, 2) Responsibility to related professions, and 3) Responsibility to society. There is an interesting distinction made between the confidentiality of diagnostic data and of treatment data of referred cases that is not too well reflected in the present code.

In 1947 Paul Meehl and Herbert McClosky took issue with Sutich's use of the concepts of "democracy" and "authoritarianism." These are stated to be political concepts and not applicable to the ethics of counseling. Furthermore this team of psychologist and political scientist object to Sutich's failure to distinguish between *ethics* and *procedures*. The latter must be accepted or not in terms of whether they are found to be effective and contributing to the client's needs, but not because they do or do not fit a system of ethics. One may question "advice" as a procedure because it often (not always) does not work but not because it is authoritarian and therefore unethical. "The most fundamental ethical commitment of a counselor is to help the client to achieve the client's end . . . . "

This series is not, unfortunately, a straightforward presentation of points of view regarding the therapist's responsibility to his client and to society. The articles, with the possible exception of that by Bixler and Seeman, are expositions of, or refutations of, the philosophy of non-directive counseling. The implications of a philosophy of human relationships are of deep significance but we were still without a code of ethics.

The 1949 conference on Graduate Education in Clinical Psychology—The Boulder Conference—gave consideration to ethical problems in both the training and practice of clinical psychology (Raimy, 1950). No code was suggested, of course, because the Hobb's Committee results were anticipated, but attention was given to 1) ethical problems in the psychologist's functioning in the dual role of scientist and practitioner, and 2) to the ethics of his inter-professional relations. Nothing definitive was proposed for the ethics of training, but there was a clear statement of the responsibility of the university for eliminating from graduate training students guilty of unethical practices. In general, this chapter of the report raises questions without answering them.

ISSUES OF THIS PAPER

This paper has arrived at a point where it can delay no longer in the statement of its major argument. In brief, this argument is that there is a conflict between a counselor's loyalties to his client and his corresponding loyalties to his society, his employing institution, his profession and himself. This conflict is outlined by a series of ethical principles that have been grouped under the headings of the basic loyalties named above. After some analysis of the principles, this paper will propose that the conflict in counseling ethics can be resolved only by recourse to a framework of values.

The statement of principles as taken directly from the Hobb's Committee Report, or as modified or added to by the writer,[4] follows.

---

[4]The wording of the principles is the same as that proposed by the A.P.A. Committee and reported in the February and May, 1951, issues of *The American Psychologist* except for material in roman type. This indicates changed wording or new material by the author.

ETHICAL PRINCIPLES IN COUNSELING

I. Responsibility to Client

1. The counselor is primarily responsible to his client and ultimately to society; these basic loyalties guide all his professional endeavors. The counselor is at all times to respect the integrity and guard the welfare of the person with whom he is working as a client.

2. The counselor must obtain his client's permission before communicating any information about the client that has been given in a counseling relationship to another person or agency such as a parent, family physician, a social agency, an employer. This principle must be observed even though the action may be perceived by the counselor as only in the interest of the client. An exception to this is contained in principle three.

3. The counselor should guard professional confidences as a trust and reveal such confidences without the client's permission only after most careful deliberation and when there is clear and imminent danger to an individual or to society; i.e., threatened suicide, homicide, or treason.

4. Psychological information, such as the results of tests or of a diagnostic appraisal, should be given to a client at such time *and in such a manner* when it is most likely to be accepted by him as part of his self-concept; i.e., *when it is most likely to be helpful to the client's efforts to solve his problems.*

5. The counselor must refer his client to an appropriate specialist when there is evidence of a difficulty with which the counselor is not competent to deal. In such cases the counselor's responsibility for the welfare of the client continues until this responsibility is assumed by the professional person to whom the client is referred. In schools or institutions referral should be made through channels, and, where children are involved, with parents' consent.

6. Clinical materials should be used in teaching and writing only when the permission of those involved is secured or *when their identity is obscured beyond likelihood of recognition.*

7. Interviews held within a counseling relationship are not to be mechanically recorded for training or other purposes without the knowledge and consent of the client. The excep-

tion may be the recording of interviews for valid research purposes under circumstances where only the research worker can identify the client in the typescript.

8. When a counselor's position in an organization is such that some departure is required from the normal expectation that counseling relationships are confidential, it is essential that the counselor make clear to the client the nature of his role before counseling is begun.

It is with this last stated principle that the counselor's conflict of loyalties becomes specific although it has been made clear in principles 1 and 3 that he has a dual responsibility to client and to society. The pinch really comes, however, when the counselor has a known responsibility to a specific organization or to an employer that may affect his complete loyalty to his client. To say that a counselor should not have a double loyalty is to be unrealistic. He has them—the question is how can he resolve them? The principles to follow make clear the variety of relationships that cloud the clear waters of single-minded loyalty to his client.

It has been suggested that the confidential nature of the interview is less to be stressed when the client is a child and that permission to transmit is not necessary for children. I doubt this assumption. A child's trust in a counselor may be betrayed as well as an adult's. A child is very much a person and the integrity of his personality must be protected while at the same time admitting that parents' consent must be obtained for treatment or referral.

II. Responsibility to Society (Principle 1, Principle 3)

9. It is unethical for a counselor, and a betrayal of his responsibility to society, *to offer services outside his area of training and experience or beyond his level of competence,* or to accept assignments of this nature that are made by his employer.

10. Where a counselor is not granted the rights of "privileged communication" in his state, he must decide for himself whether his professional ethics regarding the confidential nature of his relationship to his client are subordinate to the demands of the state as these may be made by an agent of the state or in a court of law. It follows that the counselor must be informed regarding his legal rights and limitations.

III. Responsibility to Employing Institution and to Colleagues

11. Counselors are obligated to define for themselves the nature and direction of their loyalties and responsibilities in any particular undertaking, to inform all involved of these commitments, and to carry them out conscientiously.

12. In counseling situations where a possible division of loyalties exists, as between the client and the employer of the counselor, an agreement concerning the handling of confidential material must be worked out and the nature of the agreement made known to all concerned.

13. Information obtained in counseling relationships should be discussed only in professional settings and with professional persons who are clearly concerned with the case.

14. Case records prepared for the counselor or *for professional communication should not be shown to a client.*

15. A counselor should not accept a private fee or other form of remuneration for professional work with a person who is entitled to his services through an institution or agency.

IV. Responsibility to Self and to the Profession

16. It is desirable in counseling, where sound inter-personal relationships are essential to effective endeavor, that a counselor be aware of the inadequacies in his own personality which may bias his appraisals of others or distort his relationships with them. He should refrain from undertaking any activity where his personal limitations and preconceptions are likely to result in inferior professional services, or harm a client.

17. The counselor must distinguish between his own values and those held by his client or his client's associates in order to guard against a subtle imposition of his own values and moral code upon his client.

18. In situations where referral is indicated and the client refuses referral, the counselor must carefully weigh the possible harm to the client, to himself and his profession, that might ensue from continuing the relationship. If the client is in clear and imminent danger, the counselor should insist on referral or refuse to continue the relationship.

19. Counseling activities, such as administering diagnostic tests, encouraging self-revelations, or engaging in psychotherapy, should be undertaken only with serious intent and not in casual relationships.

Lest I be misunderstood may the first principle—first for the Committee and first in my list—be repeated: "The counselor is *primarily* responsible to his client and *ultimately* to society . . . . The counselor *is at all times* to respect the integrity and guard the welfare of the person with whom he is working as a client" (italics mine).

It is clear the client comes first but there is all too often a second and a third to be considered. It is difficult to point out where the shoe pinches most. I believe that for many school, college, or institutionally employed counselors there is greatest danger of unethical conduct in communicating officially to one's superior what is confidential and in discussing case information too freely and casually with colleagues. In some situations the unauthorized mechanical recording of case data that is played back to others is an equally grave violation of ethics.

Where pressure is placed upon a counselor for the transmittal of interview information what *is* his recourse? Sometimes recommendations for constructive or protective action can be made without divulging the reason for such action and thus violating confidences. Sometimes the client's permission for transmittal of information can be secured. But at other times the issue cannot be avoided— and it is as sharp an issue ethically when a colleague asks us for information that should not be shared as it would be if we were under oath and in a witness chair. There is a clear ethical question in both cases with a difference only in the first situation possessing a more subtle temptation to violate confidences.

It is clear that there is frequently a real question as to whom the counselor's loyalty is due. Is it due the client and not the employer, the client and not the colleague, the client and not the professional training need, the client and not the state? The answer lies in the judgment of the counselor. He and he alone can decide. The profession has said "Here is the code of ethics—you apply it. Upon you rests the responsibility of deciding who must be protected in these matters of confidential information and interprofessional relationships—the client, the employer, or the state." Sometimes it is simpler than that but much harder—who gets hurt, someone else or you?

ETHICS WITHIN A VALUE SYSTEM

In the ethical judgments that must be made by the counselor some system of values must be employed. One doesn't decide in terms of logic—the logic may lead in opposing directions—one decides in terms of this value or that. The relation of values to psychotherapy in general is crucial. A discussion by Arnold Green of the University of New Hampshire of social values inherent in the practice of psychotherapy starts out with this statement: "The history of modern psychotherapy can be viewed as an unsuccessful struggle to evaluate the role of social values" (Green, 1946). Green is speaking here of social values in the life of both the client and the counselor, for later he states that one of the shortcomings of modern psychotherapy is the failure to distinguish between three value areas—that of the therapist, that of the client, and that of the persons and groups with whom the client is interacting. The therapist must be aware of the values held by the client's associates but he must also, in matters of ethics, be aware of the values held by his own associates. All of us "maintain a series of relations with others whose values comprise effective limits to the implementation of our own."

Incidentally, Green contends that modern psychotherapy is sociologically naive—that it does not realize what social values are being recognized in the process of therapy. He criticizes the nondirective counselor for believing that he is doing something that he is not doing but at the same time proposes that the non-directive approach is best equipped of all therapies for dealing with a modern social trend toward separateness rather than wholism. To point up Green's provocative analysis this proposition might be made—there may be debate as to whether or not a science considers values but there is no doubt that the practice of a therapy does.

Values enter deeply into the field of ethics, for ethical principles in any field are based upon the value system of that field of endeavor. In psychology, and in the application of psychology in counseling, we now have a code of ethics. Such a code is a crystallization of the value system of our profession. This paper has tried to suggest that the adoption of this code, excellent as it is, will not solve the ethical problems of the counselor. For the code clearly shows the several obligations and loyalties that the counselor must attempt to reconcile. In general these loyalties are grouped into two categories and the perplexing question can be stated as follows—"Which is to be elevated, the integrity of the individual or the welfare of the state?" It is no weakness of our code that this problem remains to be resolved. Not at all, for counselors clearly have loyalties to others than the client, even though these loyalties are secondary. Responsibilities to society, employer, and colleague are clearly a part of our code and these may conflict with the counselor's responsibility to the client. When this happens what values determine the counselor's decision?

For some, there is little conflict, for the will of the state or of society is paramount. The individual is never as important as the group. The state or the institution exists for the protection and welfare of the individual and must at all costs be preserved. The fact that the state or the group punishes when its values are rejected doubtless influences all of us, but some individuals cleave to conformity as a matter of principle rather than because of fear. They will also be loyal to their employer and will rationalize any harm that comes to their client because of information about the client that has been transmitted to the employer.

To other counselors the reverse always seems true—the individual is always more important than a social institution and must be protected at all costs. Institutional or group welfare is sacrificed in favor of the individual as a matter of deep principle. For most counselors, however, no consistency is possible and each situation presenting a conflict of loyalties must be analyzed anew. Sometimes the group or employer is favored, and at other times the client is protected, even at cost to the counselor. Both types of decisions may be individually defensible but one observation should be made. It takes more courage and strength of conviction to take a stand to protect the client than it does to make a decision to protect the employer. Courage is variable too, however, a variable in any man's life. Because this is true it ill fits any of us to be critical of a colleague when he was not as courageous as we thought he should have been. *We* have lacked courage too at times—"He that is without sin among you, let him first cast a stone."

What system of values does the counselor have recourse to when an ethical conflict arises? To whose, indeed, but his own. Each man has his own pattern of values, with limits, indeed, that are set by his state, his society, his immediate associates, but for all that, a man's beliefs are his own. Back of these personal values, which sometimes must be pitted against those of his society, is another set of values. These are part of our great human heritage, great principles of truth and mercy and justice that are as yet, and perhaps always will be, only dimly understood. Certainly the life of man is more than he can see and hear or even understand. Each of us in his own way is trying to apprehend truths that are part of the ultimate. So it is with some of the values that transcend that which is legalized or accepted by a man's associates.

A counselor to be ethical has to do more than observe a code of ethics. He must be great within himself because he relates himself to God and the greatness of the Infinite. He must consider how important or unimportant he is as compared with principles for which men have in centuries past suffered and died. Some men have formerly believed in the great truths of life but their experiences have soured them. They could not live up to greatness. Some men have gotten too big for their intellectual britches and have discarded all but that which they can understand. For these we can be truly sorry but for the young in age or spirit there is still greatness possible—greatness of faith in the unseen, of belief in the intangible, of expectation of the impossible.

Henry Luce spoke recently in Texas to a group of eminent jurists on Justice Oliver Wendell Holmes. He proposed that Holmes had a cynical philosophy of life and that the influence of this cynicism had done harm to the legal profession. He closed with these words:

And now, gentlemen, if I have spoken extravagantly, I ask your indulgence and plead that if your profession is in want of anything, it is not in want of sobriety, caution, discretion, prudence; if it is in want of anything, it is in want of extravagance, enthusiasm, heroism, and these qualities I would willingly incite (Luce, 1951).

I close with a paraphrase of this—spoken gently and with affection for all of you who are my colleagues. I propose that our profession is not in want of a respect for evidence and scientific truth, nor in want for a drive to serve individuals and to advance human welfare. We are aware of our technical and knowledge limitations and have a great discontent with the imperfectness of much that we do. If this profession is in want of anything it is in a neglect of the proposition that man is spiritual as well as intellectual in nature—it is in a failure to recognize that man has a relationship to the Infinite as well as to other men. The profession has established a code of ethics but its application calls for decisions that will require great personal courage and depth of conviction. It is at this point that the counselor may have to have recourse to the great values and principles of the human race in order to resolve the ethical conflict. The counselor may truly have to think more of others than of himself. Counselors need to strengthen their moral courage as well as their understandings and skills, for it is the constellation of all these qualities that provides true professional competence.

REFERENCES

Bixler, R., & Seeman, J. Suggestions for a code of ethics for consulting psychologists. *J. Abnorm. Soc. Psychol.*, 1946, 41: 486-490.

Fowerbaugh, C. C. Legal status of psychologists in Ohio. *J. Consult. Psychol.*, 1945, 9:196-200.

Green, A. W. Social values and psychotherapy. *J. Pers.*, 1946, 14:199-228.

Heermance, E. L. *Codes of Ethics, A Handbook.* Burlington, Vermont: Free Press, 1924.

Ichheiser, G. Misinterpretations of personality in everyday life and the psychologist's frame of reference. *Charact. & Pers.*, 1943, 12:145-160.

Luce, H. R. Holmes was wrong. *Fortune,* June 1951.

Meehl, P. E., & McClosky, H. Ethical and poligical aspects of applied psychology. *J. Abnorm. Soc. Psychol.*, 1947, 43:91-98.

Pound, R. What is a profession? *Rev. of Reviews*, 1936, 94:84-85.

Principles of medical ethics. *J. Clin. Psychol.*, 1945, 1:336-342.

Raimy, V. C. (Ed.) *Training in Clinical Psychology.* New York: Prentice-Hall, 1950.

Sargent, Helen. Professional ethics and problems of therapy. *J. Abnorm. Soc. Psychol.*, 1945, 40:47-60.

School & Soc., 1950, 72:396

Sutich, A. Toward a professional code for psychological consultants. *J. Abnorm. Soc. Psychol.*, 1944, 39:329-350.

Thorne, F. C. Principles of personality counseling. Brandon, Vermont: *Journal of Clinical Psychology*, 1950.

Wrenn, C. G. Trends and predictions in vocational guidance. *Occupations,* May 1947, 503-515.

Wrenn, C. G., & Darley, J. G. Student personnel work as a profession; I and II. In E. G. Williamson (Ed.) *Trends in Student Personnel Work.* Minneapolis: University of Minnesota Press, 1950.

22

ON THE PHILOSOPHICAL NEUTRALITY OF COUNSELORS

Robert L. Browning, Ph.D., and Herman J. Peters, Ph.D.

There appears to be an urgent demand among guidance counselors for a clarification of the relationship between the counselor's
basic philosophy and his counseling procedures. *Can* a counselor
remain philosophically neutral, on the one hand, and *should* the
counselor do so, on the other hand. Is Vordenberg's dictum true
that "Regardless of the *kind* of personal philosophy evolved by
the counselor, it must surely affect the techniques he uses and the
evaluation of the effectiveness of his work" (Vordenberg, 1953)?

DEMANDS FOR THE CONSIDERATION OF
THE INFLUENCE OF PHILOSOPHY OF COUNSELING

After giving a survey of the inadequacies of the current attempts
to develop a philosophical foundation and direction for guidance,
Donald Walker and Herbert Peiffer issue a call to action. They say,
". . . we would urge close and careful attention to the problems of
the goals of counseling, both at the general theoretical level and as
they affect the progress of the individual counseling case. . . . We
are handicapped by the fact that in psychotherapy we are, to some
extent, the victims of our disease orientation, our bias against
value judgments and our contradictory cultural goals" (Walker and
Peiffer, 1957, p. 209). Mathewson says that the old myth of economic man is inadequate. He says, "A new myth may be forming;
we cannot tell what it may be and perhaps we cannot hasten its

Reprinted by permission of the authors and *Educational Theory*, 1960, *10:*
142-147.

formation, or even consciously affect its form. But unless we wish to take a completely passive position in the determination of our national destiny, it seems necessary to think about and to choose between alternative sets of social and moral values, especially in the education and guidance of our youth" (Mathewson, 1955, p. 26).

Arbuckle (1953) compares the counselor and the surgeon, saying that the philosophy of the surgeon may have very little effect on the recovery or death of a patient. "The attitude and the philosophy of the counselor, however, are all-important and in any research it is difficult to keep such an inconsistent factor consistent." In Arbuckle's thinking the personal point of view must include a consideration of every aspect in the development of the student— ". . . his intellect, his emotions, his physical being, his moral values, his skills and aptitudes, his means of recreation, his esthetic and religious values, his social adjustment, and his environmental situation" (Arbuckle, 1953, p. 3). This is a big order! The fulfillment of such a goal in guidance is greatly complicated by the fact that the counselor, in dealing with the counselee's development along such broad lines, is confused about whether or not his own loyalties, his own philosophy of life, should be shared, or whether, in fact, he can keep himself from sharing it!

"Counseling involves the interaction of two personalities through the medium of speech and other symbolic behavior. It is reasonable to suppose, therefore, that the structure of each of these personalities will have a marked influence on the interaction. It may be hypothesized further that the ways in which the personality structure of each of the counseling participants is symbolized in the speech of the interview will also have a marked effect upon the interaction.

"If it is true that the counselor's personality influences the direction, course, and outcome of the counseling interaction, it might be profitable to speculate about the kinds of counselor personality traits which are likely to facilitate counseling and those which are not" (Arbuckle, 1953).

Strang states,

"The counselor should be himself but not impose himself. He should be genuine and sincere. He is likely to fail if he tries to play a role that is not natural for him. If a person cannot risk being himself in the counseling relationship, he should not try to be a counselor. Moreover, he is consciously or unconsciously influenced by his theory of counseling; his attitude toward school policies, his outlook on life, his attitude toward people. In short, his counseling is an expression of his personality, not merely a technic applied at will" (Strang, 1953).

Pepinsky and Pepinsky, writing in 1954, state,

"There is no denying that the counselor's behavior, also, is subject to change as a function of his experience in working with clients" (p. 173).

A little later under this same topic, "The Primary Function of Interaction," they go on to say,

"Indeed, the more closely we examine the counselor's motives, the more they become suspect! It appears to be, at best, nonsense and, at worst, a delusion to try to maintain that the counselor does or ought to leave his own needs parked outside the door while he interviews a client. We can state only that the explicit function of the counseling relationship—to help the client to change—should not be interfered with or destroyed" (Pepinsky & Pepinsky, 1954, p. 74).

Perhaps the greatest single influence on counselors to be philosophically neutral has come from the work of Carl Rogers. His non-directive theory of psychotherapy was built on the belief that man could be trusted to work his way through to insights and new orientation if he could have a genuinely permissive relationship with the counselor in which he could open his inner life to himself and the helping person. Early research by Rogers led him to state that, "One can read through a complete recorded case or listen to it, without finding more than a half dozen instances in which the therapist's views on any point are evident. . . One could not determine his diagnostic views, his standards of behavior, his social class" (Rogers, 1947, p. 358). Rogers did not, at that time, comment on the effect of the half dozen times and the absolute inevitability of such sharing of values. More recently, but only after a number of years of general confusion about the issue, has he addressed himself more directly to this pressing concern. In 1957, he said, in answer to certain articles challenging his position, that, "One cannot engage in psychotherapy without giving operational evidence of an underlying value orientation and view of human nature. It is definitely preferable, in my opinion, that such underlying views be open and explicit, rather than covert and implicit" (Rogers, 1957, p. 199). Rogers' insistence upon as much neutrality as possible has been a helpful research technique and allowed him and his associates to see deeply into the inner dynamics of the self. From his research there is ample evidence that the self, when free from threat or attack, is able to consider "hitherto rejected perceptions, to make new differentiations and to reintegrate the self in such a way as to include them" (Rogers, 1947, p. 365). Rogers' method seems honestly to help the person change. ". . . as changes occur in the perception of self and in the perception of reality, changes occur in the behavior" (Rogers, 1947, p. 363). The fact that persons often integrate their lives on levels that are not ultimately satisfactory but which only give the illusion of well-being must now be faced by Rogers and others.

ATTEMPTS TO CLARIFYING THE RELATIONSHIP OF BASIC PHILOSOPHY TO COUNSELING

One of the most powerful attempts to do away with philosophical relativism has been made by the humanistic psychotherapist and author, Erich Fromm, in his several writings, especially in *The Sane Society*. Fromm seeks to establish a solid foundation for the development of mental health for all men in whatever society. He observes that man has not only physiological and anatomical commonalities but that he is governed universally by certain basic psychic factors as well. His system of right and wrong is therefore built squarely upon whether or not man as man, in his essential being, is having his basic human needs fulfilled.

Fromm's inclusion in his list of basic needs of the necessity for a "frame of orientation and devotion" has led him to be most sympathetic toward the insights of the great religions and philosophies of the past and present. He is sensitive also to the moral standards propagated in our varying societies, because he believes that whole cultures can become full of defects which can and do tend to make men mentally ill. Societal arrangements, therefore, often must be changed before man's needs can be met. This observation forces counselors to be concerned with social, political, and religious philosophies which have created and are sustaining, often, such unhealthy social structures.

Fromm's theory is an attempt to build on what man's needs are objectively and not on what man feels his needs to be. This concept challenges in many ways the goal of non-directive counseling which tends to center on the process of man's expression of his inner feelings of need without reference to the fact that such needs are often a result of cultural defects which will not and can-not bring ultimate health to the client. This is true because of the very nature of his human condition, and the breadth of his needs which are in the area of ultimate loyalties and basic, undergirdling frames of orientation, about which most counselors feel insecure and from which discussions they tend to steer clear!

A similar trend to that of Fromm's can be seen in the writings of Kurt Lewin. He stated as far back as 1935 that, "The individual psychical experiences, the actions and emotions, purposes, wishes and hopes, are rather embedded in quite definite psychical structures, spheres of the personality, and whole process" (Lewin, 1935, p. 54).

Also to be found in Fromm and Lewin thought is an emphasis on man's freedom and the necessity to broaden the range of that freedom in psychotherapy as well as in intelligent political action. Lewin observed that often the individual area of freedom is very small due to the vectors and forces in his field of psychic experience, built on past identifications, inhibitions and loyalties. Yet, this freedom existed. Man as man had qualities beyond the realm of the animal. Therapy should help man use his freedom to find the paths to growth, and to overcome the psychic barriers.

One of the most dramatic and controversial attempts to deal with the question of philosophy in psychotherapy has been made by Dr. Viktor E. Frankl, the Director of the Neurological Polyclinic in Vienna and a Professor of Psychiatry at the University of Vienna. Frankl's point of view grows out of the emphasis in existentialist philosophy on man's actual conditions of existence. Man in his essence is endowed with certain capacities for freedom, for decision making, for determining his destiny. Man is a responsible being with the power to transcend his own situation and to prophesy the results of his decisions. His intellectual powers and his psychic powers are qualitatively different from other animals. Frankl joins Fromm, at this point, in that he is seeking to analyze man's basic need for a value system on which he can base his decisions, as a result of which he will increase his freedom and his meaning.

He recognizes the significance of both individual psychology, stemming from Adler, and psychoanalysis, stemming from Freud. He maintains, however, that psychotherapy will be incomplete until man has a "psychotherapy of the mind" which deals with philosophical issues. Differing with Freud and others, he says, "The individual's philosophical attitude is part and parcel of his psychological one and emerges in every case" (Frankl, 1955, p. 34). He also believes, against the stream of thought in psychotherapy, that, "In no case should the intellectual problems of a person be written off as a 'symptom' " (p. 33).

Frankl honestly discusses the many profound problems related to his point of view, and pushes ahead, along with Fromm, to establish certain fundamental values inherent in man's situation. And yet, he maintains that existential analysis must not interfere with the ranking of values. ". . . what values he elects is and remains the patient's own affair. Existential analysis must not be concerned with what the patient decides for, what goals he sets himself, but only that he decides at all . . . The physician should never be allowed to take over the patient's responsibility; he must never anticipate decisions or impose them upon the patient. His job is to make it possible for the patient to reach decisions; he must endow the patient with the capacity for deciding" (Frankl, 1955, p. 270).

Such a view has been given great impetus by the philosophical writings of Martin Buber. Buber's philosophy urges man to relationships of trust with other men—very much like that between the counselor and the client in a permissive setting; and yet, he believes that real trust must allow and encourage honest dialogue between both parties. When there is a real meeting of persons (Buber describes this meeting in terms of an I-Thou relationship— very similar to Schweitzer's "reverence for life" concept) each person is bringing his full self to the dialogue. He must "be willing . . . to say what is really in his mind about the subject of conversation. And that means further that on each occasion he makes the contribution of his spirit without reduction and without shifting ground" (Buber, 1957, p. 112).

Dialogue on a philosophical level, on the level of the quest for ultimate meaning, is a basic need for every human being. The counselor must be sensitive, nevertheless, to the existential situation in which the client finds himself at any given time.

Gordon Allport emphasizes the profundity of this renewed interest in studying the basic conditions of man's existence. He says, "Existentialism calls for a doctrine of an active intellect, for

more emphasis upon appropriate functions, including self-objecti-
fication and oriented becoming. In particular it calls for a wider and
fresher view of anxiety, of courage, and of freedom (Allport, 1955,
p. 80). Allport stresses the fact that Freud and his followers have
dealt mostly with the anxiety in man aroused by feelings of guilt
and fear of punishment and not at all the anxiety which comes
from a fear of *nonbeing* (death—either actual or psychological, in
the Buber sense of being not in relation; not affirmed and confirmed by others).

Allport believes that the consideration of philosophical matters
has been greatly de-emphasized in counseling, to the detriment of
our whole concept of personality structure. Philosophic and religious decisions have to do with what he terms *Intentional Characteristics* which become a part of the personality. He believes that,
"Intentional characteristics represent above all else the individual's
primary modes of addressing himself to the future. As such they
select stimuli, guide inhibitions and choices, and have much to do
with the process of adult becoming. Relatively few theories of
personality recognize the pre-emptive importance of intentional
characteristics" (Allport, 1955, p. 89).

So, we are seeing a powerful movement within the guidance
field, psychotherapy, philosophy, theology, and psychology for a
deeper view of man's problems of existence, his wide and deep
needs, his essential freedom of being, and his finite situation which
forces him to go beyond knowledge to an ultimate devotion—built
on faith (not an irrational faith, but faith, nonetheless).

Buber, in his William Alanson White Lectures given at the Washington School of Psychiatry, says that the counselor or educator
"cannot wish to impose himself, for he believes in the effect of the
actualizing forces . . . The propagandist who imposes himself, does
not really believe even in his own cause, for he does not trust it to
attain the effect of its own power, without his special methods"
(Buber, 1957, p. 111). While Buber believes so strongly in the
power of honest meeting between persons in an I-Thou relationship of mutual trust and confirmation, even with differences of
loyalties, he is very cautious about the right of the psychotherapist
to embark upon a "treatment of the essential in man." He agrees
with the late Viktor von Weizsaecker who said that it is not the
privilege of the therapist or counselor to deal with the final destiny
of man.

Returning to the area of guidance and student personnel services, it is becoming equally well established that basic educational

philosophy does inevitably influence the procedures of the guidance counselor. If he is thoroughly pragmatic in his orientation of religious or metaphysical beliefs that the student brings to the counseling situation, he may feel that value judgments must be left out of the considerations. Of course, with this Pragmatic Philosophy which seems on the surface to be a neutral position, goes a basic commitment just as much so as the student may have, with his religious commitment. It seems to us that considerations of ultimate values cannot be avoided by the counselor as a person, and that he must operate from some philosophical point of view—some form of Idealism, Realism (Christian or otherwise), Pragmatism, Naturalism, or Existentialism (again religious or otherwise).

It seems imperative that guidance counselors and educators must join other leaders in education, psychology, psychotherapy, philosophy and religion in doing basic research in this field.

In this spirit of scientific inquiry (even with its obvious limitations in the area of ultimate values) and also in the spirit of dialogue (with free discussion of important questions related to man's basic needs and his basic conditions of existence) we should proceed to clarify and come to decisions about the foundation and goals of counseling.

Recently, Williamson has stated that, "I have further argued for making explicit our own value orientations as individual counselors, not in order that we may adopt a counselor's orthodox creed, but rather that we may responsibly give societal and moral direction to our individual work in terms of the explicitly desired goals chosen by our student clients" (Williamson, 1958, p. 528).

When guidance counselors, psychotherapists, or religious counselors admit that they are not philosophically neutral, then we will be able to study more systematically the effect of our philosophical loyalties upon our counseling.

REFERENCES

Allport, G. W. *Becoming: Basic Considerations for a Psychology of Personality.* New Haven: Yale Univer. Press, 1955.

Arbuckle, D. S. *Student Personnel Services in Higher Education.* New York: McGraw-Hill, 1953.

Arbuckle, D. S. *Teacher Counseling.* Cambridge, Mass.: Addison-Wesley, 1950.

Buber, M. William Alanson White memorial lectures. *Psychiatry,* 1957, *20(2):* 95-114.

Buber, M. The teacher and teaching. Unpublished manuscript. In collection compiled by Dr. Ross Snyder, Univer. of Chicago.

Frankl, V. E. *The Doctor and the Soul.* New York: Alfred Knopf, 1955.

Fromm, Erich. *The Sane Society.* New York: Rinehart, 1955.

Lewin, K. *A Dynamic Theory of Personality.* New York: McGraw-Hill, 1935.

Mathewson, R. H. *Guidance Policy and Practice.* New York: Harper, 1955.

Oates, W. E. *The Religious Dimensions of Personality.* New York: Association Press, 1957.

Pepinsky, H. B., & Pepinsky, Pauline N. *Counseling: Theory and Practice.* New York: Ronald, 1954.

Rogers, C. R. Some observations on the organization of personality. *Amer. Psychologist,* 1947, *2:* 358-368.

Rogers, C. R. A note on the nature of man. *J. Counsel. Psychol.,* 1957, *4:* 199-203.

Strang, Ruth. *The Role of the Teacher in Personnel Work.* (4th ed.) New York: Teachers College (Columbia University), 1953.

Tillich, P. *Systematic Theology.* Vol. 1. Chicago: University of Chicago Press, 1952.

Vordenberg, W. The impact of personal philosophies on counseling. *Personnel Guid. J.,* 1953, *31:* 439-440.

Walker, D., & Peiffer, H. The goals of counseling. *J. Counsel. Psychol.,* 1957, *4:* 204-209.

Weitz, H. Counseling as a function of the counselor's personality. *Personnel Guid. J.,* 1957, *35:* 276-280.

Williamson, E. G. Value orientation in counseling. *Personnel Guid. J.,* 1958, *36:* 520-528.

23

CHANGE IN VALUES: A GOAL IN COUNSELING

Joseph Samler, Ph.D.

It seems a safe statement in an otherwise hazardous paper that psychologists are no longer defensive about being concerned with values. Hobbs' summary is only the most recent in a series of essays on ethics, values, science, and psychology (1959). In her presentation of concepts of positive mental health, Marie Jahoda devotes a brief section to the value dilemma (1958). In the last three years, Williamson has written a number of articles on values and counseling. Patterson's chapter on Values and Psychotherapy in his current *Counseling and Psychotherapy* (1959) cites 52 references to pertinent literature. Wrenn's contributions and Meehl's great clarity on this problem are well known. The current puzzling courtship of religion by psychotherapy (or the other way around) is a related phenomenon.

ON THE DERIVATION OF VALUES

We are at the core, here, of man's search for meaning in life, of his attempt to provide structure where in fact none may exist. Out of this overwhelming need, answers inevitably arose. For millennia they came from the wisdom and intuition of the noblest (a most value-laden term) among us.

The second Isaiah and the other Hebrew prophets, Jesus, the deeply perceptive poets, novelists, playwrights and our modern-day moral leaders, supplied the need out of their own deep feeling

---

Reprinted by permission of the author and the *Journal of Counseling Psychology*, 1960, 7: 32-39.

and identification with humankind. The nature of the values thus adduced is well known. They are absolute and final and not readily subject to question. They are an integral part of given institutions and to question them is to attack the institutions. Since this not infrequently brings personal guilt and anxiety into play, it is done at some hazard.

As against values thus derived, and in spite of the unnerving cold shower Hobbs' clarity provides, is the method of science. Its disadvantages in the field of values are clearly evident. Out of the scientific-instrumental approach flow values which are relative by definition, take context into account, represent stages in progress, and are, therefore, open-ended. They are necessarily partial, tentative and qualified. Wheelis' (1958) informed exposition of the etiology of these different value systems warrants the attention of all who are concerned with this problem.

Hobbs' (1959) conclusion (which sounds somehow regretful) seems to be that psychology, as a science, has no major contribution to make to value organization. But psychology is *not* any other science; it is the science of man, the science of human behavior. Also courage can be taken from his statement that he is as yet highly tentative about some of his formulations and that he is not yet able to let the problem alone. "For a science of man," Ashley Montagu cites Julian Huxley as saying, "the problem is not whether or not to have anything to do with values, but how to devise methods of studying them and discovering how they work."

There is another aspect of this general problem that does not relate to choice between traditional and scientifically derived value systems. Maslow probably has been most articulate about it, although he is joined by others. This point is that the prime disease of our time is valuelessness. It is a state variously described as amorality, rootlessness, emptiness, alienation, hopelessness, the lack, in short, of something to believe in and be devoted to. We are confronted with a vacuum in values which must be filled. The point of view is that traditional values have failed and in Maslow's terms, we "need a validated, usable system of human values that we can believe in and devote ourselves to because they are true rather than because we are exhorted to believe and have faith" (1959).

THREE BASIC PROPOSITIONS

Yet with all of the disadvantages of the scientific method in the derivation of values granted, a number of points remain stubbornly in mind: That for the first time in the history of man there is a systematic means of exploring his needs and their fulfillment; that its appeal is widespread and has captured the interest and devotion of highly intelligent and creative workers; that its methodology is increasing in its sophistication; and that there is already a body of substantive information about the nature and condition of man.

Therefore, the first in a series of propositions:

1. Man's increasing scientific knowledge about himself should supply the basic data for derivation of his values.

Obviously we lack the tightly designed researches with findings validated at high levels of confidence, but we are not without theoretical contributions out of which we can identify necessary lines of research and testable hypotheses. The contributions by psychological workers are too well known to cite extensively, but they should be called to attention even if only to remind ourselves that we are least of all without such ideas.

The characteristics of Erich Fromm's productive personality are very much in point here as in his formulation of human needs in society. Sullivan's mature personality belongs here. Probably there would be a certain amount of difficulty in living in a world of Goldstein's and Maslow's self-actualizing people, but their validity and force are indubitable. Sorokin and Ashley Montagu and Shoben have contributed in this area. Of very great interest is Maslow's well known hierarchy of needs with its strong instinctoid overtones. Needs, it may be granted, are without undue difficulty translatable into values, also capable of hierarchical ordering.

With these contributions in mind, it is possible to offer, however tentatively, a second proposition:

2. The theoretical models of the psychologically healthy person, his orientation to himself and others, the choices he makes, and his criteria for making these choices, offer us meaningful material for value determinations.

A third proposition reaches for even if it does not quite grasp the horn of another dilemma:

3. Values should be subject to explicit examination as criteria for choice, as determinants of behavior.

Here I have learned from John E. Smith's descerning essay on

Jacob's study (1958), and it is congruent with our current professions relative to mental health, specifically with the importance of bringing unconscious motivation into awareness. Smith's emphasis is on the critical response which requires a standard or criterion in accordance with which the actual judgment or evaluation is made.

We have a choice of a kind here. If we do not examine our value predispositions, or indeed our valuelessness, our beliefs and behavior must flow from our present value orientation which exists at various levels of awareness and clarity and understanding. All of this affects our ability to move toward or away from them.

Thus far this paper (a) urged the need for values derived from man's increasing knowledge about himself, at least as a goal if not as an immediate program, (b) called attention to theoretical models of the well-functioning individual and (c) made Smith's point that in final analysis, values must stand as the referent points, as the criteria for choice. All of these have pertinence in considering the particular enterprise, the learning task we call counseling.

VALUES AND THE COUNSELING TASK

It is hardly news that we have yet to define clearly and cleanly the job of counseling, its distinguishing characteristics relative to psychotherapy, or the appropriate range of effort in such specific goals as vocational counseling or marriage counseling. But it can be agreed that in some measure personality appraisal, evaluation of misperception, examination of self-acceptance, resulting change of behavior, acceptance of responsibility, and assumption of independence are common to all counseling tasks. Differential goals are also, of course, to be noted, e.g., reduction in guilt, acceptance of appropriate feelings of dependence, and the experience of feeling.

Whatever the true nature of these tasks, it seems quite a circumspect statement that the counselor plays a central role in them. For some workers in therapy and counseling he is clarifier of feelings, for others teacher and mentor, for still others a vehicle for safe reliving of the past and its examination. He is other things still, depending on what one feels actually takes place in the consulting room, and of course, the nature and cause and effect of behavior change in counseling or therapy are still largely unknown. Probably it is these different and partial theoretical views of counseling interaction that compel us to assign differing behavior to the counselor. The fourth proposition is based upon the idea now gain-ing increasing acceptance that as Sullivan's participant observer, as himself his most useful tool, the counselor is in effect an instrument which itself must be calibrated.

4. The counselor's values must be held in awareness.

In his usual comprehensive fashion C. H. Patterson (1959) has pulled together the literature on this problem. As against a previously adopted fancied neutrality, he cites theory and research relative to the impossibility of keeping the therapist's values out of his work. The evidence indicates that the influence can be unintended and quite below awareness levels. Logic compels us to the same conclusion, for to say that the counselor manifests no values is to require that he have no feelings and whatever great drama this may be it is not counseling. The unreality of such a devastating neutrality requires no comment. The least we can learn from this is that the counselor's awareness of his values is of prime importance.

The impression is gained in moving among professional colleagues and in reading that this need for search of self is accepted readily enough. It seems to be, in fact, the preferred style but whether this is only the cut of cloth or really integrated personality style is an open question. To be sure, life is a great teacher and the practicum leader's comments on taped interviews may go some distance, but it is doubtful that much light is shed in the dark area of unconscious motivation by these means. Yet how many counselors have been subject to the systematic and painful and enriching (and expensive) experience of truly investigating their behavior and its motivation, that is to say their values? The point that short of analytic procedures, we have been remiss in investigating and putting into effect systematic self-exploration methods, is defended elsewhere (Samler, 1959).

The point comes home in its specifics. Williamson points out in a recent article (1959) that in vocational counseling the counselor takes for granted that choice of occupation should reflect the individual's optimum potential, that interests should be capitalized, that university training is the *summum bonum,* and that job stability is much to be preferred to job hopping, which at times in fact is seen as a clinical symptom. The point Dean Williamson makes is that these values which determine basic counselor attitudes and behavior probably are quite out of the counselor's awareness.

It seems useful to note that these are relatively "safe" value areas. That is, we do not deal here with the counselor's own deeply rooted value system relating to this regard for himself, the nature and extent of his guilt, his strong feelings of dependence and so on, although connections there may be. Yet these value assumptions also are in quite a mysterious and unlighted area.

Like the apocryphal story of the paranoid patient who was advised he could continue in his delusions if only he kept his mouth shut, it may be possible to have behavioral change without fundamental change in values, but this is hardly an acceptable counseling goal. It is only making the obvious explicit to say that behavior constitutes a reflection, sometimes twisted and distorted as in peculiar mirrors, of values. How is it possible, for instance, to divorce values from Tyler's description of counseling which reads in part "a process by which each person can be helped to develop and understand his own characteristic life pattern, his own identity," or from the core of Super's statement relative to vocational counseling—"helping a person develop and accept an integrated and adequate picture of himself and his role in the world of work."

The next proposition, therefore, is that,

5. Values are at the heart of the counseling relationship, are reflected in its content, and affect the process.

It is clear that the very availability of counseling has deeply imbedded in it a particular value orientation. *All* counseling by definition is for the benefit of the counselee (with society's needs in mind, to be sure) and, therefore, the behavior, attitudinal set and basic relationship of the counselor to his client is characterized at least by interest, probably by concern, and possibly by a form of love. The need for respecting the client is a counseling byword. As a silent preceptor, advocate of a particular way of relating to others, and as a respecting and expert helper, the counselor at the very least affects client attitudes. The literature is abundant on this point.

The counseling process as such is aimed at providing insight, changing behavior, and the exercise of choice along lines leading to more adequate functioning and greater comfort in living in terms of specified values. In vocational counseling, Super's phrase in his definition "helping the individual develop and accept an adequate picture of himself," is value loaded, as are other personality oriented counseling definitions. If the counselor functions along these lines he is inevitably, one way or another, addressing himself to the client's values. This is perhaps best illustrated by the studied observation not of a psychologist, but by the economist, researchers, and general gad-fly Eli Ginsberg (1951). In assessing the situation of vocational counseling he and his colleagues point out that:

The connection between occupational choice process and work satisfaction is not contained in the specific decision which the individual reaches, but in how he clarifies the goals and values which are associated with the satisfactions he seeks in work. This clarification is an essential part of his occupational decision making, for he cannot make a choice without determining, at least preliminarily, what he wants to get out of work. If he fails to clarify his goals and values and fails to crystallize his choice, it is more than likely that his work experience will prove frustrating. Not knowing what he wants from work, he will be unable to choose from among such alternatives as he may have. *True crystallization and specification cannot take place until a clarification of goals and values has been made.* (Italics supplied)

Equally significant is understanding of the differential value systems of occupations. Here our colleagues in related fields have contributed heavily to understanding of social, class, and occupational expectations, roles, and their related values. It is difficult to conceive of counseling related to psychological realities which does not take these data into account.

We need not deal with the problem only on presumptive grounds. In his 1958 APA paper in this area, Paul Meehl, without offering his own support, cites workers (e.g., Wolpe, Herzberg, Maeder, Phillips, Frankl, Ellis, Thorpe) who, in his words "not only permit but who encourage a detailed consideration of value problems. These practitioners prefer not to treat the patient's value-orientation as merely a symptom or derivative of something else . . . but rather conceive that a patient's value orientation may itself be one of the important determiners of his unhappiness."

Proposition 6. "Intervention" by the counselor in the client's values is an actuality and should be accepted as a necessary part of the process.

Almost the question answers itself. If the counseling task is in a context of values, and if counseling goals must explicate and integrate them, then the counselor's activity in this area should be taken for granted. But I doubt that many will be satisfied with this abstraction. Specifics may help:

Given a highly talented 17-year-old youngster in educational and vocational counseling from a lower socio-economic stratum, I submit that the counselor assumes a given attitude set. This has to do with the client's self-actualization to be sure, and will allow for unique solutions. But for the generality of cases, the desirability of college will be very much in his mind. He has set a goal, tentative to be sure, for the youngster—it is obviously value oriented. I submit that the counselor will work toward that goal for and with the youngster.

Given impulsive and acting-out behavior with another client of whatever age, the role of the worker and his goals for the client are quite clear—more rational behavior and repression of some impulses.

One can list a set of troubles, the therapies of choice and their underlying value orientation:

for the demanding and infantile—assumption of responsibility;
for the vocationally disoriented—assumption of a working role
congruent with the picture the client will develop of himself;
for the guilt-ridden—tolerance for himself and life's reality;
for the unloved and unloving—self-acceptance and kindliness;
for the achievement and power-ridden—appreciation of the rich
resources in human beings;
for the highly controlling—reduction of anxiety and a more
trusting and optimistic outlook.

The point I am making is that these goals in terms of change in client behavior and the accompanying assumption of congruent values are clearly in the minds of the workers, and that they will address their efforts toward these ends.

In an oft-quoted article Gardner Murphy (1955) also addressed himself to this central issue. To the dilemma of activity relative to client values, Murphy's answer is unequivocal and along three lines. He feels that the counselor "cannot help conveying directly or indirectly to every client what he himself sees and feels, and the perspective in which his own life is lived." Second, "it is not true that the wise man's sharing of a philosophy of life is an arrogant imposition upon a defenseless client." Third, in addressing himself to our work, he says "it is often said that all philosophies are subjective and arbitrary, and that one system of values is as good as another. But if you believed that, you would not have chosen personnel and guidance as a way of life. Your experience, moreover, has shown you that some values, such as those of sympathy, tenderness, generosity, and self-control resonate to the deeper chords of human nature, and that they are for that reason intensely practical and dependable."

In Meehl's paper referred to before (1958), the therapists he cites, he states, "are willing to step into a pedagogical role and engage in direct behavioral retraining. Some would pay only incidental attention to cognitive issues; others view cognitive clarification—including persuasion and intellectual argument—as fundamental to the therapeutic process." Those who heard this thoughtful paper will recall that he goes on to say:

> In the course of ordinary secular psychotherapy there occur, from time to time, exchanges between patient and therapist which are not defensive intellectualizations but which (whatever they may be called with the therapist's preferred theoretical scheme) are, in their actual verbal structure, rather like a segment out of one of the Platonic dialogues. I suspect that one reason why so many therapists are skittish about getting involved in this kind of thing is that they lack talent and training for the Socratic dialogue, and that this deficiency, together with their own personal ambiguity about the value-question, makes them feel unsafe if they treat any such material in its own right, rather than as a derivative calling for a psychodynamic interpretation at some other level.

It is of the greatest possible interest that the same point is made in very much the same way by Allen Wheelis (1958) in the rich context of his novelette-essay-autobiography.

Proposition 7. Promotion of given values and counseling technique are now seen as constituting an indissoluble unit. They should be regarded as separable.

It seems to me that the actuality of counselor intervention in client values is beyond dispute. While such intervention is now accomplished through a basic relationship technique, it does not follow that this must be our only means. Even if methods determine ends it is still for consideration whether these are immutably the only proper means at our disposal.

We know that in their behavior, defenses, and values, human beings change least of all by exhortation, but this does not mean that the person to whom high achievement or power is a prime value and a way of maintaining self-respect, should not change; it only means that exhortation will not work with him. We have found that it is possible for people to learn to be loving, to like people (a value), but only by living through the experience of themselves being loved, being allowed suspiciously to test the lover-therapist in a thousand different ways. We have changed a value, in awareness, with full intention of doing so, but we have done it in a very particular way.

To the client who for the best of reasons has put a tight lid on his feelings, and is defended by intellect and emptiness, the therapist may sometimes want to say "try feeling, only the learning is painful," but he will not, because it will not work. But the encouraged experience, as it were, of creeping up on feeling, can work. The value is identified and sought out, change is encouraged, but again, the way of achieving it is very particular.

Probably the examples can be multiplied many times. There is a cause and effect relationship between the experience of being accepted and feeling the concern of another and increase in self-esteem, but it should not follow that this is the only way of achieving the desired effect in change in values. One is a very special kind of learning, a particular rich experience, but it is still a technique, and it should be seen as such. I keep on wondering whether if we deny the goal (specified change in values) and emphasize the means (our present relationship techniques), we are not selling ourselves short on the possibility of finding other ways of helping.

This proposition is based in part on the discerning discussion by Meehl and McClosky (1947) of the relationship between ethics and technique in therapeutic work. It is tempting to cite any number of sharp and clear paragraphs in this discussion. It is required reading for all of us concerned with this problem.

If we can separate out technique of choice from the necessary goal of change in values, the inevitable question arises as to which values. It is this critical question that prompts the last proposal:

Proposition 8. Drawing upon the available models of the mature personality, it should be possible to develop testable hypotheses relative to the values to be supported in counselor-client interaction.

The hazards in this are tremendous: Jahoda (1958) points out for instance that:

"While it is easy to speculate about the relation of each criterion to a vast number of high values, we do not know whether such relations actually obtain. Does self-actualization really benefit the development of the species, as Fromm would claim? Is interpersonal competence a prerequisite for the happiness of the individual? Is happiness or productivity the value underlying an active orientation to problem-solving?"

Yet what recourse have we other than the dictum that the individual will develop his own? More than that: the omniscient answers that these questions appear to require are not really necessary. We do not need to solve them for the next few millennia, the job is difficult enough if we get answers that are better than any others and that will work for the next 25 years or for that part of such a period until better answers emerge. In any case, the models provide the best answers that theory making and clinical experience have yet made available to us.

I do not want to be mistaken. The notion, for example, of a congress of psychologists determining by vote whatever values should be, scares the daylight out of me as well. This is not the way. Our faith must be put on the scientific derivation of desirable behavior, orientation to life, and their underlying values.

Should we embark on such an enterprise, after coming to terms with the values implicit in it, it would follow that the professed neutrality of the counselor relative to his client's values would have to be abandoned in favor of an affirmation of given values. The attendant possibility might arise of opening up the important process of values as referent points.

Least of all am I concerned with the shibboleth of democracy and authoritarianism in the counseling relationship. These ghosts were laid by Meehl and McClosky in 1947, and what is required is a courageous editor nowhere available to reprint that sterling article. An affirmative stand in values is contrary also to Patterson's summation (1959, p. 74). He says in part about the counselor that:

"He would not feel that the counseling relationship is the place to teach moral or ethical standards, or a philosophy of life. He is confident, as apparently some are not, that the client in the therapeutic relationship will be aware of an influence by social realities. He will leave to the family, the church and the school, as institutions representing the moral and ethical standards of society, the teaching of such standards."

These three sentences appear to represent the orthodox opinion in the field and yet I believe they must be subject to serious examination. They bypass the reality that values are in fact learned in the consulting room. But more important, they disregard the counseling situation as a learning experience of the greatest possible import, ethically bound as are very few others, constantly under the scrutiny of a highly self-conscious professional community. It is not an opportunity to be lightly dismissed. It is an opportunity for the learning of values to be affirmed, explored, and made the subject of our most serious concern.

The written word takes on a finality that goes beyond intention. Personal experience and consideration of these serious problems argue a greater tentativeness then these propositions offer. But the unequivocal certitude of a great deal of present thinking on values, counselor role, and client change, is too troublesome to leave alone. This much is certain: We must examine our present value commitments and carry them sharply in awareness. In the light of our growing knowledge of human behavior we must ourselves map the country and travel a road of our own choosing. We should be able to accept without quibbling the objective in counseling of modification of client behavior and therefore of attitudes and values. With the purpose unequivocally clear our task remains that of determining how it can best be accomplished whatever our present commitments.

REFERENCES

Ginsberg, E., et al. *Occupational choice, an approach to a general theory.* New York: Columbia Univer. Press, 1951.

Hobbs, N. Science and ethical behavior. *Amer. Psychol.,* 1959, *14*:217-225.

Jahoda, Marie. *Current concepts of positive mental health.* Monograph Series No. 1, Joint Commission on Mental Health, New York: Basic Books, 1958.

Maslow, A. H. (Ed.) *New knowledge in human values.* New York: Harper, 1959.

Meehl, P. E. Some technical and axiological problems in the therapeutic handling of religious and valuational material. Unpublished paper delivered at APA convention, 1958.

Meehl, P. E., & McClosky, H. Ethical and political aspects of applied psychology. *J. abnorm. soci. Psychol.,* 1947, *42*:91-98.

Montagu, M. F. *The direction of human development: Biological and social bases.* New York: Harper, 1955.

Murphy, G. The cultural context of guidance. *Personnel Guid. J.,* 1955, *34*:4-9.

Patterson, C. H. *Counseling and psychotherapy: Theory and practice.* New York: Harper, 1959.

Samler, J. Basic approaches to mental health, an attempt at synthesis. *Personnel Guid. J.,* 1959, *37*:638-643.

Smith, J. E. *Value convictions and higher education.* New Haven: Edward W. Hazen Foundation, 1958.

Wheelis, A. *The quest for identity.* New York: Norton, 1958.

Williamson, E. G. The meaning of communication in counseling. *Personnel Guid. J.,* 1959, *38*:6-14.

24

ARE ALL MIDDLE-CLASS VALUES BAD?

Ben N. Ard, Jr., Ph.D.

"Middle class values" have become, it would seem, the favorite whipping post (if not scapegoat) for some years now as being the basic, underlying cause of quite a few personal problems, various mental illnesses (so-called), countless family problems (generation gaps), and many social problems (including some penal and racial difficulties). A lot of counseling and psychotherapy has been thrown out as based upon "middle class values."

Ghetto blacks have claimed that it takes blacks to counsel blacks; drug users have claimed only an addict (or ex-addict) can deal with addicts; "liberated" women claim they must have only other "liberated" women as their counselors or therapists; homosexuals, etc., etc., etc. It takes one to know one (and presumably counsel one) seems to be a basic assumption. Competence has been replaced by color as a necessary ingredient in the counselor's or therapist's armamentarium. Must all counselors or therapists be of the same sex, same color, same religion, same background, and always have the same (presumably un-middle-class) values as the client?

Frank Riessman, *et al*, in their book on *Mental Health of the Poor* (1964, p. vii), have stated: "We question the widely prevalent notion that psychotherapy is not the treatment of choice for blue collar people. This idea seems rooted in a very static, middle-class centered view of therapy," Reissman, et al (1964, p. viii), went on to say that "Low income groups may have considerably more potential for the basic aspects of psychotherapy than has

This paper is a much expanded version of an earlier one by the same title, which appeared in *The Family Coordinator, 21:* 223-224, April, 1972.

hitherto been recognized. Characteristics of the poor that make them inappropriate for psychotherapy have been overemphasized to the exclusion of positive indications."

What specific values are at issue here? John Clausen, using adolescent drug users as a basis for an extended discussion of these and related matters, came to many relevant conclusions (Clausen, 1957). As Clausen has indicated, the existence of differences in the values which serve as goals for persons of different class origins has been illustrated by many descriptive studies of social class, but relatively few scientists have attempted to study value orientations. Perhaps the studies of Allison Davis and his collaborators have most clearly indicated dominant value differences between lower-class and middle-class children and adults, white and negro.

"The lower-class pattern of life puts a high premium on immediate physical gratification, on free expression of aggression, on spending and sharing. Cleanliness, respect for property, sexual control, achievement—highly valued by the middle class—are of lesser importance to the lower class family. The middle-class child is encouraged and pressured to work for relatively distant goals; his parents take for granted that he will achieve these goals, and the child too comes to take his ultimate rewards for granted." (Clausen, 1957, pp. 257-258).

Counseling in ghetto or slum schools is frequently difficult because educational attainment is not highly prized in lower-class street society; thus it becomes almost impossible to motivate the lower-class adolescent toward school objectives, (Clausen, 1957, p. 258).

"In summary, the adolescent growing up in an urban slum is subject to anything but a coherent pattern of life which permits learning the 'proper' rules of conduct through consistent guidance by a more or less constant circle of concerned adults. Instead, he is exposed to all manner of deviant patterns, to occasional indulgences and sharp frustrations, and to a type of social control which stresses avoiding consequences rather than developing 'controls from within'." (Clausen, 1957, p. 262.)

What are the consequences for counseling and psychotherapy of these differences in values between lower-class and middle-class clients? The authorities are not all agreed. We have already noted the lower class tendency toward more immediate impulse gratification. There is apparently a lack of agreement among those who have been interested in this phenomenon as to whether the lower-class pattern is more conducive to mental health than is the deferred gratification pattern of the middle class, (Schneider & Lysgaard, 1933). But, as Clausen (1957, p. 263) has noted, "We shall simply observe that in a society where the achievement of substantial success rests in part upon learning to defer some gratifications and to accept substitutes for others, the pattern of demanding immediate satisfactions may in the long run produce the most frustration."

Although we have drawn heavily on Clausen's (1957) study of adolescent drug users in the discussion so far, his observations have much wider application than just to drug use. As Leighton has put it:

"The problem here is of course broader than that of drug use and involves the gulf between middle-class professionals and lower-class patients, a gulf resting on disparity in basic premises about life as well as on manifest differences of attitudes and conduct. This difference has been noted many times by therapists of various types as well as by teachers and social workers [see, for instance, Jules V. Coleman, "Mental Health Consultation to Agencies Protecting Family Life," in *The Elements of a Community Mental Health Program* (New York: Milbank Memorial Fund, 1956)], and suggests research with a view to finding ways and means for developing communication between middle and lower classes. Much of importance to the better functional integration of society might arise from this." (Leighton, *et al,* 1957, p. 276)

Perhaps, in the social criticisms of psychiatrists, college professors, psychologists, social workers, marriage and family counselors, sociologists, and other assorted "liberals" (intelligentsia or not), the time has come to question whether or not in the blanket harping against "middle-class values" the baby is being thrown out with the bad bath water. Are all middle-class values really that bad?

There are many middle-class values which do, indeed, figure prominently in many of the aforementioned problem areas of personal problems, mental illnesses, family problems, social problems, penal problems and racial problems. Now all values may need to be questioned, examined, and challenged from time to time, but particularly when acting on these values causes consequences which are harmful or detrimental to human beings. There has developed in the fields mentioned above a tendency to be ultra-critical of *all* "value judgments" but particularly of "middle-class values." The whole counter-culture movement (or alternative culture, or radical or revolutionary sub-culture) seems to be aimed at undermining *all* middle-class cultural values. (Cf. Roszak, 1969; Adler, 1972; Kluckhohn, 1958.)

What is needed now is not more polemics, nor more apologetics, but a reasoned examination of values in general, and middle-class values in particular (as the "dominant" values of our culture). What would seem to be needed is a sorting out of the consequences of acting upon various middle-class values, and where these are found to be self-defeating or harmful, the replacement of such values by more human, rational values (perhaps more cross-cultural in nature). (Cf. Opler, 1956; Gorney, 1972; Cattell, 1972; Maslow, 1971; Hemming, 1970.)

However, *some* of the much maligned middle-class values may be necessary for a technologically advanced society such as ours to survive, e.g., punctuality, a certain minimum of reliability, accountability (if not responsibility), as well as a minimum of orderliness (which is not the same as a compulsive form of orderliness). While cleanliness may not be next to godliness, a certain amount of cleanliness is necessary if large numbers of people are to survive in our increasingly urban centers.

A certain amount of postponement of instant satisfaction in the "here and now" may be necessary to learn practically any discipline, if we are to continue to have doctors, engineers, scientists, etc. This does not mean that a Puritanical rejection of all "pleasure" is desirable. The learning of a minimum of skills (reading, writing, arithmetic, etc.) is necessary for a literate if not an enlightened electorate. *All* the values that "schools" stand for are not necessarily *completely* bad. However, *all* people do *not* "have to go to college."

Neither do *all* people *have* to live in the traditional forms of marriage and the family, or become parents. Sex is a positive value for human beings who are healthy psychologically, although middle-class values have traditionally been anti-sex in our culture. (Ard, 1974). Indiscriminate, instant intimacy is *not* the *only* alternative to middle-class conventionalities regarding sex, however.

Just because we are middle-class (as a lot of counselors and psychotherapists are), does *not necessarily* mean that we always have to think "middle-class." On the other hand, instead of reflexly rejecting *all* middle-class values, if not *all* "value judgments," what would seem to be needed at this juncture in time is a more rigorous examination of all values and their consequences, with a view to rejecting the self-defeating ones but *not* rejecting *all* values, probably not even *all* middle-class values.

REFERENCES

Adler, Nathan. *The Underground Stream: New Life Styles and the Antinomian Personality.* New York: Harper & Row, 1972.

Ard, Ben N., Jr. *Treating Psychosexual Dysfunction.* New York: Jason Aronson, 1974.

Cattell, Raymond B. *A New Morality from Science: Beyondism.* New York: Pergamon Press, 1972.

Clausen, John A. Social patterns, personality, and adolescent drug use, *in* Leighton, A. E., *et al* (Eds.). *Explorations in Social Psychiatry.* New York: Basic Books, 1957, pp. 230-277.

Coleman, Jules V. Mental health consultation to agencies protecting family life, *in The Elements of a Community Mental Health Program.* New York: Milbank Memorial Fund, 1956.

Gorney, Roderic. *The Human Agenda.* New York: Simon & Schuster, 1972.

Hemming, James. *Individual Morality.* London: Panther Modern Society, 1970.

Kluckhohn, Clyde. Have there been discernable shifts in American values during the past generation? *in* Morrison, Elting E. (Ed.). *The American Style.* New York: Harper & Brothers, 1958.

Leighton, A. E., *et al* (Eds.). *Explorations in Social Psychiatry.* New York: Basic Books, 1957.

Maslow, A. H. *The Farther Reaches of Human Nature.* New York: Viking Press, 1971.

Masserman, Jules H. (Ed.). *Psychoanalysis and Human Values.* New York: Grune & Stratton, 1960.

Opler, Marvin K. *Culture, Psychiatry and Human Values.* Springfield, Illinois: Thomas, 1956.

Riessman, Frank, *et al* (Eds.). *Mental Health of the Poor: New Treatment Approaches for Low-Income People.* New York: Free Press, 1964.

Roszak, Theodore. *The Making of a Counter Culture.* Garden City, New York: Anchor, 1969.

Schneider, Louis & Lysgaard, Sverre. The deferred gratification pattern. *American Sociological Review,* 1933, *18:* 142-149.

25

PSYCHOLOGICAL DATA AND HUMAN VALUES

Abraham H. Maslow, Ph.D.

Humanists for thousands of years have attempted to construct a naturalistic, psychological value system that could be derived from man's own nature, without the necessity of recourse to authority outside the human being himself. Many such theories have been offered throughout history. They have all failed for mass practical purposes exactly as all other theories have failed. We have about as many scoundrels in the world today as we have ever had, and many more neurotics, probably, than we have ever had.

These inadequate theories, most of them, rested on psychological assumptions of one sort or another. Today practically all of these can be shown, in the light of recently acquired knowledge, to be false, inadequate, incomplete or in some other way, lacking. But it is my belief that certain developments in the science and art of psychology, in the last few decades, make it possible for us for the first time to feel confident that this age-old hope may be fulfilled if only we work hard enough. We know how to criticize the old theories; we know, even though dimly, the shape of the theories to come, and most of all, we know where to look and what to do in order to fill in the gaps in knowledge, that will permit us to answer the age-old questions, "What is the good life? What is the good man? How can people be taught to desire and prefer the good life? How ought children to be brought up to be sound adults? etc." That is, we think that a scientific ethic may be possible, and we think we know how to go about constructing it.

Reprinted by permission of the author and publisher from Abraham H. Maslow. *Toward A Psychology of Being.* Princeton, New Jersey: VanNostrand, 1962.

The following section will discuss briefly a few of the promising lines of evidence and of research, their relevance to past and future value theories, along with a discussion of the theoretical and factual advances we must make in the near future. It is safer to judge them all as more or less probable rather than as certain.

FREE CHOICE EXPERIMENTS: HOMEOSTASIS

Hundreds of experiments have been made that demonstrate a universal inborn ability in all sorts of animals to select a beneficial diet if enough alternatives are presented from among which they are permitted free choice. This wisdom of the body is often retained under less usual conditions, e.g., adrenalectomized animals can keep themselves alive by readjusting their self-chosen diet. Pregnant animals will nicely adjust their diets to the needs of the growing embryo.

We now know this is by no means a perfect wisdom. These appetites are less efficient, for instance, in reflecting body need for vitamins. Lower animals protect themselves against poisons more efficiently than higher animals and humans. Previously formed habits of preference may quite overshadow present metabolic needs (Young, 1961). And most of all, in the human being, and especially in the neurotic human being, all sorts of forces can contaminate this wisdom of the body, although it never seems to be lost altogether.

The general principle is true not only for selection of food but also for all sorts of other body needs as the famous homeostasis experiments have shown (Cannon, 1932).

It seems quite clear that all organisms are more self-governing, self-regulating and autonomous than we thought 25 years ago. The organism deserves a good deal of trust, and we are learning steadily to rely on this internal wisdom of our babies with reference to choice of diet, time of weaning, amount of sleep, time of toilet training, need for activity, and a lot else.

But more recently we have been learning, especially from physically and mentally sick people, that there are good choosers and bad choosers. We have learned, especially from the psychoanalysts, much about the hidden causes of such behavior and have learned to respect these causes.

In this connection we have available a startling experiment (Dove, 1935), which is pregnant with implications for value theory. Chickens allowed to choose their own diet vary widely in their ability to choose what is good for them. The good choosers become stronger, larger, more dominant than the poor choosers, which means that they get the best of everything. If then the diet chosen by the good choosers is forced upon the poor choosers, it is found that *they* now get stronger, bigger, healthier and more dominant, although never reaching the level of the good choosers. That is, good choosers can choose better than bad choosers what is better for the bad choosers themselves. If similar experimental findings are made in human beings, as I think they will be (supporting clinical data are available aplenty), we are in for a good deal of reconstruction of all sorts of theories. So far as human value theory is concerned, no theory will be adequate that rests simply on the statistical description of the choices of unselected human beings. To average the choices of good and bad choosers, of healthy and sick people is useless. Only the choices and tastes and judgments of healthy human beings will tell us much about what is good for the human species in the long run. The choices of neurotic people can tell us mostly what is good for keeping a neurosis stabilized, just as the choices of a brain injured man are good for preventing a catastrophic breakdown, or as the choices of an adrenalectomized animal may keep *him* from dying but would kill a healthy animal.

I think that this is the main reef on which most hedonistic value theories and ethical theories have foundered. Pathologically motivated pleasures cannot be averaged with healthily motivated pleasures.

Furthermore any ethical code will have to deal with the fact of constitutional differences not only in chickens and rats but also in men, as Sheldon (1942) and Morris (May et al., 1958) have shown. Some values are common to all (healthy) mankind, but also some other values will *not* be common to all mankind, but only to some types of people, or to specific individuals. What I have called the basic needs are probably common to all mankind and are, therefore, shared values. But idiosyncratic needs generate idiosyncratic values.

Constitutional differences in individuals generate preferences among ways of relating to self, and to culture and to the world, i.e., generate values. These researches support and are supported by the universal experience of clinicians with individual differences. This is also true of the ethnological data that makes sense of cultural diversity by postulating that each culture selects for exploitation, suppression, approval or disapproval, a small segment of the range of human constitutional possibilities. This is all in line with the biological data and theories and self-actualization theories which show that an organ system presses to express itself, in a word, to function. The muscular person likes to use his muscles, indeed, *has* to use them in order to self-actualize, and to achieve the subjective feeling of harmonious, uninhibited, satisfying functioning which is so important an aspect of psychological health. People with intelligence must use their intelligence, people with eyes must use their eyes, people with the capacity to love have the *impulse* to love and the *need* to love in order to feel healthy. Capacities clamor to be used, and cease their clamor only when they *are* used sufficiently. That is to say, capacities are needs, and therefore are intrinsic values as well. To the extent that capacities differ, so will values also differ.

BASIC NEEDS AND THEIR HIERARCHICAL ARRANGEMENT

It has by now been sufficiently demonstrated that the human being has, as part of his intrinsic construction, not only physiological needs, but also truly psychological ones. They may be considered as deficiencies which must be optimally fulfilled by the environment in order to avoid sickness and subjective ill-being. They can be called basic, or biological, and likened to the need for salt, or calcium or vitamin D because—

1. The deprived person yearns for their gratification persistently.
2. Their deprivation makes the person sicken and wither.
3. Gratifying them is therapeutic, curing the deficiency-illness.
4. Steady supplies forestall these illnesses.
5. Healthy (gratified) people do not demonstrate these deficiencies.

But these needs or values are related to each other in a hierarchical and developmental way, in an order of strength and of priority. Safety is a more prepotent, or stronger, more pressing, more vital need than love, for instance, and the need for food is usually stronger than either. Furthermore, all these basic needs may be considered to be simply steps along the path to general self-actualization, under which all basic needs can be subsumed.

By taking these data into account, we can solve many value

problems that philosophers have struggled with ineffectually for centuries. For one thing, it looks as if there were a single ultimate value for mankind, a far goal toward which all men strive. This is called variously by different authors self-actualization, self-realization, integration, psychological health, individuation, autonomy, creativity, productivity, but they all agree that this amounts to realizing the potentialities of the person, that is to say, becoming fully human, everything that the person *can* become.

But it is also true that the person himself does not know this. We, the psychologists observing and studying, have constructed this concept in order to integrate and explain lots of diverse data. So far as the person himself is concerned, all *he* knows is that he is desperate for love, and thinks he will be forever happy and content if he gets it. He does not know in advance that he will strive on *after* this gratification has come, and that gratification of one basic need opens consciousness to domination by another, "higher" need. So far as he is concerned, the absolute, ultimate value, synonymous with life itself, is whichever need in the hierarchy he is dominated by during a particular period. These basic needs or basic values therefore may be treated both as ends and as steps toward a single end-goal. It is true that there is a single, ultimate value or end of life and also it is just as true that we have a hierarchical and developmental system of values, complexly interrelated.

This also helps to solve the apparent paradox of contrast between Being and Becoming. It is true that human beings strive perpetually toward ultimate humanness, which itself may be anyway a different kind of Becoming and growing. It's as if we were doomed forever to try to arrive at a state to which we could never attain. Fortunately we now know this not to be true, or at least it is not the only truth. There is another truth which integrates with it. We are again and again rewarded for good Becoming by transient states of absolute Being, by peak-experiences. Achieving basic-need gratifications gives us many peak-experiences, each of which are absolute delights, perfect in themselves, and needing no more than themselves to validate life. This is like rejecting the notion that a Heaven lies someplace beyond the end of the path of life. Heaven, so to speak, lies waiting for us through life, ready to step into for a time and to enjoy before we have to come back to our ordinary life of striving. And once we have been in it, we can remember it forever, and feed ourselves on this memory and be sustained in times of stress.

Not only this, but the process of moment-to-moment growth is itself intrinsically rewarding and delightful in an absolute sense. If they are not mountain peak-experiences, at least they are foothill-experiences, little glimpses of absolute, self-validative delight, little moments of Being. Being and Becoming are not contradictory or mutually exclusive. Approaching and arriving are both in themselves rewarding.

I should make it clear here that I want to differentiate the Heaven ahead (of growth and transcendence) from the "Heaven" behind (of regression). The "high Nirvana" is quite different from the "low Nirvana" even though most clinicians confuse them (see also Weisskopf, 1958).

SELF-ACTUALIZATION: GROWTH

I have published in another place a survey of all the evidence that forces us in the direction of a concept of healthy growth or of self-actualizing tendencies (Maslow, 1954). This is partly deductive evidence in the sense of pointing out that unless we postulate such a concept, much of human behavior makes no sense. This is on the same scientific principle that led to the discovery of a hitherto unseen planet that *had* to be there in order to make sense of a lot of other observed data.

There is also some direct evidence, or rather the beginnings of direct evidence, which needs much more research to get to the point of certainty. The only direct study of self-actualizing people I know is the one I made, and it is a very shaky business to rest on just one study made by just one person when we take into account the known pitfalls of sampling error, of projection, etc. However, the conclusions of this study have been so strongly paralleled in the clinical and philosophical conclusions of Rogers, Fromm, Goldstein, Angyal, Murray, Moustakas, C. Buhler, Horney, Jung, Nuttin and many others that I shall proceed under the assumption that more careful research will not contradict my findings radically. We can certainly now assert that at least a reasonable, theoretical, and empirical case has been made for the presence within the human being of a tendency toward, or need for growing in a direction that can be summarized in general as self-actualization, or psychological health, and specifically as growth toward each and all of the sub-aspects of self-actualization, i.e., he has within him a pressure toward unity of personality, toward spontaneous expressiveness, toward full individuality and identity, toward seeing the truth rather than being blind, toward being creative, toward being good, and a lot else. That is, the human being is so constructed that he presses toward fuller and fuller being and this means pressing toward what most people would call good values, toward serenity, kindness, courage, honesty, love, unselfishness, and goodness.

Few in number though they be, we can learn a great deal about values from the direct study of these highly evolved, most mature, psychologically healthiest individuals, and from the study of the peak moments of average individuals, moments in which they become transiently self-actualized. This is because they are in very real empirical and theoretical ways, most fully human. For instance, they are people who have retained and developed their human capacities, especially those capacities which define the human being and differentiate him from, let us say, the monkey. (This accords with Hartman's (1959) axiological approach to the same problem of defining the good human being as the one who has more of the characteristics which define the concept "human being.") From a developmental point of view, they are more fully evolved because not fixated at immature or incomplete levels of growth. This is no more mysterious, or a priori, or question begging than the selection of a type specimen of butterfly by a taxonomist or the most physically healthy young man by the physician. They both look for the "perfect or mature or magnificent specimen" for the exemplar, and so have I. One procedure is as repeatable in principle as the other.

Full humanness can be defined not only in terms of the degree to which the definition of the concept "human" is fulfilled, i.e., the species norm. It also has a descriptive, cataloguing, measurable psychological definition. We now have from a few research beginnings and from countless clinical experiences some notion of the characteristics both of the fully evolved human being and of the well-growing human being. These characteristics are not only neutrally describable; they are also subjectively rewarding, pleasurable and reinforcing.

Among the objectively describable and measurable characteristics of the healthy human specimen are—

1. Clearer, more efficient perception of reality.
2. More openness to experience.
3. Increased integration, wholeness, and unity of the person.
4. Increased spontaneity, expressiveness; full functioning; aliveness.

5. A real self; a firm identity; autonomy, uniqueness.
6. Increased objectivity, detachment, transcendence of self.
7. Recovery of creativeness.
8. Ability to fuse concreteness and abstractness.
9. Democratic character structure.
10. Ability to love, etc.

These all need research confirmation and exploration but it is clear that such researches are feasible.

In addition, there are subjective confirmations or reinforcements of self-actualization or of good growth toward it. These are the feelings of zest in living, of happiness or euphoria, of serenity, of joy, of calmness, of responsibility, of confidence in one's ability to handle stresses, anxieties, and problems. The subjective signs of self-betrayal, of fixation, of regression, and of living by fear rather than by growth are such feelings as anxiety, despair, boredom, inability to enjoy, intrinsic guilt, intrinsic shame, aimlessness, feelings of emptiness, of lack of identity, etc.

These subjective reactions are also susceptible of research exploration. We have clinical techniques available for studying them.

It is the free choices of such self-actualizing people (in those situations where real choice is possible from among a variety of possibilities) that I claim can be descriptively studied as a naturalistic value system with which the hopes of the observer absolutely have nothing to do, i.e., it is "scientific." I do not say, "He ought to choose this or that," but only, "Healthy people, permitted to choose freely, are observed to choose this or that." This is like asking, "What are the values of the best human beings," rather than "What should be their values?" or, "What ought they be?" (Compare this with Aristotle's belief that "it is the things which are valuable and pleasant to a good man that are really valuable and pleasant.")

Furthermore, I think these findings can be generalized to most of the human species because it looks to me (and to others) as if most people (perhaps all) tend toward self-actualization (this is seen most clearly in the experiences in psychotherapy, expecially of the uncovering sort), and as if, in principle at least, most people are capable of self-actualization.

If the various extant religions may be taken as expressions of human aspiration, i.e., what people would like to become if only they could, then we can see here too a validation of the affirmation that all people yearn toward self-actualization or tend toward it. This is so because our description of the actual characteristics of self-actualizing people parallels at many points the ideals urged by the religions, e.g., the transcendence of self, the fusion of the true, the good and the beautiful, contribution to others, wisdom, honesty and naturalness, the transcendence of selfish and personal motivations, the giving up of "lower" desires in favor of "higher" ones, the easy differentiation between ends (tranquility, serenity, peace) and means (money, power, status), the decrease of hostility, cruelty and destructiveness and the increase of friendliness, kindness, etc.

1. One conclusion from all these free-choice experiments, from developments in dynamic motivation theory and from examination of psychotherapy, is a very revolutionary one that no other large culture had even arrived at, namely, that our deepest needs are not, in themselves, dangerous or evil or bad. This opens up the prospect of resolving the splits within the person between Apollonian and Dionysian, classical and romantic, scientific and poetic, between reason and impulse, work and play, verbal and preverbal, maturity and childlikeness, masculine and feminine, growth and regression.

2. The main social parallel to this change in our philosophy of human nature is the rapidly growing tendency to perceive the culture as an instrument of need-gratification as well as of frustration and control. We can now reject, as a localism, the almost universal mistake that the interests of the individual and of society are of *necessity* mutually exclusive and antagonistic, or that civilization is primarily a mechanism for controlling and policing human instinctoid impulses (Marcuse, 1955). All these age-old axioms are swept away by the new possibility of defining the main function of a healthy culture as the fostering of universal self-actualization.

3. In healthy people only is there a good correlation between subjective delight in the experience, impulse to the experience, or wish for it, and "basic need" for the experience (it's good for him in the long run). Only such people uniformly yearn for what is good for them and for others, and then are able wholeheartedly to enjoy it, and approve of it. For such people virtue is its own reward in the sense of being enjoyed in itself. They spontaneously tend to do right because that is what they *want* to do, what they *need* to do, what they enjoy, what they approve of doing, and what they will continue to enjoy.

It is this unity, this network of positive intercorrelation, that falls apart into separateness and conflict as the person gets psychologically sick. Then what he wants to do may be bad for him; even if he does it he may not enjoy it, even if he enjoys it, he may simultaneously disapprove of it, so that the enjoyment is itself poisoned or may disappear quickly. What he enjoys at first he may not enjoy later. His impulses, desires, and enjoyments then become a poor guide to living. He must accordingly mistrust and fear the impulses and the enjoyments which lead him astray, and so he is caught in conflict, dissociation, indecision; in a word, he is caught in civil war.

So far as philosophical theory is concerned, many historical dilemmas and contradictions are resolved by this finding. Hedonistic theory does work for healthy people; it does not work for sick people. The true, the good and the beautiful do correlate some, but only in healthy people do they correlate strongly.

4. Self-actualization is a relatively achieved "state of affairs" in a few people. In most people, however, it is rather a hope, a yearning, a drive, a "something" wished for but not yet achieved, showing itself clinically as drive toward health, integration, growth, etc. The projective tests are also able to detect these trends as potentialities rather than as overt behavior, just as an X-ray can detect incipient pathology before it has appeared on the surface.

This means for us that that which the person *is* and that which the person *could be* exist simultaneously for the psychologist, thereby resolving the dichotomy between Being and Becoming. Potentialities not only *will* be or could be; they also *are.* Self-actualization values as goals exist and are real even though not yet actualized. The human being is simultaneously that which he is and that which he yearns to be.

GROWTH AND ENVIRONMENT

Man demonstrates *in his own nature* a pressure toward fuller and fuller Being, more and more perfect actualization of his humanness in exactly the same naturalistic, scientific sense that an acorn may be said to be "pressing toward" being an oak tree, or that a tiger can be observed to "push toward" being tigerish, or a horse toward being equine. Man is ultimately not molded or shaped into humanness, or taught to be human. The role of the environment is ultimately to permit him or help him to actualize *his own* potentialities, not *its* potentialities. The environment does not give him potentialities and capacities; he *has* them in inchoate or embryonic form, just exactly as he has embryonic arms and legs. And creativeness, spontaneity, selfhood, authenticity, caring for others, being able to love, yearning for truth are embryonic potentialities belonging to his species-membership just as much as his arms and legs and brain and eyes.

This is not in contradiction to the data already amassed which shows clearly that living in a family and in a culture are absolutely necessary to *actualize* these psychological potentials that define humanness. Let us avoid this conclusion. A teacher or a culture doesn't create a human being. It doesn't implant within him the ability to love, or to be curious, or to philosophize, or to symbolize, or to be creative. Rather it permits, or fosters, or encourages or helps what exists in embryo to become real and actual. The same mother or the same culture, treating a kitten or a puppy in exactly the same way, cannot make it into a human being. The culture is sun and food and water: it is not the seed.

"INSTINCT" THEORY

The group of thinkers who have been working with self-actualization, with self, with authentic humanness, etc., have pretty firmly established their case that man has a tendency to realize himself. By implication he is exhorted to be true to his own nature, to trust himself, to be authentic, spontaneous, honestly expressive, to look for the sources of his action in his own deep inner nature.

But, of course, this is an ideal counsel. They do not sufficiently warn that most adults don't know how to be authentic and that, if they "express" themselves, they may bring catastrophe not only upon themselves but upon others as well. What answer must be given to the rapist or the sadist who asks "Why should I too not trust and express myself?"

These thinkers as a group have been remiss in several respects. They have implied without making explicit that if you can behave authentically, you will behave well, that if you emit action from within, it will be good and right behavior. What is very clearly implied is that this inner core, this real self, is good, trustworthy, ethical. This is an affirmation that is clearly separable from the affirmation that man actualizes himself, and needs to be separately proven (as I think it will be). Furthermore, these writers have as a group very definitely ducked the crucial statement about this inner core, i.e., that it must in some degree be inherited or else everything else they say is so much hash.

In other words, we must grapple with "instinct" theory or, as I prefer to call it, basic need theory, that is to say, with the study of the original, intrinsic, in part heredity-determined needs, urges, wishes and, I may say, values of mankind. We can't play both the biology game and the sociology game simultaneously. We can't affirm both that culture does everything and anything, and that man has an inherent nature. The one is incompatible with the other.

And of all the problems in this area of instinct, the one of which we know least and should know most is that of aggression, hostility, hatred, and destructiveness. The Freudians claim this to be instinctive; most other dynamic psychologists claim it to be not directly instinctive, but rather an ever-present reaction to frustration of instinctoid or basic needs. The truth is that we don't really know. Clinical experience hasn't settled the problem because equally good clinicians come to these divergent conclusions. What we need is hard, firm research.

THE PROBLEMS OF CONTROL AND LIMITS

Another problem confronting the morals-from-within theorists is to account for the easy self-discipline which is customarily found in self-actualizing, authentic, genuine people and which is not found in average people.

In these healthy people we find duty and pleasure to be the same thing, as is also work and play, self-interest and altruism, individualism and selflessness. We know they are that way, but not how they get that way. I have the strong intuition that such authentic, fully human persons are the actualization of what many human beings could be. And yet we are confronted with the sad fact that so few people achieve this goal, perhaps only one in a hundred, or two hundred. We can be hopeful for mankind because in principle anybody could become a good and healthy man. But we must also feel sad because so few actually do become good men. If we wish to find out why some do and some don't, then the research problem presents itself of studying the life history of self-actualizing men to find out how they get that way.

We know already that the main prerequisite of healthy growth is gratification of the basic needs. (Neurosis is very often a deficiency disease, like avitaminosis.) But we have also learned that unbridled indulgence and gratification has its own dangerous consequences, e.g., psychopathic personality, "orality," Irresponsibility, inability to bear stress, spoiling, immaturity, certain character disorders. Research findings are rare but there is now available a large store of clinical and educational experience which allows us to make a reasonable guess that the young child needs not only gratification; he needs also to learn the limitations that the physical world puts upon his gratifications, and he has to learn that other human beings seek for gratifications, too, even his mother and father, i.e., they are not only means to his ends. This means control, delay, limits, renunciation, frustration-tolerance and discipline. Only to the self-disciplined and responsible person can we say, "Do as you will, and it will probably be all right."

REGRESSIVE FORCES: PSYCHOPATHOLOGY

We must also face squarely the problem of what stands in the way of growth; that is to say, the problems of cessation of growth and evasion of growth, of fixation, regression, and defensiveness, in a word the attractiveness of psychopathology, or as other people would prefer to say, the problem of evil.

Why do so many people have no real identity, so little power to make their own decisions and choices?

1. These impulses and directional tendencies toward self-fulfillment, though instinctive, are very weak, so that, in contrast with all other animals who have strong instincts, these impulses are very easily drowned out by habit, by wrong cultural attitudes toward them, by traumatic episodes, by erroneous education. Therefore, the problem of choice and of responsibility is far, far more acute in humans than in any other species.

2. There has been a special tendency in Western culture, historically determined, to assume that these instinctoid needs of the human being, his so-called animal nature, are bad or evil. As a consequence, many cultural institutions are set up for the express purpose of controlling, inhibiting, suppressing and repressing this original nature of man.

3. There are two sets of forces pulling at the individual, not just one. In addition to the pressures forward toward health, there are also fearful-regressive pressures backward, toward sickness and weakness. We can either move forward toward a "high Nirvana" or backward to a "low Nirvana."

Psychological Data and Human Values

I think the main factual defect in the value theories and ethical theories of the past and the present has been insufficient know-ledge of psychopathology and psychotherapy. Throughout history, learned men have set out before mankind the rewards of virtue, the beauties of goodness, the intrinsic desirability of psychological health and self-fulfillment, and yet most people perversely refuse to step into the happiness and self-respect that is offered them. Nothing is left to the teachers but irritation, impatience, disillu-sionment, alternations between scolding, exhortation and hope-lessness. A good many have thrown up their hands altogether and talked about original sin or intrinsic evil and concluded that man could be saved only by extra-human forces.

Meanwhile there lies available the huge, rich, and illuminating literature of dynamic psychology and psychopathology, a great store of information on man's weaknesses, and fears. We know much about *why* men do wrong things, *why* they bring about their own unhappiness and their self-destruction, *why* they are perverted and sick. And out of this has come the insight that human evil is largely (though not altogether) human weakness or ignorance, understandable and also curable.

I find it sometimes amusing, sometimes saddening that so many scholars and scientists, so many philosophers and theologians, who talk about human values, of good and evil, proceed in complete disregard of the plain fact that professional psychotherapists every day, as a matter of course, change and improve human nature, help people to become more strong, virtuous, creative, kind, lov-ing, altruistic, serene. These are only some of the consequences of improved self-knowledge and self-acceptance. There are many others as well that can come in greater or lesser degree (Maslow, 1954; Rogers, 1960).

The subject is far too complex even to touch here. All I can do is draw a few conclusions for value theory.

1. Self-knowledge seems to be the major path of self-improve-ment, though not the only one.

2. Self-knowledge and self-improvement is very difficult for most people. It usually needs great courage and long struggle.

3. Though the help of a skilled professional therapist makes this process much easier, it is by no means the only way. Much that has been learned from therapy can be applied to education, to family life, and to the guidance of one's own life.

4. Only by such study of psychopathology and therapy can one learn a proper respect for and appreciation of the forces of fear, of

regression, of defense, of safety. Respecting and understanding these forces makes it much more possible to help oneself and others to grow toward health. False optimism sooner or later means disillusionment, anger and hopelessness.

5. To sum up, we can never really understand human weakness without also understanding its healthy trends. Otherwise we make the mistake of pathologizing everything. But also we can never fully understand or help human strength without also understanding its weaknesses. Otherwise we fall into the errors of overoptimistic reliance on rationality alone.

If we wish to help humans to become more fully human, we must realize not only that they try to realize themselves but that they are also reluctant or afraid or unable to do so. Only by fully appreciating this dialectic between sickness and health can we help to tip the balance in favor of health.

REFERENCES

Cannon, W. B. *Wisdom of the Body.* New York: Norton, 1932.

Dove, W. F. A study of individuality in the nutritive instincts. *American Naturalist,* 1935, *69*: 469-544.

Hartman, R. The science of value. In A. H. Maslow (Ed.) *New Knowledge in Human Values.* New York: Harper, 1959.

Marcuse, H. *Eros and Civilization.* Boston: Beacon, 1955.

Maslow, A. H. *Motivation and Personality.* New York: Harper, 1954.

May, R., et al. (Eds.) *Existence.* New York: Basic Books, 1958.

Rogers, C. R. *A Therapist's View of Personal Goals.* Wallingford, Pennsylvania: Pendle Hill Pamphlets, 1960.

Sheldon, W. H. *The Varieties of Temperament.* New York: Harper, 1942.

Weisskopf, W. Existence and values. In A. H. Maslow (Ed.) *New Knowledge in Human Values,* New York: Harper, 1959.

Young, P. T. *Motivation and Emotion.* New York: Wiley, 1961.

26

ETHICS, ETHOS AND ACTUALIZATION

Nathan Adler, Ph.D.

The intense interest in the marathon and Gestalt therapies is more an expression of a new social movement than of a scientific dialogue. This opinion is reinforced by the assertion, made by a leader of marathon therapy at the 1968 annual convention of the American Psychological Association, that this new movement could remake the world. These therapies differentiate themselves from older therapies by their proud assertion that they are "not detached, cool, and objective"; they encourage "constructive aggression" and "marital fighting" and focus upon and support the active role of the change agent who acknowledges that he finds a stage for his own self-realization. They repudiate conflict models, or social pressure models, and see instead a process that abjures "adjustment" and "insight," or "maturity," for a process of "growth," "risk taking," and "stepping into the unknown."

What shall we assume about their time perspective? What do they make of past, present, and future? Is the 24-hour marathon therapy session with its "excitement," "intimacy," and "reciprocity," experienced as immediate involvement and "happenings?"

The last five years have seen a growing enthusiasm and a proliferation of new therapeutic schools and techniques under the banner of encounter therapy, marathon therapy, Gestalt therapy, leaderless, sensitivity training groups, and the behavior therapies. At the same time, criticism of older "established" models and

From *The Underground Stream: New Life Styles and the Antinomian Personality* [New York: Harper & Row, 1972], pp. 107-123. © 1972 by Nathan Adler. Reprinted by permission of the publisher.

schools has been intensified. We are confronted not only with the enthusiasm of the new practitioners and consumers, but with widespread and mounting concern for the issues of ethical standards in the practice of psychology. The challenge to the validity of the "medical model" (Szasz, Albee and others) and the alternative "sociological," "existential," and humanistic models are fundamental issues that extend beyond the policing functions of a guild or profession.

A rather constricted view, and one that I believe falsifies the underlying problems, orients itself solely to the ethical issue. The following statement appeared in the March 1968 issue of *The American Psychologist:*

The science and profession of psychology change, and the ethical standards and procedures must reflect such change. Are the ethical standards as currently written sufficient to deal with current practices in consumer and industrial psychology, behavior modification based on principles of learning and reinforcement, and a variety of new group procedures and techniques?

In order to consider revisions of the ethical standards, the Committee on Scientific and Professional Ethics and Conduct calls for examples of incidents of current practice so that it can bring its standards up to date. Psychologists have been aware of their need to deal with urgent and changing problems in relation to selective service, the expanding adolescent population, special services associated with drug roles and drug abuse, the sex "revolution," and similar current sources of stress. Many have been dismayed by therapists who offer LSD to adolescent patients or challenge and chide the patient's fear of loss of control. Some have wondered whether the techniques of theater of the absurd and the alienation effects of Brecht are appropriate in the practice in Gestalt therapy, psychodrama, and the encounter therapies.

Partisans of these newer methods have countered such questions by challenging what they construe as the authoritarian role of the "establishment." They invoke rhetorical appeals to academic freedom, to the defense of innovation, progress, and growth, and see themselves as contemporary Galileos confronting the eternal inquisitors of the establishment.

The issue raised by these new modes and the problems that ensue cannot be resolved by procedures that review and modify the ethical code of a profession. Such innovations assert psychological values and roles that are also epidemic in the larger community. Slogans of self-actualization and self-realization have become modish on many campuses and have become a rationale for the hippie scene. The assertion of these values can be seen in the call to the 1968 Annual Workshop of the American Academy of Psychotherapy:

The theme of the 1968 Annual Workshop is personal (not professional) growth of the psychotherapies—the theme, in brief, of *A New Beginning.* We are proposing in this theme that, in addition to our usual concerns with enlarging technique, and discovering growth-impasses that obstruct our work through the encountering that is part of the workshop, that we share with one another our secrets.

The secrets refer to the ways in which we keep ourselves alive, zestful, growing persons in a social system that grinds one down if one lets it; the ways in which we enlarge ourselves as entire persons, rather than letting our social and professional functions devour us. Thus, we hope that people will share and show such matters as ways of becoming more vitally embodied; ways of mediating new ways to be a psychotherapist.

I, for one, believe that the times are calling for a new profession, a westernized version of the eastern guru; the guide and teacher and exemplar who can help oversocialized people get out of their roles and minds and fixated values in order to become "reborn" — again and again and again. I think that we psychotherapists may be the professionals who can most readily grow to that status. At least many of our patients (I now call them "fellow-seekers") are asking us to help them discover new potentialities beyond those activated by usual (or deviant) socialization. I believe we can best train ourselves experimentally, through encounters with gurus of our own choosing, through various "ways of growth," and through sharing our findings and experiences.

Can we cope with the issues raised by this appeal within the framework of ethical problems and the modification of an ethical code? Shall committees review ethical codes with each new-look therapeutic procedure? An ethical code that is so tendentious that it reflects only short-term goals and standards quickly becomes obsolete. It is open to question whether we are confronted with an obsolete and inadequate code or whether the issue, as an "ethical" problem, is a pseudo-issue that displaces the basic problem and deflects us from the significant area of concern. An ethical code for effective governance cannot be a particularized manual. Rather, it should assert broad and general values central to the profession and the community of which the profession is a part. It should be an open-ended system defined ideally not by specific rules, but by the accumulation of cases and traditions in a "common law."

Whether techniques are modified or innovations are assimilated, it should be possible to affirm the central and basic values of a profession independent of "schools." Unless these basic values are themselves challenged such a consensus is possible. A code based upon commonly held values can define a body of principles rather than regulations. Certainly there should appear to be common assent to such principles as that the welfare of the client is the primary concern of the professional psychologist. The psychologist is always concerned with safeguarding his client's welfare and will never act in an exploitative or self-aggrandizing way in relations with his client. Principles further can establish boundaries of competence and integrity that delineate the components of adequate training with the knowledge available in the field. They also can acknowledge that the profession as the guardian and transmitter of knowledge and as the source of sanction that gives the individual his authority, his status, and his license must be protected. This is not to assert merely guild behavior and guild standards. To protect the identity of a profession is to protect and keep uncontaminated the profession's source of knowledge.

Such a view is defensible when shared and common values do exist. If psychologists share a common vocabulary and model and if their procedures and operations are accepted as derived from such a model, they would not be forced into polemical issues formulated as the defense of academic freedom or of innovation and creativity against the vitiating bonds of the bureaucratic "establishment." Certainly such abuses are potential. We are aware, for example, despite Freud's views about nonmedical psychoanalysts, of the guild practices of the American Psychoanalytic Association. The attacks against the innovative procedures of Sister Kenny in the treatment of poliomyelitis are cited as an example of the dangers of such reactionary political power that tries to pass as the defense of science. And we are often reminded by the new enthusiasts of Freud's struggle against the established university and clinical authorities. But, if this last instance is to be used to make a case, it should be clear that the issue was not an ethical problem but the introduction of a new paradigm that altered the fundamental perspectives of the scientific community.

If we examine Jourard's appeal for a new profession and his call to become "reborn," we are confronted not with the problem of ethics, but with a rejection of the central ethos that makes the fabric of meaning for a culture. The new therapies can be understood as symptoms, not as treatment procedures. They express an antinomian crisis in psychotherapy which is similar to that expressed in the drug and sex scenes and in existential theologies and resurgent mysticism. In some professional circles Tarot cards and astrology are accepted as offering a valid conceptual framework for the study of man.

We are not concerned with the problem of quacks who offer shortcuts and panaceas. Such problems are perennial, and attempts to curb quacks' activities and to protect the public are always ineffective because those who seek magic will continue to find ways to bestow their patronage. Nor are we faced only with the same old resistances and hostility to the constructs of psychoanalysis. We always have these with us, though they may now use the new modes to reinstate the discarded techniques of suggestion, abreaction, and catharsis. (Some of the new psychotherapies use techniques of rapid intervention, but these procedures often depend upon inferences derived from psychoanalysis.)

We are instead considering those new therapies which are a flight from psychoanalysis. These therapies are a response to the disappointment and overenthusiastic acceptance of psychoanalysis in the 1930s and 1940s, when psychoanalysis was becoming Americanized. The new therapies seek solutions in either technocratic scientism or in recoil from rational secular values, both of which are part of the climate of this time.

The alienation is apparent when the underlying issues of ethics and the new therapies question the validity of the parameters within which psychotherapy has customarily operated. Wordsworth defined poetry as "emotion remembered in tranquility." This statement, I believe, can stand as well as a definition for psychotherapy. In a culture in equilibrium mutuality of contract is assumed. It does not have to be improvised or extracted by exercises of touching, rehearsals of role-playing, or the pseudo-communion of orgies. In a stable culture the self is defined as much by its limits and renunciations as by its releases and discharges. It does not seek epiphanies and actualization. When the culture is not questioned, both patient and therapist accept as given the structure of the world and the legitimacy of their assigned status and role position. They see their task as finding a way back into the social fabric that is the "nature" of the world and of "natural" behavior.

The problem at the heart of the nihilistic ethos, the other face of enthusiasm and mysticism—and this is the crucial issue, not the technology of psychotherapy—is the repudiation of ideas, abstractions, and theories that give meaning to a universe. The myths and rituals by which man construes his person and his place have lost their power. Nietzsche described the situation as that which occurs "when man begins to doubt cognitive modes of experience and the law of causation seems to suspend itself." The individual's body image is threatened with dissolution, his spatial sense and identity becomes ambiguous and unstable, and his figure-ground relation to his surroundings becomes confused and uncertain. It is a process of depersonalization and unselving. The hippies themselves speak of "ego death."

It is in this context that we must consider the return to the abreaction model and the rejection of rational insight-at-a-distance perspectives. It is not only disappointment with the results of psychotherapy that is the issue, but also the loss of morale and the transvaluation of ethos. A professional and scientific transaction would be an expression of analytic rigor rather than of ideology and morale. It would systematically scrutinize "anomalies" and try to account for them on theoretical grounds. Modifications in procedure would be a function of corrections in theory as these anomalous incidents were incorporated within an adequate theory.

If we see the issue as one of an ethical code, which sections must we change? What do we wish to modify in the definition of acceptable and good practice? What are the changing boundaries of integrity and competence?

Kuhn's study *The Structure of Scientific Revolution* argues that "normal science" presupposes a conceptual and instrumental paradigm accepted by an entire scientific community.

Kuhn remarks that "normal science proceeds without rules only so long as the relevant scientific community accepts without question the particular problem-solution already achieved." It is clear that rules and standards of practice are a function of the underlying model invoked and that rules become an issue whenever models are challenged. It is such a situation that we now face. The new modes in psychotherapy express, beyond the customary resistance, processes which reflect both a direct expression of the contemporary ideological crisis and some positive factors that are a measure of the changing perspectives of the scientific community. If we can differentiate these factors, we can more effectively clarify the issues of ethics, ethos, and methodology.

He examines the crises which cannot be resolved within these models and the ways in which these lead to new models and refinements of theory. His historic examination and the regularities he posits in the development of scientific changes are relevant to our present concerns and can illuminate our problems.

According to Kuhn, problems, standards, and legitimate methods are perceived univocally when one model is dominant. Schools become differentiated when standards, methods, and choice of problems are under attack and the validity of the stabilized model is challenged and debated. The more precise and meticulous the model, the more sensitive an indicator it provides of those anomalous results which theory may not have predicted or cannot account for. It is an attempt to account for these anomalies that theoretical and procedural modifications that lead to the change of the paradigm are undertaken.

In examining the psychological innovations now being promulgated, we must question the systematic context from which they derive and the anomalies in experimental and clinical data of which they are aware and which they believe the established models cannot explain. What are the refinements in theory and in prediction and explanation that these innovative procedures claim to achieve?

Kuhn notes that one measure of a scientific crisis and one of its typical effects is the tendency to return to elements antecedent to the established model. The reversion to systems of abreaction, suggestion, and catharsis, questioned since the 1920s, is an expression of the crises facing the psychotherapeutic model. Usually a novel theory emerges after pronounced and persistent failure of the paradigm in the normal problem-solving activity in which the discipline is engaged. But in psychology, given the variability of our training and the competition between schools, can we assert that failure is a function of the model? Or is it the range of training standards in the various "schools"? Given data can be subsumed under alternate theoretical constructs, and so long as the tools work adequately, one is not compelled to seek alternatives. The demand for retooling, the blurring of the paradigm, and the loosening of the rules for normal research are other indicators of the developing crisis. The crisis will be resolved with the emergence of a new paradigm.

Kuhn demonstrates that the crisis period in these scientific revolutions is marked by individual, eccentric, estranged behavior. Practitioners commit themselves to new perspectives and new institutional frameworks. Polarization occurs, communication breaks down, and there is no longer a shared vocabulary or framework to adjust differences. Does the question of ethics arise when the real issue is the choice of competing, or uncompatible, models which we have failed to make explicit? The choice cannot be determined by evaluating procedures of the "normal" model since it is the model which is the issue. As a consequence, we become involved in sterile, futile polemics and debate. Each group uses its model to argue in its model's defense, invokes the rhetoric of polemic and persuasion rather than evidence, and asserts aesthetic orientations rather than data. Instead of talking of logic and evidence, they offer testimonials and manifestos.

Models have normative as well as cognitive functions. The facts, operations, and measurements that scientists manipulate are not raw data, "given" experience. They are an abstraction, which is preselected as a function of a specific model, and a product of specific styles of perception. As Kuhn observed, "Far more clearly than the immediate experience from which they in part derive, operations and measurements are paradigm-determined." It follows then that scientists with different paradigms engage in different manipulations. Their activity and perception is rooted in constructs. Different models involve differently ordered universes. "Proponents of competing paradigms practice their trades in different worlds; they see different things when they look from the same point in the same direction."

Kuhn concludes that neither proof nor error is at issue. The transfer of allegiance from one to another model is essentially a conversion experience. Resistance to such conversion is not necessarily a violation of scientific standards; it is an expression of the feeling that the older model will solve the problems and puzzles and that by precise work the difficulties can be isolated and overcome. This "orthodoxy" can only be countered if it can be demonstrated that the new model solves anomalies, quantifies more precisely, and is more elegant.

ANTINOMIAN THERAPIES

Have the new therapies, as alternatives to the traditional methods, offered such data, or have we heard instead testimonials that tell more of evangelical zeal than they do of scientific conduct? The new therapies, with styles and values consonant with the current hippie ethos, are themselves more symptoms than cure.

Modish ideologies of self-actualization and self-realization encourage experimentation with drugs, sexual hyperactivity, and spiritual exercises in the name of new life styles to counter the loss of boundaries, the identity of confusion and diffusion that are parts of the process of unselving and renewal with which the drug counter culture is involved.

In humanist and existentialist therapies, "marathon" and "encounter" groups, and sensitivity training self-help groups, pathology and acting-out find sanction. We cannot speak of specific procedures and techniques of intervention and their underlying strategies until we differentiate psychotherapy as ideological commitment from psychotherapy as theoretically grounded scientific procedure.

The choice of therapist or therapeutic school is often an irrational procedure. It may be the expression of the symptom and the choice of defense. Some individuals do seek therapists and modes within the Establishment and indicate by their choice their wish to reject certain roles. Others turn to the "new-look" therapies not so much to initiate a "cure" as to legitimate their acting-out and to find a larger stage upon which to amplify their symptoms. These therapies offer the same alienation disguised as affect and the same uprooting rationalized as acts of release and pseudo-control. Unless a case can be made for homeopathic strategies in psychotherapy, these procedures are more malady than remedy.

One of the fundamental axioms of "established" psychotherapy is that therapy takes place within a framework of deprivation and that the patient's wishes are not to be indulged or gratified. It is characteristic of the antinomian therapies that they are driven to overcome insensibility and unselving by indiscriminate consumption of sensations.

The devouring of sensation is a characteristic hippie motivation. It is reflected in the phrase to be "turned on," whether to another person, to faceless sex, to drugs, to rock and roll, or to God.

Because one is essentially uninvolved, one reaches, by means of drugs, light shows, or rock and roll, for immediacy and a sense of presence. If one can achieve a sense of presence, one can then establish both the field and the boundaries of the self.

One of the flower children in the Haight-Ashbury, an eager spectator to the drama of fire engines, ladders, and a burning building, exclaimed, "Wow, I smelled *real* smoke!" Similarly, I heard a hippie eagerly exclaim, "I tasted tear gas!" Such primitive responses indicate either stimulus hunger or an effort to overcome the refractory phase produced by satiation. They represent one form of the "peak experiences," of the "B type of cognition," to which Maslow refers. Maslow and these hippies all refer to the total attention, fascination, and absorption in which "the figure becomes all figure and the ground, in effect, disappears" and in which "the percept had become for the moment the whole of Being." Both express syncretic thinking, fusion, and isolation rather than individuation, differentiation, and objectification. Maslow defines a "peak experience" as a situation in which the subject "perceives the world as if it were independent of him and of all human beings." This is not so much a definition of a peak experience as of a "happening" in an empty field.

Individuation is one of the basic goals of therapy. But individuation (and differentiation of self and object) requires postponement, delay, inhibition, and time binding—all of which are necessary to achieve a social self, control over impulses, and capacity to cope with objects.

Today, as in former times of turbulence, values are shifting and unstable, and cognitive modes of experience and laws of causality appear to be suspended. The givenness of the appropriate ratio of impulse gratification and control is challenged. A sound theory of therapy makes a place for release and control. It seeks the widest range of both individuation *and* socialization.

Therapy that is oriented toward the release of impulses focuses on the private self. Therapy oriented toward control focuses on the social self and its relation to the community of others. All therapies place themselves on the continuum between these two poles. In my opinion, the ideal therapeutic system is one which permits the widest range.

It is no longer fashionable in the circle of naked marathon therapy to maintain that it appears to be a useful therapeutic goal to support the growth of the ego as administrator and negotiator between impulse and the other, rather than to encourage total surrender to impulse or total submission to the other. Therapy implies a system of mediation rather than merely games of release. But to what ends and what goals? Accepting status and role position as "natural" requires the internalization of a culture. When commitment to a plausible and viable public can no longer be acknowledged, the orgy becomes the basis for communion and the prototype of the community. Private "rights" supersede civic "rituals."

The antinomian character, a product of both alienation and loss, is an adaptive groping towards new forms of value and integration. It is expressed in the ideologies of confrontation and encounter therapy, in many of the alleged sensitivity-training sessions in which blindfolded subjects grope for texture and touch in a charade that mirrors their actual disorientation and loss of "contact," and in marathon therapies that encourage physical assault and examination of the secretions of nose and ear.

Proponents of self-actualization maintain that their ethos is to replace the ethos of the "well-adjusted man"; the self-actualizer would become the ideal for our age as the saint, the hero, the gentleman, the knight and the mystic were for other ages. But it should be noted that these earlier images are defined in terms of roles, whereas the self-actualizer has no functional role and no referent other than the encapsulated self. It is this lack of role definition that characterizes the antinomian character and the underlying alienation. The uprooted self is either spectator or possessed actor, but the interrelated functions of self as agent and self as agency remain unbridged.

The demand that one remain true to one's reified, inner nature (that pure spirit imprisoned in the flesh) is an assertion that can only grow out of a polarization and rupture of the constructs of self and other. This demand tells more about the politics of confrontation and encounter than about a psychology of the self and the ways it develops in a social field.

If words like "self" and "transcendence" are to be assimilated into a scientific vocabulary and dialogue, rather than echoing an ancient gnostic dualism, they must have a social reference. And if, as an achievement of self-actualization or self-realization, one is to transcend the person, can transcendence mean anything other than self-limitation, the accommodation to the other, and the awareness and consciousness that are a function of this limitation? As Schachtel remarks, "the doubt and search for identity always go together with alienation from others and from the world around us," and "the preoccupation with reified identity directs attention away from what [one] *does* to what [one] supposedly *is* and releases one from responsibility and obligation."

It is a basic goal of all schools of psychotherapy to help the individual achieve perspective, to see himself as others see him, to differentiate the components of the self as the spectator and actor, and to distinguish the self as agent from the self as agency. Perhaps the key difference is that where older therapies speak of differentiation, the self-actualizing therapies imply dissociation, and see dissociation as a positive value. Self-actualization, or the psychology of being, appears to be enmeshed in a dualistic ethos. On the one hand, self-actualization seeks to overcome primitive, behavioristic, stimulus-response models and to replace them with an organismic orientation and a systems approach to the study of personality. If self-actualization sustained such a position, it might help create that psychology of affect of which we still understand so little. Instead, it becomes entwined, and is even further distorted by its enthusiastic disciples, in a secular evangelism that in the encounter therapies is committed solely to drive-release and expressions of other-directed conformism. A vocabulary influenced by and borrowed from Maslow is used to justify models of diffusion and release and strategies of kicks and being turned-on. If the intention was to reassert the values of impulse acceptance and to clarify the fears people have in encountering and acknowledging their drives, these values would be within the mainstream of psychotherapy and its psychology. But instead, the gnostic bias leads alternately to hyperactivism, detachment, and to quietism. In maintaining that they are living rather than preparing to live, the self-actualizers become constricted to a psychology of "spontaneous" happenings. Their hedonism is associated with the sense that they cannot really influence their lives. Fatalism dons hedonistic clothes, and they bow to "destiny" and toy with an astrology that is half shamefaced conviction and half put-on. As they say, "Everyone has his Karma."

The less bizarre of the new therapies do call to our attention the fact that therapy is not an informational and explanatory process alone, but an emotional experience and resolution. But an emotional experience implies no *folie à deux* and no reciprocal, symmetrical interchange. Verbal, analytic, conceptual devices may not be the only means for inducing conduct reorganization and behavior change. But the appeal to raw experience prior to concepts and abstractions merely involves other implicit concepts and abstractions which, since they remain unexamined, may be even more vitiating. Among these implicit concepts are the reified self, its biologic and nonsocial nature, an a priori commitment to the Dionysian as opposed to Apollonian values, and a psychology of release, abreaction, and catharsis that is a reversion to the cruder techniques of the early years of the century. Old resistances return in the name of innovation.

An "old saw" has it that one pays the doctor because he knows what not to do. As I listen to the enthusiasm of my students speaking of self-actualization and self-realization, it seems important to call attention to these ideological movements as dead ends rather than as progressive developments in psychotherapy or psychology. Even before naked marathon therapy, it was possible to report on the Emperor's new clothes.

The hippie scene requires no new techniques or special modifications. As I have suggested, the choice of therapist or school is itself often symptomatic. If the therapist is sensitive and tactful, he always refrains from imposing his own values and biases. But what is crucial is the achievement of a mutuality that is usually assumed in a culture but which can no longer be taken for granted. And most important, it cannot be wooed by substitutes of physical touch and gratification. Mutuality can be achieved in the quiet offer of acceptance and of recognition of the patient's otherness just as it can be lost and disrupted if the therapist is critical and frightened and has to impose "establishment" values on the patient. It can also be lost when the boundaries between patient and therapist break down. We should adopt the rule of the life guard at the public beach, "Reach, throw, row—then go." One need not agree with the patient so long as one hears what he says and recognizes him. But even more important, one must acknowledge the need for a unitary system of belief which is the ground of a culture, and for a common vocabulary for personal and corporate existence which defines *identity* and *public* and *membership*. Both patient and therapist must honestly commit themselves to this task.

REFERENCES

Albee, G. W. The Clinical Psychologist *Newsletter,* Division 12, American Psychological Association, *20* (1968).

Federn, Ernst. "How Freudian are the Freudians?" *Journal of the History of Behavioral Sciences* (July 1967), pp. 269-281.

Gollan, Stuart E. "Committee on Professional Ethics and Conduct," *Amer. Psychologist, 23, 2* (1968): 210-211.

Jourard, Sidney, Department of Psychology, University of Florida.

Kuhn, Thomas S. *The Structure of Scientific Revolutions.* Chicago: University of Chicago Press, 1962.

Maslow, Abraham A. *Towards a Psychology of Being.* Princeton, N.J.: Van Nostrand, 1962.

Nietzsche, Friedrich. *The Birth of Tragedy.* New York: Doubleday, 1956.

Schachtel, Ernest. "On Alienated Concepts of Identity." *The American Journal of Psychoanalysis, 121, 2* (November 1961): 120-131.

27

SOME CONSTRUCTIVE FEATURES
OF THE CONCEPT OF SIN

O. Hobart Mowrer, Ph.D.

As long as one adheres to the theory that psychoneurosis implies no moral responsibility, no error, no misdeed on the part of the afflicted person, one's vocabulary can, of course, remain beautifully objective and "scientific." But as soon as there is so much as a hint of personal accountability in the situation, such language is, at the very least, wide of the mark and, conceivably, quite misleading. Therefore, if "moral judgment" does enter the picture, one might as well beard the lion and use the strongest term of all, *sin*. This is the strategy involved in the present and following chapter.

But there is also a deeper objective here. "Sickness," as we shall see increasingly in later chapters [of *The Crisis in Psychiatry and Religion*], is a concept which generates pervasive pessimism and confusion in the domain of psychopathology; whereas sin, for all its harshness, carries an implication of promise and hope, a vision of new potentialities. Just so long as we deny the reality of sin, we cut ourselves off, it seems, from the possibility of radical redemption ("recovery").

In some ways it is perhaps not surprising that we are assembled here today to explore the question of whether real guilt, or

---

One of four papers comprising a symposium on "The Role of the Concept of Sin in Psychotherapy" held at the 1959 meeting of the American Psychological Association, in Cincinnati, Ohio (*American Psychologist*, 1959, 14: 356) and later published in the *Journal of Counseling Psychology*, 1960, 7: 185-188. This paper has also appeared, without authorization, in *Catholic Mind*, 1960, 58: 151-155.

sin, is relevant to the problem of psychopathology and psychotherapy. For half a century now we psychologists, as a profession, have very largely followed the Freudian doctrine that human beings become emotionally disturbed, not because of their having done anything palpably wrong, but because they instead lack insight. Therefore, as would-be therapists we have set out to oppose the forces of repression and to work for understanding. And what *is* this understanding, or insight, which we so highly prize? It is the discovery that the patient or client has been, in effect, *too* good; that he has within him impulses, especially those of lust and hostility, which he has been quite unnecessarily inhibiting. And health, we tell him, lies in the direction of recognizing and expressing these impulses.

But there are now widespread and, indeed, ominous signs that this logic and the practical strategies it seems to demand are ill-founded. The situation is, in fact, so grave that, as our presence here today suggests, we are even willing to consider the possibility that misconduct may, after all, have something to do with the matter and that the doctrine of repression and insight are more misleading than helpful.

However, as soon as we psychologists get into a discussion of this problem, we find that our confusion is even more fundamental than might at first appear. We find that not only have we disavowed the connection between manifest misconduct and psychopathology; we have, also, very largely abandoned belief in right and wrong, virtue and sin, in general.

On other occasions when I have seen this issue under debate and anyone has proposed that social deviousness is causal in psychopathology, there is always a chorus of voices who clamor that sin cannot be defined, that it is culturally relative, that it is an unscientific concept, that it is a superstition—and therefore not to be taken seriously, either in psychopathology or in ordinary, everyday experience. And whenever an attempt is made to answer these objections, there are always further objections—often in the form of reductions to absurdity—which involve naivety or sophistry that would ill-become a schoolboy. Historically, in both literate and non-literate societies, human beings are supposed to have reached the age of discretion by early adolescence; yet here we have the spectacle of grown men and women soberly insisting that, in effect, *they* cannot tell right from wrong—and that no one else can.

Now I realize how futile it is to try to deal with this kind of attitude in a purely rational or logical way. The subversive doctrine that we can have the benefits of orderly social life without paying for it, through certain restraints and sacrifices, is too alluring to be counteracted by mere reason. The real answer, I believe, lies along different lines. The unassailable, brute fact is that personality disorder is the most pervasive and baffling problem of our time, and if it should turn out that persons so afflicted regularly display (or rather hide) a life of too little, rather than too much, moral restraint and self-discipline, the problem would take on an empirical urgency that would require no fine-spun argument.

Sin used to be—and, in some quarters, still is—defined as whatever one does that puts him in danger of going to Hell. Here was an assumed cause-and-effect relationship that was completely metaphysical and empirically unverifiable, and it is small wonder that it has fallen into disrepute as the scientific outlook and method have steadily gained in acceptance and manifest power. But there is a very tangible and very present Hell-on-this-earth which science has not yet helped us understand very well, and so I invited your attention to the neglected but very real possibility that it is this Hell—the Hell of neurosis and psychosis—to which sin and unexpiated guilt lead us and that it is this Hell that gives us one of the most, perhaps the most realistic and basic criteria for defining sin and guilt. If it proves empirically true that certain forms of conduct characteristically lead human beings into emotional instability, what better or firmer basis would one wish for labeling such conduct as destructive, self-defeating, evil, sinful?[1]

If the Freudian theory of personality disorder were valid, one would expect neurotic and psychotic individuals to have lead exemplary, yea saintly lives—to have been just too good for this world. The fact is, of course, that such individuals typically exhibit lives that have been disorderly and dishonest in extreme degree. In fact, this is so regularly the case [see Chapters 8 and 13] that one cannot but wonder how so contrary a doctrine as that of

---

[1]There is, admittedly, an element of circularity in the above argument. If it is maintained that mental illness is caused by unacknowledged and unexpiated sin, or real guilt, then it adds nothing to our knowledge to *define* sin as that which causes mental illness. In fact, there is a sense in which such a definition is not only circular but misleading (see Chapter 13 [*The Crisis in Psychiatry and Religion*]). Obviously, what is needed is an *independent criterion for identifying* sin or guilt—cf. Chapters 10-11 and Mowrer, 1961.

Freud ever gained credence. Freud spurned The Wish and exalted Reality. What he regarded as Reality may yet prove to have been the biggest piece of wishfulness of all.

Or, it may be asked, how is it if sin and psychic suffering are correlated that not all who sin fall into neurosis or psychosis? Here the findings of the Kinsey studies are likely to be cited, showing that, for example, many persons have a history of sexual perversity who are later quite normal. In other words, the argument is that since sin and persistent suffering do not always go hand-in-hand, there is perhaps no relationship at all. The answer to this question is surely obvious. Some individuals, alas, simply do not have enough character, or conscience, to be bothered by their sins. These are, of course, the world's psychopaths. Or an individual may have been caught in his sin and punished for it. Or it may have weighed so heavily on his conscience that he himself has confessed it and made appropriate expiation. Or, quite conceivably, in some instances the individual, without either detection or confession, may have set upon a program of service and good works which has also brought him peace and redemption. In other words, there is, surely, no disposition on the part of anyone to hold that sin, as such, necessarily dooms a person to interminable suffering in the form of neurosis or psychosis. The presumption is rather that sin has this effect only where it is acutely felt but not acknowledged and corrected.

Also, it is sometimes contended that individuals who eventually come to the attention of psychotherapists have, to be sure, been guilty of major errors of conduct; but, it is held, the illness was present first and the misconduct was really just an expression or symptom thereof. If this were true, where then would we draw the line? Is there no such thing as moral responsibility and social accountability at all? Is every mean or vicious thing that you or I do, as ordinary individuals, not sin but rather an expression of "illness?" Who would seriously hold that a society could long endure which consistently subscribed to this flaccid doctrine?

Then there is, of course, the view that, in the final analysis, all psychopathology—or at least its profounder forms—have a constitutional or metabolic basis. One must, I believe, remain open-minded with respect to this possibility—indeed, perhaps even somewhat hopeful with respect to it; for how marvelous it would be if all the world's madness, stupidity, and meanness could be eliminated through biochemistry. But over the years we have seen one approach after another of this kind come into prominence, with much heralding as the long-awaited break-through on the problem of mental disease, only to fade out as manifestly not quite the panacea we had imagined it to be. Some of us may, at this point, even suspect that today the main incentive for keeping the biochemical hypothesis alive is not so much the supporting empirical evidence, which is meager enough, but instead the fact that it at least obliquely justifies the premise that the whole field of mental disorder is the proper and exclusive domain of medicine. Also, and again somewhat obliquely, it excuses the clergy from facing squarely the responsibilities that would devolve among them if neurosis and psychosis should indeed turn out to be essentially moral disorders.

The conception of personality disturbance which attaches major etiological significance to moral and interpersonal considerations thus faces formidable resistance, from many sources; but programs of treatment and prevention which have been predicated on these other views have gotten us nowhere, and there is no clear reason to think they ever will. Therefore, in light of the total situation, I see no alternative but to turn again to the old, painful, but also promising possibility that man is preeminently a social creature and that he lives or dies, psychologically and personally, as a function of the openness, community, relatedness, and integrity which by good action he attains and by evil action destroys.

As long as we could believe that the psychoneurotic's basic problem was not evil but a kind of ignorance, it did not seem too formidable a task to give him the requisite enlightenment or insight. But mental hospitals are now full of people who have had this kind of therapy, in one guise or another, and found it wanting, and if we are thus forced to reconsider the other alternative, the therapeutic or redemptive enterprise, however clear it may be in principle, is by no means simple in practice. If the problem is genuinely one of morality, rather than pseudo-morality, most of us in the secular healing professions, of psychology, psychiatry, or social work, find ourselves reduced to the status of laymen, with no special training or competence for dealing with or even approaching the problem in these terms. We know something, of course, about procedures for getting disturbed persons to talk about themselves, free-associate, "confess," but the whole aim of this strategy has been insight, not redemption and personal reformation. And clergymen themselves have so often been told, both by their own leaders and by members of the secular healing professions, that they must recognize their own "limitations" and know when to "refer" that they, too, lack the necessary confidence and resources for dealing with these problems adequately [cf. Chapters 11, 12].

Many present-day psychoanalysts will offer no serious objection to the way in which classical Freudian theory and practice have been evaluated in this paper, but they will insist that many "advances" have been made since Freud's time and that these put the whole problem in a very different light. If we ask, "Precisely what *are* those advances?" we are told that they have to do with the new emphasis upon "ego psychology" rather than upon "the unconscious." But what did Emalian Gutheil (1958) tell us at our convention last year in Washington about ego psychology? He said that although analysts now recognize the ego as much more important than formerly, they know next to nothing about the conditions for modifying or strengthening it, and the same position has been voiced earlier by Lawrence Kubie (1956) and in one of his very last papers (1937) even by Freud himself [see also Chapter 13].

Therefore, I do not see how we can avoid the conclusion that at this juncture we are in a real crisis with respect to the whole psychotherapeutic enterprise. But I do not think we are going to remain in this crisis, confused and impotent, indefinitely. There is, I believe, growing realism with regard to the situation on the part of both psychologists and psychiatrists, on the one hand, and ministers, rabbis, and priests, on the other, and I am hopeful and even confident that new and better ways of dealing with the situation are in the making.

What, precisely, these ways will be I do not know, but I venture the impression that Alcoholics Anonymous provides our best present intimation of things to come and that the therapeutic programs of the future, whether under religious or secular auspices, will, like AA, take guilt, confession, and expiation seriously and will involve programs of *action* rather than mere groping for "insight."

REFERENCES

Freud, S. Analysis terminable and interminable. In Collected Papers. Vol. 5. London: Hogarth, 1950.

Kubie, L. S. Some unsolved problems of psychoanalytic psychotherapy. In Fromm-Reichmann & Moreno (eds.), Progress in psychotherapy. New York: Grune & Stratton, 1956.

Gutheil, E. Pseudoneurotic symptoms in psychosis. Amer. Psychol., 1958, 13: 350.

28

SIN AND PSYCHOTHERAPY

Albert Ellis, Ph.D.

One of the most challenging and lucid of recent thinkers on the subject of psychotherapy has been the eminent psychologist, O. Hobart Mowrer. Vigorously condemning the Freudian attitudes regarding the id, ego, and superego, Professor Mowrer has for the last decade upheld the thesis that if the psychotherapist in any way gives his patients the notion that they are not responsible for their sins, he will only encourage them to keep sinning; and that they cannot become emotionally undisturbed, since at bottom disturbance is a moral problem, unless they assume full responsibility for their misdeeds—and, what is more, stop their sinning.

In a recent symposium in which I participated with Dr. Mowrer, he made some excellent points with which I heartily agree (Mowrer, 1960a): namely, that psychotherapy must largely be concerned with the patient's sense of morality or wrongdoing; that classical Freudianism is mistaken in its implication that giving an individual insight into or understanding of his immoral or anti-social behavior will usually suffice to enable him to change that behavior; that if any Hell exists for human beings it is the Hell of neurosis and psychosis; that man is pre-eminently a social creature who psychologically maims himself to the degree that he needlessly harms others; that the only basic solution to the problem of

This chapter is an expanded version of two previously published articles: "There is No Place for the Concept of Sin in Psychotherapy" *(J. Consult. Psychol.,* 1960, 7: 188-192) and "Mowrer on 'Sin'" *(Amer. Psychologist,* 1960, 15: 713). Reprinted by permission of the author and publisher from Albert Ellis, *Reason and Emotion in Psychotherapy*. New York: Lyle Stuart, 1962.

emotional disturbance is the correction or cessation of the disturbed person's immoral actions; and that the effective psychotherapist must not only give his patient insight into the origins of his mistaken and self-defeating behavior but must also provide him with a highly active program of working at the eradication of this behavior.

On the surface, then, it would appear that I am in close agreement with Mowrer's concepts of sin and psychotherapy. This, however, is not true: since one of the central theses of rational-emotive psychotherapy is that there is no place whatever for the concept of sin in psychotherapy and that to introduce this concept in any manner, shape, or form is highly pernicious and antitherapeutic. The rational therapist holds, on the contrary, that no human being should ever be blamed for anything he does; and it is the therapist's main and most important function to help rid his patients of every possible vestige of their blaming themselves, blaming others, or blaming fate and the universe.

My pronounced differences with all those who would advocate making patients more guilty than they are, in order presumably to get them to change their antisocial and self-defeating conduct, can perhaps best be demonstrated by my insistence on a more precise and reasonably operational definition of the terms "sin" and "guilt" than is usually given by those who uphold this concept.

In their recent *Comprehensive Dictionary of Psychological and Psychoanalytical Terms,* English and English (1958) give a psychological definition of "sin" as follows: "Conduct that violates what the offender believes to be a supernaturally ordained moral code." They define a "sense of guilt" in this wise: "Realization that one has violated ethical or moral or religious principles, together with a regretful feeling of lessened personal worth on that account." English and English do not give any definition of "blame" but Webster's *New World Dictionary* defines it as: 1. "a blaming; accusation; condemnation; censure. 2. responsibility for a fault or wrong."

The beauty of these definitions, if one pays close attention to them, is that they include the two prime requisites for the individual's feeling a sense of sin, or guilt, or self-blame: (a) I have done the wrong thing and am responsible for doing it; and (b) I am a blackguard, a sinner, a no-goodnik, a valueless person, a louse, for having done this wrong deed. This, as I have shown my patients for the last several years, and as I and my co-author, Dr. Robert A. Harper, have noted in several recent publications on rational-emotive psychotherapy (Ellis, 1957; Ellis and Harper, 1961a, 1961b), is the double-headed essence of the feeling of sin, guilt, and blame: not merely the fact that the individual has made a mistake, an error, or a wrong move (which we may objectively call "wrongdoing") but the highly insidious, and I am convinced quite erroneous, belief or assumption that he is worthless, no good, valueless as a person for having done wrong.

I fully accept Hobart Mowrer's implication that there is such a thing as human wrongdoing or immoral behavior. I do not, as a psychologist, believe that we can have any absolute, final, or God-given standards of morals or ethics.

However, I do believe that, as citizens of a social community, we must have some standards of right and wrong. My own feeling is that these standards are best based on what I call long-range or socialized hedonism—that is, the philosophy that one should primarily strive for one's own satisfactions while, at the same time, keeping in mind that one will achieve one's own best-good, in most instances, by giving up immediate gratifications for future gains and by being courteous to and considerate of others, so that they will not sabotage one's own ends. I am also, however, ready to accept almost any other rationally planned, majority-approved standard of morality that is not arbitrarily imposed by an authoritarian clique of actual men or assumed gods.

With Mowrer and almost all ethicists and religionists, then, I accept it as fact that some standard of morality is necessary as long as humans live in social groups. But I still completely reject the notion that such a standard is only or best sustained by inculcating in individuals a sense of sin or guilt. I hold, on the contrary, that the more sinful and guilty a person tends to feel, the less chance there is that he will be a happy, healthy, or law-abiding citizen.

The problem of all human morality, it must never be forgotten, is not the problem of appeasing some hypothetical deity or punishing the individual for his supposed sins. It is the very simple problem, which a concept of sin and atonement invariably obfuscates, of teaching a person (a) not to commit an antisocial act in the first place, and (b) if he does happen to commit it, not to repeat it in the second, third and ultimate place. This problem, I contend, can consistently and fully be solved only if the potential or actual wrongdoer has the philosophy of life epitomized by the internalized sentences: (a) "If I do this act it will be wrong," and (b) "Therefore, how do I *not* do this act?" Or: (a) "This deed I have committed is wrong, erroneous, and mistaken." (b) "Now, how do I *not* commit it again?"

If, most objectively, and without any sense of self-blame, self-censure, or self-guilt, any human being would thoroughly believe in and continually internalize these sentences, I think it would be almost impossible for him to commit or keep committing immoral acts. If, however, he does not have this objective philosophy of wrongdoing, I do not see how it is possible for him to prevent himself from being immoral, on the one hand, or for him to be moral and emotionally healthy, on the other. For the main alternatives to the objective philosophy of nonblaming morality which I have just outlined are the following:

1. The individual can say to himself: (a) "If I do this act it will be wrong," and (b) "If I do this wrong act, I will be a sinner, a blackguard." If this is what the individual says to himself, and firmly believes, he will then perhaps be moral in his behavior, but only at the expense of having severe feelings of worthlessness—of deeply feeling that he is a sinner. But such feelings of worthlessness, I submit, are the essence of human disturbance: since disturbance basically consists of intense anxiety (that is, the feelings following from the internalized sentence, "I am worthless and therefore I cannot live comfortably and safely in a world filled with much more worthwhile persons") or sustained hostility (that is, the feeling often following from the sentence, "He is more worthwhile than I, and I cannot live comfortably and compete with him, and therefore I hate him").

So, at best, if a human being remains moral mainly because he would feel guilty and worthless if he did not so remain, he will most probably never be able to rid himself of his underlying feelings of worthlessness and his fear of these feelings showing through if he did, by some chance, prove to be fallible and did behave immorally. We have, then, a moral individual who keeps himself so only by plaguing himself with feelings of sin and worthlessness. And since none of us are angels, and all must at some time make mistakes and commit immoral acts, we actually have a moral individual who actively (as well as potentially) hates himself. Or we would have, as Mowrer might well put it if he were more precise about what a sense of sin actually is and what it does to human beings, an individual who perpetually keeps himself on the verge of or actually in the Hell of neurosis or psychosis.

2. The self-blaming or guilty individual can say to himself, as I contend that most of the time he does in actual practice: (a) "If I do this act it will be wrong," and (b) "If I am wrong I will be a sinner." And then, quite logically taking off from this wholly irrational and groundless conclusion, he will obsessively-compulsively keep saying to himself, as I have seen patient after patient say, "Oh, what a terrible sinner I will be (or already am). Oh, what a terrible person! How I deserve to be punished!" And so on, and so forth.

In saying this nonsense, and thereby equating his potential or actual act of wrongdoing with a concomitant feeling of utter worthlessness, this individual will never be able to focus on the simple question, "How do I *not* do this wrong act?" or "How do I not repeat it now that I have done it?" He will, instead, keep focusing senselessly on "What a horrible sinner, what a blackguard I am!!" Which means, in most instances, that he will—ironically enough—actually be diverted into doing the wrong act or repeating it if he has already done it. His sense of sin will tend literally to drive him away from not doing wrong and toward "sinning." Or, in other words, he will become a compulsive wrongdoer.

To make matters still worse, the individual who blames himself for acting badly (or, sometimes, for even thinking about acting badly) will usually feel (as blamers normally do) that he should be punished for his poor behavior. His internalized sentences therefore will tend to go somewhat as follows: "I committed a horrible crime. I am therefore a terrible sinner and must atone for my sins, must punish myself for this crime. But if I keep doing badly, keep committing these kinds of crimes, I will certainly be caught or will have to keep being anxious about the danger of being caught. My being caught and punished or my being anxious about being caught will itself be a hard, punishing thing. Therefore, maybe it would be better if I kept committing crimes like this, in order to punish myself, and thereby atone for my sins."

In other words, the individual who construes his misdeeds as sins will often compulsively drive himself to more misdeeds in order, sooner or later, to bring punishment for these sins on his own head.

3. The self-blaming person (or, synonymously, the person with a pronounced sense of sin) may say to himself the usual sequence: (a) "If I do this act it will be wrong," and (b) "If I am wrong, I am a worthless sinner." Then, being no angel and being impelled, at times, to commit wrong deeds, and being prepared to condemn himself mercilessly (because of his sense of sin) for his deeds, he will either refuse to admit that he has done the wrong thing or admit that he has done it but insist that it is not wrong. That is to say, the wrongdoer who has an acute sense of sin will either repress thoughts about his wrongdoing or psychopathically insist that he is right and the world is wrong.

Any way one looks at the problem of morality, therefore, the individual who sanely starts out by saying (a) "It is wrong to do this act" and then who insanely continues (b) "I am a sinner or a blackguard for doing (or even for thinking about doing) it" can only be expected to achieve one or more of four most unfortunate results: (1) a deepseated feeling of personal worthlessness; (2) an obsessive-compulsive occupation with a consequent potential re-performance of the wrong act for which he is blaming himself; (3) denial or repression of the fact that his immoral act was actually committed by him; and (4) psychopathic insistence that the act was committed but was not really wrong.

To make matters infinitely worse, the individual who has a sense of sin, guilt, or self-blame inevitably cannot help blaming others for their potential or actual wrongdoings—and he therefore becomes angry or hostile to these others. And he cannot help blaming fate, circumstances, or the universe for wrongly or unjustly frustrating him in the attainment of many of his desires—and he consequently becomes self-pitying and angry at the world.

In the final analysis, then, blaming, in all its insidious ramifications, is the essence of virtually all emotional disturbances; and, as I tell my patients on many occasions, if I can induce them never, under any circumstances, to blame or punish anyone, including and especially themselves, it will be virtually impossible for them ever to become seriously upset. This does not mean that no child or adult should ever be objectively or dispassionately penalized for his errors or wrongdoings (as, for example, psychologists often penalize laboratory rats by shocking them when they enter the wrong passage of a maze); but merely that no one should ever be *blamefully* punished for his mistakes or crimes.

There are several other reasons why, almost invariably, giving an individual a sense of sin or of self-worthlessness in connection with his wrongdoing will not make for less immorality or greater happiness or mental health. Let me briefly mention some of these reasons:

For one thing, guilt and self-blame induce the individual to bow nauseatingly low to some arbitrary external authority, which in the last analysis is always some hypothetical deity; and such worship renders him proportionately less self-sufficient and self-confident. Secondly, the concept of guilt inevitably leads to the unsupportable sister concept of self-sacrifice for and dependency upon others—which is the antithesis of true mental health. Thirdly, guilty individuals tend to focus incessantly on past delinquencies and crimes rather than on present and future constructive behavior. Fourthly, it is psychophysically impossible for a person to concentrate adequately on changing his moral actions for the better when he is obsessively focused upon blaming himself for his past and present misdeeds. Fifthly, the states of anxiety created in an individual by his self-blaming tendencies induce concomitant breakdown states in which he cannot think clearly of anything, least of all constructive changes in himself.

The full measure of the harmfulness of self-blaming is perhaps best seen in regard to its interference with the reestablishment of mental health once it has set the wheels of emotional disturbance in working order. The vicious circle usually goes somewhat as follows. Jim Jones, who is a fairly normal, fallible human being, first demands that he be perfect and infallible, because he very falsely equates making mistakes with being incompetent and e-quates being incompetent with being worthless (that is, blame-worthy). Naturally, he does not achieve perfection or infallibility; and, in fact, just because he is so overconcerned about being error-less, and focuses on *how* rather than on *what* he is doing, he tends to make many more mistakes than he otherwise would make if he did not blame himself and consider himself worthless for being error-prone.

So Jim Jones excoriates himself severely for his mistakes and develops some kind of neurotic symptom—such as severe anxiety or hostility against those he thinks are less incompetent than he. Once he develops this symptom, Jim soon begins to notice that he is afflicted with it, and then he blames himself severely for having the symptom—for being neurotic. This second-level self-blaming of course causes him to be still more neurotic.

Thus, where he was originally anxious about his potential incompetence, and then became more anxious because his original anxiety drove him to become actually incompetent, he now goes one step further, and becomes anxious about being anxious. In the process—naturally!—he tends to become still more incompetent, since he is even less than ever focused on problem solving and more than ever concentrated on what a terrible person he is for being such a poor problem-solver.

Finally, after he has become anxious (that is, self-blaming) about (a) the possibility of being incompetent, (b) actual incompetence, stemming from (a), and (c) his anxiety or acute panic state resulting from both (a) and (b), Jim sees that he is terribly disturbed and goes for psychotherapeutic aid. But here again he is smitten down by his self-blaming tendencies and tends to sabotage his therapeutic efforts in several significant ways:

1. The more the therapist helps him see what he is doing to himself—that is, the more insight he is helped to acquire into how he is blaming himself—the more he tends to blame himself for being so stupid or incompetent or sick. Otherwise stated, the more he sees how he is blaming himself, the more he may, especially at the beginning of therapy, blame himself for blaming himself. He thereby may actually become considerably worse before he starts to get better.

2. As soon as he sees that therapy requires that he do something in order to get better—which it always does, since it is no magic formula for self-improvement without effort on the part of the patient—he frequently starts worrying about whether he is going to be able (meaning, competent enough) to do what he has to do to help himself. His internalized sentences may therefore run something along these lines: "My therapist is showing me that I have to see what I am doing to create my disturbances, and to challenge and contradict my own negative thinking in this connection. From what I can see, he is perfectly right. But wouldn't it be awful if I tried to do this kind of challenging of my own nonsense and failed! Wouldn't it be terrible if I proved to him and myself that I *couldn't* do what I have to do! Perhaps, since it would be so awful to try and to fail, I'd better not even try, and in that way at

least save face."

In telling himself these kinds of sentences, the patient often gives himself an excuse to give up trying to cure himself early in the game; and he either continues therapy in a half-hearted and ineffective manner, or he gives it up entirely by convincing himself that "Well, maybe it works with other people, but obviously not with me. I guess I'm just hopeless."

3. If the patient continues in therapy for a while, and if he begins surely but fairly slowly to improve (as is usually the case, since he has become so habituated for so many years to mistaken patterns of thinking and acting), he then often starts to tell himself: "How disgusting! Here I've been going for therapy for quite a while now and I'm still not better. Why, considering how I blew up the other day, I'm probably just as bad as I was when I started! How stupid! Obviously, I'm not really trying at all—in which case I'm idiotically wasting my time and money in therapy—or I'm trying and I just haven't got what it takes to get better. Other people I know have made much greater strides in equal or lesser periods of time. I guess I really *am* no good!"

4. Sometimes the patient is sorely disappointed with his own progress in therapy but, realizing that if he frankly admits that he has not been working too hard or consistently to help himself, he will mercilessly blame himself, he fails to face his own avoidance of the problem and bitterly starts resenting his therapist for not helping him enough. Knowing little but a basic philosophy of blame, he cannot conceive that neither he nor his therapist could be reprehensible (though either or both of them might be responsible) for his lack of progress; so he is faced with the choice of hating one of the two—and in this instance picks the therapist, and either quits therapy completely (telling himself that all therapists are no damn good) or keeps shopping around for another, and perhaps another, and perhaps still another therapist. In any event, he refuses to admit that probably *he* is responsible—though not blameworthy—for his lack of progress, and that he'd therefore better get back to the task of therapy with more effort and much less blaming.

The vicious circle, in instances like these, is now complete. First the individual upsets himself by his self-excoriating philosophy; then he blames himself (or others) for his becoming so upset; then, if he goes for therapeutic help, he again blames himself (or others) for his not immediately becoming completely cured. Under such triply self-blaming blows, it is virtually certain that he will not only become, but often forever remain, exceptionally disturbed.

It should be quite patent, then, that giving an individual a sense of sin, guilt or self-blame for his misdeeds is enormously disadvantageous. This is not to say that blame *never* helps human beings to correct their mistaken or criminal behavior. It certainly seems to work with many children and with some adults. But often it is highly ineffective—as shown by the fact that after thousands of years of censuring, ridiculing, jailing, killing, and otherwise severely blaming and punishing human beings for their immoralities, we still have not greatly reduced the quantity or quality of wrongdoing that goes on in this world.

Even, moreover, when blame is effective, and people do commit significantly fewer misdeeds because of harsh social sanctions which are leveled against them in their formative and later years, it is most dubious whether the game is worth the candle. For the toll, in terms of the immense amounts and intense degrees of anxiety and hostility that ensue, is so great as to call into question almost any amount of morality which is thereby achieved.

The concept of sin (as distinguished from the objective appraisal of wrongdoing) is so humanly inhuman that it would be difficult even to conceive a more pernicious technique for keeping mankind moral. And because any deity-positing religion almost by necessity involves endowing those members who violate the laws of its gods with a distinct concept of blameworthiness or sinfulness, I am inclined to reverse Voltaire's famous dictum and to say that, from a mental health standpoint, if there were a God it would be necessary to uninvent Him.

It is sometimes objected, when rational therapists talk of the distinction between "sin" and "wrongdoing," that they are merely quibbling and that the two are essentially the same. Thus, Mowrer (1960b), in a recent issue of the *American Psychologist,* argues that because "sin" is a stronger word than "wrongdoing" or "irresponsibility" it is better for the neurotic individual to admit his "sins" than to accept his "wrongdoings." Says Mowrer:

"The only way to resolve the paradox of self-hatred and self-punishment is to assume, not that it represents merely an 'introjection' of the attitudes of others, but that the self-hatred is realistically justified and will persist until the individual, by radically altered attitude *and action,* honestly and realistically comes to feel that he now deserves something better. As long as one remains, in old-fashioned religious phraseology, hard-of-heart and unrepentant, just so long will one's conscience hold him in the vise-like grip of 'neurotic' rigidity and suffering. But if, at length, an individual confesses his past stupidities and errors and makes what poor attempts he can at restitution, then the superego (like the parents of an earlier day—and society in general) forgives and relaxes its stern hold; and the individual once again is free, 'well'."

In upholding the concept of individual (if not original) "sin," Mowrer is contending that the neurotic individual must, if he is to get well, accept the following syllogism: (a) Sinning is unjustified; (b) I have sinned; (c) therefore, I must justify my existence by acknowledging my sins, changing my ways, and becoming a non-sinner.

At first blush, this seems like a perfectly valid syllogism. But, as Mowrer himself suggests, it rarely works because "there is some evidence that human beings do not change radically unless they first acknowledge their sins, but we also know how hard it is for one to make such an acknowledgment unless he has *already changed.* In other words, the full realization of deep worthlessness is a severe ego 'insult', and one must have some new source of strength, it seems, to endure it. This is a mystery (or is it only a mistaken observation?) which traditional theology has tried to resolve in various ways—without complete success. Can we psychologists do better?"

I am sure that psychologists can do better—if they avoid the trap which Mowrer, by insisting on replacing the naturalistic words, "wrongdoing" and "responsibility," with the moralistic word, "sin," has got himself into.

Let us first see what is wrong with Mowrer's syllogism and why, because of the manner in which it is stated, it virtually forces the individual to think that he is "worthless" and consequently to be unable to change his immoral behavior. Mowrer's premise is that sinning is unjustified or that the sinner's "self-hatred is realistically justified." By this statement he appears to mean two important things, only the first of which can be objectively validated: (a) the sinner's act is mistaken or wrong (because it is, in some early or final analysis, self- or society-defeating); and (b) therefore, the sinner is personally blameworthy or integrally worthless for performing this mistaken or wrong act.

Although (a) may be a true observation, (b) is an arbitrary value judgment, or moralistic definition, that can never possibly be objectively validated and that, as Epictetus, Hartman (1959), Lewis (1949), Mead (1936), and other writers have shown, is philosophically untenable. No matter how responsible, in a causative sense, an individual may be for his mistaken or wrong behavior, he becomes a villain or a worthless lout only if members of his social group *view* or *define* him as such and if, more importantly, he *accepts* their moralistic views. Where Mowrer, for example, obviously thinks that the average murderer should hate himself, I (for one) believe that he should fully acknowledge and deplore his murderous act, but that he should in no way despise him*self* for committing this act.

The paradox, therefore, that Mowrer posits—that the neurotic sinner will not get better until he acknowledges and actively repents his sins and that he will not acknowledge his sins until he gets better—is a direct and "logical" result of explicitly or implicitly including the concept or personal worthlessness in the definition of "sin." Naturally (as noted previously in this chapter), if someone believes that his acts are sinful—meaning (a) that he is wrong (self- or socially-defeating) for perpetrating them, and (b) that he is blameworthy or worthless for being wrong—he will not dare acknowledge that he has sinned; or he will make invalid excuses for so doing; or he will feel so worthless after his acknowledgment that he will hardly have the energy or efficiency to change his wrong or mistaken behavior.

How can the non-moralistic and rational psychologist help his neurotic patients resolve this paradox? Very simply: by taking the objective and "weaker" (that is, unmoralistic) words, such as "wrongdoing" and "irresponsibility," that Mowrer abandons in place of "sin," and putting them into his original syllogism. The syllogism then becomes: (a) Wrongdoing is self- or society-defeating; (b) I have made a mistake or committed a wrong act; (c) therefore, I'd better stop being self-defeating by acknowledging my wrongdoing and take considerable time and effort to work at not repeating it, so that eventually I'll become a less frequent wrongdoer.

If the neurotic wrongdoer states his syllogism in this form, he will never think that he is quite worthless, will never experience any ego "insult," and will easily be able to acknowledge his wrongdoings *before* he has changed and stopped committing them. The artificial problem that was created by his feeling he was a sinner and therefore blaming himself immediately for any wrongdoing that he may have perpetrated is no longer created when a misdeed is viewed as a serious mistake rather than as a heinous crime.

Although I still agree heartily with Hobart Mowrer that the healthy and happy human being should have a clear-cut sense of wrongdoing, and that he should not only try to understand the origin of his antisocial behavior but to do something effective to become more morally oriented, I contend that giving anyone a sense of sin, guilt, or self-blame is the worst possible way to help him be an emotionally sound and adequately socialized individual.

A rational psychotherapist certainly helps show his patients that they have often behaved wrongly, badly, and self-defeatingly by performing antisocial actions, and that if they continue to act in this kind of self-defeating manner they will inevitably continue to defeat their own ends. But he also shows them that this is no reason why they should feel sinful or guilty or self-blaming about the actions for which they may well have been responsible. He helps his patients to temporarily accept themselves as wrongdoers, acknowledge fully their responsibility for their acts, and then focus intently, in their internalized sentences and their overt activities, on the only real problem at hand—which is: How do I not repeat this wrong deed next time?

If, in this thoroughly objective, non-guilty manner, we can teach patients (as well as the billions of people in the world who, for better or worse, will never become patients) that even though human beings can be held quite accountable or responsible for their misdeeds, no one is ever to blame for anything he does, human morality, I am sure, will be significantly improved and, for the first time in human history, civilized people will have a real chance to achieve sound mental health. The concept of sin is the direct and indirect cause of virtually all neurotic disturbance. The sooner psychotherapists forthrightly begin to attack it the better their patients will be.

REFERENCES

Ellis, A. Outcome of employing three techniques of psychotherapy. *J. Clin. Psychol.*, 1957, 13:334-350.

Ellis, A., & Harper, R. A. *A guide to rational living.* Englewood Cliffs, N.J.: Prentice-Hall, 1961a.

Ellis, A., & Harper, R. A. *Creative marriage.* New York: Lyle Stuart, 1961b.

English, H. B., & English, Ava C. *A comprehensive dictionary of psychological and psychoanalytical terms.* New York: Longmans, Green, 1958.

Hartman, R. S. *The measurement of value.* Crotonville, N.Y.: General Electric Co., 1959.

Lewis, C. L. The nature of ethical disagreement. In H. Feigl & W. Sellars (Eds.) *Readings in philosophical analysis.* New York: Appleton-Century-Crofts, 1949.

Mead, G. H. *Mind, self and society.* Chicago: Univer. of Chicago Press, 1958.

Mowrer, O. H. Some constructive features of the concept of sin. *J. counsel. Psychol.*, 1960a, 7:185-188.

Mowrer, O. H. "Sin," the lesser of two evils. *Amer. Psychologist*, 1960b, 15:301-304.

29

NOTHING'S UGLIER THAN SIN

Ben N. Ard, Jr., Ph.D.

What should a counselor do when faced with religious values which say that a given client's sex act is bad, harmful and sinful, while science says there is no scientific evidence to indicate that such is the case? Counselors and psychotherapists frequently face just such issues in their practices (Ard, 1974).

Clients often bring such dilemmas to counselors (regarding masturbation, petting, premarital intercourse, etc.) and counselors need to think through the probable consequences—for the counselor as well as the client—of taking various courses of action. Sitting on the fence and refusing to deal with such matters as values involving sex will not resolve the counselor's problem.

As a specific illustration, what should a counselor do when a clients feels guilty about some sexual act such as masturbation (and states that his religious values hold such acts to be bad, harmful, and sinful) and in counseling asks the counselor: "Is masturbation *really* bad and harmful?" Science says that masturbation is a natural, normal phenomenon in our society (Dearborn, 1961; Ellis, 1958). This instance poses a problem for the counselor; in a society where sexual behavior and attitudes are changing (Reiss, 1960), along with values in general, counselors may expect to face many such dilemmas in their counseling practice. What legitimate stances are open to professional counselors in that "never never land" where values, sex and science are so closely intertwined?

Historically, counselors were expected (at least by some people) to "guide" their clients (hence the old term "guidance"), of what-

---

This article is an expanded version of one by the same title that appeared in *Rational Living, Vol. 2,* No. 1, p. 4-6, Spring, 1967.

ever age in school or college, into the "proper" paths. This meant that counselors functioned *in loco parentis* (or in place of the parents) in colleges and schools and reinforced the conventional values (derived ultimately from the religious values) of Christian middle-class parents, in the main.

Some members of the counseling profession grew to feel that there was something not quite right about this traditionally moralistic approach and came to the conclusion that counselors should not make "value judgments," but should be philosophically "neutral." People who take this "neutralist" position argue that the counselor "is no moralist, that he has no business becoming involved in the moral, religious, or political beliefs of his client, and that he has no right, in the course of his practice, to make value judgments about his client, to moralize or preach at him, or to try to dictate to him some good way of life" (London, 1964, p. 4).

This "neutralist" position has been very influential in counseling circles, particularly among those counselors who like to feel that they are "non-directive," although their most famous leader, Carl Rogers, has shown some recent concern for "the good life" as one of his goals (Rogers, 1961, pp. 183-196). It could probably be fairly said that this "neutralist" position is widely popular nowadays among counselors, if not the dominant position.

Now along comes Mowrer, a psychologist, in the *Personnel and Guidance Journal* (April, 1964), with the suggestion that "science" seems to give no support for "morality" and "virtue" (Mowrer, 1964, p. 748). Mowrer has suggested, as a different approach from the widespread "neutralist" point of view, that counselors should become actively concerned with "unredeemed sin" and thereby "help" clients to admit their "real guilt" and to seek necessary "atonement" (Mowrer, 1964, p. 750).

Karl Menninger, a psychiatrist, has also sought to re-introduce the concept of sin in his recent book, *Whatever Became of Sin?* (1973). Mowrer has also collected together and edited a series of papers on *Morality and Mental Health* (1967) and also discussed the matter further in his book *The Crisis in Psychiatry and Religion* (1961).

I would like to suggest that this return to "moralistic" counseling, as advocated by Mowrer, Menninger, et al, would *not* best meet the needs of counselors or their clients in our pluralistic society. In fact, it would be, in effect, a return to the Dark Ages.

For the religious counselor who works in a parochial school or college with clients of a single religious faith, this "moralistic" approach might seem to have some value (within the context of their *assumed* values regarding "sin" and the function of "guilt"), but for *most* professional counselors, who have to function in a more pluralistic setting, Mowrer and Menninger's moralistic approach will probably alienate more clients than it will help.

Many young people today come to counselors with their problems *precisely* because they *already know* what their church, parents, deans, priests and religious counselors say *should* be done (or *not* done), but the clients still want to talk the matter over with someone who does *not* moralize, who does not "have an axe to grind," as some college students have said to me.

To illustrate some of the problems involved for counselors—whether they take a "moralist," "neutralist," or "pluralist" position—let us look at an imaginary case Mowrer himself presented, of a college student who feels guilty about playing cards (bridge) because her parents taught her that such behavior is sinful. Mowrer criticized what he considered the "scientific" approach of a Freudian counselor who might try to "shrink" a rigid, unrealistic conscience (or "strong" superego); the Freudian counselor might essentially conclude that "Everyone knows that playing bridge is not really a sin" (Mowrer, 1964, pp. 751-752).

A "neutralist" might maintain that the girl simply has to work out her problem herself, with the counselor not taking any stand on the issue *per se*, but trying to establish the kind of relationship wherein the girl would feel free to come to her own conclusions without any hint of the counselor's views on the question. He presumably (according to the "neutralist" view) should not answer her questions as to whether or not he feels that card-playing is a sin, but reflect the question back to her: that is, it is her decision to make.

Mowrer took the position that the girl did not have the right to continue to take money for college expenses from her parents without telling them of her decision in this matter (Mowrer, 1964, p. 752). But surely counselors can work with clients having such value dilemmas without adopting Mowrer's approach. Surely college students can differ with their parents on some "moral" matters, and still accept money from them for college expenses.

As Kirkendall has pointed out, "Young adults are sometimes in an agony because their parents are making them choose between what the parents call loyalty to them, and freedom and a life in their own right" (Kirkendall, no date, p. 11). The young adult must choose the path which frees him as an individual, Kirkendall held. If the parents cannot see their way clear to freeing their grown children, then the break should come, he said.

Albert Ellis has perhaps stated the clearest opposition to the use of the concept of sin in counseling or psychotherapy (Ellis, 1962, pp. 132-146). He has stated that "there is no place whatever for the concept of sin in psychotherapy, and to introduce this concept in any manner, shape, or form is highly pernicious and anti-therapeutic" (Ellis, 1962, p. 133). In fact, "The more sinful and guilty a person tends to feel, the less chance there is that he will be a happy, healthy, or law-abiding citizen" (Ellis, 1962, p. 134).

In the rational therapy that Ellis provides, the self-defeating nature of feelings of guilt, self-blame, and sin are forthrightly pointed out to the client: "The concept of sin (as distinguished from the objective appraisal of wrongdoing) is so humanly inhuman that it would be difficult even to *conceive* a more pernicious technique for keeping mankind moral" (Ellis, 1962, p. 142). Ellis has contended that "giving anyone a sense of sin, guilt, or self-blame is the worst possible way to help him to be an emotionally sound and adequately socialized individual" (1962, p. 145). Finally, Ellis concluded that "the concept of sin is the direct and indirect cause of virtually all neurotic disturbance" (1962, p. 146). If this is true, then the sooner counselors forthrightly begin to demolish the concept of sin, rather than augmenting and increasing its sway, the better off their clients will be.

For a philosophical analysis of the whole concept of guilt, we may turn to the recent work of Walter Kaufmann, *Without Guilt and Justice* (1973). Kaufmann has stated quite clearly that ". . . guilt feelings involve beliefs and even strenuous convictions. These convictions could be, and are, false and irrational, and there-fore guilt feelings are open to criticism" (1973, p. 112). Kaufmann puts the crux of the matter in a succinct sentence: "Guilt feelings are a contagious disease that harms those who harbor them and endangers those who live close to them. The liberation from guilt spells the dawn of autonomy" (1973, p. 114).

Some authorities have tried to avoid some of the problems inherent in the concept of guilt, conscience, or superego by pos-tulating two kinds of guilt or conscience or superego; thus we have seen such concepts as a "benevolent superego" as well as the tyrannical (usual) superego, neurotic guilt and authentic guilt, intrinsic guilt (Maslow, in this text), the "humanistic conscience" (Fromm, 1947), etc. But Walter Kaufmann has clearly stated that man is "caught in the spurious alternative between the bad conscience and the good conscience. *I reject the good conscience as well as the bad*." (1973, p. 125).

One of the basic reasons that guilt feelings are self-defeating for those who have them as well as harmful to others is that "Guilt feelings are a form of resentment. The person who harbors them is therefore a menace" (Kaufmann, 1973, p. 126). So we need to help people eliminate their guilt feelings, for their own sake and for our sake as well.

Some people assume as a basic premise that guilt feelings are necessary for the protection of society. People would run amok if they had no guilt feelings, many people assume without question. Walter Kaufmann has dealt with this question and has said, "Thus the question that I have set out to answer involves a false premise, namely, that guilt feelings do protect society. There is no evidence that they accomplish much in this way (1973, p. 127).

In his extensive treatment of the subject, Walter Kaufmann has concluded that "Only reason can decide what is irrational; and I have tried to show that guilt feelings *are* irrational" (1973, p. 132).

"Millions have discovered that one can care for one's fellow men and refrain from monstrous crimes without belief in hell or God. Surely, self-criticism and a social conscience can survive the death of guilt" (1973, p. 136). A final conclusion from Walter Kaufmann points the way: "To liberate oneself, one must break the chains of guilt" (1973, p. 137).

The whole question of the relationship of values and science in the counseling area is coming in for some analysis in several books. (Cf. Anderson, *Beyond Freud*, 1957; Buhler, *Values in Psychotherapy*, 1962; London, *The Modes and Morals of Psychotherapy*, 1964; Maslow, *New Knowledge in Human Values*, 1959; Masserman, *Psychoanalysis and Human Values*, 1960; Patterson, *Counseling and Psychotherapy: Theory and Practice*, 1959). One particularly significant conclusion, which is pertinent here, is that all values do not have to be subjectivistic and moralistic (i.e., derived from religious beliefs), some values may be objective (i.e., derived from science). That is, an objective system of ethics can be developed which is based on the findings of science. As Maslow has stated, "For the first time in history, many of us feel, such a system—based squarely upon valid knowledge of the nature of man, of his society, and of his works—may be possible" (1959, p. viii).

Psychology, the basic science which provides so much for counseling as an applied profession, thus provides the basis for some resolution of this dilemma regarding values, sex, and science. As Erich Fromm has said, "Psychology must not only debunk false ethical judgments, but can, beyond that, be the basis for building objective and valid norms of conduct" (Fromm, 1947, p. vii).

Thus, the importance of the counselor's need to think this whole area through critically is indicated, because "the value judgments we make determine our actions, and upon their validity rests our mental health and happiness" (Fromm, 1947, p. viii).

REFERENCES

Anderson, Camilla M. *Beyond Frued.* New York: Harper, 1957.

Ard, Ben N., Jr. *Treating Psychosexual Dysfunction.* New York: Jason Aronson, 1974.

Buhler, Charlotte. *Values in Psychotherapy.* New York: Free Press of Glencoe, 1962.

Dearborn, Lester W. Autoeroticism in Ellis, Albert & Abarbanel, Albert (Eds.). *The Encyclopedia of Sexual Behavior.* New York: Hawthorn, 1961, 204-216.

Ellis, Albert. New light on masturbation in *Sex Without Guilt.* New York: Lyle Stuart, 1958, 15-25.

Ellis, Albert. *Reason and Emotion in Psychotherapy.* New York: Lyle Stuart, 1962.

Fromm, Erich. *Man For Himself.* New York: Rinehart, 1947.

Kaufmann, Walter. *Without Guilt and Justice.* New York: Wyden, 1973.

Kirkendall, Lester A. Searching for the roots of moral judgments. Unpublished (mimeographed) article. No date.

London, Perry. *The Modes and Morals of Psychotherapy.* New York: Holt, Rinehart, & Winston, 1964.

Maslow, Abraham H. (Ed.). *New Knowledge in Human Values.* New York: Harper, 1959.

Maslow, Abraham H. Some basic propositions of a growth and self-actualization psychology, in this text.

Masserman, Jules H. (Ed.). *Psychoanalysis and Human Values.* New York: Grune & Stratton, 1960.

Menninger, Karl. *Whatever Became of Sin?* New York: Hawthorn, 1973.

Mowrer, O. Hobart. *The Crisis in Psychiatry and Religion.* Princeton, New Jersey: Van Nostrand, 1961.

Mowrer, O. Hobart. Science, sex and values in *Personnel and Guidance Journal,* April, 1964, 746-753.

Mowrer, O. Hobart (Ed.). *Morality and Mental Health.* Chicago: Rand McNally, 1967.

Patterson, C. H. *Counseling and Psychotherapy: Theory and Practice.* New York: Harper, 1959.

Reiss, Ira L. *Premarital Sexual Standards in America.* Glencoe, Illinois: Free Press of Glencoe, 1960.

Rogers, Carl R. *On Becoming A Person.* Boston: Houghton Mifflin, 1961.

30

PSYCHOTHERAPY AND THE OBJECTIVIST ETHICS

Nathaniel Branden, Ph.D.

The belief that moral values are the province of faith and that no rational, scientific code of ethics is possible, has had disastrous effects in virtually every sphere of human activity. But there is one profession for which the consequences of this belief have been particularly acute: the science of psychology.

As a theoretical discipline, psychology is concerned with studying and defining the nature of consciousness or mind; the volitional and automatic functions of mind, the source and nature of emotions, the principles of character-formation, the principles of motivation. As a therapeutic discipline, it is concerned with the diagnosis and treatment of the malfunctions of consciousness, of mental and emotional disturbances, of character and motivational disorders.

Central to the science of psychology is the issue or problem of *motivation*. The base of the science is the need to answer two fundamental questions: Why does a man act as he does? What would be required for a man to act differently? These questions are directed, not only at man's physical actions, but at the actions of his consciousness—at the whole of his mental life.

The key to motivation lies in the realm of *values.*

Within the context of his inherent needs and capacities as a specific kind of living organism, it is man's premises—specifically

This paper was orginally delivered before the Michigan Society of Consulting Psychologists, November 24, 1965. It is based on material which appeared in the *Objectivist Newsletter* and *Who Is Ayn Rand?* (New York: Random House, 1962).

his *value*-premises—that determine his actions and emotions. Whether his value-premises are rational or contradictory and self-defeating, whether they are held consciously or subconsciously, whether they are explicit or implicit, whether they were chosen independently and by deliberation or were uncritically absorbed from other men by a process of cultural osmosis—it is a man's notion of what is for him or against him, what is conducive or inimical to his welfare, that determines the goals he will pursue and the emotions he will experience.

An *emotion* is the psychosomatic form in which man experiences his estimate of the relationship of things to himself. An emotion is a *value*-response. It is the automatic psychological result of a man's value-judgments.

Man's value-judgments are not innate. Having no innate knowledge of what is true or false, man can have no innate knowledge of what is good or evil. His values, and his emotions, are the product of the conclusions he has drawn or accepted, that is: of his *basic premises.*

If man chooses values that are consonant with the facts of reality and the needs of his own nature, these values will work in the service of his life. If he chooses values that are in contradiction to the facts of reality and to his nature, they will work for his destruction. No man whose values were *consistently* irrational could continue to exist. The majority of men hold values that are part-rational, part-irrational—part-consonant with and part-inimical to man's nature and needs—and they spend their lives in anxiously precarious fluctuation between life and destruction, neither dying immediately nor achieving their full human potential; they pay the price of their unresolved contradictions in frustration, in misery and in neurosis.

The existence of neurosis, of mental and emotional disturbances, is one of the most eloquent proofs that man *needs* an integrated, objective code of moral values—that a haphazard collection of subjective or collective whims will not do—that a rational ethical system is as indispensable to man's psychological survival as it is to his existential survival.

The paradox—and the tragedy—of psychology today is that *values* is the one issue specifically banned from its domain.

The majority of psychologists—both as theoreticians and as psychotherapists—have accepted the premise that the realm of science and the realm of ethics are mutually inimical, that morality is a matter of faith, not of reason, that moral values are inviolately subjective, and that a therapist must cure his patients without appraising or challenging their fundamental moral beliefs.

Ladies and gentlemen, it is this premise that I ask you to challenge.

Guilt, anxiety and self-doubt—the neurotic's chronic complaints—entail *moral* judgments. The psychotherapist must deal with such judgments constantly. The conflicts that torture patients are *moral* conflicts: Is sex evil, or is it a proper human pleasure?—Is the profit motive evil, or do men have the right to pursue their own interests?—Must one love and forgive everybody, or is it ever justifiable to feel violent indignation?—Must man blindly submit to the teachings of his religious authorities, or dare he subject their pronouncements to the judgment of his own intellect?—Is it one's duty to remain with the husband or wife one despises, or is divorce a valid solution?—Should a woman regard motherhood as her noblest function and duty, or may she pursue an independent career?—Is man "his brother's keeper," or does he have the right to live for his own happiness?

It is true that patients frequently repress such conflicts and that the repression constitutes the major obstacle to the conflict's resolution. But it is not true that merely bringing such conflicts into conscious awareness guarantees that the patients will resolve them. The answers to moral problems are not self-evident; they require a process of complex philosophical thought and analysis.

Nor does the solution lie in instructing the patient to "follow his deepest feelings." That frequently is the policy that brought him to disaster in the first place. Nor does the solution lie in "loving" the patient, and, in effect, giving him a moral blank-check (which is one of the approaches most commonly advocated today). Love is not a substitute for reason, and the suspending of all moral estimates will not provide the patient with the code of values that his mental health requires. The patient feels confused, he feels uncertain of his judgment, he feels he does not know what is right or wrong; if the therapist, to whom the patient has come for guidance, is professionally *committed* to not knowing, the impasse is total.

To the extent that the therapist acts on the principle that he must be silent in moral issues, he passively confirms and sanctions the monopoly on morality held by mysticism—more specifically, by religion. Yet no conscientious therapist can escape the knowledge that religious teachings frequently are instrumental in *causing* the patient's neurosis.

in fact, there is *no way* for a psychotherapist to keep his own moral convictions out of his professional work. By countless subtle indications he reveals and makes the patient aware of his moral estimate—through his pauses, his questions, the things he chooses to say or not to say, etc. But because—for both parties—this process of communication is subconscious, the patient is being guided emotionally rather than intellectually; he does not form an independent, self-conscious appraisal of the therapist's value-premises; he can only accept them, if he accepts them at all, on *faith*, by *feeling*, without reasons or proof, since the issues are never named explicitly. This makes of the therapist, in effect, a religious authority—a subliminal religious authority, as it were.

A therapist who approaches moral problems in this manner will, most commonly, encourage conformity to and the acceptance of the prevailing moral beliefs of the culture, without regard for the question of whether or not those beliefs are compatible with psychological health. But even if the values the therapist communicates are rational, the method of "persuasion" is not—and thus fails to bring the patient any closer to authentic, *independent* rationality.

A code of ethics or morality is a code of values to guide one's choices and actions.

Effective psychotherapy requires a conscious, rational, scientific code of ethics—a system of values based on the facts of reality and geared to the needs of man's life on earth.

It is this that Ayn Rand has provided in her philosophy of Objectivism. For a detailed presentation of the Objectivist ethics, I refer you to Miss Rand's celebrated *Atlas Shrugged* (1957), to my own *Who is Ayn Rand?* (Branden, 1962), and to her most recent work, *The Virtue of Selfishness* (Rand, 1964).

My purpose here is not a detailed exposition of the Objectivist ethics, but rather a presentation of the base or foundation of this system of ethics: the method of deriving and justifying the Objectivist standard of value.

Ayn Rand does not begin by taking the phenomenon of "values" as a given; that is, she does not begin merely by observing that men pursue various values and by assuming that the first question of ethics is: What values ought man to pursue? She begins on a far deeper level, with the question: What are values and why does man need them? What are the facts of reality—the facts of existence and of man's nature—that necessitate and give rise to values?

A *value* is that which one acts to gain and/or keep. A value is the object of an action. " 'Value' presupposes an answer to the question: of value to whom and for what? 'Value' presupposes a standard, a purpose and the necessity of action in the face of an alternative. Where there are no alternatives, no values are possible." (p. 1012)[1] An entity who—by its nature—had no purposes to achieve, no goals to reach, could have no values and no need of values. There would be no "for what." An entity incapable of initiating action, or for whom the consequences would always be the same, regardless of its actions—an entity not confronted with alternatives—could have no purposes, no goals, and hence no values. Only the existence of alternatives can make purpose—and therefore values—possible and necessary.

"There is only one fundamental alternative in the universe; existence or non-existence—and it pertains to a single class of entities; to living organisms. The existence of inanimate matter is unconditional, the existence of life is not: it depends on a specific course of action. Matter is indestructible, it changes its forms, but it cannot cease to exist. It is only a living organism that faces a constant alternative: the issue of life or death. Life is a process of self-sustaining and self-generated action. If an organism fails in that action, it dies; its chemical elements remain, but its life goes out of existence. It is only the concept of 'Life' that makes the concept of 'Value' possible. It is only to a living entity that things can be good or evil" (pp. 1012-13).

It is only a living entity that can have needs, goals, *values*—and it is only a living entity that can generate the actions necessary to achieve them.

A plant does not possess consciousness; it can neither experience pleasure and pain nor have the concepts of life and death; nevertheless, plants can die; a plant's *life* depends on a specific course of action. "A plant must feed itself in order to live; the sunlight, the water, the chemicals it needs are the values its nature has set it to pursue; its life is the standard of value directing its actions. But a plant has no choice of action; there are alternatives in the conditions it encounters, but there is no alternative in its function; it acts automatically to further its life, it cannot act for its own destruction" (p. 1013).

Animals possess a primitive form of consciousness; they cannot

---

[1] This and all subsequent quotations are from Rand (1957).

know the issue of life and death, but they can know pleasure and pain; an animal's life depends on actions automatically guided by its sensory mechanism. "An animal is equipped for sustaining its life; its senses provide it with an automatic code of action, an automatic knowledge of what is good for it or evil. It has no power to extend its knowledge or to evade it. In conditions where its knowledge proves inadequate, it dies. But so long as it lives, it acts on its knowledge, with automatic safety and no power of choice, it is unable to ignore its own good, unable to decide to choose the evil and act as its own destroyer"(p. 1013).

Given the appropriate conditions, the appropriate physical environment, all living organisms—with one exception—are set by their nature to originate automatically the actions required to sustain their survival. The exception is *man*.

Man, like a plant or an animal, must act in order to live; man, like a plant or an animal, must gain the values his life requires. But man does not act and function by automatic chemical reactions or by automatic sensory reactions; there is no physical environment on earth in which man could survive by the guidance of nothing but his involuntary sensations. And man is born without innate ideas; having no innate knowledge of what is true or false, he can have no innate knowledge of what is good for him or evil. *Man has no automatic means of survival.*

Man's basic means of survival is his mind, his capacity to reason. Reason is the faculty that identifies and integrates the material provided by the senses.

For man, survival is a question—a problem to be *solved*. The perceptual level of his consciousness—the level of passive sensory awareness, which he shares with animals—is inadequate to solve it. To remain alive, man must *think*—which means: he must exercise the faculty which he alone, of all living species, possesses: the faculty of abstraction, of *conceptualizing*. The conceptual level of consciousness is the human level, the level required for man's survival. It is upon his ability to think that man's life depends.

"But to think is an act of choice. The key to . . . human nature is the fact that *man is a being of volitional consciousness.* Reason does not work automatically; thinking is not a mechanical process; the connections of logic are not made by instinct. The function of your stomach, lungs or heart is automatic; the function of your mind is not. In any hour and issue of your life, you are free to think or to evade that effort. But you are not free to escape from your nature, from the fact that *reason* is your means of survival—

so that for *you,* who are a human being, the question 'to be or not to be' is the question 'to think or not to think' " (p. 1012).

A being of volitional consciousness, a being without innate ideas, must discover, by a process of thought, the goals, the actions, the values on which his life depends. He must discover what will further his life and what will destroy it. If he acts against the facts of reality, he will perish. If he is to sustain his existence, he must discover the *principles of action* required to guide him in dealing with nature and with other men. His need of these principles is his need of a code of values.

Other species are not free to choose their values. Man is. "A code of values accepted by choice is a code of morality" (p. 1013).

The reason of man's need for morality determines the purpose of morality as well as the standard by which moral values are to be selected. Man needs a moral code in order to live; that is the purpose of morality—for every man as an individual. But in order to know what are the values and virtues that will permit him to achieve that purpose, man requires a standard. Different species achieve their survival in different ways. The course of action proper to the survival of a fish or an animal, would not be proper to the survival of man. Man must choose *his* values by the standard of that which is required for the life of a *human being*—which means: he must hold *man's life* (man's survival *qua* man) as his standard of value. Since reason is man's basic tool of survival, this means: the life appropriate to a rational being—or: that which is required for the survival of man *qua* rational being.

"All that which is proper to the life of a rational being is the good; all that which destroys it is the evil" (p. 1014).

To live, man must think, he must act, he must *produce* the values his life requires. This, metaphysically, is the human mode of existence.

"Man's life, as required by his nature, is not the life of a mindless brute, of a looting thug or a mooching mystic, but the life of a thinking being—not life by means of force or fraud, but life by means of achievement—not survival at any price, since there's only one price that pays for man's survival: reason" (p. 1014).

Thinking is man's basic virtue, the source of all his other virtues. Thinking is the activity of perceiving and identifying that which exists—of integrating perceptions into concepts, and concepts into still wider concepts, of constantly expanding the range of one's knowledge to encompass more and more of reality.

Evasion, the refusal to think, the willful rejection of reason, the willful suspension of consciousness, the willful defiance of reality, is man's basic vice—the source of all his evils.

Man, like every other living species, has a specific manner of survival which is determined by his nature. Man is free to act against the requirements of his nature, to reject his means of survival, his mind; but he is not free to escape the consequences: misery, anxiety, destruction. When men attempt to survive, not by thought and productive work, but by parasitism and force, by theft and brutality, it is still the faculty of reason that they are secretly counting on: the rationality that some moral man had to exercise in order to create the goods which the parasites propose to loot or expropriate. Man's life depends on thinking, not on acting blindly; on achievement, not on destruction; nothing can change that fact. Mindlessness, passivity, parasitism, brutality are not and cannot be principles of survival; they are merely the policy of those who do not wish to face the issue of survival.

"Man's life" means: life lived in accordance with the *principles* that make man's survival *qua* man possible.

Just as man is alive, physically, to the extent that the organs within his body function in the constant service of his life, so man is alive, as a total entity, to the extent that his *mind* functions in the constant service of his life. The mind, too, is a vital organ—the one vital organ whose function is volitional. A man encased in an iron lung, whose own lungs are paralyzed, is not dead; but he is not living the life proper to man. Neither is a man whose *mind* is volitionally paralyzed.

If man is to live, he must recognize that facts are facts, that A is A, that *existence* exists—that reality is an absolute, not to be evaded or escaped—and that the task of his mind is to perceive it, that *this* is his primary responsibility. He must recognize that his life requires the pursuit and achievement of rational values, values consonant with his nature and with reality—that life is a process of self-sustaining and self-generated action. He must recognize that *self*-value is the value without which no others are possible, but it is a value that has to be earned—and the virtue that earns it, is thinking. "To live, man must hold three things as the supreme and ruling values of his life: Reason—Purpose—Self-esteem. Reason, as his only tool of knowledge—Purpose, as his choice of the happiness which that tool must proceed to achieve—Self-esteem, as his inviolate certainty that his mind is competent to think and his person is worthy of happiness, which means: is worthy of living" (p. 1018).

The cardinal principle at the base of Ayn Rand's ethical system is the statement that "it is only the concept of 'Life' that makes the concept of 'Value' possible. It is only to a living entity that things can be good or evil." This is the identification that cuts through the Gordian knot of past ethical theorizing, that dissolves the mystical fog in the field of morality, and refutes the contention that a rational morality is impossible and that values cannot be derived from facts.

It is the nature of living entities—the fact that they must sustain their life by self-generated action—that makes the existence of *values* possible and necessary. For each living species, the course of action required is specific; what an entity *is* determines what it *ought* to do.

By identifying the context in which values arise existentially, Ayn Rand refutes the claim—especially prevalent today—that the ultimate standard of any moral judgment is "arbitrary," that *normative* propositions cannot be derived from *factual* propositions. By identifying the genetic roots of "value" epistemologically, she demonstrates that not to hold man's life as one's standard of moral judgment is to be guilty of a *logical contradiction.* It is only to a living entity that things can be good or evil; life is the basic value that makes all other values possible; the value of life is not to be justified by a value beyond itself; to demand such justification—to ask: Why *should* man choose to live?—is to have dropped the meaning, context and source of one's concepts. "Should" is a concept that can have no intelligible meaning, if divorced from the concept *and value* of life.

If life—existence—is not accepted as one's standard, then only one alternative standard remains: *non*-existence. But non-existence—death—is not a standard of value: it is the negation of values. The man who does not wish to hold life as his goal and standard is free not to hold it; but he cannot claim the sanction of reason; he cannot claim that his choice is as valid as any other. It is not "arbitrary," it is not "optional," whether or not man accepts his nature as a living being—just as it is not "arbitrary" or "optional" whether or not he accepts reality.

What are the major virtues man's survival requires, according to the Objectivist ethics? Rationality—Independence—Honesty—Integrity—Justice—Productiveness—Pride.

Rationality is the unreserved commitment to the perception of reality, to the acceptance of reason as an absolute, as one's only guide of knowledge, values and action. Independence is reliance upon one's own mind and judgment, the acceptance of intellectual responsibility for one's own existence. Honesty is the refusal to seek values by faking reality, by evading the distinction between the real and the unreal. Integrity is loyalty *in action* to the judgment of one's consciousness. Justice is the practice of identifying men for what they *are,* and treating them accordingly—of rewarding the actions and traits of character in men which are pro-life and condemning those which are anti-life. Productiveness is the act of supporting one's existence by translating one's thought into reality, of setting one's goals and working for their achievement, of bringing knowledge or goods into existence. Pride is moral ambitiousness, the dedication to achieving one's highest potential, in one's character and in one's life—and the refusal to be sacrificial fodder for the goals of others.

If life on earth is the standard, then it is not the man who *sacrifices* values who is moral, but the man who *achieves* them; not the man who renounces, but the man who creates; not the man who forsakes life, but the man who makes life possible.

The Objectivist ethics teaches that man—every man—is an end in himself, not a means to the ends of others. *He is not a sacrificial animal.* As a living being, he must exist for his own sake, neither sacrificing himself to others nor sacrificing others to himself. The achievement of his own happiness is man's highest moral purpose.

To live for his own happiness imposes a solemn responsibility on man: he must learn what his happiness objectively requires. It is a responsibility that the majority of men have not chosen to assume. No belief is more prevalent—or more disastrous—than that men can achieve their happiness by the pursuit of any random desires they experience. The existence of such a profession as psychotherapy is an eloquent refutation of that belief. Happiness is the consequence of living the life proper to man *qua* rational being, the consequence of pursuing and achieving consistent, life-serving values.

Thus, Objectivism advocates an ethics of *rational self-interest.*

Only reason can judge what is or is not objectively to man's self-interest; the question cannot be decided by feeling or whim. To act by the guidance of feelings and whims is to pursue a course of self-destruction; and self-destruction is not to man's self-interest.

To think is to man's self-interest; to suspend his consciousness, is not. To choose his goals in the full context of his knowledge, his values and his life, is to man's self-interest; to act on the impulse of the moment, without regard for his long-range context, is not. To exist as a productive being, is to man's self-interest; to attempt to exist as a parasite, is not. To seek the life proper to his nature, is to man's self-interest; to seek to live as an animal, is not.

In the light of the foregoing, let us turn now to a consideration of the issue of mental health.

It is a bromide of modern psychology that mental health cannot be defined. That which we call "healthy" or "normal," psychologists commonly declare, is determined by the culture or society in which one happens to live; what is health in one society is not healthy in another; it is all "relative"—there can be no universal and objective standard of mental health, they declare, just as there can be no universal and objective standard of moral values.

Psychological relativism is a corollary of moral relativism—and contains the same fallacies.

Just as the nature of mental health is not determined by *individual* preference, so it is not determined by social, cultural or historical preference; it is determined by the nature of man. That some hallucinating savage lives on an island where hallucinations are fashionable, does not alter the fact that hallucinations are the proof and the product of an aberrated mind. A leper cannot make himself healthy by joining a leper colony where his disease is shared by everyone; neither can a schizophrenic. Health is not adherence to a statistical norm. A healthy *body* is one whose organs function efficiently in maintaining the life of the organism; a diseased body is one whose organs do not. The standard by which health and disease are to be measured is *life,* for it is only the alternative of life or death that makes the concept of health or disease meaningful or possible. Just as medical science evaluates man's body by the standard of whether or not his body is functioning as man's life requires, so psychological science must uphold the standard of life in appraising the health or disease of a man's consciousness. The health of man's consciousness must be judged, like the health of any other organ, by how well it performs its proper function; and the function of consciousness is perception, cognition, and the initiation and direction of action.

An unobstructed consciousness, an integrated consciousness, a thinking consciousness, is a *healthy* consciousness. A blocked consciousness, an evading consciousness, a self-blinding consciousness, a consciousness disintegrated by fear or immobilized by depression, a consciousness dissociated from reality, in an *unhealthy* consciousness.

A psychologist cannot—and should not attempt to—force his views on a patient who is unwilling to accept them. Nothing can compel a mind to work, to think, to accept reason; that is a matter of a man's own choice. But this does not mean that health or disease—good or evil—are subjective and "personal." If a physician sees a patient who suffers from pneumonia wandering with inadequate clothing in the rain, he does not say: "It seems to me that is bad for the patient—but who am I to pass value-judgments?" But as psychotherapy is currently practiced, psychologists utter the equivalent of such statements every day, as when they declare that one must not "tamper" with a patient's religious beliefs. Or again: if an individual came to a physician and requested to be cured of a disease that had already infected two-thirds of the population, the physician would not reply: "Adjust to your environment. Do you want to be a non-conformist?" But what might a modern psychologist reply to *his* patient?

Neurotic and psychotic manifestations are the *symptoms* of a mind's malfunctioning. In order to learn whether a particular action or belief *is* an expression of such malfunctioning, it may be necessary to evaluate and interpret that action or belief in a social, cultural or historical context. This is an issue of *diagnosis*—not of the nature of mental health. It is *not* an indication of neurosis, for instance, for a man to believe, in the sixth century, that the earth is flat; but to believe it in the twentieth century, *is*. The diagnostician has to take into consideration the knowledge available to the patient (or person being studied). Ignorance or honest errors of knowledge are not intrinsic signs of disease; only errors due to evasion, to the rejection of available evidence, are. The concept of mental health pertains to the manner in which a consciousness *functions;* this determines the degree of its health.

I have said that man is a being of volitional consciousness. This means that man is free to exercise his rational faculty—or to suspend it; to act in accordance with his best, clearest and most conscientious judgment—or to act against it, moved by blind feelings; to preserve his intellectual independence and integrity—or to surrender in parasitical fear to the authority of others. This principle has the most profound implications for psychology in general, and psychotherapy in particular.

Man is the one living species who must, by volitional effort, make himself into an entity that is *able* to live and *worthy* of living. Self-esteem is the conviction that one has succeeded at this task. Self-esteem is the conviction that one is able to live and worthy of living—which means: that one's mind is competent to think and one's person is worthy of happiness.

Self-esteem is the hallmark of mental health. It is the consequence, expression and reward of a mind fully committed to reason. Commitment to reason is commitment to the maintenance of a full intellectual focus, to the constant expansion of one's understanding and knowledge, to the principle that one's actions must be consistent with one's convictions, that one must never attempt to fake reality, or place any consideration above reality, that one must never permit oneself contradictions—that one must never attempt to subvert or sabotage the proper function of consciousness.

In order to deal with reality successfully—to pursue and achieve the values which his life requires—man needs self-esteem: he needs to be confident of his efficacy and worth. Anxiety and guilt, the antipodes of self-esteem and the insignia of mental illness, are the disintegrators of thought, the distorters of values and the paralyzers of action. When a man of self-esteem chooses his values and sets his goals, when he projects the long-range purposes that will unify and guide his actions, it is like a bridge thrown to the future, across which his life will pass, a bridge supported by the conviction that his mind is competent to think, to judge, to value, and that *he* is worthy of enjoying values.

This sense of control over reality, of control over one's own existence, is not the result of special skills, ability or knowledge. It is not dependent on particular successes or failures. It reflects one's fundamental relationship to reality, one's conviction of fundamental efficacy and worthiness. It reflects the certainty that, in essence and in principle, one is right for reality.

It is this psychological state that traditional morality makes impossible, to the extent that a man accepts its tenets. And this is one of the foremost reasons why a psychotherapist cannot be indifferent to the question of moral values in his work.

Neither mysticism nor the creed of self-sacrifice is compatible with mental health or self-esteem. These doctrines are destructive existentially *and psychologically.*

(1) The maintenance of his life and the achievement of self-esteem require of man the fullest exercise of his reason—but morality, men are taught, rests on and requires *faith.*

Faith is the commitment of one's consciousness to beliefs for which one has no sensory evidence or rational proof.

When a man rejects reason as his standard of judgment, only one alternative standard remains to him: his feelings. A mystic is a man who treats his feelings as tools of cognition. Faith is the equation of *feeling* with *knowledge.*

To practice the "virtue" of faith, one must be willing to suspend one's sight and one's judgment; one must be willing to live with the unintelligible, with that which cannot be conceptualized or integrated into the rest of one's knowledge, and to induce a trancelike illusion of understanding. One must be willing to repress one's critical faculty and hold it as one's guilt; one must be willing to drown any questions that rise in protest—to strangle any thrust of reason convulsively seeking to assert its proper function as the protector of one's life and cognitive integrity.

Remember that all of man's knowledge and all his concepts have a hierarchical structure. The foundation and starting point of man's thinking are his sensory perceptions; on this base, man forms his first concepts, then goes on building the edifice of his knowledge by identifying and integrating new concepts on a wider and wider scale. If man's thinking is to be valid, this process must be guided by *logic,* "the art of non-contradictory identification"—(p. 1016)—and any new concept man forms must be integrated without contradiction into the hierarchical structure of his knowledge. To introduce into one's consciousness any idea that cannot be so integrated, an idea not derived from reality, not validated by a process of reason, not subject to rational examination or judgment—and worse: an idea that clashes with the rest of one's concepts and understanding of reality—is to sabotage the integrative function of consciousness, to undercut the rest of one's convictions and kill one's capacity to be certain of anything. This is the meaning of John Galt's statement in *Atlas Shrugged* that "the alleged shortcut to knowledge, which is faith, is only a short circuit destroying the mind" (p. 1018).

There is no greater self-delusion than to imagine that one can render unto reason that which is reason's and unto faith that which is faith's. Faith cannot be circumscribed or delimited; to surrender one's consciousness by an inch, is to surrender one's consciousness in total. Either reason is an absolute to a mind or it is not—and if it is not, there is no place to draw the line, no principle by which to draw it, no barrier faith cannot cross, no part of one's life faith cannot invade: then one remains rational only until and unless one's *feelings* decree otherwise.

Faith is a malignancy that no system can tolerate with impunity; and the man who succumbs to it, will call on it in precisely those issues where he needs his reason most. When one turns from reason to faith, when one rejects the absolutism of reality, one undercuts the absolutism of one's consciousness—and one's mind becomes an organ one cannot trust any longer. It becomes what the mystics claim it to be: a tool of distortion.

(2) Man's need of self-esteem entails the need for a sense of control over reality—but no control is possible in a universe which, by one's own concession, contains the supernatural, the miraculous and the causeless, a universe in which one is at the mercy of ghosts and demons, in which one must deal, not with the *unknown,* but with the *unknowable;* no control is possible if man proposes, but a ghost disposes; no control is possible if the universe is a haunted house.

(3) His life and self-esteem require that the object and concern of man's consciousness be reality and this earth—but morality, men are taught, consists of scorning this earth and the world available to sensory perception, and of contemplating, instead, a "different" and "higher" reality, a realm inaccessible to reason and incommunicable in language, but attainable by revelation, by special dialectical processes, by that superior state of intellectual lucidity known to Zen-Buddhists as "No-Mind," or by death.

There is only one reality—the reality knowable to reason. And if man does not choose to perceive it, there is nothing else for him to perceive; if it is not of this world that he is conscious, then he is not conscious at all.

The sole result of the mystic projection of "another" reality, is that it incapacitates man psychologically for this one. It was not by contemplating the transcendental, the ineffable, the undefinable—it was not by contemplating the nonexistent—that man lifted himself from the cave and transformed the material world to make a human existence possible on earth.

If it is a virtue to renounce one's mind, but a sin to use it; if it is a virtue to approximate the mental state of a schizophrenic, but a sin to be in intellectual focus; if it is a virtue to denounce this earth, but a sin to make it livable; if it is a virtue to mortify the flesh, but a sin to work and act; if it is a virtue to despise life, but a sin to sustain and enjoy it—Then no self-esteem or control or efficacy are possible to man, *nothing* is possible to him but the guilt and terror of a wretch caught in a nightmare universe, a universe created by some metaphysical sadist who has cast man into a maze where the door marked "virtue" leads to self-destruction and the door marked "efficacy" leads to self-damnation.

(4) His life and self-esteem require that man take pride in his power to think, pride in his power to live—but morality, men are taught, holds pride, and specifically intellectual pride, as the gravest of sins. Virtue begins, men are taught, with humility; with the recognition of the helplessness, the smallness, the impotence of one's mind.

Is man omniscient?—demand the mystics. Is he infallible? Then how dare he challenge the word of God, or of God's representatives, and set himself up as the judge of—anything?

Intellectual pride is not—as the mystics preposterously imply it to be—a pretense at omniscience or infallibility. On the contrary, precisely because man must *struggle* for knowledge, precisely because the pursuit of knowledge requires an *effort,* the men who assume this responsibility properly feel pride.

Sometimes, colloquially, pride is taken to mean a pretense at accomplishments one has not in fact achieved. But the braggart, the boaster, the man who affects virtues he does not possess, is not proud; he has merely chosen the most humiliating way to reveal his humility.

Pride (as an emotional state) is one's response to one's power to achieve values, the pleasure one takes in one's own efficacy. And it is this that mystics regard as evil.

But if doubt, not confidence, is man's proper moral state; if self-distrust, not self-reliance, is the proof of his virtue; if fear, not self-esteem, is the mark of perfection; if guilt, not pride, is his goal—then mental illness is a moral ideal, the neurotics and psychotics are the highest exponents of morality, and the thinkers, the achievers, are the sinners, those who are too corrupt and too arrogant to seek virtue and psychological well-being through the belief that they are unfit to exist.

Humility is, of necessity, the basic virtue of a mystical morality; it is the only virtue possible to men who have renounced the mind.

Pride has to be earned; it is the reward of effort and achievement; but to gain the virtue of humility, one has only to abstain from thinking—nothing else is demanded—and one will feel humble quickly enough.

(5) His life and self-esteem require of man loyalty to his values, loyality to his mind and its judgments, loyalty to his life—but the essence of morality, men are taught, consists of self-sacrifice: the

sacrifice of one's mind to some higher authority, and the sacrifice of one's values to whomever may claim to require it.

It is not necessary, in this context, to analyze the almost countless evils entailed by the precept of self-sacrifice. Its irrationality and destructiveness have been thoroughly exposed in *Atlas Shrugged*. But there are two aspects of the issue that are especially pertinent to the subject of mental health.

The first is the fact that *self*-sacrifice means—and can only mean—*mind*-sacrifice.

A sacrifice means the surrender of a higher value in favor of a lower value or of a nonvalue. If one gives up that which one does not value in order to obtain that which one does value—or if one gives up a lesser value in order to obtain a greater one—this is not a sacrifice, but a *gain*.

All of man's values exist in a hierarchy; he values some things more than others; and, to the extent that he is rational, the hierarchical order of his values is rational: that is, he values things in proportion to their importance in serving his life and well-being. That which is inimical to his life and well-being, that which is inimical to his nature and needs as a living being, he *dis*values.

Conversely, one of the characteristics of mental illness is a distorted value structure; the neurotic does not value things according to their objective merit, in relation to his nature and needs; he frequently values the very things that will lead him to self-destruction. Judged by objective standards, he is engaged in a chronic process of self-sacrifice.

But if sacrifice is a virtue, it is not the neurotic but the rational man who must be "cured." He must learn to do violence to his own rational judgment—to reverse the order of his value hierarchy—to surrender that which his mind has chosen as the good—to turn against and invalidate his own consciousness.

Do mystics declare that all they demand of man is that he sacrifice his *happiness?* To sacrifice one's happiness is to sacrifice one's desires; to sacrifice one's desires is to sacrifice one's values; to sacrifice one's values is to sacrifice one's judgment; to sacrifice one's judgment is to sacrifice one's mind—and it is nothing less than this that the creed of self-sacrifice aims at and demands.

If his judgment is to be an object of sacrifice—what sort of efficacy, control, freedom from conflict, or serenity of spirit will be possible to man?

The second aspect that is pertinent here, involves not only the creed of self-sacrifice but *all* the foregoing tenets of traditional morality.

An irrational morality, a morality set in opposition to man's nature, to the facts of reality and to the requirements of man's survival, necessarily forces men to accept the belief that there is an inevitable clash between the moral and the practical—that they must choose either to be virtuous or to be happy, to be idealistic or to be successful, but they cannot be both. This view establishes a disastrous conflict on the deepest level of man's being, a lethal dichotomy that tears man apart; it forces him to choose between making himself *able* to live and making himself *worthy* of living. Yet self-esteem and mental health require that he achieve *both*.

If man holds life on earth as the good, if he judges his values by the standard of that which is proper to the existence of a rational being, then there is no clash between the requirements of survival and of morality—no clash between making himself able to live and making himself worthy of living; he achieves the second by achieving the first. But there *is* a clash, if man holds the renunciation of this earth as the good, the renunciation of life, of mind, of happiness, of self. Under anti-life morality, man makes himself worthy of living to the extent that he makes himself unable to live—and to the extent tl at he makes himself able to live, he makes himself unworthy of living.

The answer given by many defenders of traditional morality is: "Oh, but people don't have to go to extremes!"—meaning: "We don't expect people to be *fully* moral. We expect them to smuggle *some* self-interest into their lives. We recognize that people have to live, after all."

The defense, then of this code of morality is that few people will be suicidal enough to attempt to practice it consistently. *Hypocrisy* is to be man's protector against his professed moral convictions. What does *that* do to his self-esteem?

And what of the victims who are insufficiently hypocritical?

What of the child who withdraws in terror into an autistic universe because he cannot cope with the ravings of parents who tell him that he is guilty by nature, that his body is evil, that thinking is sinful, that question-asking is blasphemous, that doubting is depravity, and that he must obey the orders of a supernatural ghost because, if he doesn't, he will burn forever in hell?

Or the daughter who collapses in guilt over the sin of not wanting to devote her life to caring for the ailing father who has given her cause to feel only hatred?

Or the adolescent who flees into homosexuality because he has been taught that sex is evil and that women are to be worshipped, but not desired?

Or the businessman who suffers an anxiety attack because, after years of being urged to be thrifty and industrious, he has finally committed the sin of succeeding, and is now told that it shall be easier for the camel to pass through the eye of a needle than for a rich man to enter the kingdom of heaven?

Or the neurotic who, in hopeless despair, gives up the attempt to solve his problems because he has always heard it preached that this earth is a realm of misery, futility and doom, where no happiness or fulfillment is possible to man?

If the advocates of these doctrines bear a grave moral responsibility, there is a group who perhaps, bears a graver responsibility still: the psychologists and psychiatrists who see the human wreckage of these doctrines, but who remain silent and do not protest—who declare that philosophical and moral issues do not concern them, that science cannot pronounce value judgments—who shrug off their professional obligations with the assertion that a *rational* code of morality is impossible, and, by their silence, lend their sanction to spiritual murder.

Mental health requires of man that he place no value above perception, which means: no value above consciousness, which means: no value above reality.

Every neurosis entails a break with reality. A neurotic is a man who, when his desires clash with reality, considers reality expendable. This is the attitude that the psychotherapist must seek to correct. But he cannot do so except by challenging (a) the patient's manner of using his consciousness, the abuses to which he subjects it, the evasions, the emotion-worshipping, the policy of mental inertia, and (b) the values that create the patient's emotions and set his purposes and goals.

If the patient is to be cured of his neurosis, he must learn to distinguish between a *thought* and a *feeling,* between a *fact* and a *wish,* and to recognize that nothing but destruction can result from sacrificing one's sight of reality to any other consideration. He must learn to seek his sense of self-esteem in the productive use of his mind, in the achievement of rational values, on whatever his level of ability. He must learn that the approval of others cannot be a substitute for self-esteem, and that only anxiety is possible to those who attempt such a substitution. He must learn not to seek the fraud of unearned love, and not to grant it. He must learn not to be afraid to question and challenge the prevalent beliefs of his culture. He must learn to reject the claims of those who demand his agreement *on faith*. He must learn to fight for his own happiness and to deserve it. He must learn that the irrational *will not work*—and that so long as any part of him desires it, that desire is the cause of his suffering.

He must learn to live as a rational being—and for guidance at this task, he needs a code of rational moral principles.

This is the reason I consider the Objectivist ethics indispensable to the practice of psychotherapy.

REFERENCES

Branden, N. *Who is Ayn Rand?* New York: Random House, 1962.

Rand, Ayn. *Atlas shrugged.* New York: Random House, 1957.

Rand, Ayn. *The virtue of selfishness.* New York: New American Library, 1964.

31

THE CASE AGAINST RELIGION:
A PSYCHOTHERAPIST'S VIEW

Albert Ellis, Ph.D.

Before we can talk sensibly about religion—or almost anything else!—we should give some kind of a definition of what we are talking about. Let me, therefore, start with what I think are some legitimate definitions of the term *religion*. Other concepts of this term, of course, exist; but what *I* am talking about when I use it is as follows.

According to Webster's New World Dictionary, religion is: "1. belief in a divine or superhuman power or powers to be obeyed and worshipped as the creator(s) and ruler(s) of the universe. 2. expression of this belief in conduct and ritual."

English and English (1958), in their *Comprehensive Dictionary of Psychological and Psychoanalytical Terms*, define religion as "a system of attitudes, practices, rites, ceremonies, and beliefs by means of which individuals or a community put themselves in relation to God or to a supernatural world and often to each other, and from which the religious person derives a set of values by which to judge events in the natural world."

The *Columbia Encyclopedia* notes that "when a man becomes conscious of a power above and beyond the human, and recognizes a dependence of himself upon that power, religion has become a factor in his being."

These, then, are the definitions of religion which I accept and which I shall have in mind as I discuss the religious viewpoint in this paper. Religion, to me, must include some concept of a supernatural deity and some dependence on this deity. When the term

Reprinted by permission of the author and *The Independent,* October 1962, pp. 1-7.

is used merely to denote a system of beliefs, practices, or ethical values which are not connected with any assumed higher power, then I believe it is used loosely and confusingly: since such a non-supernatural system of beliefs can more accurately be described as a philosophy of life or a code of ethics, and it is misleading to confuse a believer in this general kind of philosophy or ethical code with a true religionist.

Every atheist, in other words, has *some* kind of philosophy and *some* code of ethics; and many atheists, in fact, have much more rigorous life philosophies and ethical systems than have most deists.

SOMEONE IS RELIGIOUS . . .

It therefore seems silly to say that someone is religious because he happens to be philosophic or ethical; and unless we rigorously use the term religion to mean some kind of *faith unfounded on fact*, or dependency on some assumed superhuman entities, we broaden the definition of the word so greatly as to make it practically meaningless.

If religion is defined as man's dependence on a power above and beyond the human, then, as a psychotherapist, I find it to be exceptionally pernicious. For the psychotherapist is normally dedicated to helping human beings in general and his patients in particular to achieve certain goals of mental health, and virtually all these goals are antithetical to a truly religious viewpoint.

Let us look at the main psychotherapeutic goals. On the basis of twenty years of clinical experience, and in basic agreement with most of my professional colleagues (such as Braaten, 1961; Dreikurs, 1955; Fromm, 1955; Goldstein, 1954; Maslow, 1954; Rogers, 1957; and Thorne, 1961), I would say that the psychotherapist tries to help his patients be minimally anxious and hostile, and to this end, he tries to help them to acquire the following kinds of personality traits:

1. *Self-interest*. The emotionally healthy individual should primarily be true to himself and not masochistically sacrifice himself for others. His kindness and consideration for others should be derived from the idea that he himself wants to enjoy freedom from unnecessary pain and restriction, and that he is only likely to do so by helping create a world in which the rights of others, as well as himself, are not needlessly curtailed.

2. *Self-direction.* He should assume responsibility for his own life, be able independently to work out most of his problems, and while at times wanting or preferring the cooperation and help of others, not *need* their support for his effectiveness or well-being.

3. *Tolerance.* He should fully give other human beings the right to be wrong; and, while disliking or abhorring some of their behavior, still not blame *them*, as persons, for performing this dislikeable behavior. He should accept the fact that all humans are remarkably fallible, never unrealistically expect them to be perfect, and refrain from despising or punishing them when they make inevitable mistakes and errors.

4. *Acceptance of uncertainty.* The emotionally mature individual should completely accept the fact that we all live in a world of probability and chance, where there are not nor probably ever will be any absolute certainties, and should realize that it is not at all horrible—indeed, in many ways it is fascinating and exciting—to live in such a probabilistic, uncertain world.

5. *Flexibility.* He should remain intellectually flexible, be open to change at all times, and unbigotedly view the infinitely varied people, ideas, and things in the world around him.

6. *Scientific thinking.* He should be objective, rational, and scientific, and be able to apply the laws of logic and of scientific method not only to external people and events, but to himself and his interpersonal relationships.

7. *Commitment.* He should be vitally absorbed in something outside of himself, whether it be in people, things, or ideas, and should preferably have at least one major creative interest, as well as some outstanding human involvement, which is highly important to him, and around which he structures a good part of his life.

8. *Risk-taking.* The emotionally sound person should be able to take risks: to ask himself what he would really like to do in life, and then to try to do this, even though he has to risk defeat or failure. He should be adventurous (though not necessarily foolhardy); be willing to try almost anything once, just to see how he likes it; and look forward to some breaks in his usual life routine.

9. *Self-acceptance.* He should normally be glad to be alive, and to like himself just *because* he is alive, *because* he exists, and because he (as a living being) invariably has some power to enjoy himself, to create happiness and joy. He should not equate his worth or value to himself on his extrinsic achievements, or on what *others* think of him, but on his personal existence; on *his* ability to think, feel, and act, and thereby to *make* some kind of

an interesting, absorbed life for himself.

These, then, are the kind of personality traits which a psychotherapist is interested in helping his patients achieve and which he is also, prophylactically, interested in fostering in the lives of millions who will never be his patients.

How, now, does religion—by which, again, I mean faith unfounded on fact, or dependence on some supernatural deity—help human beings to achieve these healthy traits and thereby to avoid becoming anxious, depressed, and hostile?

The answer, of course, is that it doesn't help at all, and in most respects it seriously sabotages mental health. For religion, first of all, is not self-interest: it is god-interest.

The religious person must, by virtual definition, be so concerned with whether or not his hypothesized god loves him, and whether he is doing the right thing to continue to keep in this god's good graces, that he must, at the very best, put himself second, and must sacrifice some of his most cherished interests to appease this god. If, moreover, he is a member of any organized religion, then he must choose his god's precepts first, those of his church and its clergy second, and his own views and preferences third.

NO VIEWS OF HIS OWN

In a sense, the religious person must have *no* real views of his own; and it is presumptuous of him, in fact, to have any. In regard to sex-love affairs, to marriage and family relations, to business, to politics, and to virtually everything else that is important in his life, he must try to discover what his god and his clergy would like him to do; and he must primarily do *their* bidding.

Masochistic self-sacrifice is an integral part of almost all organized religions: as shown, for example, in the various forms of ritualistic self-deprivation that Jews, Christians, Mohammedans, and other religionists must continually undergo if they are to keep in good with their assumed gods.

Masochism, indeed, stems from an individual's deliberately inflicting pain on himself in order that he may guiltlessly permit himself to experience some kind of sexual or other pleasure; and the very essence of most organized religions is the performance of masochistic, guilt-soothing rituals, by which the religious individual gives himself permission to enjoy life.

Religiosity, to a large degree, essentially *is* masochism, and both are forms of mental sickness.

In regard to self-direction, it can easily be seen from what has just been said that the religious person is by necessity dependent and other-directed rather than independent and self-directed. If he is true to his religious beliefs, he must first bow down to his god; second, to the clergy who run this god's church; and third, to all the other members of his religious sect, who are eagle-eyedly watching him to see whether he deflects an iota from the conduct his god and his church define as proper.

If religion, therefore, is largely masochism, it is even more dependency. For a man to be a true believer and to be strong and independent is impossible; religion and self-sufficiency are contradictory terms.

Tolerance, again, is a trait that the firm religionist cannot possibly possess. "I am the Lord thy God and thou shalt have no other Gods before me," sayeth Jehovah. Which means, in plain English, that whatever any given god and his clergy believe must be absolutely, positively true; and whatever any other person or group believes must be absolutely, positively false.

Democracy, permissiveness, and the acceptance of human fallibility are quite alien to the real religionist—since he can only believe that the creeds and commands of his particular deity should, ought, and must be obeyed, and that anyone who disobeys them is patently a knave.

Religion, with its definitional absolutes, can never rest with the concept of an individual's doing wrong or making mistakes, but must inevitably add to this the notion of his sinning and of his deserving to be punished for his sins. For, if it is merely *desirable* for you to refrain from harming others or committing other misdeeds, as any non-religious code of ethics will inform you that it is, then if you make a mistake and do commit some misdeeds, you are merely a wrongdoer, or one who is doing an undesirable deed and who should try to correct himself and do less wrong in the future. But if it is god-given, absolutistic law that you *shall* not, *must* not, do a wrong act, and you actually do it, you are then a miserable sinner, a worthless being, and must severely punish yourself (perhaps eternally, in Hell) for being a wrongdoer, being a fallible human.

Religion, then, by setting up absolute, god-given standards, must make you self-depreciating and dehumanized when you err; and must lead you to despise and dehumanize others when they act badly. This kind of absolutistic, perfectionistic thinking is the prime creator of the two most corroding of human emotions: anxiety and hostility.

If one of the requisites for emotional health is acceptance of uncertainty, then religion is obviously the unhealthiest state imaginable: since its prime reason for being is to enable the religionist to believe in a mythical certainty.

Just because life is so uncertain, and because millions of people *think* that they cannot take its viscissitudes, they invent absolutistic gods, and thereby pretend that there is some final, invariant answer to things. Patently, these people are fooling themselves—and instead of healthfully admitting that they do not *need* certainty, but can live comfortably in this often disorderly world, they stubbornly protect their neurotic beliefs by insisting that there *must* be the kind of certainty that they foolishly believe that they need.

This is like a child's believing that he *must* have a kindly father in order to survive; and then, when his father is unkindly, or perhaps has died and is nonexistent, he dreams up a father (who may be a neighbor, a movie star, or a pure figment of his imagination) and insists that this dream-father actually exists.

The trait of flexibility, which is so essential to proper emotional functioning, is also blocked and sabotaged by religious belief. For the person who dogmatically believes in god, and who sustains this belief with a faith unfounded in fact, which a true religionist of course must, clearly is *not* open to change and *is* necessarily bigoted.

If, for example, his scriptures or his church tell him that he shall not even covet his neighbor's wife—let alone having actual adulterous relations with her!—he cannot ask himself "*Why* should I not lust after this woman, as long as I don't intend to do anything about my desire for her? What is *really* wrong about that?" For his god and his church have spoken; and there is no appeal from this arbitrary authority, once he has brought himself to accept it.

Anytime, in fact, anyone unempirically establishes a god or a set of religious postulates which have a superhuman origin, he can thereafter use no empirical evidence whatever to question the dictates of this god or these postulates, since they are (by definition) beyond scientific validation.

The best he can do, if he wants to change any of the rules that stem from his religion is to change the religion itself. Otherwise, he is stuck with the absolutistic axioms, and their logical corollaries, that he himself has initially accepted on faith. We may therefore note again that, just as religion *is* masochism, other-directedness, intolerance, and refusal to accept uncertainty, it also is mental and emotional inflexibility.

In regard to scientific thinking, it practically goes without saying that this kind of cerebration is quite antithetical to religiosity. The main canon of the scientific method—as Ayer (1947), Carnap (1953), Reichenbach (1953) and a host of other modern philosophers of science have pointed out—is that, at least in some final analysis, or in principle, all theories be confirmable by some form of human experience, some empirical referent. But all religions which are worthy of the name contend that their superhuman entities cannot be seen, heard, smelled, tasted, felt, or otherwise humanly experienced, and that their gods and their principles are therefore distinctly beyond science.

To believe in any of these religions, therefore, is to be unscientific at least to *some* extent; and it could well be contended that the more religious one is, the less scientific one tends to be. Although a religious person need not be *entirely* unscientific (as, for that matter, a raving maniac need not be either), it is difficult to see how he could be perfectly scientific.

While a *person* may be both scientific and religious (as he may also be at times sensible and at other times foolish), it is doubtful if an individual's *attitude* may simultaneously be truly pious and objective.

In regard to the trait of commitment, the religious individual may—for once!—have some advantages. For if he is truly religious, he is seriously committed to his god, his church, or his creed; and to some extent, at least, he thereby acquires a major interest in life.

Religious commitment also frequently has its serious disadvantages; since it tends to be obsessive-compulsive; and it may well interfere with other kinds of healthy commitments—such as deep involvements in sex-love relations, in scientific pursuits, and even in artistic endeavors. Moreover, it is a commitment that is often motivated by guilt or hostility, and may serve as a frenzied covering-up mechanism which masks, but does not really eliminate, these underlying disturbed feelings. It is also the kind of commitment that is based on falsehoods and illusions, and that therefore easily can be shattered, thus plunging the previously committed individual into the depths of disillusionment and despair.

Not all forms of commitment, in other words, are equally healthy. The Grand Inquisitors of the medieval Catholic church were utterly dedicated to their "holy" work, and Hitler and many of his associates were fanatically committed to their Nazi doctrines. But this hardly proves that they were emotionally stable human beings.

When religious individuals are happily committed to their faith, they often tend to be fanatically and dogmatically committed in an obsessive-compulsive way that itself is hardly desirable. Religious commitment may well be better for a human being than no commitment to anything. But religion, to a large degree, is *fanaticism*—which, in turn, is an obsessive-compulsive, rigid form of holding to a viewpoint that invariably masks and provides a bulwark for the underlying insecurity of the obsessed individual.

In regard to risk-taking, it should be obvious that the religious person is highly determined *not* to be adventurous nor to take any of life's normal risks. He strongly believes in unvalidateable assumptions precisely *because* he does not want to risk following his *own* preferences and aims, but wants the guarantee that some higher power will back him.

Enormously fearing failure, and falsely defining his own worth as a person in terms of achievement, he sacrifices time, energy, and material goods and pleasures to the worship of his assumed god, so that he can at least be sure that this god loves and supports him. All religions worthy of the name are distinctly inhibiting; which means, in effect, that the religious person sells his soul, surrenders his own basic urges and pleasures, so that he may feel comfortable with the heavenly helper that he himself has invented. Religion, then, is' needless inhibition.

Finally, in regard to self-acceptance, it should again be clear that the religious devotee cannot possibly accept himself just because he is alive, because he exists and has, by mere virtue of his aliveness, some power to enjoy himself. Rather, he must make his self-acceptance utterly contingent on the acceptance of his definitional god, the church and clergy who also serve this god, and all other true believers in his religion.

If all these extrinsic persons and things accept him, he is able— and even then only temporarily and with continued underlying anxiety—to accept himself. Which means, of course, that he defines himself only through the reflected appraisals of others and loses any real, existential self that he might otherwise keep creating. Religion, for such an individual, consequently *is* self-abasement and self-abnegation—as, of course, virtually all the saints and mystics have clearly stated that it is.

If we summarize what we have just been saying, the conclusion seems inescapable that religion is, on almost every conceivable count, directly opposed to the goals of mental health—since it basically consists of masochism, other-directedness, intolerance, refusal to accept uncertainty, unscientific thinking, needless inhibition, and self-abasement.

In the one area where religion has some advantage in terms of emotional hygiene—that of encouraging hearty commitment to a cause or project in which the person may be vitally absorbed—it even tends to sabotage this advantage in two important ways: (a) it drives most of its adherents to commit themselves to its tenets for the wrong reasons—that is, to cover up instead of to face and rid themselves of their basic insecurities; and (b) it encourages a fanatic, obsessive-compulsive kind of commitment that is, in its own right, a form of mental illness.

If we want to look at the problem of human disturbance a little differently, we may ask ourselves "What are the main irrational ideas which people believe and through which they drive themselves into severe states of emotional sickness?"

EXPLORING THE QUESTION

After exploring this question for many years, and developing a new form of psychotherapy which is specifically directed at quickly unearthing and challenging the main irrational ideas which make people neurotic and psychotic, I have found that these ideas may be categorized under a few major headings (Ellis, 1962; Ellis and Harper, 1961a, 1961b). Here, for example, are five irrational notions, all or some of which are strongly held by practically every seriously disturbed person; and here, along with these notions, are the connections between them and commonly held religious beliefs.

Irrational idea No. 1 is the idea that it is a dire necessity for an adult to be loved or approved by all the significant figures in his life. This idea is bolstered by the religious philosophy that if you cannot get certain people to love or approve you, you can always fall back on god's love. The thought, however, that it is quite possible for you to live comfortably in the world *whether or not* other people accept you is quite foreign to both emotionally disturbed people and religionists.

Irrational idea No. 2 is the idea that you must be thoroughly competent, adequate, and achieving in all possible respects, otherwise you are worthless. The religionist says that no, you need not be competent and achieving, and in fact can be thoroughly inadequate—as long as god loves you and you are a member in good standing of the church. But this means, of course, that you must be a competent and achieving religionist—else you are no damned good.

Irrational idea No. 3 is the notion that certain people are bad, wicked, and villainous and that they should be severely blamed and punished for their sins. This is the ethical basis, of course, of virtually all true religions. The concepts of guilt, blaming, and sin are, in fact, almost synonymous with that of revealed religion.

Irrational idea No. 4 is the belief that it is horrible, terrible, and catastrophic when things are not going the way you would like them to go. This idea, again, is the very core of religiosity; since the religious person invariably believes that just because he cannot stand being frustrated, and just because he must keep worrying about things turning out badly, he needs a supreme deity to supervise his thoughts and deeds and to protect him from anxiety and frustration.

Irrational idea No. 5 is the idea that human unhappiness is externally caused and that people have little or no ability to control their sorrows or rid themselves of their negative feelings. Once again, this notion is the essence of religion: since real religions invariably teach that only by your trusting in god and relying on and praying to him will you be able to control your sorrows or counteract your negative emotions.

Similarly, if we had the time to review all the other major irrational ideas that lead humans to become and to remain emotionally disturbed, we would quickly find that they are coexterminous with or are strongly encouraged by religious tenets.

If you think about the matter carefully, you will see that this close connection between mental illness and religion is inevitable and invariant: since neurosis or psychosis is something of a high-class name for childishness or dependency; and religion, when used correctly, is little more than a synonym for dependency.

In the final analysis, then, religion *is* neurosis. This is why I remarked, at a symposium on sin and psychotherapy held by the American Psychological Association a few years ago, that from a mental health standpoint Voltaire's famous dictum should be reversed: for if there were a God, it would be necessary to un-invent Him.

If the thesis of this article is correct, religion goes hand in hand with the basic irrational beliefs of human beings. These keep them dependent, anxious, and hostile, and thereby create and maintain their neuroses and psychoses. What then is the role of psycho-therapy in dealing with the religious views of disturbed patients? Obviously, the sane and effective psychotherapist should not—as many contemporary psychoanalytic Jungian, client-centered, and existentialist therapists have contended he should—go along with his patient's religious orientation and try to help these patients live successfully with their religions: for this is equivalent to trying to help them live successfully with their emotional illnesses.

EXCLUSIVE HOMOSEXUALITY

If a man is fearfully fixated on exclusive homosexuality, or obsessively engaged in hating his boss, or compulsively dependent on the love of his mother, no sensible psychotherapist would try to enable him to retain his crippling neurotic symptoms and still lead a happy life.

The effective therapist, instead, would of course try to help this man live successfully *without* his symptoms—and to this end would keep hammering away at the basic irrational philosophies of life which cause the patient to manufacture and to hang on to his manifestations of emotional illness.

So will the therapist, if he himself is not too sick or gutless, attack his patient's religiosity. Not only will he show this patient that he is religious—meaning, as we previously noted, that he is masochistic, other-directed, intolerant, unable to accept uncer-tainty, unscientific, needlessly inhibited, self-abasing, and fanatic—but he will also quite vigorously and forcefully question, chal-lenge, and attack the patient's irrational beliefs that support these disturbed traits.

This is what is done in my own system of psychotherapy, which is called rational-emotive psychotherapy. Where other systems of therapy largely try to give the patient insight into the origins of his self-defeating beliefs (as, for example, the Freudians do) or try to help him accept himself with his self-sabotaging behavior (as the existential and client-centered therapists do), in rational therapy we give him insight and accept him in spite of his failings—but we also, and I think more importantly, clearly show him how he keeps maintaining his early-acquired irrationalities by indoctrinating himself over and over with nonsensical internalized sentences which challenge and contradict these internalized philosophies, by logically parsing and analyzing them, and by convincing himself that he must give them up if he is to regain emotional health.

Rational-emotive psychotherapy, in other words, goes distinctly beyond the usual insight-producing and patient-accepting methods of treatment in that it actively depropagandizes the patient, and teaches him how to keep depropagandizing himself for the rest of his life, so that the highly irrational, and essentially superstitious and religious, beliefs that he acquired from his parents and his culture can be thoroughly combatted until they are truly nonexistent.

THE DISTURBED INDIVIDUAL

RT, as rational therapy is called for short, literally teaches the disturbed individual how he can apply the methods of scientific thinking to himself and his personal relationships with others; and it usually does so with many fewer sessions of psychotherapy than the more conventional psychoanalytic and other schools use. It is, however, an unusually depth-centered and thoroughgoing form of treatment, in that it is not interested in symptom removal or in release of feelings, but in an extensive and intensive reorganization of the patient's basic philosophy of life. While valuing the patient himself and his inalienable, existential right to happiness, it vigorously and most directly attacks his self-sabotaging values and his self-repeated irrational internal verbalizations which uphold these values. This is not the place to give the details of the theory and practice of rational-emotive psychotherapy, since they may be found in my recent book, *Reason and Emotion in Psychotherapy* (1962).

Not that RT is the only method of helping human beings to change their fundamental irrational and superstitious ideas about themselves, others, and the world. Various other depropagandizing techniques, including books, lectures, and works of literature, as well as other modes of psychotherapy, can also be most useful in this respect. The main point is, however, that the vast majority of people in contemporary society are basically irrational and religious in their thinking and feeling—and hence are more or less emotionally sick.

All true believers in *any* kind of orthodoxy—whether it be religious, political, social, or even artistic orthodoxy—are distinctly disturbed, since they are obviously rigid, fanatic, and dependent individuals (Hoffer, 1951). And many liberal religionists of various groups are distinctly less, but still quite definitely, emotionally childish. For that, again, is what all manner of religion essentially is: childish dependency. And that is what effective psychotherapy, along with all the other healing arts and informative sciences, must continue uncompromisingly to unmask and eradicate.

REFERENCES

Ayer, A. J. *Language, Truth and Logic.* New York: Dover Publications, 1947.

Braaten, L. J. The main theories of "existentialism" from the viewpoint of a psychotherapist. *Mental Hygiene,* 1961, *45:* 10-17.

Carnap, R. Testability and meaning. In H. Feigl and M. Brodbeck (Eds.) *Readings in the Philosophy of Science.* New York: Appleton-Century-Crofts, 1953.

Dreikurs, R. *The Adlerian Approach on the Changing Scope of Psychiatry.* Chicago: Author, 1955.

Ellis, A. *Reason and Emotion in Psychotherapy.* New York: Lyle Stuart, 1962.

Ellis, A., & Harper, R. A. *Creative Marriage.* New York: Lyle Stuart, 1961.

Ellis, A., & Harper, R. A. *A Guide to Rational Living.* Englewood Cliffs, New Jersey: Prentice-Hall, 1961.

Fromm, E. *The Sane Society.* New York: Rinehart, 1955.

Hoffer, E. *The True Believer.* New York: Harper, 1951.

Maslow, A. H. *Motivation and Personality.* New York: Harper, 1954.

Reichenback, H. The verifiability theory of meaning. In H. Feigl and M. Brodbeck (Eds.) *Readings in the Philosophy of Science.* New York: Appleton-Century-Crofts, 1953.

Rogers, C. R. The necessary and sufficient conditions of therapeutic personality change. *J. Consult. Psychol.,* 1957, *21:* 459-461.

Thorne, F. C. Personality: a clinical eclectic view. Brandon, Vermont: *Journal of Clinical Psychology,* 1961.

32

MENTAL HEALTH AND RELIGION

Ben N. Ard, Jr., Ph.D.

What is the relationship between mental health and religion? Does psychotherapy cause individuals to lose their religion? Erich Fromm, in his book *Psychoanalysis and Religion* (1950), touches upon these and other topics of interest to anyone concerned with mental health as well as ethics. Fromm is to be complimented for bringing this moot subject out into the open and discussing it frankly. The basis of the book consists of the Terry Foundation lectures at Yale University. In this presentation of his views Fromm continues the work he started in *Man for Himself* (1947), in which, among other things, he dealt with psychological maturity as a basis for an objective standard of ethics. The central problem in *Psychoanalysis and Religion* (1950) is the conflict, or lack of conflict, between religion and psychoanalysis. The problem centers around the question: Is psychoanalysis a threat to religion?

Fromm admits his views are not representative of orthodox psychoanalytic thinking. His views then may be taken to be those of a worker in the broader field of psychotherapy, where they will be of interest to non-analytic psychiatrists, psychologists, social workers, counselors, and those interested in ethics. Anyone concerned with the aims and goals of psychotherapy will find many valuable insights in this book. Since Fromm admittedly does not speak for orthodox psychoanalysis, the more generic term *psychotherapy* will be used to contrast with religion, rather than the more restrictive term, psychoanalysis.

Probably ever since psychotherapy has been instituted with the

Reprinted, with the permission of the author and the publisher, from *Rational Living,* Vol. 7, No. 1, pp. 7-12, Spring, 1972.

aim of helping gain mental health for those in need of it, some workers in the field have wondered about the goals toward which the patient or client and the psychotherapist might be said to be striving. Implicit goals have always been inherent in any psychotherapy but it has been only fairly recently that concern over the values and aims of psychotherapy has become explicit. The concept of psychological maturity has been brought more and more to the front of these discussions in the writings of Horney (1950), Overstreet (1949), Saul (1947), and Maslow (1950), to mention only a few examples.

The above mentioned authors use different terminology, of course, but if *psychological maturity* may be taken as the broad generic term and understood to be the goal of psychotherapy, the question arises: Can religion have a place in this psychological maturity? If the psychologically mature person has no religion, the conflict is obvious and irreconcilable. The answer given to the question depends upon the meaning or interpretation given to religion and to psychological maturity. In other words, it might be said to be primarily a matter of definition of terms.

Fromm gives the aim of therapy as the "optimal development of a person's potentialities and the realization of his individuality" (1950, p. 74). This will serve as a good working definition of psychological maturity. Fromm correctly sees that this view is based on the premise that there are laws inherent in human nature, or human functioning, which operate in any culture. He says that "these laws cannot be violated without serious damage to the personality" (1950, p. 74). He also states that, "If someone violates his moral and intellectual integrity he weakens or even paralyzes his total personality" (1950, p. 74). What the psychologically ill person needs is "someone who can help him uncover the reasons for this waste of his best human powers and thus regain their use" (1950, p. 73). This is the function of the psychotherapist then: to help the patient or client help himself toward psychological maturity.

With regard to religion, as contrasted with psychological maturity, Fromm's definition is of more dubious value. His definition, in fact, is such that it makes it impossible to properly distinguish between a secular philosophy of life, or ethical orientation, and religion. Before going into any specific criticism of Fromm's definition of religion, perhaps a few words on the matter of definitions in general might not be out of order.

In regard to definitions in general we may say that they are, in one sense, primarily a matter of classification. In other words, the sameness or difference of the phenomenona in question help determine their classification and thereby their definition. Now with regard to religion and philosophy: if they are essentially the same, one definition is sufficient to cover both, or, in other words, they are merely two different words for essentially the same kind of phenomena. However, if they are two different kinds of phenomena, then a definition which equates them by subsuming them under the same rubric or classification is a mistaken definition. It is simply not in accord with the facts of the case.

Perhaps an analogy will make this point clearer. If astronomy and astrology were assumed to be the same merely because they both dealt with similar phenomena it would be, again, a mistake. Even though they both do deal with similar materials or areas they differ fundamentally as to method. Hence any proper definition must distinguish between them and not so loosely define the phenomena in question that they both will be included in the same classification. So it is with religion and philosophy. In astrology we have a psuedo-science; in astronomy, an actual science. Though they both may deal with stars, astrology is not scientific, whereas astronomy is. *Mutatis mutandis* with religion and philosophy. Although both the latter may be said, in one sense, to deal with the "soul," or "psyche," of man, they certainly go about it in fundamentally different ways. Therefore they should be defined differently.

Fromm defines religion as "any system of thought or action shared by a group which gives the individual a frame of orientation and an object of devotion" (1950, p. 21). Now if "an object of devotion" is interpreted to mean *any* aim or idea (1950, p. 24), then the definition obviously cannot distinguish between a religion in the usual sense of the word and a secular "philosophy of life" or ethical orientation, and it is inadequate to define religion in a way that would make it indistinguishable from philosophy. Surely such extended usage of the word religion can hardly be distinguished from a misuse of the same. Certainly one cannot justifiably say that *any* system of ethics or values must *necessarily* be called a religion.

If, on the other hand, Fromm's "object of devotion" is taken to mean something like "the All" (1950, p. 95), or God (1950, p. 24), then his analysis leads us in the direction of pure, unadulterated mysticism. If "God" is taken to mean merely a symbol of man's own powers which he tries to realize in his life (1950, p. 37), it might prove compatible with psychological maturity. But it would be very difficult, if not impossible, to disentangle this unusual use of the word "god" from its age-old meanings. In fact, this would seem to be a hedge, an attempt to avoid any conflict between psychotherapy and religion by simply redefining one's terms.

If God is taken in the more usual sense of some being, both visible and tangible, as concrete as another man, then Fromm's definition smacks of the fundamentalists' notion of the old man with a long white beard who sits on a throne up in the sky, interfering with the rainfall (1950, p. 2), and so forth. Belief in such a concept hardly seems compatible with psychological maturity.

Mystical orientations toward life have been criticized because they defy empirical verification and can be a serious social liability by causing conflicts among those who are trained to conform to them (Zipf, 1949, p. 203).

Such mystical statements as "to be at one with the All (Fromm, 1950, p. 95), can be shown to be meaningless when analyzed rigorously. [For an excellent presentation of the contribution of logical empiricism in this field, see Arthur Pap, *Elements of Analytic Philosophy* (1949).] Such religious or mystical experiences cannot be translated into meaningful knowledge for those not experiencing them themselves. They should not, therefore, be made the basis of an ethical orientation. Freud has objected to religion because it puts morality on shaky grounds (1928). As Fromm has noted, "If the validity of ethical norms rests upon their being God's commands, the future of ethics stands or falls with the belief in God" (1950, p. 13).

If a mystic "experiences" a contact with "the All" or God in the presence of others who are not mystics, but scientists, the latter cannot verify his experience even at the time it occurs. Of course, when they say they do not see or "feel" anything, the mystic may nevertheless insist that "it" is still there. Hence his statements are either false or unverifiable (and therefore meaningless), depending upon how he defines what he experiences. If he is willing to submit his "experiences" to rigorous empirical testing they will be proven false [Pap (1949, pp. 95-97, 114-148, 197-202) on meaning and verifiability]. However, if a person wishes to continue to believe in mystical "explanations" he may of course do so in spite of anything anyone could say. Mental institutions are full of individuals whose experiences of hallucinations, delusions, and illusions are real enough to them but there is no objective evidence that their experiences exist outside of their own imaginations. It is customary in our culture, however, not to put an individual into a mental institution if the objects of his hallucinations, delusions, or illusions are of a religious nature. He is usually thought of as a religious saint or prophet, frequently founding a new sect.

To take another example, which may prove more palatable to some—if a man "sees" a magician pull a rabbit out of a hat, after waving a wand over the hat, he can believe the wand "caused" the rabbit to appear if he wants to, as the magician implies by his actions, but such belief will not enable the man to predict the future (i.e., be scientific) as well as *not* believing in the wand but instead looking for false compartments, sleight of hand, and other paraphernalia of the magician's trade. Any theory may be put forward as a possible explanation, but only the theory that is *verifiable* is suitable for adoption as a basis for further action.

Mysticism is a poor basis for an ethical or philosophical orientation, because most modern, civilized men have had no mystical experiences. In fact, if we take religious conversion as one example, there have been a decreasing number of mature people (i.e., past adolescence and before senility) who have had such an experience in the last few years, according to church records. This does not deny, of course, that a mystical experience may greatly impress anyone having one. It is just not experienced by very many mature people these days and therefore cannot serve as a basis for our ethics.

A person who has an hallucination may be momentarily convinced that what he "saw" really was objectively there; a man may sincerely believe that he saw a woman actually sawed in half by a magician; a person may believe he "walked and talked with God," but in all these cases sincerety is not enough. *Verifiability* is ultimately the only justifiable criterion by which we, the other people concerned, can judge the validity of any person's belief.

The trouble with the ethical systems of religions lies in the fact that they are usually "revealed," or are arrived at by "intuition" or "communion with the Divine," or some other such mystical experience. Since their origin is thus dubious they serve as a poor foundation for ethical practice.

The relatively new science of psychotherapy in its possible conflict with religion is merely continuing what was started when science itself started. The history of the conflict between science and religion has been covered elsewhere in many volumes and scarcely needs further documentation here. [Max Otto, *Science and the Moral Life* (1949, Chapter 10), Andrew Dickson White,

A History of the Warfare of Science with Theology in Christendom (1897), John William Draper, *History of the Conflict Between Religion and Science* (1927)]. It would hardly seem necessary to mention this matter here except for the fact that religious people have continually tried to deny this conflict by delineating the interests of religion in ever decreasing areas. However, no matter where the line has been drawn in the past, with science excluded on one side and religion resolute on the other, with every step forward that science has taken, religion has taken a step back. When will the inevitability of this conflict impress itself on us all? Why is not the inevitable defeat of religion by science accepted? Religion has held ethics to its bosom as its last child *but ethics do not have to be religious.* Personal ethics or a philosophical orientation of a secular nature should *not* be regarded as a religion. Once this is seen, the ultimate decline of religion should be obvious, as education and science combine to apply reason to ever-increasing areas in man's life.

Criticizing Fromm for his use, and therefore definition, of such words as religion and philosophy may seem a trivial point but it may prove more important than it looks at first sight. By extending the meaning of religion until it includes *any* frame of reference or ethical philosophy of life, Fromm has attempted, in effect, to define the conflict between psychotherapy and religion away. Since nearly everyone would agree that the psychologically mature person needs to have (and does have) some philosophy of life, psychotherapy, with its aim of psychological maturity, is thus seemingly in no conflict with this redefined "religion." However, in his naive misuse of language, Fromm reserves the word "religion" for the wider class, thereby creating the need for a new couple of terms (i.e., authoritarian and non-authoritarian), in order to express the necessary distinction of subclasses which he has in no way eliminated by this misleading play with words.

Fromm is not the only one who has tried to avoid the conflict between science and religion by defining away any possibility of conflict. The so-called "modern" theologians are at one with Fromm in defining religion vaguely; by stretching the definition of religion until it excludes nothing it therefore necessarily follows that the word religion, thus used, includes no definite meaning. Hence there could be no conflict with anything. The fallacy of such an approach is obvious to anyone who is not trying to hold on to some religion at all costs.

Zipf has said that if an individual wishes to alter his environment (which we may suppose is Fromm's wish), his action must be meaningful in terms of the language of his environment (1949, p. 313). Otherwise, his environment will not respond according to the individual's intentions. Thus, for example, if the manipulation refers only to inanimate material, then the manipulation must be in terms of the invariant language of physics, if the manipulation is to succeed. On the other hand, if the manipulation refers to the "other fellow" as a social human being (as in Fromm's case), and not as a mere lump of matter, then the manipulation must be in terms of the language of his culture as well as in terms of the language of physics.

In one sense the above observation gives us an objective measuring stick for definitions. If Fromm's use of words is to succeed in causing the "other fellow" to take some desired action, then the words used must be meaningful to the other fellow in his cultural context. Now religion in our culture has meant something quite different from what Fromm says it means. Therefore, if we are going to refer to a phenomenon in our culture (i.e., religion), we must use the word as it is used in our culture, if we want to communicate, which it is assumed Fromm wants to do. How can a usage of a word be judged incorrect except by being contrasted with correct usage?

Now it might be said that we have criticized Fromm's definition without giving an adequate definition in its stead. However, one may be able to recognize a proposed definition of a frequently employed term as inadequate without necessarily being able to, or having to, in one sense, give an adequate definition oneself. In this instance Fromm tries in vain to wipe out a real difference by stretching a word (religion) to cover two separate and distinct phenomena (religion and philosophy) that clearly need to be distinguished.

As a result of Fromm's use of the word religion, and his subsequent subdivision of it into authoritarian and non-authoritarian (or humanist) religions, religious people of even such an authoritarian religion as Roman Catholicism, not to mention the various Protestant fundamentalist sects, will be unchanged after reading Fromm's excellent book, because they will conceive of themselves as falling within the non-authoritarian or humanist classification. Every religious person will insist that *his* religion is humanistic and consequently will miss the points of value which otherwise might have been obtained from reading Fromm's analysis of this topic. If Fromm would use the word religion as it is normally used, and use philosophic orientation, or philosophy of life, or some such phrase, for the ethical beliefs which the psychologically mature person has, this effect would be avoided. [For the point of view that man can exist quite adequately without religions or Gods, the reader is referred to Hector Hawton, *Men Without Gods* (1948), James H. Leuba, *God or Man?* (1933), Amber Blanco White, *Ethics for Unbelievers* (1949).]

Some religious people of more modern bent might say that Fromm's conception of humanistic religion could be translated into empirically verifiable terms and would thus be admissible. However, to call by the name of religion any ethical orientation which is devoid of any theological or supernatural reference would seem to the present writer to be going to too great lengths merely to preserve the word religion for the psychologically mature person when it is not necessary and can be harmful. It all we mean by "religion" is an ethical orientation, or philosophy of life, why confuse the issue by bringing in this word "religion" with all its mystical, unverifiable, and supernatural connotations?

A psychologically mature person can lead a full, happy, productive life, with optimal development of all his healthy potentialities, including the realization of his unique individuality, without ever having any need of religion. He does need a philosophy of life, but this phrase has none of the connotations that the word religion has. However, in all fairness to Fromm, it would seem that leaving the concept of religion out of the picture of the psychologically mature person is a position he has not reached as yet. He has tried to gloss over the contradiction involved in conceiving the psychologically healthy person as being mature, with all that implies, and yet at the same time subscribing to the restrictions of religious belief. This from the same man who had said, in *Man for Himself* (1947, p. 244), where he discussed the contradiction between the conventional (i.e., religious) ethics of our society and the ethics necessary for the psychologically mature person, "It is the obligation of the student of the science of man not to seek for 'harmonious' solutions, glossing over this contradiction, but to see it sharply."

No more fitting close to this paper could be found than the words of Max Otto:

"If it is true that religion regarded as allegiance to the supernatural—and that is the basic demand of our religions, implicit when not explicit—has been outgrown as we have become better acquainted with nature and human nature, why not forget about those religions and concentrate upon the problem of a good life in a good world?" (1949, pp. 144-145).

REFERENCES

Draper, John William. *History of the Conflict Between Religion and Science.* New York: Appleton, 1875.

Freud, Sigmund. *The Future of an Illusion.* London: Hogarth, 1928.

Fromm, Erich. *Man for Himself.* New York: Rinehart, 1947.

Fromm, Erich. *Psychoanalysis and Religion.* New Haven: Yale University Press, 1950.

Hawton, Hector. *Men Without Gods.* London: Watts, 1948.

Horney, Karen. *Neurosis and Human Growth.* New York: Norton, 1950.

Leuba, James H. *God or Man?* New York: Henry Holt, 1933.

Maslow, A. H. Self-actualizing people: a study of psychological health, in Werner Wolff (Ed.). *Personality Symposium No. 1.* New York: Grune & Stratton, 1950, 11-34.

Otto, Max C. *Science and the Moral Life.* New York: New American Library, 1949.

Overstreet, Harry. *The Mature Mind.* New York: Norton, 1949.

Pap, Arthur. *Elements of Analytic Philosophy.* New York: Macmillan, 1949.

Saul, Leon. *Emotional Maturity.* Philadelphia: Lippincott, 1947.

White, Amber Blanco. *Ethics for Unbelievers.* London: Routledge & Kegan Paul, 1948.

White, Andrew Dickson. *A History of the Warfare of Science with Theology in Christendom.* New York: George Braziller, 1955.

Zipf, G. K. *Human Behavior and the Principle of Least Effort.* Cambridge, Massachusetts: Addison-Wesley, 1949.

APPENDIX A

ETHICAL STANDARDS

American Personnel and Guidance Association

PREAMBLE

The American Personnel and Guidance Association is an educational, scientific, and professional organization dedicated to service to society. This service is committed to profound faith in the worth, dignity, and great potentiality of the individual human being.

The marks of a profession, and therefore of a professional organization, can be stated as follows:

1. Possession of a body of specialized knowledge, skills, and attitudes known and practiced by its members.

2. This body of specialized knowledge, skills, and attitudes is derived through scientific inquiry. and scholarly learning.

3. This body of specialized knowledge, skills, and attitudes is acquired through professional preparation, preferably on the graduate level, in a college or university as well as through continuous in-service training and personal growth after completion of formal education.

4. This body of specialized knowledge, skills, and attitudes is constantly tested and extended through research and scholarly inquiry.

5. A profession has a literature of its own, even though it may, and indeed must, draw portions of its content from other areas of knowledge.

6. A profession exalts service to the individual and society above personal gain. It possesses a philosophy and a code of ethics.

Reprinted by permission of the American Personnel and Guidance Association from "Ethical Standards," *Personnel and Guidance Journal*, October 1961, pages 206-209.

461

7. A profession through the voluntary association of its members constantly examines and improves the quality of its professional preparation and services to the individual and society.

8. Membership in the professional organization and the practice of the profession must be limited to persons meeting stated standards of preparation and competencies.

9. The profession affords a life career and permanent membership as long as services meet professional standards.

10. The public recognizes, has confidence in, and is willing to compensate the members of the profession for their services.

The Association recognizes that the vocational roles and settings of its members are identified with a wide variety of academic disciplines and levels of academic preparation. This diversity reflects the pervasiveness of the Association's interest and influence. It also poses challenging complexities in efforts to conceptualize:

a. the characteristics of members;

b. desired or requisite preparation or practice; and

c. supporting social, legal and/or ethical controls.

The specification of ethical standards enables the Association to clarify to members, future members, and to those served by members the nature of ethical responsibilities held in common by its members.

The introduction of such standards will inevitably stimulate greater concern by members for practice and preparation for practice. It will also stimulate a general growth and identification with and appreciation for both the common and diverse characteristics of the definable roles within the world of work of Association members.

There are six major areas of professional activity which encompass the work of members of APGA. For each of these areas certain general principles are listed below to serve as guide lines for ethical practice. These are preceded by a general section which includes certain principles germane to the six areas and common to the entire work of the Association members.

SECTION A: GENERAL

1. The member exerts what influence he can to foster the development and improvement of his profession and continues his professional growth throughout his career.

2. The member has a responsibility to the institution within

which he serves. His acceptance of employment by the institution implies that he is in substantial agreement with the general policies and principles of the institution. Therefore, his professional activities are also in accord with the objectives of the institution. Within the member's own work setting, if, despite his efforts, he cannot reach agreement as to acceptable ethical standards of conduct with his superiors, he should end his affiliation with them.

3. The member must expect ethical behavior among his professional associates in APGA at all times. He is obligated, in situations where he possesses information raising serious doubt as to the ethical behavior of other members, to attempt to rectify such conditions.

4. The member is obligated to concern himself with the degree to which the personnel functions of non-members with whose work he is acquainted represent competent and ethical performance. Where his information raises serious doubt as to the ethical behavior of such persons, it is his responsibility to attempt to rectify such conditions.

5. The member must not seek self-enhancement through expressing evaluations or comparisons damaging to other ethical professional workers.

6. The member should not claim or imply professional qualifications exceeding those possessed and is responsible for correcting any misrepresentations of his qualifications by others.

7. The member providing services for personal remuneration shall, in establishing fees for such services, take careful account of the charges made for comparable services by other professional persons.

8. The member who provides information to the public or to his subordinates, peers, or superiors has a clear responsibility to see that both the content and the manner of presentation are accurate and appropriate to the situation.

9. The member has an obligation to ensure that evaluative information about such persons as clients, students, and applicants shall be shared only with those persons who will use such information for professional purposes.

10. The member shall offer professional services only, through the context of a professional relationship. Thus testing, counseling, and other services are not to be provided through the mail by means of newspaper or magazine articles, radio or television programs, or public performances.

SECTION B: COUNSELING

This section refers to practices involving a counseling relationship with a counselee or client and is not intended to be applicable to practices involving administrative relationships with the persons being helped. A counseling relationship denotes that the person seeking help retain full freedom of choice and decision and that the helping person has no authority or responsibility to approve or disapprove of the choices or decisions of the counselee or client. "Counselee" or "client" is used here to indicate the person (or persons) for whom the member has assumed a professional responsibility. Typically the counselee or client is the individual with which the member has direct and primary contact. However, at times, "client" may include another person(s) when the other person(s) exercise significant control and direction of the individual being helped in connection with the decisions and plans being considered in counseling.

1. The member's *primary* obligation is to respect the integrity and promote the welfare of the counselee or client with whom he is working.

2. The counseling relationship and information resulting therefrom must be kept confidential consistent with the obligations of the member as a professional person.

3. Records of the counseling relationship including interview notes, test data, correspondence, tape recordings, and other documents are to be considered professional information for use in counseling, research, and teaching of counselors but always with full protection of the identity of the client and with precaution so that no harm will come to him.

4. The counselee or client should be informed of the conditions under which he may receive counseling assistance at or before the time he enters the counseling relationship. This is particularly true in the event that there exist conditions of which the counselee or client would not likely be aware.

5. The member reserves the right to consult with any other professionally competent person about his counselee or client. In choosing his professional consultant the member must avoid placing the consultant in a conflict of interest situation, i.e., the consultant must be free of any other obligatory relation to the member's client that would preclude the consultant being a proper party to the member's efforts to help the counselee or client.

6. The member shall decline to initiate or shall terminate a

counseling relationship when he cannot be of professional assistance to the counselee or client either because of lack of competence or personal limitation. In such instances the member shall refer his counselee or client to an appropriate specialist. In the event the counselee or client declines the suggested referral, the member is not obligated to continue the counseling relationship.

7. When the member learns from counseling relationships of conditions which are likely to harm others over whom his institution or agency has responsibility, he is expected to report the *condition* to the appropriate responsible authority, but in such a manner as not to reveal the identity of his counselee or client.

8. In the event that the counselee or client's condition is such as to require others to assume responsibility for him, or when there is clear and imminent danger to the counselee or client or to others, the member is expected to report this fact to an appropriate responsible authority, and/or take such other emergency measures as the situation demands.

9. Should the member be engaged in a work setting which calls for any variation from the above statements, the member is obligated to ascertain that such variations are justifiable under the conditions and that such variations are clearly specified and made known to all concerned with such counseling services.

SECTION C: TESTING[1]

1. The primary purpose of psychological testing is to provide objective and comparative measures for use in self-evaluation or evaluation by others of general or specific attributes.

2. Generally, test results constitute only one of a variety of pertinent data for personnel and guidance decisions. It is the member's responsibility to provide adequate orientation or information to the examinee(s) so that the results of testing may be placed in proper perspective with other relevant factors.

3. When making any statements to the public about tests and

---

[1] Regarding the preparation, publication, and distribution of tests reference should be made to "Tests and Diagnostic Techniques"—Report of the Joint Committee of the American Psychological Association, American Educational Research Association, and National Council of Measurements Used in Education. Supplement to *Psychological Bulletin*, 1954, 2:1-38.

testing care must be taken to give accurate information and to avoid any false claims or misconceptions.

4. Different tests demand different levels of competence for administration, scoring, and interpretation. It is therefore the responsibility of the member to recognize the limits of his competence and to perform only those functions which fall within his preparation and competence.

5. In selecting tests for use in a given situation or with a particular client the member must consider not only general but also specific validity, reliability, and appropriateness of the test(s).

6. Tests should be administered under the same conditions which were established in their standardization. Except for research purposes explicitly stated, any departures from these conditions, as well as unusual behavior or irregularities during the testing session which may affect the interpretation of the test results, must be fully noted and reported. In this connection, unsupervised test-taking or the use of tests through the mails are of questionable value.

7. The value of psychological tests depends in part on the novelty to persons taking them. Any prior information, coaching, or reproduction of test materials tends to invalidate test results. Therefore, test security is one of the professional obligations of the member.

8. The member has the responsibility to inform the examinee(s) as to the purpose of testing. The criteria of examinee's welfare and/or explicit prior understanding with him should determine who the recipients of the test results may be.

9. The member should guard against the appropriation, reproduction, or modifications of published tests or parts thereof without express permission and adequate recognition of the original author or publisher.

SECTION D: RESEARCH AND PUBLICATION

1. In the performance of any research on human subjects, the member must avoid causing any injurious effects or after-effects of the experiment upon his subjects.

2. The member may withhold information or provide misinformation to subjects only when it is essential to the investigation and where he assumes responsibility for corrective action following the investigation.

3. In reporting research results, explicit mention must be made of all variables and conditions known to the investigator which might affect interpretation of the data.

4. The member is responsible for conducting and reporting his investigations so as to minimize the possibility that his findings will be misleading.

5. The member has an obligation to make available original research data to qualified others who may wish to replicate or verify the study.

6. In reporting research results or in making original data available, due care must be taken to disguise the identity of the subjects, in the absence of specific permission from such subjects to do otherwise.

7. In conducting and reporting research, the member should be familiar with, and give recognition to, previous work on the topic.

8. The member has the obligation to give due credit to those who have contributed significantly to his research, in accordance with their contributions.

9. The member has the obligation to honor commitments made to subjects of research in return for their cooperation.

10. The member is expected to communicate to other members the results of any research he judges to be of professional or scientific value.

SECTION E: CONSULTING AND PRIVATE PRACTICE

Consulting refers to a voluntary relationship between a professional helper and help-needing social unit (industry, business, school, college, etc.) in which the consultant is attempting to give help to the client in the solving of some current or potential problem.[2]

1. The member acting as a consultant must have a high degree of self-awareness of his own values and needs in entering a helping relationship which involves change in a social unit.

2. There should be understanding and agreement between consultant and client as to directions or goals of the attempted change.

3. The consultant must be reasonably certain that he or his

---

[2]This definition is adapted from "Dimensions of the Consultant's Job" by Ronald Lippitt, *The Journal of Social Issues*, Vo. XV, No. 2, 1959.

organization have the necessary skills and resources for giving the kind of help which is needed now or that may develop later.

4. The consulting relationship must be one in which client adaptability and growth toward self-direction are encouraged and cultivated. The consultant must consistently maintain his role as a consultant and not become a decision maker for the client.

5. The consultant in announcing his availability for service as a consultant follows professional rather than commercial standards in describing his services with accuracy, dignity, and caution.

6. For private practice in testing, counseling, or consulting the ethical principles stated in all previous sections of this document are pertinent. In addition, any individual, agency, or institution offering educational and vocational counseling to the public should meet the standards of the American Board on Professional Standards in Vocational Counseling, Inc.

SECTION F: PERSONNEL ADMINISTRATION

1. The member is responsible for establishing working agreements with supervisors and with subordinates especially regarding counseling or clinical relationships, confidentiality, distinction between public and private material, and a mutual respect for the positions of parties involved in such issues.

2. Such working agreements may vary from one institutional setting to another. What should be the case in each instance, however, is that agreements have been specified, made known to those concerned, and whenever possible the agreements reflect institutional policy rather than personal judgment.

3. The member's responsibility to his superiors requires that he keep them aware of conditions affecting the institution, particularly those which may be potentially disrupting or damaging to the institution.

4. The member has a responsibility to select competent persons for assigned responsibilities and to see that his personnel are used maximally for the skills and experience they possess.

5. The member has a responsibility for constantly stimulating his staff for their and his own continued growth and improvement. He must see that staff members are adequately supervised as to the quality of their functioning and for purposes of professional development.

6. The member is responsible for seeing that his staff is informed

of policies, goals, and programs toward which the department's operations are oriented.

SECTION G: PREPARATION FOR PERSONNEL WORK

1. The member in charge of training sets up a strong program of academic study and supervised practice in order to prepare the trainees for their future responsibilities.

2. The training program should aim to develop in the trainee not only skills and knowledge, but also self-understanding.

3. The member should be aware of any manifestations of personal limitations in a student trainee which may influence the latter's provision of competent services and has an obligation to offer assistance to the trainee in securing professional remedial help.

4. The training program should include preparation in research and stimulation for the future personnel worker to do research and add to the knowledge in his field.

5. The training program should make the trainee aware of the ethical responsibilities and standards of the profession he is entering.

6. The program of preparation should aim at inculcating among the trainees, who will later become the practitioners of our profession, the ideal of service to individual and society above personal gain.

APPENDIX B

ETHICAL STANDARDS OF PSYCHOLOGISTS

American Psychological Association

The psychologist believes in the dignity and worth of the individual human being. He is committed to increasing man's understanding of himself and others. While pursuing this endeavor, he protects the welfare of any person who may seek his service or of any subject, human or animal, that may be the object of his study. He does not use his professional position or relationships, nor does he knowingly permit his own services to be used by others, for purposes inconsistent with these values. While demanding for himself freedom of inquiry and communication, he accepts the responsibility this freedom confers: for competence where he claims it, for objectivity in the report of his findings, and for consideration of the best interests of his colleagues and of society.

SPECIFIC PRINCIPLES

Principle 1. Responsibility. The psychologist,[1] committed to increasing man's understanding of man, places high values on objectivity and integrity, and maintains the highest standards in the services he offers.

a. As a scientist, the psychologist believes that society will be best served when he investigates where his judgment indicates investigation is needed; he plans his research in such a way as to minimize the possibility that his findings will be misleading; and

---

Reprinted by permission of the American Psychological Association from the *American Psychologist*, *18*:58-60, 1963.

[1]A student of psychology who assumes the role of psychologist shall be considered a psychologist for the purpose of this code of ethics.

he publishes full reports of his work, never discarding without explanation data which may modify the interpretation of results.

b. As a teacher, the psychologist recognizes his primary obligation to help others acquire knowledge and skill, and to maintain high standards of scholarship.

c. As a practitioner, the psychologist knows that he bears a heavy social responsibility because his work may touch intimately the lives of others.

Principle 2. Competence. The maintenance of high standards of professional competence is a responsibility shared by all psychologists, in the interest of the public and of the profession as a whole.

a. Psychologists discourage the practice of psychology by unqualified persons and assist the public in identifying psychologists competent to give dependable professional service. When a psychologist or a person identifying himself as a psychologist violates ethical standards, psychologists who know first-hand of such activities attempt to rectify the situation. When such a situation cannot be dealt with informally, it is called to the attention of the appropriate local, state, or national committee on professional ethics, standards, and practices.

b. The psychologist recognizes the boundaries of his competence and the limitations of his techniques and does not offer services or use techniques that fail to meet professional standards established in particular fields. The psychologist who engages in practice assists his client in obtaining professional help for all important aspects of his problem that fall outside the boundaries of his own competence. This principle requires, for example, that provision be made for the diagnosis and treatment of relevant medical problems and for referral to or consultation with other specialists.

c. The psychologist in clinical work recognizes that his effectiveness depends in good part upon his ability to maintain sound interpersonal relations, that temporary or more enduring aberrations in his own personality may interfere with this ability or distort his appraisals of others. Therefore he refrains from undertaking any activity in which his personal problems are likely to result in inferior professional services or harm to a client; or, if he is already engaged in such an activity when he becomes aware of his personal problems, he seeks competent professional assistance to determine whether he should continue or terminate his services to his client.

Principle 3. Moral and Legal Standards. The psychologist in the practice of his profession shows sensible regard for the social codes and moral expectations of the community in which he works, recognizing that violations of accepted moral and legal standards on his part may involve his clients, students, or colleagues in damaging personal conflicts, and impugn his own name and the reputation of his profession.

Principle 4. Misrepresentation. The psychologist avoids misrepresentation of his own professional qualifications, affiliations, and purposes, and those of the institutions and organizations with which he is associated.

a. A psychologist does not claim either directly or by implication professional qualifications that differ from his actual qualifications, nor does he misrepresent his affiliation with any institution, organization, or individual, nor lead others to assume he has affiliations that he does not have. The psychologist is responsible for correcting others who misrepresent his professional qualifications or affiliations.

b. The psychologist does not misrepresent an institution or organization with which he is affiliated by ascribing to it characteristics that it does not have.

c. A psychologist does not use his affiliation with the American Psychological Association or its Divisions for purposes that are not consonant with the stated purposes of the Association.

d. A psychologist does not associate himself with or permit his name to be used in connection with any services or products in such a way as to misrepresent them, the degree of his responsibility for them, or the nature of his affiliation.

Principle 5. Public Statements. Modesty, scientific caution, and due regard for the limits of present knowledge characterize all statements of psychologists who supply information to the public, either directly or indirectly.

a. Psychologists who interpret the science of psychology or the services of psychologists to clients or to the general public have an obligation to report fairly and accurately. Exaggeration, sensationalism, superficiality, and other kinds of misrepresentation are avoided.

b. When information about psychological procedures and techniques is given, care is taken to indicate that they should be used only by persons adequately trained in their use.

c. A psychologist who engages in radio or television activities does not participate in commercial announcements recommending purchase or use of a product.

Principle 6. Confidentiality. Safeguarding information about an individual that has been obtained by the psychologist in the course of his teaching, practice, or investigation is a primary obligation of the psychologist. Such information is not communicated to others unless certain important conditions are met.

a. Information received in confidence is revealed only after most careful deliberation and when there is clear and imminent danger to an individual or to society, and then only to appropriate professional workers or public authorities.

b. Information obtained in clinical or consulting relationships, or evaluative data concerning children, students, employees, and others are discussed only for professional purposes and only with persons clearly concerned with the case. Written and oral reports should present only data germane to the purposes of the evaluation; every effort should be made to avoid undue invasion of privacy.

c. Clinical and other case materials are used in classroom teaching and writing only when the identity of the persons involved is adequately disguised.

d. The confidentiality of professional communications about individuals is maintained. Only when the originator and other persons involved give their express permission is a confidential professional communication shown to the individual concerned. The psychologist is responsible for informing the client of the limits of the confidentiality.

e. Only after explicit permission has been granted is the identity of research subjects published. When data have been published without permission for identification, the psychologist assumes responsibility for adequately disguising their sources.

f. The psychologist makes provision for the maintenance of confidentiality in the preservation and ultimate disposition of confidential records.

Principle 7. Client Welfare. The psychologist respects the integrity and protects the welfare of the person or group with whom he is working.

a. The psychologist in industry, education, and other situations in which conflicts of interest may arise among various parties, as between management and labor, or between the client and employer of the psychologist, defines for himself the nature and direction of his loyalties and responsibilities and keeps all parties concerned informed of these commitments.

b. When there is a conflict among professional workers, the psychologist is concerned primarily with the welfare of any client involved and only secondarily with the interest of his own professional group.

c. The psychologist attempts to terminate a clinical or consulting relationship when it is reasonably clear to the psychologist that the client is not benefiting from it.

d. The psychologist who asks that an individual reveal personal information in the course of interviewing, testing, or evaluation, or who allows such information to be divulged to him, does so only after making certain that the responsible person is fully aware of the purposes of the interview, testing, or evaluation and of the ways in which the information may be used.

e. In cases involving referral, the responsibility of the psychologist for the welfare of the client continues until this responsibility is assumed by the professional person to whom the client is referred or until the relationship with the psychologist making the referral has been terminated by mutual agreement. In situations where referral, consultation, or other changes in the conditions of the treatment are indicated and the client refuses referral, the psychologist carefully weighs the possible harm to the client, to himself, and to his profession that might ensue from continuing the relationship.

f. The psychologist who requires the taking of psychological tests for didactic, classification, or research purposes protects the examinees by insuring that the tests and test results are used in a professional manner.

g. When potentially disturbing subject matter is presented to students, it is discussed objectively, and efforts are made to handle constructively any difficulties that arise.

h. Care must be taken to insure an appropriate setting for clinical work to protect both client and psychologist from actual or imputed harm and the profession from censure.

Principle 8. Client Relationship. The psychologist informs his prospective client of the important aspects of the potential relationship that might affect the client's decision to enter the relationship.

a. Aspects of the relationship likely to affect the client's decision include the recording of an interview, the use of interview material for training purposes, and observation of an interview by other persons.

b. When the client is not competent to evaluate the situation (as in the case of a child), the person responsible for the client is informed of the circumstances which may influence the relationship.

c. The psychologist does not normally enter into a professional relationship with members of his own family, intimate friends, close associates, or others whose welfare might be jeopardized by such a dual relationship.

Principle 9. Impersonal Services. Psychological services for the purpose of diagnosis, treatment, or personalized advice are provided only in the context of a professional relationship, and are not given by means of public lectures or demonstrations, newspaper or magazine articles, radio or television programs, mail, or similar media.

a. The preparation of personnel reports and recommendations based on test data secured solely by mail is unethical unless such appraisals are an integral part of a continuing client relationship with a company, as a result of which the consulting psychologist has intimate knowledge of the client's personal situation and can be assured thereby that his written appraisals will be adequate to the purpose and will be properly interpreted by the client. These reports must not be embellished with such detailed analyses of the subject's personality traits as would be appropriate only after intensive interviews with the subject. The reports must not make specific recommendations as to employment or placement of the subject which go beyond the psychologist's knowledge of the job requirements of the company. The report must not purport to eliminate the company's need to carry on such other regular employment or personnel practices as appraisal of the work history, checking of references, past performance in the company.

Principle 10. Announcement of Services. A psychologist adheres to professional rather than commercial standards in making known his availability for professional services.

a. A psychologist does not directly solicit clients for individual diagnosis or therapy.

b. Individual listings in telephone directories are limited to name, highest relevant degree, certification status, address, and telephone number. They may also include identification in a few words of the psychologist's major areas of practice; for example, child therapy, personnel selection, industrial psychology. Agency listings are equally modest.

c. Announcements of individual private practice are limited to a simple statement of the name, highest relevant degree, certification or diplomate status, address, telephone number, office hours, and a brief explanation of the types of services rendered. Announcements of agencies may list names of staff members with their qualifications. They conform in other particulars with the same standards as individual announcements, making certain that the true nature of the organization is apparent.

d. A psychologist or agency announcing nonclinical professional services may use brochures that are descriptive of services rendered but not evaluative. They may be sent to professional persons, schools, business firms, government agencies, and other similar organizations.

e. The use in a brochure of "testimonials from satisfied users" is unacceptable. The offer of a free trial of services is unacceptable if it operates to misrepresent in any way the nature or the efficacy of the services rendered by the psychologist. Claims that a psychologist has unique skills or unique devices not available to others in the profession are made only if the special efficacy of these unique skills or devices has been demonstrated by scientifically acceptable evidence.

f. The psychologist must not encourage (nor, within his power, even allow) a client to have exaggerated ideas as to the efficacy of services rendered. Claims made to clients about the efficacy of his services must not go beyond those which the psychologist would be willing to subject to professional scrutiny through publishing his results and his claims in a professional journal.

Principle 11. Interprofessional Relations. A psychologist acts with integrity in regard to colleagues in psychology and in other professions.

a. A psychologist does not normally offer professional services to a person receiving psychological assistance from another professional worker except by agreement with the other worker or after the termination of the client's relationship with the other professional worker.

b. The welfare of clients and colleagues requires that psychologists in joint practice or corporate activities make an orderly and explicit arrangement regarding the conditions of their association

477

and its possible termination. Psychologists who serve as employers of other psychologists have an obligation to make similar appropriate arrangements.

Principle 12. Remuneration. Financial arrangements in professional practice are in accord with professional standards that safeguard the best interest of the client and the profession.

a. In establishing rates for professional services, the psychologist considers carefully both the ability of the client to meet the financial burden and the charges made by other professional persons engaged in comparable work. He is willing to contribute a portion of his services to work for which he receives little or no financial return.

b. No commission or rebate or any other form of remuneration is given or received for referral of clients for professional services.

c. The psychologist in clinical or counseling practice does not use his relationships with clients to promote, for personal gain or the profit of an agency, commercial enterprises of any kind.

d. A psychologist does not accept a private fee or any other form of remuneration for professional work with a person who is entitled to his services through an institution or agency. The policies of a particular agency may make explicit provision for private work with its clients by members of its staff, and in such instances the client must be fully apprised of all policies affecting him.

Principle 13. Test Security. Psychological tests and other assessment devices, the value of which depends in part on the naivete of the subject, are not reproduced or described in popular publications in ways that might invalidate the techniques. Access to such devices is limited to persons with professional interests who will safeguard their use.

a. Sample items made up to resemble those of tests being discussed may be reproduced in popular articles and elsewhere, but scorable tests and actual test items are not reproduced except in professional publications.

b. The psychologist is responsible for the control of psychological tests and other devices and procedures used for instruction when their value might be damaged by revealing to the general public their specific contents or underlying principles.

Principle 14. Test Interpretation. Test scores, like test materials, are released only to persons who are qualified to interpret and use them properly.

a. Materials for reporting test scores to parents, or which are designed for self-appraisal purposes in schools, social agencies, or industry are closely supervised by qualified psychologists or counselors with provisions for referring and counseling individuals when needed.

b. Test results or other assessment data used for evaluation or classification are communicated to employers, relatives, or other appropriate persons in such a manner as to guard against misrepresentation or misuse. In the usual case, an interpretation of the test result rather than the score is communicated.

c. When test results are communicated directly to parents and students, they are accompanied by adequate interpretive aids or advice.

Principle 15. Test Publication. Psychological tests are offered for commercial publication only to publishers who present their tests in a professional way and distribute them only to qualified users.

a. A test manual, technical handbook, or other suitable report on the test is provided which describes the method of constructing and standardizing the test, and summarizes the validation research.

b. The populations for which the test has been developed and the purposes for which it is recommended are stated in the manual. Limitations upon the test's dependability, and aspects of its validity on which research is lacking or incomplete, are clearly stated. In particular, the manual contains a warning regarding interpretations likely to be made which have not yet been substantiated by research.

c. The catalog and manual indicate the training or professional qualifications required for sound interpretation of the test.

d. The test manual and supporting documents take into account the principles enunciated in the *Technical Recommendations for Psychological Tests and Diagnostic Techniques.*

e. Test advertisements are factual and descriptive rather than emotional and persuasive.

Principle 16. Research Precautions. The psychologist assumes obligations for the welfare of his research subjects, both animal and human.

a. Only when a problem is of scientific significance and it is not practicable to investigate it in any other way is the psychologist justified in exposing research subjects, whether children or adults, to physical or emotional stress as part of an investigation.

b. When a reasonable possibility of injurious aftereffects exists, research is conducted only when the subjects or their responsible agents are fully informed of this possibility and agree to participate nevertheless.

c. The psychologist seriously considers the possibility of harmful aftereffects and avoids them, or removes them as soon as permitted by the design of the experiment.

d. A psychologist using animals in research adheres to the provisions of the Rules Regarding Animals, drawn up by the Committee on Precautions and Standards in Animal Experimentation and adopted by the American Psychological Association.

Principle 17. Publication Credit. Credit is assigned to those who have contributed to a publication, in proportion to their contribution, and only to these.

a. Major contributions of a professional character, made by several persons to a common project, are recognized by joint authorship. The experimenter or author who has made the principal contribution to a publication is identified as the first listed.

b. Minor contributions of a professional character, extensive clerical or similar nonprofessional assistance, and other minor contributions are acknowledged in footnotes or in an introductory statement.

c. Acknowledgment through specific citations is made for unpublished as well as published material that has directly influenced the research or writing.

d. A psychologist who compiles and edits for publication the contributions of others publishes the symposium or report under the title of the committee or symposium, with his own name appearing as chairman or editor among those of the other contributors or committee members.

Principle 18. Responsibility toward Organization. A psychologist respects the rights and reputation of the institute or organization with which he is associated.

a. Materials prepared by a psychologist as a part of his regular work under specific direction of his organization are the property of that organization. Such materials are released for use or publication by a psychologist in accordance with policies of authorization, assignment of credit, and related matters which have been established by his organization.

b. Other material resulting incidentally from activity supported by any agency, and for which the psychologist rightly assumes individual responsibility, is published with disclaimer for any responsibility on the part of the supporting agency.

Principle 19. Promotional Activities. The psychologist associated with the development or promotion of psychological devices, books, or other products offered for commercial sale is responsible for ensuring that such devices, books, or products are presented in a professional and factual way.

a. Claims regarding performance, benefits, or results are supported by scientifically acceptable evidence.

b. The psychologist does not use professional journals for the commercial exploitation of psychological products, and the psychologist-editor guards against such misuse.

c. The psychologist with a financial interest in the sale or use of a psychological product is sensitive to possible conflict of interest in his promotion of such products and avoids compromise of his professional responsibilities and objectives.

Read, every day, something no one else is reading.
Think, every day, something no one else is thinking. . . .
It is bad for the mind to be always part of a unanimity.

Christopher Morley

A SELECTED BIBLIOGRAPHY OF BASIC TEXTS
IN COUNSELING AND PSYCHOTHERAPY

Adams, J. F. *Problems in Counseling: A Case Study Approach.* New York: Macmillan, 1962.

Adams, J. F. (Ed.) *Counseling and Guidance: A Summary View.* New York: Macmillan, 1965.

Adler, N. *The Underground Stream: New Life Styles and the Antinomian Personality.* New York: Harper & Row, 1972.

American Personnel and Guidance Association. *Ethical Standards.* Washington: A. P. G. A., 1961.

American Psychological Association. *Ethical Standards of Psychologists.* Washington: A. P. A., 1953.

Anderson, Camilla M. *Beyond Freud.* New York: Harper, 1957.

Arbuckle, D. S. *Counseling: Philosophy, Theory and Practice.* Boston: Allyn & Bacon, 2nd edition, 1965.

Ard, B. N., Jr. *Treating Psychosexual Dysfunction.* New York: Jason Aronson, 1974.

Ard, B. N., Jr., & Ard, Constance C. (Eds.) *Handbook of Marriage Counseling.* Palo Alto: Science & Behavior Books, 1969.

Avila, D. L., et al. (Eds.) *The Helping Relationship Sourcebook.* Boston: Allyn & Bacon, 1971.

Bakken, C. J. *The Legal Basis for College Student Personnel Work.* Washington: A. P. G. A., 1961.

Balser, B. (Ed.) *Psychotherapy of the Adolescent.* New York: International Universities Press, 1957.

Barclay, J. R. *Foundations of Counseling Strategies.* New York: Wiley, 1971.

Barry, Ruth & Wolf, Beverly. *Modern Issues in Guidance-Personnel Work.* New York: Teachers College (Columbia University), 1957.

Barten, H. H. (Ed.) *Brief Therapies.* New York: Behavioral Publications, 1971.

Barton, A. *Three Worlds of Therapy: An Existential-Phenomenological Study of the Therapies of Freud, Jung, and*

Rogers. Palo Alto: National Press Books, 1974.

Beck, A. T. *Depression: Clinical, Experimental and Theoretical Aspects.* New York: Hoeber-Harper, 1967.

Beck, C. E. (Ed.) *Philosophical Guidelines for Counseling.* Dubuque, Iowa: William C. Brown, 2nd edition, 1971.

Beier, E. G. *The Silent Language of Psychotherapy.* Chicago: Aldine, 1966.

Bentley, J. C. (Ed.) *The Counselor's Role: Commentary and Readings.* Boston: Houghton Mifflin, 1968.

Berenson, B. G., & Carkhuff, R. R. (Eds.) *Sources of Gain in Counseling and Psychotherapy: Readings and Commentary.* New York: Holt, Rinehart & Winston, 1967.

Bergin, A. E., & Strupp, H. H. *Changing Frontiers in the Science of Psychotherapy.* Chicago: Aldine Atherton, 1972.

Berne, E. *Transactional Analysis in Psychotherapy.* New York: Grove Press, 1961.

Berne, E. *Games People Play.* New York: Grove Press, 1964.

Berne, E. *What Do You Say After You Say Hello?* New York: Grove Press, 1972.

Bingham, W. V. D., & Moore, B. V. *How to Interview.* New York: Harper, 4th edition, 1959.

Blaine, G. B., Jr., & McArthur, C. C. (Eds.) *Emotional Problems of the Student.* New York: Appleton-Century-Crofts, 1961.

Blanck, Gertrude & Blanck, R. *Ego Psychology: Theory and Practice.* New York: Columbia University Press, 1974.

Blum, M. L., & Balinsky, B. *Counseling and Psychology.* Englewood Cliffs, N.J.: Prentice-Hall, 1951.

Bordin, E. D. *Psychological Counseling.* New York: Appleton-Century-Crofts, 2nd edition, 1968.

Bowers, Margaretta K., et al. *Counseling the Dying.* New York: Thomas Nelson, 1964.

Boy, A. V., & Pine, G. J. *Client-Centered Counseling in the Secondary School.* Boston: Houghton Mifflin, 1963.

Bozarth, J. D. (Ed.) *Models and Functions of Counseling for Applied Settings and Rehabilitation Workers.* Fayetteville, Arkansas: Arkansas Rehabilitation Research and Training Center, 2nd edition, 1972.

Brammer, L. N., & Shostrom, E. L. *Therapeutic Psychology.* Englewood Cliffs, N.J.: Prentice-Hall, 2nd edition, 1968.

Branden, N. *The Psychology of Self-Esteem.* Los Angeles: Nash, 1969.

Branden, N. *Breaking Free.* Los Angeles: Nash, 1970.

Branden, N. *The Disowned Self.* Los Angeles: Nash, 1971.

Brayfield, A. H. (Ed.) *Readings in Modern Methods of Counseling.* New York: Appleton-Century-Crofts, 1950.

Bry, Adelaide (Ed.) *Inside Psychotherapy.* New York: Basic Books, 1971.

Buhler, Charlotte. *Values in Psychotherapy.* New York: Free Press, 1962.

Burton, A. (Ed.) *Case Studies in Counseling and Psychotherapy.* Englewood Cliffs, N.J.: Prentice-Hall, 1959.

Burton, A. (Ed.) *Modern Psychotherapeutic Practice: Innovations in Technique.* Palo Alto: Science & Behavior Books, 1965.

Byrne, R. H. *The School Counselor.* Boston: Houghton Mifflin, 1963.

Callis, R., et al. *A Casebook of Counseling.* New York: Appleton-Century-Crofts, 1950.

Calvin, A. D., et al. (Eds.) *Psychology.* Boston: Allyn & Bacon, 1961.

Carkhuff, R. R., & Berenson, B. G. *Beyond Counseling and Therapy.* New York: Holt, Rinehart & Winston, 1967.

Cattell, R. B. *A New Morality from Science: Beyondism.* New York: Pergamon Press, 1972.

Clifford, W. K. *The Ethics of Belief and Other Essays.* London: Watts, 1947.

Colby, K. *A Primer for Psychotherapists.* New York: Ronald, 1951.

Combs, A. R., et al. *Helping Relationships: Basic Concepts for the Helping Professions.* Boston: Allyn & Bacon, 1971.

Corsini, R. (Ed.) *Current Psychotherapies.* Itasca, Illinois: Peacock, 1973.

Cottle, W. C., & Downie, N. M. *Procedures and Preparation for Counseling.* Englewood Cliffs, N.J.: Prentice-Hall, 1960.

Cunningham, L. M., & Peters, H. J. *Counseling Theories.* Columbus, Ohio: Merrill, 1973.

Delaney, D. J., & Eisenberg, S. *The Counseling Process.* Chicago: Rand McNally, 1972.

DiCaprio, N. S. *Personality Theories: Guides to Living.* Philadelphia: Saunders, 1974.

DiLoreto, A. O. *Comparative Psychotherapy.* Chicago: Aldine Atherton, 1971.

Dugan, W. E. (Ed.) *Counseling Points of View.* Minneapolis, Minnesota: University of Minnesota Press, 1959.

Elkstein, R., & Wallerstein, R. S. *The Teaching and Learning of*

Psychotherapy. New York: Basic Books, 1958.

Ellis, A. (Ed.) *What is Psychotherapy?* Annals of Psychotherapy, Monograph #1, 1959.

Ellis, A. (Ed.) *The Place of Values in the Practice of Psychotherapy.* Annals of Psychotherapy, Monograph #2, 1959.

Ellis, A. *Reason and Emotion in Psychotherapy.* New York: Lyle Stuart, 1962.

Ellis, A. (Ed.) *Growth Through Reason: Verbatim Cases in Rational-Emotive Therapy.* Palo Alto: Science & Behavior Books, 1971.

Ellis, A. *Humanistic Psychotherapy: The Rational-Emotive Approach.* New York: Julian Press, 1973.

Ellis, A., & Harper, R. A. *A Guide to Rational Living.* Englewood Cliffs, N.J.: Prentice-Hall, 1961.

Erickson, C. E. *The Counseling Interview.* Englewood Cliffs, N.J.: Prentice-Hall, 1950.

Evraiff, W. *Helping Counselors Grow Professionally.* Englewood Cliffs, N.J.: Prentice-Hall, 1963.

Eysenck, H. J. (Ed.) *Behavior Therapy and the Neuroses.* New York: Pergamon Press, 1960.

Eysenck, H. J. (Ed.) *Experiments in Behavior Therapy.* New York: Macmillan, 1964.

Fagan, Joen & Shepherd, Irma Lee (Eds.) *Gestalt Therapy Now.* Palo Alto: Science & Behavior Books, 1970.

Farwell, Gail P., & Peters, H. J. (Eds.) *Guidance Readings for Counselors.* Chicago: Rand McNally, 1960.

Fitts, W. H. *The Experience of Psychotherapy.* Princeton, N.J.: Van Nostrand, 1965.

Ford, D. H., & Urban, H. B. *Systems of Psychotherapy.* New York: Wiley, 1963.

Frank, J. D. *Persuasion and Healing.* New York: Schocken, 1961.

Franks, Violet & Burtle, Vasanti (Eds.) *Women in Therapy: New Psychotherapies For a Changing Society.* New York: Brunner/Mazel, 1974.

Freud, Sigmund. *An Outline of Psychoanalysis.* New York: Norton, 1949.

Fromm, Erich. *Man for Himself.* New York: Rinehart, 1947.

Fromm, Erich. *Psychoanalysis and Religion.* New Haven: Yale University Press, 1950.

Fromm, Erich. *The Sane Society.* New York: Rinehart, 1955.

Fromm, Erich. *The Anatomy of Human Destructiveness.* New York: Holt, Rinehart & Winston, 1973.

Garrett, Annette. *Interviewing: Its Principles and Methods.* New York: Family Service Association of America, 2nd edition, 1972.

Giovacchini, P. L. (Ed.) *Tactics and Techniques in Psychoanalytic Therapy.* New York: Science House, 1972.

Glasser, W. *Reality Therapy.* New York: Harper & Row, 1965.

Glasser, W. *The Identity Society.* New York: Harper & Row, 1972.

Goldstein, A. P.; Heller, K.; & Sechrest, L. B. *Psychotherapy and the Psychology of Behavior Change.* New York: Wiley, 1966.

Gorney, R. *The Human Agenda.* New York: Simon & Schuster, 1972.

Gottman, J. M., & Leiblum, Sandra R. *How to do Psychotherapy and How to Evaluate it.* New York: Holt, Rinehart & Winston, 1974.

Greenwald, H. (Ed.) *Active Psychotherapy.* New York: Atherton, 1966.

Greenwald, H. *Direct Decision Therapy.* San Diego: Edits, 1973.

Hadley, J. M. *Clinical and Counseling Psychology.* New York: Knopf, 1958.

Hahn, M. E., & MacLean, M. S. *Counseling Psychology.* New York: McGraw-Hill, 1955.

Halmos, P. *The Faith of the Counselors.* New York: Schocken, 1966.

Hamrin, Shirley A., & Paulson, Blanch B. *Counseling Adolescents.* Chicago: Science Research Associates, 1950.

Hanfmann, Eugenia, et al. *Psychological Counseling in a Small College.* Cambridge: Shenkman, 1963.

Harms, E., & Schreiber, P. (Eds.) *Handbook of Counseling Techniques.* New York: Pergamon, 1964.

Harper, R. A. *Psychoanalysis and Psychotherapy: 36 Systems.* Englewood Cliffs, N.J.: Prentice-Hall, 1959.

Hemming, J. *Individual Morality.* London: Panther Modern Society, 1970. Hendrickson, D. E.

Hendrickson, D. E., & Krause, F. H. (Eds.) *Counseling and Psychotherapy: Training and Supervision.* Columbus, Ohio: Charles E. Merrill, 1972.

Henry, J. *On Sham, Vulnerability and Other Forms of Self-Destruction.* New York: Vintage Books, 1973.

Hersher, L. (Ed.) *Four Psychotherapies.* New York: Appleton-Century-Crofts, 1970.

Herzberg, A. *Active Psychotherapy.* London: Research Books,

1945.

Holland, G. A. *Fundamentals of Psychotherapy.* New York: Holt, Rinehart & Winston, 1965.

Horney, Karen. *Neurosis and Human Growth.* New York: Norton, 1950.

Jackson, D. D. (Ed.) *Communication, Family and Marriage.* Palo Alto: Science & Behavior Books, 1968.

Jackson, D. D. (Ed.) *Therapy, Communication, and Change.* Palo Alto: Science & Behavior Books, 1968.

Jahoda, Marie. *Current Concepts of Positive Mental Health.* New York: Basic Books, 1958.

Johnson, W. *People in Quandries: The Semantics of Personal Adjustment.* New York: Harper, 1946.

Jurjevich, R. (Ed.) *Direct Psychotherapy.* Coral Gables, Florida: University of Miami Press, 2 volumes, 1973.

Kaufmann, Walter. *Without Guilt and Justice.* New York: Wyden, 1973.

Kemp, C. G. *Intangibles in Counseling.* Boston: Houghton Mifflin, 1967.

Krumboltz, J. D. (Ed.) *Revolution in Counseling: Implications of Behavioral Science.* Boston: Houghton Mifflin, 1966.

Krumboltz, J. D., & Thoresen, C. A. (Eds.) *Behavioral Counseling: Cases and Techniques.* New York: Holt, Rinehart & Winston, 1969.

Langs, R. *The Technique of Psychoanalytic Psychotherapy.* New York: Jason Aronson, Volume I, 1973, Volume II, 1974.

Levine, M. *Psychiatry and Ethics.* New York: George Braziller, 1972.

Lewis, E. C. *The Psychology of Counseling.* New York: Holt, Rinehart & Winston, 1970.

Lindner, R. *Must You Conform?* New York: Grove, 1956.

Litwack, L., et al. *Critical Issues in Student Personnel Work: A Problem Casebook.* Chicago: Rand McNally, 1965.

London, P. *The Modes and Morals of Psychotherapy.* New York: Holt, Rinehart & Winston, 1964.

Loughary, J. W. (Ed.) *Counseling, A Growing Profession: Report Concerning the Professionalization of Counseling.* Washington: A. P. G. A., 1965.

Lowe, C. M. *Value Orientations in Counseling and Psychotherapy.* San Francisco: Chandler, 1969.

Mahrer, A. R. (Ed.) *The Goals of Psychotherapy.* New York: Appleton-Century-Crofts, 1967.

488

Marzolf, S. R. *Psychological Diagnosis and Counseling in the Schools.* New York: Holt, 1956.

Maslow, A. H. (Ed.) *New Knowledge in Human Values.* New York: Harper, 1959.

Maslow, A. H. *Eupsychian Management.* Homewood, Illinois: Richard D. Irwin & the Dorsey Press, 1965.

Maslow, A. H. *Toward a Psychology of Being.* Princeton, N.J.: Van Nostrand, 2nd edition, 1968.

Maslow, A. H. *Motivation and Personality.* New York: Harper & Row, 2nd edition, 1970.

Maslow, A. H. *The Farther Reaches of Human Nature.* New York: Viking Press, 1971.

Masserman, J. H. (Ed.) *Psychoanalysis and Human Values.* New York: Grune & Stratton, 1960.

Masserman, J. H. (Ed.) *Handbook of Psychiatric Therapies.* New York: Jason Aronson, 1973.

May, R. (Ed.) *Existential Psychology.* New York: Random House, 1961.

Menninger, K. *Whatever Became of Sin?* New York: Hawthorn, 1973.

McCary, J. L. (Ed.) *Six Approaches to Psychotherapy.* New York: Grove, 1956.

McGowan, J. F., & Schmidt, L. D. (Eds.) *Counseling: Readings in Theory and Practice.* New York: Holt, Rinehart & Winston, 1962.

McKinney, F. *Counseling for Personal Adjustment in Schools and Colleges.* Boston: Houghton Mifflin, 1958.

McKinney, F. *Understanding Personality: Cases in Counseling.* Boston: Houghton Mifflin, 1961.

Mosher, R. L., et al. (Eds.) *Guidance: An Examination.* New York: Harcourt, Brace & World, 1965.

Moustakas, C. E. (Ed.) *The Self: Explorations in Personal Growth.* New York: Harper, 1956.

Mowrer, O. H. *The Crisis in Psychiatry and Religion.* Princeton, N.J.: Van Nostrand, 1961.

Mowrer, O. H. (Ed.) *Morality and Mental Health.* Chicago: Rand McNally, 1967.

Mueller, Kate H. *Student Personnel Work in Higher Education.* Boston: Houghton Mifflin, 1961.

Mueller, W. J., & Kell, B. L. *Coping with Conflict: Supervising Counselors and Psychotherapists.* New York: Appleton-Century-Crofts, 1972.

Mullahy, P. *Oedipus Myth and Complex.* New York: Hermitage, 1948.

Munroe, Ruth L. *Schools of Psychoanalytic Thought.* New York: Holt, Rinehart & Winston, 1955.

Nixon, R. E. *The Art of Growing.* New York: Random House, 1962.

Opler, M. K. *Culture, Psychiatry and Human Values.* Springfield, Illinois: Thomas, 1956.

Patterson, C. H. (Ed.) *The Counselor in the School: Selected Readings.* New York: McGraw-Hill, 1967.

Patterson, C. H. *Theories of Counseling and Psychotherapy.* New York: Harper & Row, 2nd edition, 1973.

Pepinsky, H. B., & Pepinsky, Pauline N. *Counseling: Theory and Practice.* New York: Ronald, 1954.

Perez, J. F. *Counseling: Theory and Practice.* Reading, Mass.: Addison-Wesley, 1965.

Perls, F., et al. *Gestalt Therapy.* New York: Dell, 1965.

Perls, F. *The Gestalt Approach & Eye Witness to Therapy.* Palo Alto: Science & Behavior Books, 1973.

Peters, H. J., et al. (Eds.) *Counseling: Selected Readings.* Columbus, Ohio: Merrill, 1962.

Peterson, J. A. *Counseling and Values: A Philosophical Examination.* Scranton, Pa.: International Textbook, 1970.

Pietrofesa, J. J., et al. *The Authentic Counselor.* Chicago: Rand McNally, 1972.

Redl, F., & Wineman, D. *The Aggressive Child.* New York: Free Press, 1957.

Redl, F. *When We Deal With Children.* New York: Free Press, 1966.

Riessman, F., et al. (Eds.) *Mental Health of the Poor: New Treatment Approaches for Low-Income People.* New York: Free Press, 1964.

Robinson, F. P. *Principles and Procedures in Student Counseling.* New York: Harper, 1950.

Rogers, C. R. *Counseling and Psychotherapy.* Boston: Houghton Mifflin, 1942.

Rogers, C. R. *Client-Centered Therapy.* Boston: Houghton Mifflin, 1951.

Rogers, C. R. *On Becoming a Person.* Boston: Houghton Mifflin, 1961.

Rogers, C. R., & Dymond, Rosalind F. (Eds.) *Psychotherapy and Personality Change.* Chicago: University of Chicago Press, 1954.

Rothmey, J., & Roens, B. *Counseling the Individual Student.* New York: William Sloan, 1949.

Ruesch, J. *Therapeutic Communication.* New York: Norton, 1961.

Ruesch, J., & Bateson, G. *Communication: The Social Matrix of Psychiatry.* New York: Norton, 1951.

Rutledge, A. *Premarital Counseling.* Cambridge, Mass.: Schenkman, 1965.

Sahakian, W. S. (Ed.) *Psychology of Personality: Readings in Theory.* Chicago: Rand McNally, 1965.

Saltzman, G. A., & Peters, H. J. (Eds.) *Pupil Personnel Services: Selected Readings.* Itasca, Illinois: Peacock, 1967.

Satir, Virginia. *Conjoint Family Therapy.* Palo Alto: Science & Behavior Books, revised edition, 1967.

Satir, Virginia. *Peoplemaking.* Palo Alto: Science & Behavior Books, 1972.

Saul, L. J. *The Hostile Mind.* New York: Random House, 1956.

Schofield, W. *Psychotherapy: The Purchase of Friendship.* Englewood Cliffs, N.J.: Prentice-Hall, 1964.

Shertzer, B., & Stone, S. C. *Fundamentals of Counseling.* Boston: Houghton Mifflin, 2nd edition, 1974.

Shulman, L. M., & Taylor, Joan Kennedy. *When To See A Psychologist.* Los Angeles: Nash, 1969.

Siegel, M. (Ed.) *The Counseling of College Students.* New York: Free Press, 1968.

Sifneos, P. E. *Short-Term Psychotherapy and Emotional Crisis.* Cambridge: Harvard University Press, 1972.

Singer, C. *Scripts People Live.* New York: Grove Press, 1974.

Smith, G. E. *Counseling in the Secondary School.* New York: Macmillan, 1955.

Snyder, W. U. (Ed.) *Casebook of Non-Directive Counseling.* Boston: Houghton Mifflin, 1947.

Snyder, W. U. *The Psychotherapy Relationship.* New York: Macmillan, 1961.

Standal, S. W., & Corsini, R. J. (Eds.) *Critical Incidents in Psychotherapy.* Englewood Cliffs, N.J.: Prentice-Hall, 1959.

Stefflre, B. (Ed.) *Theories of Counseling.* New York: McGraw-Hill, 1965.

Stein, M. T. (Ed.) *Contemporary Psychotherapies.* New York: Free Press, 1961.

Stewart, L. H., & Warnath, C. F. *The Counselor and Society: A Cultural Approach.* Boston: Houghton Mifflin, 1965.

Sullivan, H. S. *The Psychiatric Interview.* New York: Norton, 1954.

Suttie, I. D. *The Origins of Love and Hate.* London: Kegan Paul, 1935.

The Radical Therapist Collective. *The Radical Therapist.* New York: Ballantine, 1971.

Thompson, Clara. *Psychoanalysis: Evolution and Development.* New York: Hermitage, 1950.

Tolbert, E. L. *Introduction to Counseling.* New York: McGraw-Hill, 1959.

Tosi, D. J. *Youth: Toward Personal Growth (A Rational-Emotive Approach).* Columbus, Ohio: Charles E. Merrill, 1974.

Truax, C. B., & Carkhuff, R. R. *Toward Effective Counseling and Psychotherapy.* Chicago: Aldine, 1967.

Tyler, Leona. *The Work of the Counselor.* New York: Appleton-Century-Crofts, 3rd edition, 1969.

Walker, N. *A Short History of Psychotherapy in Theory and Practice.* New York: Noonday, 1959.

Ware, Martha L. (Ed.) *Law of Guidance and Counseling.* Cincinnati: Anderson, 1964.

Warters, Jane. *Technique of Counseling.* New York: McGraw-Hill, 2nd edition, 1964.

Watzlawick, P., et al. *Pragmatics of Human Communication.* New York: Norton, 1967.

Wiener, D. N. *A Practical Guide to Psychotherapy.* New York: Harper & Row, 1968.

White, R. W. *Lives in Progress.* New York: Holt, Rinehart & Winston, 1952.

Wolberg, L. R. (Ed.) *Short-Term Psychotherapy.* New York: Grune & Stratton, 1965.

Wolberg, L. R. *Psychotherapy and the Behavioral Sciences.* New York: Grune & Stratton, 1966.

Wolberg, L. R. *The Technique of Psychotherapy.* New York: Grune & Stratton, 2 volumes, 2nd edition, 1967.

Wolpe, J., et al. (Eds.) *The Conditioning Therapies.* New York: Holt, Rinehart & Winston, 1964.

Woody, R. H. *Psychobehavioral Counseling and Theory.* New York: Appleton-Century-Crofts, 1971.

Young, Howard S. *A Rational Counseling Primer.* New York: Institute for Rational Living, 1974.

ABOUT THE EDITOR

Dr. Ben N. Ard, Jr., received his B.A. degree (1947), with a major in psychology and a minor in philosophy, from the University of California at Los Angeles, his M.S. (1954) from Oregon State University at Corvallis, and his Ph.D. (1962) from the University of Michigan at Ann Arbor. He was a fellow in marriage counseling and family life education (1953-1954) at the Merrill-Palmer Institute in Detroit, as well as a teaching fellow at the University of Michigan.

He has taught at Michigan State University, East Lansing (1956-1959), the University of Michigan (1959-1960) and was Professor of Psychology (and University Psychologist) at Central Michigan University at Mount Pleasant (1960-1963). Since 1963 he has been Professor of Counseling at San Francisco State University.

He is a licensed psychologist and also a licensed marriage, family and child counselor in private practice in San Francisco. He is also a fellow and former member of the Board of Directors of the American Association of Marriage and Family Counselors; a fellow and president (1975) of the California Association of Marriage and Family Counselors; a fellow of Society for the Scientific Study of Sex; a member of the National Council on Family Relations; and a member of the American Psychological Association.

He has three books published previously: *Counseling and Psychotherapy* (1966), a *Handbook of Marriage Counseling* (1969), and *Treating Psychosexual Dysfunction* (1974). He has published articles in *The Family Coordinator, Sexology, Marriage and Family Living, Rational Living, Marriage Counseling Quarterly, Merrill-Palmer Quarterly, Guidance Journal, Progressive World, Rehabilitation Counseling Bulletin, Journal of Marriage and Family Counseling, Journal of Sex Research, Personnel and Guidance Journal,* and *Professional Psychology.*

SUBJECT INDEX

This listing seeks to aid the reader in his search for a specific reference to a specific subject named in the text. It is by no means all-inclusive and no categorizations have been attempted.

NAME INDEX